CP

WORLDS OF MODERN CHINESE FICTION

WORLDS OF MODERN CHINESE FICTION

SHORT
STORIES &
NOVELLAS
FROM THE
PEOPLE'S
REPUBLIC,
TAIWAN &
HONG KONG

Michael S. Duke, editor

An East Gate Book
M.E. Sharpe, Inc.
Armonk, New York
London, England

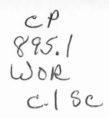

An East Gate Book

Library of Congress Cataloging-in-Publication Data

Worlds of modern Chinese fiction : short stories and novellas from the
  Poeple's Republic, Taiwan, and Hong Kong / edited by Michael S. Duke
      p.   cm.
  Translated from Chinese.
  Includes bibliographical references.
  ISBN 0-87332-757-8   ISBN 0-87332-758-6 (pbk.)
  1. Chinese fiction—20th century—Translations into English.
  2. Chinese fiction—Taiwan—Translations into English. 3. Chinese
  fiction—Hong Kong—Translations into English. I. Duke, Michael S.
  PL2658.E8W58   1991
  895.1'30108—dc20   91-2564
                                                                          CIP

Printed in the United States of America

MV   10   9   8   7   6   5   4   3   2   1

Contents

Introduction

Michael S. Duke

JUST AS premodern Chinese fiction was closely linked to the narrative conventions of traditional historiography, so the twentieth-century Chinese short story has been, and to a great extent still is, heavily influenced by the writers' involvement in the catastrophic events of modern Chinese history. Modern Chinese writers of serious fiction have called upon themselves as committed intellectuals to play a problematic role in China's historical travails from the late 1890s to the present day. Ever since Liang Qichao (1873–1929) fled into exile in Japan after the failure of the Hundred Days' Reform of 1898 and discovered the "political novel," most serious Chinese writers have believed, in the words of Lu Xun (1881–1936), that "the best way for spiritual transformation [of the Chinese people and nation] is through literature." Much of their fiction was written as part of their overall attempt to "save the nation."

The writers of the May Fourth, New Culture, and Vernacular Literature movements in the first decades of this century achieved two extremely important literary triumphs. They created a new vernacular language based on the Peking (Mandarin) dialect and enriched with vocabulary and stylistic elements from European languages. Combining traditional prose styles and the conventions of late Qing dynasty novels of social exposure with various Western influences, they completed a tendency begun in the Ming dynasty and established narrative fiction as the dominant form of modern Chinese literature. Early May Fourth writers created the modern Chinese short story in the 1920s by integrating lyrical elements from traditional Chinese poetry and essay forms with Western-style social and psychological analysis and expression.

At first their short stories, whether romantic and individualistic or realistic and socially oriented, were chiefly concerned with urban phenomena and spoke primarily for urban intellectuals. This lyrical and urban character of the modern Chinese short story did not, however, continue with the emergence of the modern Chinese novel in the 1930s. The modern Chinese novel became an increasingly rural-based panorama of social realism in which humanistic and ideologically engagé writers attempted to depict the desperate problems of poverty, ignorance, cruelty, and backwardness that cried out for solution at the time. This shift from individual to social concern and from urban to rural setting was one symptom of a striking urban-rural polarity that emerged for the first time in

Chinese social history in this century. The short story generally followed the novel's shift in subject matter and interest. The cities, especially the eastern coastal cities led by Shanghai, were depicted as the scene of political and economic oppression and moral corruption. With the arrival of a full-scale Anti-Japanese War of Aggression in 1937, modern Chinese fiction became predominantly concerned with rural life, or with the contrast between rural and urban China, and it has remained so on the mainland into the 1990s.

The mainstream of traditional or premodern Chinese literature was lyric poetry in a subjective mood. The blending of this tradition, together with a Western-influenced new consciousness of individual human personality (humanism, humanitarianism, and individualism) and China's perennial Confucian humanism, resulted in the finest works of modern Chinese fiction: the psychological and the social short story. In Jaroslav Prusek's succinct description,

> The *psychological short story* creates a complex composition by skillful stratification of various experiences and emotions relating to different times and places; and although it embodies a number of heterogeneous elements it is yet absolutely homogeneous in its spiritual atmosphere. . . . The *social short story* recasts some personal experience of the author, so that its facets reflect the most fundamental problems of human existence and of the social situation of the time. . . . This power of reflecting the whole cosmos in a single detail is a legacy which has been taken over from Chinese poetry by modern literature, especially in its concentrated form of the short story.[1]

The other side of the modern Chinese writers' commitment to truthful and ameliorative reflection of social reality in a nineteenth-century realist mode was too great a dependence on unmediated reality. This excessive reliance on life as opposed to art acted as a curb both to the imaginative transformation of raw reality and to the expression of more profound thought in fiction. C. T. Hsia coined the term "obsession with China" to describe and explain this artistic drawback in modern Chinese fiction. Modern Chinese writers have often been so concerned to get their "message" across, to make their theme understandable to even the most naive of readers, that the more imaginative, creative, or artistic elements of their craft have been sadly neglected. In periods when this freely chosen intellectual predisposition of Chinese writers has been insisted upon by the literary bureaucracy and enforced by the security apparatus of the state, the Chinese short story has often degenerated to the level of party propaganda. Such a tendency existed from the founding of the People's Republic in 1949 to 1977 and was extremely pronounced during the ten years of the Great Proletarian Cultural Revolution, 1966–76.

---

[1]Jaroslav Prusek, *The Lyrical and the Epic: Studies of Modern Chinese Literature*, ed. Leo Ou-fan Lee (Bloomington: Indiana University Press, 1980), pp. 84–85. Italics added.

Despite these artistic shortcomings, which severely hampered its success in English translation, the modern Chinese short story has always been a living literature with a voluntary reading public numbering in the hundreds of millions. Chinese readers read it in search not only of artistic experience, but also of important ideas and information about Chinese social life and individual character. Fiction still has a far greater impact on the individual and society in China today, both in the rapidly modernizing People's Republic and in the highly modernized Taiwan, than it does in the United States.

From a Western perspective, Chinese literature in this century presents an anomalous situation in which from 1919 to 1949 there flourished what has been rightly called "Modern Fiction," embodying a realism, romanticism, humanism, and social criticism familiar to Western readers since the nineteenth century. Beginning in 1942 in Yan'an and continuing from 1949 through 1977 in the People's Republic, there was a Great Return to heavy-handed didacticism under Chinese Communist Party control in which the only accepted literary mode was the "worker-peasant-soldier" fiction of either the Stalinist-inspired "Socialist Realism" or the Maoist Cultural Revolution era "Revolutionary Romanticism." From 1978 through June 1989, there was a highly successful return to the twentieth century as it is experienced throughout much of the developed and developing world. This resulted in the creation of a situation of literary pluralism not seen on the mainland since the May Fourth era, and the production of a truly "Modern Chinese Fiction."

The ten years from December 1978 to June 1989 (from the Third Plenum of the Eleventh Central Committee to the Tiananmen Massacre) thus represent a turning point in Chinese fiction comparable in scope and importance to the political and economic reforms it ushered in. For the first time since 1949, writers of serious fiction were able to abandon the pretense that they wrote for and were read by "the masses." As political restrictions on literature were increasingly relaxed, they began once again to express their individual moral and intellectual visions in narratives informed by personal esthetic standards.

Their work continued to be confronted with periodic political obstacles. Chinese writers still suffered a number of setbacks in 1981, 1983–84, and the first half of 1987. These were the periods of official denunciation campaigns, first against the spoken drama *What If I Really Were?* and the film *Bitter Love*, then against "spiritual pollution" and "literary modernism," and finally against "bourgeois liberalization." Prior to June 1989, however, the new literary and intellectual trends remained unchecked. Each setback proved briefer than the one before. Further restrictions continued to be lifted, more freedom was promised by the government in 1984 and 1985, and things just quietly returned to normal in late 1987 as the last campaign fizzled out. Writers continued to enjoy a degree of artistic freedom never before available in the People's Republic.

With increasing freedom to create and to publish came increasing artistic innovation. Although their best works remained ideologically powerful, many writers, especially those under forty, became intensely concerned with structural and linguistic artistry. They strove to create new modes of literary expression either in direct conflict or in dynamic dialogue with the received notions of literary work in China. Many writers began to experiment with nontraditional narrative forms including nonlinear plot lines or plotless narratives, multiple narrators, unreliable narrators and antiheroes, stream-of-consciousness, metafiction, and magic realism. By the end of the decade, some of their explorations of Chinese character and society equaled or surpassed the finest mainland fiction of this century. The stories from mainland China in this volume are representative of this renewed flourishing of the short story as a serious art form in contemporary China.

Since Taiwan's rupture with the mainland in 1949, the development of the short story there was no less spectacular than the economic and social transformation of the island itself. This development was an almost mirror-image contrast to the devolution of mainland literature during the same period. Starting from the "cultural desert" of the 1950s, the next two and a half decades witnessed a flowering of fiction that reached some very high levels of artistic excellence. Cut off from the socially critical literature of the May Fourth era due to the Nationalist Party's (KMT) fear of literary leftism, the decade of the 1960s saw an elaboration of the psychological short story with the rise of Western-influenced "modernist" experimentation. Both native and émigré Taiwan writers probed the personal fates and psychological agonies of individuals caught up in the maelstrom of modern Chinese history. The early 1970s saw the crowning achievement of this trend in the publication of *Taibei ren* [Wandering in the Garden, Waking from a Dream] by Bai Xianyong [Pai Hsien-yung].[2]

The turbulent decade of the 1970s, when the People's Republic replaced Taiwan in the United Nations, and many felt that the United States had too great an influence on the island's life and culture, saw the return of the social short story. Satiric and engagé realist fiction and semifictional reportage was dominated by "nativist" critiques of pressing social and political problems. Even in these socially conscious writings, however, the emphasis on linguistic artistry, well-delineated and individualized characters, and expression of the authors' personal vision was in stark contrast to the virtual absence of such traits in contemporary mainland fiction. Some of these works rival or even surpass many May Fourth writings in their linguistic sophistication, structural artistry, and production of multiple layers of meaning as well as their intellectual and emotional impact on the reader.

During the decades of the 1960s and 1970s, then, Taiwan short story writers developed a mature style of Chinese vernacular narration well suited to the

---

[2]Pai Hsien-yung and Patia Yasin, trans., *Wandering in the Garden, Waking from a Dream: Tales of Taipei Characters* (Bloomington: Indiana University Press, 1982).

modern society developing there. Their successes gave rise to a great diversity of styles among many new and excellent writers in the politically more liberal (though not yet fully democratic) 1980s. The stories from Taiwan in this volume are representative of these later works.

The British crown colony of Hong Kong was long regarded, and rightly so, as a cultural wasteland. Although the region has still not completely overcome its hyper-commercialism and the legacy of cultural philistinism, a new and vibrant literature has grown up since the mid-1970s. The short story in both its psychological and social modes has been a mainstay of this Hong Kong literary revival. The writers come from a variety of diverse backgrounds—some are refugees from the mainland, some were born in Hong Kong, and some have taken up residence in Hong Kong after becoming well-known literary figures in Taiwan. This anthology breaks new ground in offering several works by some of Hong Kong's finest short-story writers.

The twenty-five stories in this collection have been arranged on the basis of subject matter and narrative style. Despite some inevitable overlapping, they may be seen to form three more or less distinct groups. From "Blue Bottlecap" to "Dream Scenario," the first nine stories are concerned with the interrelated themes of the perception and narrative creation of time and history in individual psychology and social life. They explore the problematic relations between narrative and "real" time, history, and human life; the perception of time and history; and the production of meaning through narratives of personal or national history. From a Chinese perspective, they are the most technically advanced. They employ many modernist narrative techniques of symbolism, mythopoesis, stream-of-consciousness, and dream or dream-like sequences, and they involve various forms of quest for something in the past that might confer meaning on the characters' present lives. As a group, their unifying thematic principle is a deliberate attempt to reevaluate the received notions of twentieth-century Chinese history through an alternative and revisionist or deconstructive narrative of that history from an individual point of view. All of these stories (as well as Li Ang's "A Love Letter Never Sent") cast serious doubts on the politically dominant interpretation of the meaning of recent Chinese history, whether in the People's Republic or on Taiwan. Han Shaogong, Qiao Dianyun, Can Xue, Mo Yan, Hong Feng, and Shi Tiesheng are mainland Chinese writers who started writing after 1976. Zhang Dachun, Huang Fan, and Chen Yingzhen are Taiwan writers.

The second fourteen stories, from "The Conquerors" to "Aunty Li's Pocket Watch," are concerned with the more personal and immediate themes of love and romance (of female protagonists in six out of seven), mothers and sons, and the struggles of ordinary people in modern urban society. With the exception of the dream vision of a ghost in "The Window" and the unbelievable element of extreme conformity in "Aunty Li's Pocket Watch," these stories rely chiefly on a range of conventional narrative techniques inherited from nineteenth- and twentieth-century Chinese and Western social realism. All but one of these four-teen writers of urban fiction are from either Taiwan (Zhang Xiguo, long a resi-dent in the United States, Li Ang, Yuan Qiongqiong, Xiao Sa, and Wang Zhenhe) or Hong Kong (Xi Xi, Shi Shuqing, originally from Taiwan, Zhong Xiaoyang, Zhong Ling, currently living in Taiwan, Bai Luo, Liu Yichang, Hai Xin, and Liang Bingjun); only Chen Jiangong is from Beijing.

Unlike the first nine and last two stories, most of the themes in this group will be quite familiar to readers of twentieth-century European and American fiction. They lack much of the "exotic flavor" that some readers look for in Chinese fiction in translation, but that does not make them either derivative or less thor-oughly Chinese than stories dealing with the rural masses or the ethnic minorities on China's western borders. The problems of Taiwan and Hong Kong society today will be the problems of all of Chinese society tomorrow, and these stories both realistically and ironically delineate some of the dilemmas facing modern urban Chinese characters.

The last two stories are examples of what has been called the Chinese west-ern. Set on China's borderlands with their distinctive natural scenery, the first concerns minatory, and the last exemplary, bigger-than-life heroes. Both authors are from the mainland and have written to a great extent on the non-Han minori-ties of Inner Mongolia and Xinjiang.

Since the Tiananmen Massacre of June 1989, mainland Chinese literature has come once again under repressive political control. The main organs of all cul-tural activity, especially the literary bureaucracy and the state-controlled publica-tions, are once again in the hands of people whose literary and political beliefs and practices hark back to the era of Maoist hegemony. They were most unhappy with the increasingly pluralistic literary scene of the past decade. It is difficult to predict how long they will remain in control or what effect they will have on Chinese fiction in the 1990s. Chinese writers, intellectuals, business profession-als, students, factory workers, and urban dwellers as a whole (the Chinese read-ing public) have had too much contact with their counterparts in Hong Kong, Taiwan, Singapore, and elsewhere in the developed Western world ever to go back to living, thinking, and writing the way they did during China's enforced isolation from the mainstream of the modern world.

Many good mainland writers are now writing without publishing, while others in exile are publishing original works in Taiwan and Hong Kong. At the same time, Hong Kong, Taiwan, and overseas Chinese fiction continues to flourish. The cosmopolitan nature of that fiction and the cross-fertilization that has taken place in the past decade are certain to continue at an increasing pace in the years to come. This anthology is dedicated to the proposition that modern Chinese fiction is once again an extremely vibrant and important part of world literature. Our translations have made some of its finest recent works available to serious readers for their artistic and intellectual pleasure.

I would like to thank Professor Joseph S. M. Lau for asking me to do this editing job in the summer of 1986 and for helping me to keep in contact with the many people involved behind the scenes who suggested titles to be included and translators for them. Three people—professors David Der-wei Wang and Wong Wai-leung and Mr. Li Tuo—deserve special thanks for suggesting most of the stories from Taiwan, Hong Kong, and the People's Republic, respectively. I would also like to gratefully acknowledge the collection of a generous grant by Dr. Lau Siu-kai, director of the Centre for Hong Kong Studies, which went to cover the first retyping of the translators' manuscripts here at UBC. Finally, I thank all of the translators for their superb work.

WORLDS OF MODERN CHINESE FICTION

Blue Bottlecap

Han Shaogong

Translated by Michael S. Duke

MY STRENGTH gave out. I passed the heavy bottle of wine over and asked if he could get the cap off. He was just then struggling mightily with a chunk of pig's feet, a piece of gristle stuck between his teeth, and hadn't even got his tongue free to talk. The wine bottle just disappeared.

A hand on my left had grabbed it away. "I'll open it." The young-looking Town Elder glanced over at him and then at me with a simple, guileless smile on his plain, ruddy face.

He grabbed the wine bottle away too quickly, too abruptly; it was more than politeness. There was obviously something behind it.

There was also something funny about those two fellows across the table from us, looking at him and then smiling at me.

He just kept his head down and went on eating with some difficulty. Not until he had let out a burp of satisfaction, picked clean a nice row of false teeth that looked just like real ones, and stooped over to wash his hands did the Town Elder finally touch me lightly on the knee: "You shouldn't ask him to open bottlecaps. Come on, have some soup, it's still pretty fresh."

"Why not?"

"You'd better not mention bottlecaps."

"Why not?"

"Have some soup, have some soup; what're you doing staring at that bowl of rice?"

I was very puzzled, not about my host getting on me for eating only rice, but about that empty chair on my left. He was sitting there just a minute ago, wearing a pair of high-topped boots seldom seen around here, offering me some beef and introducing himself: Name's Chen, Chen Mengtao, work in the warehouse taking care of the tea. He even went on with me about the differences between spring tea and summer tea and about the Martial Emperor of the Han

---

The original story was published in January 1985. This translation is from Han Shaogong, *You-huo* (Lure) (Changsha: Hunan wenyi chubanshe, 1986), pp. 19–29.

dynasty—I could see that his woolen cap was resting on a slim volume called *Anecdotes of the Western Han.* What kind of strange connection did he have with bottlecaps?

After washing his hands, he came in very solemnly, clicked in his false teeth, suddenly smiled once more, and started talking to me about the Martial Emperor of the Han dynasty. I moved my chair back a little to take a good look at him and discovered that his neck was sort of frightening: the skin was loose and there were rolls of protruding flesh moving softly up and down in time to the rhythms of his speech; it made one's own neck feel uncomfortable, like you'd want to scrunch down in your collar. His eyes stared straight at you with a look of intimate friendship; they were like cat's eyes, with yellow and green circles. Inside the circles it was very, very deep and made you think of a dark tunnel that you could not see to the bottom of; a slight speck of light floated there in the tunnel sorely tempting you—tempting you to walk right in.

I felt there was something wrong, too.

As the Town Elder escorted me back into town, I asked him, "Why can't that fellow Chen open bottlecaps? Did he . . .''

"I don't know. I hear the town zoo has a new red-haired wild man; have you seen 'im?''

"I haven't seen it. How did you happen to end up here?''

"I don't know, I haven't been here long. Do you think there really are creatures like red-haired wild men? It's probably just some kind of ape, right?''

All I could do was settle down to discuss apes with him.

That day I ran into another friend who also knew Chen Mengtao, and he finally helped me to get rid of that bottlecap. It was after dinner, I was sitting on the high wooden veranda of the town guesthouse looking way out over the railing at the moss-covered, mottled old brick wall of the Fupo Temple there in the distance. Below the high temple wall, the ridge tiles were streaked with water marks, some deep and some shallow, all in close-knit lines. Silky threads of cooking smoke pushed their way through the cracks in the tiles, rose into the sky, gradually faded and drifted down again to pervade the whole horizon and all the small streets and alleyways like an amorphous wave of smoke. The roofs resembled the masts of a great ship drifting along on a wave of smoke with the two high ridges naturally forming the bow and stern of the ship.

I seemed to feel the boards swaying beneath my feet.

The newcomer was a young man who worked at the meat- and fish-processing plant. I had seen him a few times before. He was an amateur expert on regional surnames. I heard that he often went to the local police station to help with the census; on the basis of only the name someone reported, he could accurately determine whether or not that person had made a mistake about his native place; in this way he had cleared up a number of cases and earned the respect of the provincial authorities in charge of such things. He already had half a trunkfull of unofficial historical anecdotes that he had secretly collected for several years; he regarded them as a precious treasure and probably intended to hide them on some famous mountain. Whatever he thought ought to be recorded, he recorded: what village produced an arithmetic prodigy, what village dug up a giant sweet potato, or even the gossip surrounding a big blowup in one of the high-level provincial academies. At the mention of Chen Mengtao, he pursed his lips and smiled, leaned back, rolled his eyes a little as though looking both at you and at the roof, seemingly in complete control of the facts.

"You mean him? Yea, I'm pretty clear about him. He came from the penal colony. You know what a hard-labor penal camp is? There used to be one here. A lot of these bricks came from there; there was a kiln. . . ."

He went on talking (I have to omit some of his overly detailed verifications and explanations, and also add an appropriate amount of my own imagination): Chen Mengtao used to carry rocks at the penal colony. Because he was so tall it was very hard for him to carry rocks; if the carrying pole moved just a little off center he would go toppling over like an avalanche. After carrying rocks for a few days, his back was bent out of shape; he had a pained expression all the time; when he changed his clothes his shoulders and back hurt so much he would yell out loud. The clothes he took off were weighted down with big white powdery patches of salt, each blotch bigger than the next one, made from the condensation of old and new sweat. Early one morning before first light, he was awakened by a full bladder and discovered that his legs were so numb he couldn't move. When he finally felt around in the dark and discovered a pair of legs he thought were his, he discovered that they were all covered with mud; he had completely forgotten to wash his feet the day before. He couldn't move his legs, but he had to piss something awful; finally he struggled to the edge of the bed, but the hot piss trickled out through his trousers and wet the bed.

He started bawling, woke up everybody else in the shed, and got himself roundly cursed.

He decided to ask for an easier job. There was only one really easy job at that time—burying people. There were those who died of illness and those who committed suicide, and there were those who could not finish their assigned labor quota and were marched out at gunpoint for "training." When their trainers got bored, they'd always have to slap 'em and kick 'em around or use their ropes and leather belts; after a loud wail full of the most exquisite educational significance, a pile of bone and meat weighing about a hundred pounds or so would have to be returned to the yellow earth. When the guards saw that Chen Mengtao was always first in line for collective training and always bowed his head at the lowest possible angle, they decided to treat him with special care by giving him the task of burying people.

"Right, you go get ready," they'd order him.

As a matter of fact, Chen Mengtao was terribly afraid of dead people; as soon as he heard that wail, he'd start shaking and looking miserable; his tongue would roll around in his mouth for a long time without being able to form a single word. But then carrying people was a good deal lighter work than carrying rocks. Furthermore, the guards thought this particular task very unpropitious and would not go along to supervise. You could relax and take a morning nap or put on long unworn shoes and socks, drink your fill of water, revitalize your spirits, leave the tensions of the work site far behind, and go up to the quiet hillside. Slowly dig a hole and slowly fill in the dirt; didn't even matter if you sat down on the pick handle to rest until your sweat cooled. Carefree, with the carrying pole removed from your back and those unpredictable rifle barrels no longer pointed at you, you could just relax and put on weight.

With a feeling of cheerful trepidation, Chen Mengtao busily plaited a straw rope, making an altogether different use of the previously harvested rice stalks. After he finished plaiting it, he stepped on one end with his foot and pulled it hard several times to see if it could bear the weight of a man. Then he picked up another carrying pole, bent it a few times, saw that it was of good quality, held it up by his side to measure it, and, discovering that it was indeed two or three feet taller than he, was then completely satisfied. He worked with loud vivacity so that the guards could see him, and to demonstrate that he was most worthy of their trust in this occupation.

When he came face to face with the icy cold body of the deceased, however, the wrinkles on his face twitched quite uncontrollably, and he held his breath and turned his face to one side before he dared to breath. His hands would not obey orders either; for a long time they were unable to tie a knot in the rope. Fortunately he had a helper who tied a couple of loops in the rope, put one loop around the neck and one loop around the feet, and let Chen Mengtao shoulder the carrying pole and walk in front. When a person has a body temperature he's very soft, but when he's cold he's stiff and you don't even have to put a stretcher board under him; you can just hoist him up straight as you please, let him sway back and forth as you walk him up the hill to the place of eternal repose.

There was one good thing about walking in front. You didn't have to see the deceased's dark, cavernous mouth, or a copper-capped tooth, or a black piece of pickled vegetables still caught between his teeth. You could just pretend that you were carrying rocks or a wedding palanquin; but as soon as you recalled that what was following behind you step by step was really not a wedding palanquin but a life that was once warm but was now cold, you couldn't help staring straight ahead blankly. That day as they crossed the ridge of the hill and took a downward trail, he stepped off the road a bit to avoid a pile of cow dung. The carrying pole swayed violently, and one of the deceased's cold arms slipped down from his side, making a wide arc like a pendulum and just grazing the inside of Chen Mengtao's knee as if he were playfully tickling him there.

"Mama ya!!!" Chen Mengtao leaped high in the air a couple of times and fell over in a heap. The deceased's body fell just right so as to weigh down crookedly upon him and Chen fainted dead away with his arms stiff at his sides.

His partner pinched his upper lip, slapped him a few times, revived him, and got him to spit out the mud that stuck to his mouth.

After performing a few burials, he became a little more courageous and a little more experienced. The more he worked, the more proficient he became; he didn't have to dig a pit as big as a swimming pool any more, like the first time. The bottom of the pit didn't have to be made into a perfect rectangle either, it didn't have to be finely done. Going up and down the hill, everything had its prearranged pattern, right down to which foot stepped on which stone or which clump of grass and which hand grabbed onto which bunch of thatch or which tree branch. The time spent sitting on his pick handle at the top of the ridge also grew greater and greater. Chen Mengtao had sung in an amateur theater troupe and allowed that his partner had a handsome face and could play the *xiaosheng* (young man) roles. He said that he was in love once. The woman's name had the character "tao" (peach) in it, so he changed his name to "Mengtao" (dreaming of peach) just to express the steadfastness of his love. This was the absolute truth. They talked up and down about everything that way until the wind gradually grew cold and the sun inclined toward the western hills, having already changed from a small white to a large red ball; they gazed off, not without sympathy, in the direction of the work site, gathered up their tools, and headed back. On entering the shed and without undue talk, he put his pick, carrying pole, and rice stalks for plaiting mats carefully away in their appointed place in the corner of the wall, making certain they didn't become mixed up with the others' tools and were ready for use the next time.

Sometimes he was able to return a little early, stealthily dish up a small bowl of steamed meat with black bean sauce from the steamer in the kitchen, close the door, and wolf it down before everyone came back. He cleared this practice with the guards, his excuse being that in burying people he was polluted by the aura of the dead, which was very detrimental to his health, and thus he certainly needed the extra nourishment. At any rate the food money came from his family.

In the same shed with him lived several men who often failed to complete their quota of work, and they were naturally enough quite disturbed by that bundle of rice stalks in the corner of the wall. When they saw that Chen Mengtao no longer pissed on his bedding and was becoming more ruddy complected, they looked at him with an even more jaundiced eye. For some reason or other his porcelain bowl had a few more pieces of porcelain chipped off of it, and an old padded jacket flew away without the aid of wings. If he was the least bit late for dinner, that crock of salted vegetables there on the floor would be completely empty, without even a trace of green juice left over.

One day in the shed there was a pair of chopsticks that went unused and an empty bunk; everybody was feeling gloomy and didn't dare to come close to the desolate emptiness of that bunk. When his partner came to ask him to plait a grass rope, Chen Mengtao just sat there on the piss bucket without getting up, his cat eyes dark and lusterless and his two buck teeth chattering away against his lower lip.

"I . . . I can't piss."

"Go plait a rope."

"I can't . . . can't piss, what . . . can I do?"

His partner stared at him a moment and understood. The man to be buried that day was probably not some unknown he'd never had anything to do with before, like the others they'd buried earlier, but was from the bunk directly in front of Chen Mengtao's, and thus he was feeling fainthearted. Chen Mengtao didn't actually know the man very well, never talked to him much; it was just that the time when he wet his bed he had asked the man to loan him a pair of pants. He'd also talked to him once about the best place in town to buy steamed buns; they hit it off pretty well. What kind of friendship was that? But they had slept in facing bunks for several weeks; night before last Chen had even indignantly listened to him grinding his teeth, and today his straw mat was empty. Now Chen Mengtao had to rush out and plait a grass rope for that tooth-grinding head, right? He wouldn't grind his teeth on Chen's butt, would he?

His partner said, "You don't want to go? That's OK, just go find the boss and get somebody else."

Chen Mengtao grit his teeth and stared at the worn-out straw sandals in front of his bed. "I'll go carry rocks! I'll go . . . carry rocks!"

"Carry rocks? You're as skinny as a monkey; tomorrow I'll just have to come and carry you off."

"I . . . I'm stronger than Song Chaoyuan."*

"They've increased the work quota today."

"By how much?"

"By one square yard per person."

"God!"

Chen Mengtao's expression changed, the long wrinkles on his face drooped downward; his bladder feeling more stopped up than before, he painfully straightened up, stretched his long neck, sniffled slightly, and closed his eyes. He knew by now they had gone to work for some time and even if he had three bodies and six arms there was no way he could complete today's quota. And besides he couldn't piss. . . .

"You think," he caught his breath, "we have to bury him today?"

"Not bury him, we going to lay him out as an offering?"

"Cover him . . . with earth?"

"We going to cover him with rice?"

"Bury him . . . in the usual place?"

"What the hell are you talking about? If you don't want to go, don't go, but don't screw up my work. I still have to plait a rope."

---

*Otherwise unidentified character, probably someone who died in the camp.

"Tell you the truth, I really . . . I really feel weak to think of it. Just think, night before last I heard him grinding his teeth, and yesterday he even smiled at me. . . . Look at his chopsticks, his chopsticks, he stuck 'em in the shelf over my bed. I can't carry him; I really can't go. Don't yell at me; I just can't . . ."

But he did go that day anyway, only when he returned to the shed he didn't eat dinner.

Life slowly settled down to normal, just as if there had been no particularly extraordinary change. As always, everyone squatted on the ground to shovel in their rice; as always, they kept groaning about their stiff, sore arms and legs; as always, they scratched like crazy all over their bodies to dig out a couple of lice. That pair of unused chopsticks was also carried off by someone who used it to repair his carrying pole. Every day the sunlight extended itself inside through the door and then retracted itself again like a long white tongue licking away a little bit of the damp and the smell of rice straw, lapping it back out into nature, commingling it once again with the sweet smell of the rape blossoms and the intermittent honking of the geese.

Chen Mengtao was acting rather strange, seemed to be very agitated; he often looked over at other people in a most suspicious way. While they were eating, with his two buck teeth sticking out, he would raise his head and look from this face to that face, and even though it was just a momentary glance, you would still feel like he was giving you a thorough going over, like he was sizing you up in some extremely meaningful way that made you shiver.

He began enthusiastically performing good deeds and became especially solicitous toward those people who had a difficult time completing their work quotas. Asleep in bed at night, after tossing and turning he'd wake up and then go to the foot of your bed, arrange your shoes a little more neatly, or pour a little tea into your cup, or, noticing that your sleeping posture was none too good, he would lightly move your head or your feet over a little. If he carelessly woke you up, he would stoop over, bow his head, and smile that buck-toothed smile that served as his greeting, his farewell, and his apology. With that extremely short-lived and totally baseless smile coming and going on his face in a very mechanical fashion, he certainly seemed to be up to no good. After becoming accustomed to the sight of grass ropes and holes in the ground, his cat eyes seemed even deeper, as if the pupils had grown larger and only a thin yellow circle was now left hiding some sort of glossy, green light. You would feel that his gaze had already pierced right through you, successfully estimating your weight and the size of your neck, predicting your future posture, and secretly comparing your body with the height of an invisible something.

His abject meanness and his eager solicitude positively enraged the others. One night a big, strapping fellow was awakened by the clammy breath from his nostrils. He froze there in fright, then scrambled a few feet away on the bed and cursed him: "Fuck your mother, you sonovabitch Chen! Why don't you mess with somebody else; what're you doing straightening up my shoes?"

"There was some grass in your shoes. Heh, heh."

"What's that got to do with you? Piss off!"

Chen Mengtao stooped over, smiled bitterly, picked up a dirty shirt off the floor, grabbed some soap, and headed for the sink to wash it.

The owner of the shirt was frightened and said with a quivering voice, "Chen . . . Chen Mengtao . . . when did I ever cross you? What are you washing my shirt for?"

"I . . . I'm just going to wring it out a bit. Heh."

"What do you mean by that? What do you mean?"

Chen Mengtao was very sad, feeling that his services must be somehow deficient. He trudged resentfully back to his bed and fell asleep, but he tossed and turned again and often cried out. Some people look very large when they're asleep, but, strangely enough, as soon as he got under his covers he seemed to shrink, becoming as small as a child.

He began to suffer from an increasingly inexplicable guilty conscience, and the more good deeds he did, the more he was cursed by the others. His complexion grew deathly pale, his eyelids drooped, his hands and feet trembled, and much of his hair turned white, but he kept on working with all his heart. When he took his rice bowl up in line, he would often skip a few steps for no reason at all and then return to his normal gait as if some invisible person had just stepped on the heel of his foot. He rushed to take out the piss bucket and, with his height and his clumsiness, got filthy water all over his shoes, but he never complained a bit.

One day a cold wind was blowing, one's nose and fingers were extremely cold, it was torture to hide under the covers or to get out of bed. The guards talked it over a minute and agreed that everyone could buy some wine to ward off the cold. Chen Mengtao went into action immediately, generously pulling out the money his younger brother had sent him and rushing right off to the storeroom to buy the wine.

Back with the wine, he tried to take off the little metal bottlecap. He tried to bite it off, but to no avail. He got a chopstick and tried to pry it off, but it didn't budge at all. Finally he propped a hoe up on his knee and used the hoe blade to scrape it off. As he pulled down vigorously on the bottle there was a pop and the bottlecap disappeared.

He was dumbfounded. "Where's the bottlecap?"

"Where's the bottlecap?" He lifted up the grass mat; he turned over each of his shoes and shook them out.

"Where's the bottlecap?" He banged around the rakes and carrying poles in the corner of the wall and peered into the empty piss bucket, but he still could not find it.

Everybody had already taken a few big slugs of wine, and the pungent, hot feeling was rising from their stomachs and coming out on their faces. Noticing that he still had not joined them, they looked over after him; they did not see his upper body; all they saw was his rump facing them, sticking up high in the air; the center seam of his pants was pulled over crookedly to one side, and there were still two big spots of faded yellow mud. These two spots of faded yellow mud went straight out the door down to the yard and onto the road. Later on they heard that he wanted to go right on past the guardpost and straight onto the town streets, all the while talking to himself in a bemused tone:

"Where's the bottlecap? That's really something, where's my bottlecap?"

Just like that, he went insane. With the utmost calmness and amiability he started off looking for that eternally irretrievable bottlecap. This event puzzled everyone no end.

Later and later on a good deal of time went by, a number of people died and were born, a number of houses were torn down and many more were built up again. When the penal colony was disbanded, just like many other people's his case was ruled mistaken and unjust and he was given his freedom. He was sent to hospital after hospital and then, when he seemed much better, was transferred here to take care of the tea. He took down a pretty good wage, ate steamed pork with black bean sauce, and sometimes would read a few books and newspapers, listen to the radio, evaluate the performances of amateur drama troupes, or wear his high-topped leather boots into town to buy the latest science fiction magazine. Apart from searching for that bottlecap, he didn't have any other symptoms of insanity. Many good-hearted or ill-intentioned people gave him various kinds of bottlecaps, and he pinched them all between his crude, rough fingers, looked them all over, turned his richly colored cat eyes back to the people, and spoke like someone seriously discussing an academic problem: "It looks a little bit like it, but it's not."

Who knows which one he's searching for after all.

The amateur expert on regional surnames finished talking and looked at his watch, "Oh, I've been talking too much. I still want to hear what you've got to say. What sort of news have you brought this time?"

I smoked a cigarette and realized that we had actually been talking all along. Since we had been talking about it, the thing was now somewhat trivial and remote. We could immediately talk about something else, talk about the study of surnames, talk about pig's feet, talk about the nuclear disarmament negotiations, just talk and talk.

Suddenly my mind seemed quite numb. For a long time I could not think of a subject of conversation, could not think of a single sentence, not even a single word.

Once again I looked at all those roofs with the cooking smoke swirling around them; under those roofs were thousands of families. In the long, slow march of ages, who knows where these roofs were sailed in from to moor here and make up this little town. Maybe someday they'll simply sail away again one by one to make a new world, silently stealing in and silently slipping away. Taking temporary shelter in this tiny harbor, resting their poles and their oars, they entered into this pale blue stillness and repose. Right, there's not even a single word there.

Just as there is no bottlecap.

The General's Monument

Zhang Dachun

Translated by Ying-tsih Hwang and John J. S. Balcom

EXCEPT for the passing of the seasons, the General was no longer aware of the existence of time. Usually he would get up at midnight and walk to the balcony, smiling and waving as he greeted the trees and flowers in the dark garden. At dusk he would take up his field glasses and spend a considerable amount of time scanning Mt. Taiping and its environs, guessing the whereabouts of Communist or Japanese bases. If there were no fog or rain in the morning, he would dress up, and, from the south gate of the Garden of Indifference, he would take the small path up the mountain to look at the marble monument his subordinates erected for him many years later.

How the General was able to travel through the past and the future was a secret. During the last two years of his life, no one could figure out why he talked and acted so strangely. People just assumed that he couldn't stand the quietness and loneliness of retired life, and that he spent so much time buried in the glories of the past that he eventually lost his mind. Others even blamed his only son for neglecting his filial duty by allowing the old man to live too long in seclusion and thus end up crazy. Some people ardently wished to organize a fellow provincial association or some kind of foundation and invite him to accept the post of director or adviser so that he could avoid the awful boredom of idleness. Still others published a collection of writings in honor of the General on his eightieth birthday, asking him, time and again, to give an oral account of his life, so as to leave his historic testimony of a great age.

When the General could still talk, he normally expressed his appreciation very politely to those who occasionally came to show their concern for him. He even defended his son, Weiyang. During the early years he was still able to tell little lies about the frequency and duration of Weiyang's visits to the Garden of Indifference. But as time went on, the General really got confused—he wasn't certain if Weiyang had left in the morning day before yesterday or if he had just

---

The original appeared in the literary section of the *Zhongguo shibao* (China Times), October 3 and 4, 1986.

come back the night before. Gradually, he responded less and less to his guests. The reason for all responses becoming more and more irrelevant was that his mind had begun to travel even when people were around him. Once, a fellow provincial asked him how he managed to stay in such good health; he let his interlocutor stand at attention for a good fifteen minutes. Something like this also occurred at the celebration of his eighty-third birthday. As he gulped down the last bit of wine in his gold cup, he suddenly rose from his seat before the seventy-two guests who had come to celebrate his birthday and blurted out, "If you really think highly of me, Wu Zhendong,* please remove the monument from the top of the mountain, I cannot accept such fine words." The guests looked at one another in blank dismay, unable to understand what he meant. They wondered if they had heard correctly—what monument on the mountain? But no one dared to disagree with him, so they hurriedly assented to his request. The General, on the contrary, became upset. He knew very well that no one would remove the monument, so he sat down in anger. "Fuck it," he cursed, "a bunch of idiots." At that moment, Weiyang quietly stood up and, raising his hand to push away the old valet who had just come up to stop him, wove his way between the round tables covered with red table cloths and left the Garden of Indifference amid the rising clamor. The General gazed after his departing son as he disappeared among the rows of cypress trees planted outside the hall. Then he heard his old valet say haltingly, "The young master must attend a lecture tonight, he has to rush back to Taibei." He burped and nodded at the people, smiling and waving his hand as if nothing had happened. However, nobody knew that the General had already made up his mind never to talk again.

The first person to discover that the General had become mute was Shi Qi, the biographer whom the Foundation had invited to write the General's memoirs. She spent an entire day pleading with the General to make an effort to recall the state of affairs when the troops of the Northern Expedition recaptured Jiujiang in November 1926. But the General just sat there, rocking back and forth in his rocking chair, saying nothing. Finally Shi Qi turned off the tape recorder and softly patted the back of his hand. "Please take a rest then, I have to leave," she said.

Actually, the General hadn't rested at all. He skillfully used his hidden ability of penetrating time, to transport Shi Qi from Jiujiang to Nanchang. In the basement of an enamel factory they met Ma, leader of the Green Gang.† Ma disclosed, then and there, the alarming news that the Communists would lead the masses in a riot in Shanghai. The General turned his head and saw Shi Qi curled up among piles of enamelware. He smiled and said, "Don't be afraid. I'm here." He gave a few thrusts of his chin indicating that Shi Qi should pay attention to

---

*Wu means "martial," zhen means "to suppress or to pacify," and dong means "the East." The General's name is, thus, broadly symbolic.

†The Green Gang was a criminal organization similar to the Mafia.

the young man of fine bearing having a conference with Ma Zhifang: it was none other than he himself. "I wasn't even twenty-five that year." Then the General took Shi Qi by the hand and passed through another four months and twenty days. They arrived at the border of the French Concession where they saw more than two hundred bloody, decapitated heads stuck on pointed bamboo poles.* Shi Qi screamed and fainted in his arms. The General shook her to wake her up, then stood, arms akimbo, looking around at the chaotic aftermath of battle. The streets were filled with the smoke of gunpowder. "The rioters have all been executed, don't be afraid," he said. Then she opened her eyes, which were filled with fear and suspicion, to stare at him for some time before she softly patted the back of his hand, saying, "Please take a rest then, I have to leave." The General watched her perfect, round calves and delicate ankles and heard the tapping of her high-heeled shoes going down the green stone path, as she disappeared in the haze. Then he found himself standing alone on a street in the Wampoa district shouting, "Today is a great day!" His shout was a mixture of great joy and great sadness, and it was at once both very loud and very soft. The General had no way of knowing for certain if today was his twenty-fifth or eighty-third birthday.

The General once secretly attended his own funeral, which took place in his eighty-fourth year.

The funeral, as he expected, was held at the Garden of Indifference. His funeral portrait was that photograph taken when he was seventy-two, just after retiring from military service. It was hung on the north wall of the living room. All sorts of elegiac couplets and horizontally inscribed plaques filled the walls and the lateral beam of the room. He took off his reading glasses and read the first line of a couplet, but he felt so dizzy and short of breath that he simply stopped reading.

With some difficulty he spotted Weiyang in the crowd. He was wearing a white gown and silver-framed glasses; his eyes were a little swollen, apparently from crying. Though startled, the General was also pleasantly surprised. He pushed his way through the crowd to stand next to his son. Weiyang was half a head taller than him; he had to straighten his back and stand on tiptoe; only then could he see his son's face clearly. He discovered that Weiyang's mustache was already sprinkled with white. Half out of rebuke and half out of pity, the General tugged at Weiyang's cuff, saying, "I've died and you still haven't got yourself a wife. What sin did I commit that you must punish me by cutting off my lineage?" Weiyang, pulling his sleeve away, paid no attention to him.

The General sighed, blowing the handkerchief from the *qipao* of a representative from the Women's League. Then he followed the handkerchief as it blew across the floor out into the main hall, and he avoided hearing the strange tones

---

*On April 12, 1927, the Nationalist Party (KMT) under Chiang Kai-shek betrayed their Communist allies in the Northern Expedition and executed thousands of Communists and labor leaders in Shanghai.

of the chanted eulogies. He saw Shi Qi standing beneath the eaves of the corridor wiping away her tears with her fingers. Just as he was about to pick up the handkerchief and hand it to her, he heard the secretary general of the Foundation say, "It's a pleasure to see you here, Miss Shi." They greeted one another with some familiarity. Shi Qi then recovered some of her sadness and said, "Do you know how much trouble I went through in the last three months interviewing and recording, and now all for nothing." The secretary general patted Shi Qi on the shoulder and thought for a while, then he raised his eyebrows. "I've got an idea. Let me introduce you to the General's son, maybe that will help." This immediately upset the General, who said, "He doesn't know shit!" "I know him," said Shi Qi, brushing the hair back out of her face and smiling. "He is a well-known professor of sociology." "Crap, what nonsense!" said the General, jumping angrily down the steps and overturning several wreaths.

Returning from the funeral ceremony, the General became ill. He slept ten to twenty hours a day. His old valet kept watch over him at his bedside, praying to heaven, hoping the General would mutter a few words in his sleep so that he could guess what had caused the General to lose his mind. However, the General, relying upon the same determined spirit as he had for decades, refused to utter a word even when dreaming. This went on for a month until early one morning the strong fragrance of the flowering bush in the garden wafted over the green stone path, through the hallway, and into the bedroom. The General stirred, got up out of bed, and walked to the window, nodding his head as if greeting the fragrance. "Spring is here," was all he said to his valet. His old valet was astonished, his eyes filled with tears of happiness, "Your Honor, your Honor has awakened!" The General was baffled and assumed that his old valet was indeed getting senile. He became silent again and glared at his valet, angered because he had forgotten the last few days when the two of them, master and servant, had gone through thick and thin fighting for the defense of the country south of the Yangzi.

The reason the General had taken his old valet to revisit the battlefield was, without a doubt, that he had been upset at the funeral ceremony. He insisted that his old valet be a witness to the fact that Weiyang was not the right person to finish his memoirs. During those years, when he was at the height of his glory— "Weiyang, that stinking brat, was still a lonely spirit or wild ghost who had not yet found a place to be reborn!" Over the years, every time father and son clashed, the General would vigorously assert this idea. But as soon as he said it, an even greater and stronger fear would rise up inside him—the General really suspected that this son, born in his later years after the war, was the lonely spirit or wild ghost of an unknown soldier killed at the front, or the combined essence of all the injustices and evils he had perpetrated. Oppressed by this fear, he had to explain or change history for his old valet; he weaved a few new memories or erased some old memories in order to defy the invisible retribution that may have been placed upon him.

Thus, when master and servant reached Shanghai on January 20, 1932, they watched fifty members of the Japanese Youth Defense Association burn down a linen factory and burn two Chinese factory workers to death. "Actually I wasn't in Shanghai at that time. I arrived after the War of Resistance began," said the General promptly to his valet. But he could not clearly explain how he could "return" to the scene of the fire that night if he had not been present. "General, didn't you say that the Japanese burned down the factory because they wanted to get revenge on you? Didn't you have a Japanese monk beaten to death?" The General at once shook his head so as not to link that stinking monk with Weiyang. He seemed to speak sternly and forcefully for the cause of justice: "Nonsense!" But, on the other hand, the General had already seen himself, a handsome young man, rush into the flames to rescue a third Chinese who, unexpectedly, turned out to be a middleman in the Hongkou* opium business. After the incident of the fire, the General had few worries because the person he rescued later aided him with provisions and funds for his irregular troops, and finally became his father-in-law.

Lowering his voice, the General told his old valet that he never liked his father-in-law, that bastard. "But at that time—," murmured the General as he sighed, but he didn't continue. He hoped that his old valet would understand that during that time of war at home and abroad, nothing nor anyone was pure. Honor and evil, merit and murder, power and love, kindness and hatred, life and death could all be mixed together into a mass of watery mud. "I understand that, General," said the old valet. The General gritted his teeth so as not to show any expression of appreciation. He held up his chin with even greater force, staring fixedly at the flames that shot up into the sky from the factory. At the same time, deep down in the pit of his heart, he heard a shout like the crashing of a dry, rotten tree consumed in flame. "Oh, Weiyang! You vile little bastard, you never understood! You don't understand shit!"

Weiyang returned to the Garden of Indifference on Tomb-Sweeping Day.† The General, as usual, wore a padded black satin jacket and blue silk robe. He sat in front of a full-length window with a pair of field glasses looking at the mountain, which seemed to shift about in the seasonal rains. Weiyang brushed away the raindrops sparkling on his raincoat, put his hand on the back of the rocking chair, and then walked around in front. He bent over to take a closer look at the old man. The General moved his head back into the light. Weiyang just kept on examining his wrinkled forehead, his cheeks, and his dry shrunken mouth, wiping away a grain of rice still on his chin and picking a thread from the front of his jacket. After which he said to the old valet, "He doesn't look too good."

"Yes, that's right. Since February, the General has been acting as if he's lost

*Hongkou was the Japanese section of Shanghai at the time.
†The Festival of Tombs or Tomb-Sweeping Day falls on April 4 or 5 each year.

his wits. He refuses to talk.'' The old valet then walked with Weiyang over to examine the General. They both felt that the General was absolutely unaware of their presence. Weiyang brushed some raindrops from the General's lap and talked at random with the old valet about how it rained more and more each year, and other such topics. The old valet, as if influenced by Weiyang's solemn propriety, comparable only to that of a connoisseur of art, lifted his hand to smooth out what little hair remained behind the General's left ear. ''Yes, the azaleas are covered with buds, but they don't blossom,'' he responded casually. ''Taibei is even worse, the air pollution is awful,'' said Weiyang, picking at a particle of sleep beside the General's nose, ''but it's cleaner in the mountains.'' ''Yes, it is!'' ''Can he go to the bathroom by himself?'' ''Yes, yes, he can, don't worry about it. The General eats, drinks, and goes to the bathroom very well.'' ''That's good,'' Weiyang was about to smooth out the wrinkles on the General's jacket but found that the old valet had already done so; he took a breath, saying, ''That's good—ai, it's cleaner in the mountains.'' ''Indeed.'' The old valet rolled up the General's sleeve, but when he discovered a ring of dirt on the cuff of the white shirt underneath he rolled the sleeve down again, saying, ''I've planted some vegetables in the backyard. They're organic, you can take some back to Taibei with you.'' Weiyang nodded, adjusted the General's collar, and, lightly rocking the chair, said, ''Fine, first I'll visit my mother's grave; when I get back we'll have a look around together.'' They walked away from the window. After taking a few steps, Weiyang hesitated, feeling somewhat uneasy, glanced back at the General, who continued rocking back and forth in his chair, and said, ''He doesn't look too good.''

With his field glasses, the General watched Weiyang walking away in his gray raincoat. Weiyang walked very slowly with great care. Even though the weeds and leaves were wet and splashed with mud, he never dirtied his cream-colored flannel trousers. But the General himself didn't care about these matters. Throughout his lifetime he had walked with large strides, his head held high; the wind and rain beating against his bare face and his feet in the mud always made him feel great. By then he had already gone right through his field glasses, beyond their focal distance, and was standing firmly on top of the mountain waiting for his son.

''Hurry up!'' The General took off his white gloves, clenched his fists, and yelled to Weiyang, who was halfway up the mountain. He grew impatient, worrying that Weiyang wouldn't make it in time to watch the great spectacle as their Twentieth Army inflicted heavy casualties on the Japanese North China Army. The General frowned as he squinted, gazing over the smoky loess plain to the northwest where bursts of gunfire were faintly audible. As a shot whizzed over, knocking off the General's hat, Weiyang made it to the top of the cliff. The General pulled him up with one hand, then pushed him down on the fresh green grass and handed him the field glasses. ''Do you see that, that's the Seya detachment of the Tenth Division of the North China Army. We have them right where we want them." Weiyang nodded his head and pulled the burrs from his clothes. "Now look over there, directly in front of us, our tank battalions and heavy artillery from Kaifeng and Xuzhou are approaching. Keep your eyes open, it'll be like shooting ducks in a barrel, we'll kill them all tomorrow morning." "Father, I'm in a hurry to visit mother's grave," said Weiyang, glancing at his Seiko watch. "When will it be over?" he said, lowering his voice. The General, restraining his anger, glared at him, "In a few days, the Sakamoto detachment of the Fifth Division will send four battalions from that direction—you see? From the northeast—from over there! All stuck with no way out!" "Father, how long will the fighting last?" "How long?" the General suddenly jumped to his feet, "Eight years! It's not over yet, I tell you, your old man has fought all his life!" "I'm really in a hurry, Father!" said Weiyang, lifting his head and lightly wiping away the sweat on his forehead with the back of his hand. "Please, I have to go visit the grave," pleaded Weiyang. "Visit your damned mother's grave," cursed the General. "Yes," said Weiyang calmly, adjusting his silver-framed glasses. "I'm going to visit mother's grave." Once the General lost his temper that was it, he threw his gloves to the ground and stamped his foot fiercely several times, "Get back here! Your old man's going to kill you. Don't you understand, this is the history of China." "It's your history, Father." Weiyang carefully made his way back down the cliff, following his own footprints. Maintaining a tone of complete respect he said, "Besides, it's all over now." The General was so furious that his eyes seemed to pop out of his head; he stamped his feet several times. A bullet grazed the top of his head, peeling off a piece of his scalp: the General was left with a bald spot on which not a single hair grew for the rest of his days. He was thirty-seven that year. For the rest of his life he would never forget that place called Tai-er Zhuang.*

After the incident at Tai-er Zhuang, the General developed a very peculiar habit: whenever he had nothing to do, he would touch that bald spot to see if any hair had grown there without him being aware of it. He often stood in front of a small mirror, pinching his scalp between his fingernails to see if the follicles were dead or not. As he grew older, the hope that his hair would grow back diminished, but the unconscious desire to examine it had not died. Whenever he was angry, worried, or embarrassed he would run his hand lightly over his head, yet not touching it, like a woman who just had her hair permed, to test its springiness. Then he would violently scratch his head with his long fingernails until his face turned red.

The first time the General scratched his scalp open was during the summer of

---

*Tai-er Zhuang (*zhuang* means "village") in North China was the sight of a famous battle in the Anti-Japanese War of Resistance; it is especially noteworthy as one of the few battles in which the Nationalist Chinese armies defeated the Japanese, and thus it is particularly dear to the hearts of people like the General living in Taiwan after their final defeat by the Communists.

the year Weiyang entered college. He was furious; he couldn't imagine that his own son wanted to study sociology. From his point of view, sociology was the same as socialism, and socialism was the same as leftism and leftism was communism. "You're lucky that you've never had to fight in a war. If you want to study at a liberal arts school that's up to you." The General talked faster and faster, his voice ever higher in pitch, "But if you want to study that Communist nonsense, no way! Stand at attention!" Weiyang lowered his head; his chin quivered. The General paced back and forth and knocked over a tea table. The General's wife, who stood to one side, trembled with fear and didn't dare pick up the pieces of the broken porcelain on the floor. The General frothed at the mouth, "You want to study, then why don't you study history, your old man has spent his whole life fighting Communists." "That's your history, Father," Weiyang interrupted heavily. "Besides, it's all over." As he finished speaking, he turned around and walked out the door. "There's absolutely no discipline in this house," the General shouted at his wife. He scratched his head until it bled.

Before it got dark Weiyang returned to the Garden of Indifference. The General also made his way back alone from Tai-er Zhuang of forty-six years ago, from his official residence of twenty years ago, and from all the battles, large and small, in between. Father and son both looked tired; sitting across from one another at the dinner table they took turns yawning. Weiyang, as usual, reported on the recent status of his work and research. He never lost the chance to glance at his wristwatch or straighten his already impeccably neat suit and tie. When Weiyang paused from talking, the General would nod his head mechanically or take the opportunity to sip some soup or serve himself some food from one of the dishes. The actions of chewing and swallowing did not disturb his mental responses to his son, "No matter what, I will not allow you to promise that bunch from the Foundation to write or tape my memoirs or erect a monument or write a biography. What kind of talk is that, I'm not dead yet. What's more, this is not the time, the important things have all yet to be accomplished. How could we talk of merit and reward? The wrong people are in power. Moreover, your old man is unworthy of having his memoirs recorded; besides, what do you know of anything? Don't let anyone flatter you too much and make you forget who you are. Professor? Is a professor greater than a commanding officer?" "Father, I have to go, I have two classes to teach at the night school." Weiyang stood up to take the bag of greens from the old valet who had prepared it earlier. "I'll be back in a couple of days. You've really gone to a lot of trouble," he said politely, shaking his hand. "I grew this myself, it's organic. If you like it, come back for more. There's plenty in the garden." "It's cleaner here in the mountains. The air pollution is really bad in Taibei," said Weiyang, turning his head to look at his father. "Can he go to the bathroom by himself?" "Yes, yes he can," the old valet stretched out his hand toward the General as if he were introducing someone. "The General can eat, drink, and go to the bathroom on his own, everything is okay." "Don't bother to see me out." "Take care." As they were saying good-bye they didn't hear what the General was saying—he turned around, still enumerating the shortcomings of the Foundation, "What kind of talk is that, I'm not dead yet."

The General didn't sleep well that night; he clearly heard the rain stop in the middle of the night. With great difficulty he endured until the first misty light of dawn appeared, then he decided to visit his own grave.

The Korean grass on his tomb had the appearance of being newly planted compared with that on his wife's grave. The General bent down to touch the grass, feeling its strength and resilience. He pulled up a couple of sprigs, discovering that their roots had reached into the soil. He couldn't stop smiling from satisfaction, but his smile only lasted a few seconds because he realized he couldn't scratch it the same way he scratched his scalp—it was only a thin, thin layer. The grass couldn't bear up under the "iron-finger-eagle-talon" *gongfu* the General had learned earlier from his association with the Green Gang. Scratching the soil a couple of times uncovered a sheet of green plastic underneath. The General couldn't help being upset. He sat down on the tombstone and read the epitaph, "Here lies my late father, the honored general, Wu Zhendong." He sighed and wiped away the pieces of grass remaining on his fingers and said, "Fake."

Weiyang, who came to visit the grave, couldn't stand the sight of that patch of stripped-off Korean grass. He threw down the basket containing offerings of fruit, joss sticks, candles, and fresh flowers. He darted forward, his hair, pomaded with Gentleman's Hair Cream, slightly mussed. He yelled, "Look at how this grass has been dug up, there must be a wild dog in the area." Shi Qi, who had followed him, said, "I heard you were an incurable perfectionist, I guess they're right." The General was pressed against the tombstone by Weiyang. He felt the cold in his spine and was sickened by the smell of Weiyang's cologne. He wanted to push him away but felt somewhat hesitant because he hadn't been that close to his son in decades.

Weiyang used quite a bit of energy to gather up the sprigs of grass that still had roots and replanted them on the grave. He examined it left and right but couldn't get it right; his mood was completely ruined. Silently he arranged the joss sticks, candles, and fruit; he placed the fresh flowers on the bare spot where the grass had been pulled up so he wouldn't have to see the eyesore. Then he bent down and, spreading his handkerchief on the ground, knelt on it to pay his respects. Shi Qi followed him, bowing deeply. The General patted his backside and then stood to one side.

"I appreciate your accompanying me here," said Weiyang to Shi Qi from his position in front of the tombstone. "But I'm afraid I can't offer you any information of value. My father and I were never close. You know, I never was able to understand his times." The General nodded.

Shi Qi nodded her head too and said, "Can't you tell me something about your family life? For example, your childhood experiences. What was your relationship with your parents?"

"Childhood experiences?" snorted Weiyang, his nostrils flaring. He slowly walked to one side, nearly bumping the General's forehead with his chin, and then said, "Once he tried to teach me to salute, but, because I couldn't get my hand straight, he punished me. He had me stand in front of a portrait of Sun Yat-sen and told me that I wasn't to move until the father of the country smiled. I was four that year, can you call that a childhood experience?"

Shi Qi didn't respond to his question but, laughing mischievously, asked, "Well, how long did you stand there?"

"Three days, three whole days," Weiyang ground his teeth, and even the General could hear the grinding—but he couldn't remember the incident ever occurring. Shi Qi stopped smiling and looked at him, her eyes filled with a mixture of shock and doubt. "How frightening, the General was such a kind person, I never would have thought . . . !" "It never happened, the boy's lying." The General scratched his head a couple of times and then continued, "You think I'm dead, so you make up stories to betray your old man!" As he finished he gave Weiyang a slap on the left cheek. Weiyang immediately turned up the collar of his raincoat to keep away the wind, then walked toward the grave of the General's wife. He carefully bowed and knelt and then, stretching out his hand, pulled up some weeds. "My mother knelt beside me for two days and two nights. She didn't even dare wipe away her tears, so her *qipao* became wet through. She ended up catching cold, and I couldn't walk for a few months," said Weiyang.

"Didn't you have any happy experiences?"

"What was there to be happy about?" asked Weiyang and the General at the same time. Weiyang suddenly went into a trance, experiencing a subtle feeling of déjà vu. It was at once both very near and very distant, floating about, unfathomable. He calmly narrated one of his memories as a child in a stiff uniform, a soldier's hat, medals, and a gun. "My late father always wanted to mold me into the *stereotype* of a soldier, but I wasn't cut out for it. I was born an *anti-bureaucrat** and, as a result, he and I both suffered, the whole family suffered." The General didn't understand the foreign words, but he understood the word "suffer," which couldn't be confused in any language. He at once took his wallet from his pocket and found the yellowed photo in its yellowed plastic holder: it was a picture of Weiyang as a child. He was dressed in a sharp military uniform, facing a mirror, saluting with his little hand. His mouth was open and smiling. "Is this what you call suffering?" yelled the General in a fury. "Crap, stinking crap."

"My mother suffered the most." Weiyang took two steps back to look for any weeds remaining on the grave of the General's wife; they had nearly all been pulled. Only then did he speak, "My father is responsible for her death."

The General couldn't stand hearing those words; he carelessly thrust his wal-

---

*Both *stereotype* and *anti-bureaucrat* appear in English in the original, as do *conditioned*, *political sphere*, and *Well* further on; this sort of usage is typical of returned overseas students in Taiwan.

let and the photo back into his pocket and took a step forward. With his left hand he seized Weiyang's collar and with his right hand held Shi Qi by the elbow and said, "Go back with your old man and see who was responsible, who was really responsible."

That year the General had reached the age of retirement from the army, but he decided to stay on for two more years. He was greatly pleased with himself for following the old saying, "The old steed in the stable still aspires to gallop a thousand miles." Also following the old custom, he found a famous painter to become his teacher and filled in his time learning painting and calligraphy. He complained that landscape painting was flat; flower and bird painting was soft; portraits of beauties were worthless, so he decided on painting dragons, tigers, and horses. He used large sheets of paper, a coarse brush, and large hollow brush strokes. He didn't study for very long, but many people sought treasured specimens of his work. Once in a while he would send a scroll or two to Weiyang, who was then studying in the United States. Invariably the complimentary verses, which he sent in place of a letter, went something like, "The day the emperor's troops pacify the northern plains / Don't forget to tell this old man when performing the ancestral sacrifices," or "My great desire is to feed my hunger with the flesh of barbarians / To drink their blood as I laugh and talk."*

When Weiyang and Shi Qi, who were escorted by the General, got back to the Garden of Indifference, the seventy-year-old General was in the study affixing his seal to a huge tiger with a white forehead, which seemed to howl fiercely against a wind it could scarcely bear. Weiyang glanced at the complimentary verse—it was those old lines from Xin Qiji's poem "The Southland": "Whenever I look at China Beigu Tower fills my eyes / . . . How I wish I had a son like Sun Zhongmou." He immediately turned to Shi Qi and said, "I suffered most because of this painting." "Uh?" said Shi Qi, glancing at the painting and then at the General, who was absorbed in the appreciation of his own work. "That year I was in D.C.," right away Weiyang lowered his voice and whispered, "I was involved in the Diaoyutai protest movement.† A few of my classmates, who

---

*The lines of classical poetry quoted by the General are from the "patriotic poets" Lu You and Yue Fei; together with Xin Qiji, mentioned further on, they are all from the Song dynasty, whose northern territories were occupied by non-Chinese peoples. In Taiwan people like the General quoted their poetry with the implication that the Communists were barbarian usurpers who would someday be driven out by the rightful heirs to the Chinese government—the Nationalists.

†Diaoyutai refers to a small group of islands that were disputed by China and Japan in the 1970s. The PRC disputed them with Japan, but the KMT government on Taiwan did not do so vigorously enough for many "patriotic" and "left-wing" students from Taiwan who were studying in the United States. The Diaoyutai Movement was both a patriotic anti-Japanese movement and an anti-KMT movement highly critical of the government on Taiwan. It generated a great deal of heat among overseas Chinese students on both the left and the right. Zhang Xiguo's novel *Zuori zhi nu* (Yesterday's anger, 1978) provides an excellent picture of the situation at that time.

were also involved in the movement, knew of my family background and, when they saw the painting he sent me, decided to hold a struggle meeting to attack me. They wanted me to do a self-criticism; the meeting lasted a whole night." "You were that far left at the time?" "I wasn't left, ah, how should I say—," said Weiyang as he adjusted his necktie with some discomfort, "—I was rather confused." "But to hold that kind of meeting—" "At that time it was just a 'democratic practice,' that's all, nothing serious."*

"Nothing serious?" The General pointed to the old valet who had just rushed in and said to the two of them, "Now see for yourselves."

The old valet handed an air mail letter to the General, who was busy painting. The envelope carried the words "Hong Kong New Wing Gallery" in seal-style characters. The General opened the letter and while reading said, "They want to show my work . . ." but before he had finished speaking, his expression changed and his upper body trembled. He shook so much that he almost splashed the ink from the inkstone. After a while he seemed to grow calm. He took a deep breath and said to the old valet, "Have this mounted and mailed to the United States— and have my wife come here."

When the General's wife entered the room, Weiyang spoke to Shi Qi, "I've always believed that the sacrificial character of Chinese women is a political by-product." Shi Qi nodded her head with profound understanding. The General again called for their attention. The General's wife received the letter from the General's hand and exclaimed, "Wonderful." "Shit, take a closer look. Who's the vice-director of the gallery?" His wife looked again and couldn't help being surprised, "My father, he's escaped!" "You're dreaming!" The General casually took up brush and paper and, with several large hollow strokes, drew one circle, then another and another, all squeezed together, and said, "With his opium habit, he was probably thrown out." "You seem to—," Shi Qi lifted her face and stared at Weiyang, "—understand quite well." "It was only after I had been out of the country a number of years that I then began to see things clearly." Weiyang's eyes had settled on some distant point between the General and his wife and said, "The relationship between men and women in China, indeed, any ethical relationship, is *conditioned* by difficulties in the *political sphere* from which there is no escape." "Escaped or released, it's all the same, isn't it?" The General's wife could almost feel the cold hatred emanating from the General. The General stretched the paper between his fingers and, bearing down with the brush, painted a big X and hoarsely said, "You women know nothing. They released him to get at me, to create an embarrassing situation for me. They've invited me to have a show so that I can meet my father-in-law and disgrace myself. What, do they still think I'm a baby? Shit!" "A family reunion is a happy occasion, what's so disgraceful about that?" As the General's wife

---

*"Struggle meeting," and "self-criticism" are Maoist terms used by the left-wing Chinese students at the time.

spoke she began to cry, her words became weaker and weaker, and she hung her head as if she were trying to convince her embroidered shoes. "So you took part in the movement to avoid that sort of difficulty?" Shi Qi took a notebook from her leather bag and began taking notes. Weiyang smoothed out the ends of his mustache and cleared his throat just as he always did when preparing to be interviewed, and in a more measured tone said, "*Well*, ah, I think, by the logic of action, yes; but I must clarify: I was never deeply involved, I backed out almost at once and became a mere onlooker. I've always regretted that the 'Diaoyutai Movement' became a 'Unification Movement'! Of course that's another question. . . ." "Bullshit! What reunion, they want to use me." The General threw the brush and shouted, "This is called a 'United Front'! If you want to join that old bastard, go to hell!" The last two words were interrupted by the General behind the General, "Did you hear that? A 'United Front'!" "From my point of view, these things happened long ago; we ought to be able to discuss them in a rational manner and not resort to emotion." The General's wife couldn't bear it any longer and cursed, "You're not human." Then she turned around and rushed out of the room. "You can go to hell," the General kept yelling. "Well—," Shi Qi glanced at the General and the General behind the General, "To get back to our original topic, can you say anything rational about your father?" Hearing this, Weiyang pursed his lips, thought for a moment, and then said, "Frankly, we all live with contradictions."

The General had come back from the cemetery greatly confused. He thought about the word "contradiction" and its meaning, that word which he had never used. He hated that word because his lifelong enemies had skillfully made use of the law of contradiction.* This had already become a conviction of his faith as a professional soldier. The General also believed that if a man believed in something he would never have any damned contradictions. But as he thought about this, he couldn't help worrying about Weiyang. If Weiyang lived with contradictions it meant that he didn't believe in anything. In that case, the friction that had been there between father and son over the years was not limited to "hard versus soft," "pen versus sword," "new versus old," or other simple forms of opposition. What was really frightening, then, was that the General didn't know where his son really stood, what he believed in, or what he was against. Whereas by comparison, on the contrary, he felt that for Weiyang to blame his mother's death on his ignorance and tyranny was a small matter for which he shouldn't be held too much to account.

Circling the top of the mountain twice, the General made his way back along the north slope to the Garden of Indifference. Halfway down the mountain he ran into some veterans from the Engineering Corps erecting the framework of a scaffold in the center of which was an empty space. He knew they would set up a memorial made of marble on that spot. On the memorial would be carved words

---

*"Contradiction" is a Maoist political term that is naturally hated by the General.

of praise by seventy-two people, members of the Foundation, old friends from the Fellow Provincial Association, his old subordinates, and his son. The monument would be completed and unveiled much later, on the ninetieth anniversary of his birth. Weiyang would even be invited to give a seven-minute speech, the title of which would be "Some Incidents from the Life of My Late Father, General Wu."

The General stopped to greet the foreman of the crew. "Putting up a monument, huh?" he asked. "Yeah," said the foreman, lifting the front part of his shirt to wipe the sweat from his forehead. On his forearm could be seen a dark green tattoo: "Oppose the Communists, resist the Russians, save China / Kill Zhu, pull out Mao, sweep away the traitors."* "It's for a general, he died several years back."

"Oh."

"He was great, he fought all his life."

"Oh."

"I also heard he was quite a calligrapher and painted lots of paintings."

"Oh."

The General heard his achievements praised once again, but it wasn't like in the past when he would fly into a rage if someone offered too much praise. He listened patiently, nodding constantly as if he were listening to an unfamiliar piece of fleeting music. Finally he raised his hand in a salute to say good-bye and muttered, "Yes, yes, the longer a person is dead, the fewer the contradictions."

"What's that?"

As summer approached, the General said one thing, "It's getting hot." The old valet was startled, thinking he must have been mistaken, he couldn't believe his ears. When the General said it was getting hot he had already joined those gathered to celebrate the anniversary of the birth of the late General. He saw a large, fire-red silk veil fall fluttering from the monument, gliding down to rest among the baskets of flowers arranged around the monument. The crowd immediately burst into clamorous applause.

Weiyang's speech took the General completely by surprise. He's recounted the exact year the General fought a certain battle and what year he broke out of an encirclement and which year he had received a medal or promotion. Except for the pronunciation of some personal names and place names, the speech accorded with the General's memory. There was just one point that, when he heard it, he couldn't believe his ears.

"In January 1971, my mother, Madame Wu née Zhou, died of a sudden heart attack. My father was deeply grieved and kept vigil beside her bier for forty-nine

---

Zhu refers to Zhu De, a famous Communist general, and is a homophone for "pig." *Mao* refers to Mao Zedong and is a homophone for "hair." *Sha zhu ba mao* is a common phrase meaning "kill pig, pull out hair," but as a political slogan it is a homophone for "kill Zhu De and root out Mao Zedong."

days, scarcely eating a thing. From this we can see how deeply he loved my mother. . . ."

When Weiyang read this section, he was as pale and expressionless as usual. He did misread "grieved" as "grew old" without noticing the mistake. The General was astonished and scratched his scalp furiously; he didn't know if he should agree with Weiyang's statement or not.

The General spent a whole summer just lingering over the period after his wife committed suicide by swallowing sleeping pills. Sometimes he would be accompanied by his old valet, who had a new hearing aid. Their clothes were so thin that they couldn't ward off the cold of past winters. Usually they went out and came right back. In that cold wind the General would always ask, "You tell me, did I keep vigil by her bier or not?" The old valet, shivering with cold, looked at him and said, "You know if you did." "But I'm asking you!" The old valet looked again at the empty hall but he huddled, stiff with cold, and shook even more violently, "It seems you didn't!" "But I remember . . . " "If you say you did then you did, if you say no then you didn't." The General grunted and asked, "Then you tell me, did I eat?" The old valet paused and adjusted his hearing aid, "Huh? What did you say?" "I asked if I ate anything." "Yes, you ate the rice and dishes I prepared! You also drank wine to ward off the cold." "Oh? That's strange!" The General asked, "Didn't I just keep vigil by the bier and not eat anything?" The old valet shivered again and shook his head, "It's cold, General, let's go back!"

The last time the General stepped out of the Garden of Indifference was on the Double Ninth Festival. Weiyang supported him with his hand as they walked uphill against the wind. "All the leaves have fallen," said the General. "Yes," replied Weiyang. It took him quite a while to realize that the General hadn't become mute, and when he did he stopped automatically in his tracks. "Let's not go on, Father, it is cold here in the mountains." The General paid no attention and continued walking up the slope. He wanted to take his son to the dedication ceremony on the anniversary of his birth to hear what he would say six years from then.

". . . We can see how deeply he loved my mother. In a word, my father was a man with beliefs. All his life he struggled and made sacrifices for his beliefs. In this age of ours, so full of changes and contradictions, he has left us an undying example. Though he has passed away, his spirit lives on: he will be with us forever."

"You, did you mean what you said?" The General asked him, his voice trembling as he looked left and right at the son on the stage and at the one standing beside him. Weiyang, standing next to him, hesitated and said, "Don't you like what you hear?" Amidst the applause, Weiyang, on the stage, walked down into the crowd and shook hands with the guests. At last he stood next to the secretary general of the Foundation and offered him his thanks, "Without your help, I don't know what I would have said." "Don't thank me." Laughing, the secretary general said, "It was drafted by Miss Shi. It's indeed a well-written piece, each word is a gem. Very touching, very touching."

Hearing this, the General's scalp had turned a violent red, and with his hands he pushed away Weiyang who was standing next to him, supporting him. "If you don't believe any of this, how could you say it so convincingly?" he shouted. "It's only a speech," replied Weiyang as he smoothed out the wrinkles of his sleeve. "What are you against me for? What do you believe in?" The General kicked wildly in the direction of the monument. The kick caused a small gust that overturned the red veil and flower baskets. Weiyang, who had made the speech, and Shi Qi rushed to set them back in place and straighten out the red veil. "Frankly, we all live with contradictions," said Weiyang, standing next to him as he moved forward.

The General watched as the two forms of his son, from the left and right, collided, separated, and merged—sometimes clear and sometimes indistinct. Then he felt the sky and the earth begin to spin; he shouted as loud as he could and smashed his head against the monument. At that moment he heard a thunderous roar simultaneously from inside and outside his body, sundering all the contradictions in which he had been entangled. It was the first time he had ever been released from them.

The General existed omnipresently, unconcerned with praise or censure. He would wait with all his heart and mind: one day Weiyang would finally understand all these things, because they were men who could ignore time and change, or correct memory as they wished.

A Wordless Monument

Qiao Dianyun

Translated by Michael S. Duke

IN FRONT of the village there's a small stream, not very broad with shallow running water, very, very clear and as transparent as glass. Multicolored rocks on the bottom of the river, rocks come loose and drifting around under the water, and the mirror image of hills, trees, and flying birds reflected on the surface of the river can all be seen with perfect clarity. When people went to work in the fields, to market to sell firewood, or to school to study, in summer they'd wade across barefooted and in winter they'd step on the rocks to cross; it was convenient and it was inconvenient. For many years they'd said they were going to build a bridge, and for just that many years they didn't build one. After all, we'd got on fine for hundreds of years without a bridge, and that proved we could go right on living without a bridge. No need to look for trouble and hardship; we had no quarrel with ourselves; as long as we could take it easy for a while, we'd just as well take it easy. Why not?

On the other side of the river there was a grave mound, very, very big, as big as a small hill. How old was that grave? Don't know. There was a ginkgo tree on top of the grave; the old folks say trees like that can live for more than a thousand years. It seems true enough; the tree can shade over half an acre of land. In front of the grave was a stone stele, very high and very thick with a stone cap of dragons carved on the top of it. The words on the stele had become blurred from a thousand years of wind and rain. What was written on it? Couldn't make it out. Nobody went to look at it, and nobody felt like looking at it. The affairs of the living were such a tangled mess we could never get 'em straight, and we could hardly take care of ourselves; who had any heart left over to mess around with the affairs of the dead? And besides, what good would it have done to make out those words? Could we eat 'em or drink 'em or make revolution with 'em?

This translation is from *Lianhe wenxue* (Unitas), no. 6 (1987): 194–99.

Later on came a burst of revolution,* and first we attacked the living. We
attacked them one bunch after another. Out of forty-five families in the entire
village, forty-two came under attack. The more people we attacked, the more
actively everybody went on attacking everybody else. To atone for their crimes
and curry favor, those who were attacked yesterday risked everything to attack
others today. You attacked me and I attacked you. Although it wasn't very pretty
to be attacked, still there was some sweetness amid the bitterness: when one
person was being attacked, everybody sat around and watched the excitement;
resting up like that was a might lighter work than learning from Dazhai.† This
was known as "the individual suffering for the well-being of the group" and
was in perfect accord with revolutionary principles. After we'd attacked all of
the living several times over, there was nobody left to attack, so we'd have to go
back to the fields and work like hell. That was an awful prospect! And besides, if
we didn't keep on with the revolution, the higher-ups wouldn't let us off the
hook. What could we do? Who could we attack? Well then! It was the turn of
that big grave mound. No doubt about it! The guy under there was certainly a big
villain, certainly a no-good scoundrel, certainly a high official, certainly a capitalist roader.‡ If he was a small fry, a good sort, a commoner, or a revolutionary,
would he be buried in such a big grave? When the higher authorities heard our
idea they sent down an order of commendation: Good! Outstanding! Overall
direction absolutely correct, should be attacked without mercy, attack the hell
out of it!

And so everybody let out a whoop and entered the fray:

Cut down the big tree!

Rake open the grave!

Push over the stele!

Stomp on him with ten thousand feet; never mind that he's been dead for a
thousand years, we mustn't let him rise again.

Take the stele and lay it across the stream.

Revolution is good! Our little old stream has been given a revolutionary
bridge.

Revolution is good! The lowly commoners trample on the body of a high
official from a thousand years ago!

From that time on, when the villagers went to work in the fields, to market to
sell firewood, or to school to study, they no longer had to wade across barefooted
or jump across on the rocks. They felt right proud as they walked across on the
bridge. How about it, look who's oppressing who? Who told you to be so evil

---

*The Great Proletarian Cultural Revolution began in 1966 and did not officially end
until 1977, but it was most violently carried out from 1966 to 1969.

†Dazhai is a famous oil field that was hailed as a model of socialist labor during the
Cultural Revolution.

‡A "capitalist roader" was anyone accused of wanting to turn away from the "socialist road" in economic development.

when you were alive? Who told you to be so cruel? Who told you to be so highfalutin? Some people deliberately stamped their feet harshly a few times; some deliberately gouged around with their picks and hoes; and some people even paused to piss on the bridge! Why? To vent their hatred, to feel happy. Vent what hatred? Happy about what? Nobody gave it a thought. And they didn't need to think about it. To be able to knock down something that was standing, able to walk on top of it, able willfully to stamp their feet on it, able wantonly to piss on it, that was victory, that was power, that was venting your hatred, feeling good, glorious, and happy; what need was there to ask why any more?!

It wasn't that people didn't think at all. They thought, all right, they thought a lot. They thought about the man in the grave. He certainly didn't learn from Dazhai, certainly had not eaten in a communal mess hall, certainly had buckets of oil and bushels of grain, certainly didn't eat dried sweet potato leaves, certainly rode in a sedan chair when he went out, certainly had several concubines, his concubines were certainly very fair skinned and very tender, tender as a cucumber, if you scratched them with your fingernail, oil would ooze out, certainly . . .

When anybody walked on the bridge, he'd start cursing out loud.

"I'll teach you to be so highfalutin!"

"I'll teach you to eat and dress well!"

"I'll teach you to keep several wives for yourself and not give each of us one!"

"I'll teach you . . ."

Everybody walked over laughing gaily and cursing angrily.

Everybody walked back laughing gaily and cursing angrily.

Every day the stone stele bore the people's cruel stamping; every day it heard their taunts and curses. It bore them all in silence, never said a word nor put up the least resistance.

All of a sudden, to everyone's surprise, the little bridge was transformed in appearance; it had been washed clean and a pale layer of ink traces had been left on it. Who? Up to what? People suddenly thought of ghosts and ghostly emanations. Their scalps went numb and their skin crept with gooseflesh as though they were about to suffer immediate retribution and be struck down by a great calamity. Thus they put their heads together and secretively whispered about it everywhere.

"In life the man in the grave was a high official and now he's a high official up in Heaven; you think he's going to let us off easy after we broke open his grave?!"

"At midnight last night, he dispatched a troop of heavenly soldiers and heavenly generals wearing golden helmets and golden armor to come riding down on the clouds!"

"They came down riding white horses. Last night I came out to piss and saw a big herd of white horses in the sky, kicking and clopping as they rushed along; scared me shitless!"

The village was nervous as hell.

Quite a few people locked their front gates tight, knelt down in their yards, kowtowed to the Lord of Heaven, and tried to vindicate themselves: "This really shouldn't be blamed on us, we had no grudge or enmity with the man in the grave and never thought to rake open his tomb! It should all be blamed on the higher authorities for offending the heavenly principles and forcing us to open the grave; if we didn't do it they would've denounced us. If You're displeased You should go and be displeased with the higher authorities, even if You have to smite them with heavenly thunder and lightning!"

When the higher authorities heard the news, they were hopping mad; they dispatched a team to investigate and called upon the people to expose and inform on the offender. There was a reward for informing; but if you had knowledge and didn't report it, your crime would be twice as great. The power of the law is boundless; even if Sun the Monkey King were alive today he would find it hard to escape the Buddha's palm.* Besides, as long as there was merit to be gained, naturally there were people willing to gain it or who wanted to gain it. If you didn't gain merit what should you gain? Thus everybody started informing and finally they exposed somebody.

It's him, it must be him! A worthy scion of the landlord class, a traitor to the poor and lower-middle peasants, an inveterate enemy of the revolution, one of Liu Shaoqi's little vermin.† When we raked the grave, everybody joyfully vied for the chance to rake it; but he acted like he was raking open his own mother and father's grave. He said he had a stomach-ache and asked for time off; he even cried, said his stomach hurt so bad it made him cry. Everybody beams with happiness and pride when they walk back and forth across the little bridge. But he's the only one who still jumps across on the rocks, never lets his feet touch the bridge, and even sighs out loud watching the happy masses cross the bridge. He doesn't cross over on the bridge, and he doesn't let Little Sun cross over on the bridge either; three times a day he carries Little Sun back and forth to school on his back over the rocks.

Xu Shuge, an old school master. Him with a white beard already and still up to such shenanigans. The fellow's mind's too deeply poisoned and there's no cure for him. His son's been struggled to death, his daughter-in-law's married into another family, and he still won't repent.

What's he trying to do? What's he been up to already? Drag him out! First we made him recite the official policies. He had 'em down pat: "Leniency for confession, severity for resistance." He said confession, but he buttoned his lips

---

*In the popular Ming novel, *Journey to the West*, Sun Wukong, the Monkey King, tries unsuccessfully to fly off of the Buddha's palm.

†Liu Shaoqi was chairman of the Republic when he was purged by Mao Zedong during the Cultural Revolution. He was known as the "number one capitalist roader," and anyone associated with his policies might be vilified as vermin.

tight as a tick and wouldn't spit out a single word of honest confession. No matter, that's easily taken care of. If the old man won't confess, there's still the little kid. Drag out his grandson, Little Wen. Good, with a meat cleaver flashing in the sun and sawing away on his neck, the little counterrevolutionary wasn't as stubborn as the old counterrevolutionary. He started crying and told us: "Grampa made a rubbing of the bridge stone."

What's he want to make a rubbing of the bridge for? He's up to no good, keeping records for a future restoration of the overthrown classes! After his death, he intends to curry favor with the high officials of the nether world; plans to collaborate with them to come back to this world to counterattack and regain power. How venomous! How vicious! How sneaky! If we didn't have a lot of sharp eyes around here, his plot might have even succeeded. We have to make him give it up! Hand it over! He won't give it up? Search for it! If we have to dig three feet under the ground, we've got to find it. We overturned his trunks and rifled his closets; even poked around in every rat hole in his house. We didn't find a pinch of salt in his crocks or a grain of rice in his larder. The old buzzard's living on wind and dew and still has the nerve to get up to such malevolent practices, still has the money to pull off such a nefarious scheme; he must be possessed by devils. Where did he hide it? The interrogators wore their tongues out asking questions and pounded the table till it collapsed, but the old fart remained steely-hearted and reactionary to the core; he just would not say!

The whole village was furious. Even those who believed in Heaven were full of righteous indignation: "His mother's . . . . . . , messing around like that, scaring our souls half to death, making us kowtow to the Lord of Heaven for nothing! We can't let him off easy. We have to give him a taste of revolution."

And so we had a meeting for three days straight. For three days and three nights, we made war on him, made war on the counterrevolutionary, eating and sleeping and attacking him in revolving shifts. It was really hot and heavy, really lively. We hadn't sung local opera in the village for over ten years, and the kids kept asking us what opera was like. How good did opera look anyway? This was a better play than any opera, better looking than any play acting, and you didn't have to buy a ticket; just watch, watch to your heart's content, watch until you'd seen enough. Pushing, squeezing, tying down, beating, hanging, forced kneeling . . . all the eighteen techniques of the martial arts were used on him, and they even invented a nineteenth martial technique: beard pulling. Pulled out his beard one whisker at a time, pulled out one whisker and asked him once; if he didn't answer, they pulled out another one and pulled out another one, just kept on pulling them out one at a time. It was marvelous to watch; an old man turned into an old lady, nothing like it in traditional opera. The old fool just wouldn't talk, refused to atone for his crime; he even laughed out loud, laughed with tears streaming down his face. Was he crazy? Crazy my ass! He was just acting crazy and simple-minded as a form of resistance, trying to play act his way out of trouble. He'll not get off so easily. The evil of his crime was so great, he was more Liu Shaoqi than Liu Shaoqi himself, rotten to the core. Rotten? No matter how bad he is, no matter how stubborn he is, no bull is so big that there's not a way to trap it. Put a dunce cap on his head, put him under surveillance, practice dictatorship on him, give him the hardest labor duties, struggle him to death, tire him to death, anger him to death; see who's more terrible than who. Is the revolution something easily provoked? Easily bullied? As long as you don't die, that's just how long you're going to have to take what we dish out.

A praying mantis should forget about trying to stop a wagon—there's no way. Everybody walked over the revolutionary bridge as before, only now they had another thing to laugh about when they walked up on the bridge. They laughed at that stupid prick Xu Shuge. Never mind that he'd read a belly full of books, he read 'em all for nothing, read himself into a bookworm, read himself silly. He didn't even know which side of a person's ass to kiss, never flattered the living but ran off to kiss up to a ghost. No matter how high an official that fellow in the grave was, he's been moldered into slop for eight hundred years. He's not one of today's living officials; no matter how much you care about him, lean to his side, and protect him, can he even give you a fart to smell for your reward? If Xu Shuge doesn't even understand that, isn't even clear about such simple things, he really drank all of that ink for nothing.

Year after year everybody walked back and forth over the stone stele, walked back and forth without cease. The surface of the bridge was first worn down to a shiny finish, and then it was covered with a layer of mud by all those feet walking back and forth. The stone stele was no longer a stone stele, it had truly become a little bridge. After the people had walked over it so many times, they got used to it, took it for granted, it was no longer anything new, and they lost all interest in the origin of this little bridge. Gradually they forgot everything, forgot that the bridge under their feet was a stone stele, forgot the big grave mound that was originally behind the stone stele, and forgot about Xu Shuge's beard. They forgot everything about everything, and they didn't laugh any more either.

The bridge was just a bridge. As long as it was convenient for going back and forth, why should they remember that the bridge was made from a stone stele, why should they remember the big grave behind the stone stele, and why should they remember Xu Shuge's beard? What good was there in remembering all of that? If a body didn't have anything to do, he'd just as well take a nap and rest his mind.

Several years went by and the events surrounding the little bridge died away, were buried, and completely forgotten.

We say what's past is past; who could have known that something dead and buried would be stirred up again?

One day a little automobile suddenly pulled up, its black paint shining, long and flat, the spitting image of a dung beetle, with smoke still farting out the rear. And so our village that had been peaceful for so many years grew lively again. The men didn't go into the fields and the women didn't cook; they all picked up or pulled along their kids and shouted back and forth as they gathered around to look at this rare, newfangled object. Just as if they were trying to get a look at a three-legged man or a one-legged cow, row upon row of them jostled and pushed their way up to the front, pushing and cursing because nobody wanted to move aside for anybody.

Several people were disgorged from the dung beetle's mouth. There was a white-haired old fellow wearing spectacles; he certainly looked to be a high official. The high official first led his military escort over to the big grave mound to look at how the grave had been raked over. He sighed and sighed as if it was his family's ancestral grave site, as if somebody had ruined his family's geomantic tradition. His military escort dug around in the ground near the grave, picked up some pieces of broken plates and jars and put them in the car, treating them like something precious, like they'd picked up a pile of fifty-cent coins. What do they want those things for? Ancient objects! Ha, ha, ancient objects? City folks make a big fuss about things they seldom see. Of the rocks in the river, the mud in the fields, the little stream in front of the village, the big hill behind the village, which one of 'em hasn't been here since the creation, which one of 'em isn't ancient? If you want 'em, take 'em all back; you can even take all of us livin' on top of these ancient objects back home with you too; that'd be just fine. People couldn't hold back their laughter. They laughed at the high official with the spectacles until he shook his head back and forth like a child's toy rattle and got all red in the face.

Later on all those officials ran up onto the bridge, shoveled the dirt off the bridge, washed the mud off the bridge; bit by bit they shoveled and washed, wiping the stone stele sparkling clean just like washing a new bride's face; only thing they didn't do was rub on some facial makeup. The old official in the spectacles walked up onto the bridge, knelt down, and then went down on all fours to shine a mirror with a handle on it up and down; inch by inch he shined it for a long, long time, shined it on the entire bridge like someone trying to catch lice, but he didn't find anything, didn't even catch a single louse; then he started crying and took out a cloth and wiped his tears. At seventy or eighty years old, with no one hitting him, with no illnesses or other calamities, not going broke or anything, what was he crying about? He was crying with genuine grief, too, as if his young wife had just died; it was downright laughable. Maybe city people are just naturally born with so many tears!

Later on, after the high official with the spectacles had done crying, he asked the people to carry the stone stele back to its original place and stand it up in the original manner. Don't you wish! We neither drink nor eat off you; if we had that much strength we'd go shovel manure to build up the soil. As soon as they heard him, everybody took off in a flash; it was as if they all had the power of invisibility; in the wink of an eye not a soul was left in sight. The bespectacled high official shook his head and sighed. Then he pulled out a wad of cash and everybody suddenly clambered back out from under the ground. Quickly clustering around the stele, they almost came to blows as they pushed and fought for a chance to carry it. Fetching ropes, fetching carrying poles, laughing, and shouting, they carried it with joyful enthusiasm as though they were carrying a wedding palanquin. They grew happier and happier as they walked along. Thanks be to Heaven and Earth, lucky for us we went up and raked away the grave that time; if we hadn't used the stele for a bridge how'd we ever have such a windfall as this here? It's a damned sight better than selling firewood, just walking a few feet to pick up such a load of cash; it'll be good for a whale of a lot of salt, enough for a family to eat for half a year. Good deals like this are mighty damn hard to find; what a shame they come along too rarely; if good deals like this came along every day, that'd sure as hell be mighty fine, mighty damn fine!

What about Xu Shuge? We didn't see hide nor hair of him. The next day, the old coot showed up and handed in the ink rubbing he'd made of the stele's inscription. The bespectacled old high official looked that inscription up and down and back and forth, looking and looking and getting happy and smiling; he even forgot he was a high official and started bowing to Xu Shuge; bending his waist and stretching his back down until his head damn near hit the ground, he bowed three times in a row to Xu Shuge. Social morality is really screwed up these days, plum turned upside down; rocks in the ditch are rolling uphill and mountain piglets are swallowing tigers; high officials have started in bowing to the common folk; what kind of morality is that? Xu Shuge started crying. When we pulled out his beard, he laughed, but now, when it didn't hurt or even itch, he starts in bawling. He cried until the tears were streaming down his face and then bent at the waist and returned those three bows. What on earth?! They went on in front of everybody like a bride and groom bowing to Heaven and Earth, bowing back and forth without even as much as a blush. Unfortunately, they were men and both oldsters to boot; if they had'a been a young man and women bowing like that it would'a been worth watching, but that show didn't satisfy nobody!

The high official with the spectacles said Xu Shuge had saved a national treasure and handed him five hundred dollars cash. Xu Shuge got red in the face and said he didn't want it. He really put on a good show, wouldn't take it for the life of him. He even said he hadn't fulfilled the responsibility of a true Chinese; said a whole heap of fine-sounding words; that's what scholars are good for, they sure know how to string pretty words together. The two of 'em kept handing that five hundred bucks back and forth, back and forth for the longest time, all the while piling up a couple of big bushels full of fine-sounding phrases. Xu Shuge wouldn't take it, wouldn't take it, wouldn't take it until he finally took it. Not want money? Huh, the hypocrite! Who don't know how to act drunk when he's not? What's a little bit, what's only twenty or thirty cents? But this was five hundred bucks. Seeing he wasn't drugged out of his mind, it'd be damned strange if he hadn't taken it.

The dung beetle rolled off farting smoke as it went.

Xu Shuge suddenly became a rich man in the village. Shit, we busted our asses carrying that stone stele back and forth for a few measly bucks, but attacking him all those times actually made him a fortune. Wait a minute! Wait just a minute! If it hadn't been for all of us rubbing the characters clean off of that stele, would that piece of paper of his be worth a fart? Five hundred? It wouldn't even be worth fifty cents, not even five cents; if he gave it to us to wipe our asses we'd say it was too dirty. Thanks to everybody, you walked over it and I walked over it and we rubbed it up to five hundred bucks. Well then? He's got to express some consideration, he's got to show a little gratitude.

Everybody started following Xu Shuge around. If he was in the fields they surrounded him in the fields and if he went home they followed him home. Day and night they smiled at him, smiled and smiled and smiled, hundreds of smiling eyes staring straight at his bulging pockets. You think you're going to have it all to yourself? No way! You've got to share the wealth with everybody.

How about it? A sensible person is easy to deal with!

How about it? You ought to give us half!

How about it? You should share and share alike!

How about it? You ought to stand a few drinks for everybody!

How about it . . . ?

How about it . . . ?

Every time they said "How about it" they laughed; the laughter was false, but the hatred was real. Xu Shuge laughed too, just the way he laughed back then when they were pulling out his beard. Somebody would "How about it?" a while and he'd laugh a while, then somebody else'd "How about it?" again and he'd laugh again. The old fart laughed all right, but he didn't cough up a dime, just kept sawing the melon without ever opening it up to share it out, acting like a muddleheaded monk. We don't care if you're a hard knot on an elm tree, as long as the axe is sharp enough you'll soon split open. You can't be so unfair. Xu Shuge's house was pelted with rocks in the middle of the night. When he came out of his door in the early morning, Xu Shuge stepped right into fresh dog shit. In his vegetable garden, Xu Shuge's garlic was pulled up all over the place and there were holes everywhere. Everybody went on smiling right at him again; he ought to get the message; he ought to understand that people are made of flesh and blood. But Xu Shuge didn't seem to understand anything, didn't seem to know anything, didn't act like anything had happened; he just went on smiling back at everybody, smile for smile.

Suddenly Xu Shuge disappeared and wasn't seen for three days and three nights. The old coot was probably scared shitless, afraid we'd kidnap him, and ran away. Or was he dead? Everybody in the village was afraid of everybody else: "human life is a matter touching Heaven" and not something to be played with! Better not miss beating the skunk to death and come away reeking with stench. If the higher-ups didn't go along with it, goddamn, if they didn't cut off your head at least they'd send you to prison for a long time. Everybody dragged the deep pools, searched the hilltops and scoured the forests, but they didn't find so much as a hair off his head. The old fart was gone without a trace, not even a corpse. Somebody must have done him in for the money, cut his body up into pieces and buried 'em. Damn scary business.

Who did it? The whole village was gossiping away: so and so threw rocks at his house, so and so put dog shit on his front doorstep, so and so pulled up his garlic, so and so . . . Before the higher-ups had even come along to interfere, the accusations were flying hot and heavy. So and so bought some new clothes; where'd he get the money? So and so was smoking cigarettes wrapped in tinfoil; where'd he get the money? So and so was eating meat; where'd he get the money? So and so . . . The more they saw, the more they thought, and the more they accused each other. You accused me and I accused him and he accused you, the whole village was turned into a gang of bloody murderers. The whole village was nervous as hell; they all boarded up their doors before it was even dark and stopped having anything to do with each other. A human heart is under the skin and a tiger's heart is under his pelt, who could tell who was the murderer; better not get yourself implicated with him; extreme caution was in order.

There's no wall that doesn't let in the wind. When people talk at home the walls have ears, and when they gab on the road there are eavesdroppers in the grass. When somebody accused somebody else of being the murderer, that somebody else always knew about it. Your mother's! Incriminating the innocent, trying to get me killed are you? I'm not somebody to provoke lightly, my blood is red and hot too! People started going to other people's houses to question 'em, arguing, cursing, and fighting; one head after another was busted open and the blood flowed freely, but nobody was willing to stop. If we die here we die and if we're taken to court we die, so we might as well fight for our lives! The whole village was crying and shouting wildly enough to scare off the chickens and the dogs; everybody said he'd been wronged, everybody wanted to redress the wrong and wreak vengeance; they acted out a play that was much better than real stage plays, and you didn't even have to buy a ticket.

After a few days Xu Shuge came back with some workers. The village finally settled down; actually they were even more unsettled. Everybody ran over to Xu Shuge's house, each one trying to outdo the others in venting a belly full of angry resentment. "Damn you, people said I killed you! If you really hadn't turned up, they'd probably cut off my head and a good man would die for lack of evidence!"

"Damn you, some people put your blood onto me, said I cut you up into little pieces!"

"Damn you, I ate a little meat and they said I killed you and took your money!"

"Damn you, my buddies gave me a pack of good smokes and I almost smoked myself into a murder charge!''

"Damn you . . .''

Xu Shuge laughed, none too long and none too short, didn't say who was right nor who was wrong, didn't say anything; he just led the workers over to our little stream where they started in building a bridge. When the five hundred dollars were all gone the bridge was completed. It was a nice broad bridge, flat and sturdy. The cement bridge took the stone stele's place and was much easier to walk over.

When everybody walked over that real bridge and talked about the bespecta- cled high official and that old character Xu Shuge, they all had something in common to talk about again, and their former suspicions and enmities fell by the wayside. Those two old geezers were really weird, downright ridiculous. That bespectacled old high official was sure cracked not to remain at home and enjoy the good life, but rather run all the way up here to this godforsaken old mountain village to cry, to bow, and to pass out money; a true case of weeping at the opera—worrying about the ancients. Saying that rubbing was a national treasure, bullshit! Could it protect us from cold and hunger, or would it ward off the foreigners' guns? The fever must'a drove him crazy. How much meat could we cut off with five hundred dollars? Enough to make our mouths water for years. So happy to buy a piece of black smudgy paper, as if he'd come upon a big treasure! Xu Shuge's not a normal person either. Could any right living person treat money like it wasn't even money? After being struggled against and beaten and having his beard pulled out, he finally comes into five hundred bucks, and he spends it all to build a bridge without even keeping a cent for himself; can't even go out every day and buy himself a steamed white flour roll! And he doesn't even know how to show off properly. You built a bridge, but when everybody walks over it who's going to thank you for it? If you gave somebody one or two hundred, or even thirty or fifty, or even three fifty, or even if you gave somebody a good cigarette, anybody would have a good word for you; but what asshole's going to say shit about you now? They were a couple of real idiots, a couple of jerks, they both studied themselves stupid; fools, what good did all that reading and studying do 'em?!

After everybody got through laughing, they all began to regret their past actions, to regret 'em like the devil. Back then if they had secretly made a rubbing, how wonderful that would have been! Hot damn, they could have sold one piece of smudgy black paper for five hundred bucks—as much as you make for selling a passel of hog's heads; enough to convince a gal to marry you, what luck! If you'd made ten or twenty copies, good Lord, how much money that would'a been! You'd be rich as Croesus, you'd have enough to take yourself ten wives, screw one every day, you could pleasure yourself silly, pleasure yourself to death!

After they'd done regretting, they set in hating, hating Xu Shuge. That old fart was no damned good. He knew all along it was worth money; if he'd only given us all a hint on the sly, told us to make a few rubbings, then we'd have all had money to spend. A relative is a relative and a neighbor is a neighbor; Master Guan Yu always helped the people of his native Shanxi,* but that old fart wouldn't even help his native district. Scholars are all treacherous at heart, always vicious, always ruthless; they want everything just for themselves. Pulling out your beard served you right, we weren't the least bit unfair. Considering how malicious you were, the next time we'll pull out your hair too!

The laughter, the regrets, and the hate, everything, disappeared and was gradually forgotten as the days went by, just as though a big wind had blown through and when the wind subsided not a track was left in the dust.

Only the little stream now had a cement bridge that would last for a thousand years.

Only the stone stele in front of the big ruined grave mound would never have any inscription.

From that time on, every day at dawn and at dusk no matter whether it was clear or cloudy, summer or winter, Xu Shuge would walk up slowly with the aid of a walking stick, stand in front of the stone stele, look up and read that wordless monument just as though the stele was still covered with elegant essays in a beautiful script. He would read the stele for a long, long time, reading it very conscientiously, with great emotion, reading it out loud, reading and reading and reading until the tears streamed down his face.

In order to commemorate this stone monument that was originally wordless, then had words carved on it, and today, a thousand years later, was made wordless again, I have written down this record.

---

*Master Guan Yu, or Guan Gong, a hero of the popular Ming novel *Romance of the Three Kingdoms* and the Chinese God of War, was a native of Xie County in Shanxi Province.

The Hut on the Hill

Can Xue

Translated by Michael S. Duke

ON THE barren hill behind my house there is a hut built of wooden planks. At home every day I clean up my drawer. When I'm not cleaning up my drawer, I sit in a big armchair, put my hands on my knees, and listen to the whistling sounds: the wind beating fiercely on the pine plank roof of the hut, the echo of wolves howling in the valley.

"You never ever finish cleaning up your drawer," Mama says, looking at me with a phony smile.

"Everyone's hearing's gone bad." Holding back my anger, I continue, "There are so many thieves pacing around outside our house in the moonlight. I turned on the light and saw that someone had poked countless holes in the window. In the next room the sound of you and father snoring was unusually loud, causing all the bottles and jars to jump around in the cupboards. I pressed my feet against the bed frame, turned my swollen head sideways, and heard the person locked up in the hut pounding furiously on the wooden door; this sound persisted until dawn."

"Every time you come into my room looking for something I tremble with fear." Mama stares at me cautiously as she retreats toward the door. I notice that one side of her face is twitching ridiculously in fright.

One day I decided to climb the hill and see what is really up there. I started out as soon as the wind stopped. I climbed for a long time, the sun beat down making me dizzy and blurring my vision, every pebble shimmered with tiny white sparks. Coughing, I reeled around on the hill. The salty sweat on my eyebrows dripped into my eyes. I didn't see anything. I didn't hear anything. When I got home I stood outside my room for a while and saw that the person in the mirror was wearing shoes completely covered with mud, and that her eyes were ringed with two black halos.

The original appeared in *Renmin wenxue*, no. 8 (1985). This translation was first published in *Renditions*, nos. 27–28 (Autumn 1987) and is reprinted by permission. The translator wishes to thank the editors of *Renditions* for their valuable assistance.

"This is some sort of disease." I hear my family laughing furtively in some dark corner.

By the time my eyes adjust to the darkness of the room, they have already hidden themselves somewhere—laughing as they disappear. I discover that they took advantage of my absence to tip up my drawer and make a big mess out of it, dumping several dead moths and dragonflies onto the floor; they know very well those are my favorite things.

"They helped you clean up your drawer when you weren't here," my little sister tells me with a blank stare, as her left eye turns green.

"I hear wolves howling," I say, deliberately trying to frighten her, "a whole pack of wolves running back and forth around the house. Some of them can even stick their heads through the crack in the door. These things come with the dark. When they're asleep in this house, everybody's feet break out in a cold sweat. Look how damp the quilts are."

My mind is in a turmoil because some of my things are missing from my drawer. Mother lowers her eyes and pretends to know nothing about it, but I can feel her hostile stare on the back of my head. Whenever she stares at the back of my head, the point on my scalp she stares at tingles and swells. I know they have buried my box of *go* pieces next to the well out back; they've done this countless times before. Every time I dig it up in the middle of the night. While I'm digging, they always turn on the light and poke their heads out of the window, unmoved by my resistance.

At dinner I tell them: "There's a little hut on the top of the hill."

They are all noisily slurping their soup with their heads down and probably don't hear a word I say.

"There was a whole pack of rats scurrying frantically about in the wind." I raise my voice and put my chopsticks down. "Gravel from the hillside came crashing down against the wall behind our house and you were all so frightened when you heard it that your feet were covered in cold sweat. Do you remember? Just look at your quilts and see. As soon as the sun comes out, you hang them out to dry; the clotheslines are always loaded down with your quilts."

My father glares at me suddenly with one eye, a very familiar wolf's eye. I have a sudden revelation: every night my father turns into one of those wolves that run around our house howling mournfully.

"There's a dazzling white light everywhere." I dig my fingers into Mother's shoulder and shake her. "It's so bright that it makes my eyes water; you can't see anything at all. But as soon as I return to my room, sit in the big armchair, and put my hands on my knees, I can see the pine plank roof so clearly. That image is so close, you must have seen it too. In fact, everyone in the family has seen it. There really is someone crouching in there; he's got two big purple smudges under his eyes, too, from staying up all night."

"Every time you make that noise digging at that granite by the side of the well, your mom and I are suspended in mid-air; we shiver and shake all over, feeling around with our bare feet, but we can't touch the ground." Father turns his face toward the window to avoid my gaze. The pane is pockmarked with fly specks. "There's a pair of scissors I dropped at the bottom of the well. In my dreams I secretly resolve to fish them up. But when I wake up I always discover that I've made a mistake, that I never really dropped any scissors; your mother always swears that I made a mistake, but I can't get those scissors out of my mind; the next time I remember them again. I'll be lying down and suddenly I'll feel a sense of regret because the scissors are rusting at the bottom of the well; why don't I go fish them out? I've been worrying about this for several decades now, you can see the wrinkles on my face are like knife cuts. One time I actually tried to lower the bucket down the well, but the rope was heavy and slippery, my hands went limp, and the bucket made a tremendous racket as it plummeted into the well. I ran back into the house, glanced at myself in the mirror, and saw that the hair on my left temple had turned completely white."

"The north wind is so fierce." I scrunch up my shoulders, my face breaks out in black and blue blotches. "Little pieces of ice have formed in my stomach. When I sit in the big armchair, I can hear them endlessly clinking in there."

I always want to clean up my drawer properly, but Mama is always secretly against it. The tap-tapping of her footsteps pacing back and forth in the next room makes me imagine all sorts of weird things. In order to forget that sound, I take out a deck of cards and start counting: "One, two, three, four, five . . ." The pacing stops suddenly, however, and Mother pokes her little blackish green face into the room and says in a low drone: "I had a very vulgar dream and my back is still covered in cold sweat."

"And also the soles of your feet," I add. "The soles of everyone's feet are covered in cold sweat. You hung the quilts out to dry yesterday. It's quite common."

Little Sister sneaks in to tell me that Mother always wants to break my arms because the sound I make opening and closing my drawer drives her crazy. That sound hurts her so much that she sticks her head in cold water; she soaks it until she catches a terrible cold.

"That's no accident." Little Sister's gaze is always a perfect blank; it pierces through me and makes the back of my neck break out in little red bumps. "Take Father, for example; he's been talking about those scissors for twenty years or more. Everything has a long history."

I oil the sides of my drawer and open and close it very gently until it makes absolutely no sound. I try this for several days and the sound of pacing in the next room ceases. I've fooled her. It appears you can get by deceitfully in many things as long as you are a bit careful. I become very excited and set out to work energetically through the night; my drawer looks like it's just about to be completely cleaned up, but suddenly the electric light bulb goes out. Mother snickers in the next room.

"The light coming from your room irritates me so much that my veins are pounding like a drum. Look here,'' she says, pointing to her temple; a fat round worm is lying there. ''I would rather have scurvy. There's something drumming inside me all the time, making noises everywhere; you've never had such a feeling. Your father even contemplated suicide because of an illness like this.'' She reaches out and rests her fat hand on my shoulder; her hand feels as if it had been frozen, it never stops dripping.

Someone near the well is up to no good. I can hear him letting the bucket down over and over again; it makes a loud, clattering sound as it hits the sides of the well. At dawn, he slams the bucket down and runs away. I open the door to the next room and see Father sleeping soundly; one of his hands, bulging with dark tendons, is painfully clawing the edge of the bed while he moans miserably in his dreams. Mother, her hair in disarray, is mechanically sweeping the floor. She tells me that at the crack of dawn a big swarm of long-horned beetles flew in the window, smashed into the wall, and fell all over the floor. She got out of bed to clean them up, but when she was putting on her slippers, a beetle hiding in one of her slippers bit her, and her entire leg has swollen up like a lead post.

''He,'' Mother says, pointing at Father sleeping soundly, ''dreamed that he was the one who was bitten.''

''In the hut on the hill someone is also moaning right now. The black wind is blowing some wild grape leaves around.''

''Did you hear that?'' In the half-light Mother concentrates her entire attention and puts her ear to the floor. ''These creatures knocked themselves out when they hit the floor. They burst in just at the crack of dawn.''

That day I actually climbed up hill again. I remember it perfectly clearly. At first I sat in the rattan chair with my hands on my knees, then I opened the door and walked into the white light. When I climbed up the hill, all I could see were the sparks from the white pebbles; there were no wild grapes, there was no hut.

White Dog and the Swings

Mo Yan

Translated by Michael S. Duke

GAOMI Dongbei Xiang once produced a species of large gentle white dog, but now after several generations it's very difficult to find a pure breed. Today everybody raises mongrels, and even if a white one is occasionally seen, somewhere on its body will be a patch of colored fur betraying its mixed blood. But if the patch of colored fur doesn't cover too much of the dog's body and isn't located in too prominent a place, everybody will habitually refer to it as a "white dog" without being too critical about the discrepancy between the name and the reality.

I was on the stone steps under the bridge washing my face in the crisp, clean water, just as a "white dog" whose body was completely white except for two black front paws walked dejectedly over the dilapidated stone bridge across the little river near my old home. It was the seventh lunar month and the low-lying Gaomi Dongbei Xiang was unbearably hot. When I got down off the bus from the county seat to the rural townships, the sweat had already soaked through my clothes, and my face and neck were covered with thick yellow dust. After washing my face and neck I wanted to strip down to nothing and dive into the river, but when I saw people walking this way in the distance on the brown dirt road through the fields that lead up to the stone bridge, I gave up the idea, stood up, and wiped my face and neck with one of a set of matching handkerchiefs my fiancée had given me. It was already past noon, the sun was declining slightly to the west, and a few gusts of breeze wafted over from the southeast. Those gentle and refreshing southeast breezes made one feel very comfortable, made the tips of the sorghum lightly sway back and forth, made the fur ruffle up the back of the "white dog" who was coming closer and closer, wagging his tail. He came up close and I saw his two black front paws.

The black-pawed white dog walked to the end of the bridge, stopped, looked back toward the road, raised his chin, and looked over at me with turbid canine

The original was first published in 1985. This translation is from Mo Yan, *Touming de hong luobo* (The crystal carrot) (Beijing: Zuojia chubanshe, 1986), pp. 265–90.

eyes. The dog's eyes had a look of far-off desolation that held some sort of vague intimation, and the hint of that far-off desolation called up a dim feeling of confusion from somewhere deep in my heart.

After I left home to go to school, my parents also moved to another province to live with my elder brother; I had no more relatives in my old home, so I never came back again. All of a sudden it's been ten years, neither a long nor a short time. Just before summer vacation, my father came to the college where I was teaching and couldn't help becoming very emotional when he talked about our old home. He wanted me to go back there and take a look around; I said I was busy with my work and couldn't get away, but he just shook his head disapprovingly. After my father left, I always felt uneasy. Finally I decided to put off everything I was doing and come back.

The white dog looked back again at the brown dirt road then lifted his head to look at me; his canine eyes remained turbid. Just as I was looking at his black paws, about to recall something in astonishment, he sucked in his bright red tongue and barked at me. Then he crouched near a piling at the end of the bridge, lifted one leg, and pissed in his accustomed manner. His business done, he walked slowly down the path I had taken under the bridge, stood by my side, wagged his tail between his legs, stuck out his tongue, and lapped up some water.

He seemed to be waiting for someone, displaying an air of leisureliness in his drinking as if he really wasn't thirsty. The look of indifference on the dog's face was reflected on the surface of the river while fish kept swimming by under the dog's nose. Neither the dog nor the fish were afraid of me; I distinctly smelled the stench of the dog and the fish and even had the disgusting idea of kicking him into the water after the fish, but I decided I ought to have better "canine manners." Just then the dog curled up his tail, lifted his head, glanced coldly over at me, and strode deliberately up to the end of the bridge. I watched him as he ruffled up the fur around his neck and ran with nervous excitement toward the road. On both sides of the dirt road were long fields of sorghum with gray-green tassels. A small blue sky full of pure white clouds scudding by hung over the checkerboard countryside. I walked to the top of the bridge and picked up my traveling bag, intending to cross the bridge quickly. This place was still about six miles from my village, and I hadn't let anybody there know I was coming; better hurry on in there early and make it easy for them to find a place for me to eat and sleep. Just as I was thinking about that, I saw the white dog trot out of the sorghum field beside the road, leading the way for a person carrying a big load of sorghum leaves.

I'd worked around in a village for nearly twenty years and naturally knew those sorghum leaves made first-class fodder for horses and cattle; I also knew that stripping the old leaves off the sun-ripening sorghum wouldn't hurt it's productivity. As I watched that far-off bundle of sorghum leaves hobbling over, I felt sorry for the person carrying it. I know all too well what it feels like to push your way through those dense and windless sorghum fields cutting leaves. Needless to say, your whole body is drenched with sweat and your lungs feel like they're going to explode, but the worst thing is the way the dry little hairs on the sorghum leaves scratch against your sweat-soaked skin. I heaved a relaxed sigh that I wasn't carrying that bundle.

Gradually I could make out the person who was trudging forward all bent over by the weight of the sorghum bundle. A blue shirt, black pants, brown plastic sandals on skinny black crow's feet; if she didn't have long hair I wouldn't have been able to tell it was a woman, even though she was quite near when she first came out of the field. She walked along with her head parallel to the ground and her neck stuck way out, probably to lessen the pain of the load on her back. She used one hand underneath to hold the carrying pole up on her back while the other hand reached back to hold it from the top. The sun beat down on the shiny beads of sweat on her neck and forehead. The sorghum leaves were fresh and green as leeks. She moved along slowly and deliberately, finally coming onto the bridge. The bridge was just about as wide as the bundle of leaves on her back, so I stepped back down to the place where the dog had just left his calling card and stood there watching them cross the bridge.

Suddenly I felt that there was an invisible cord between her and the white dog; as the white dog bumped along, one step fast and one step slow, that cord alternately pulled up tight and slacked off. Coming up in front of me, he glanced over at me again with that detached canine look. That look of vague intimation in the dog's eyes suddenly took on an extraordinary clarity: those black paws of his stripped the veil of confusion from my mind and made me remember her. The pungent smell of her sweat and the sound of her panting for breath as she struggled past me with her head bent low remains forever in my memory. Dropping the heavy sorghum leaves down off her back, she stretched her body out slowly. The big bundle of leaves behind her came almost up to the level of her breasts. I looked at the place on the bundle of leaves that came in contact with her body; it was noticeably concave, and the spot where she pulled it most forcefully was a mass of wet crumpled leaves. I knew that the places on her body that had crumpled the sorghum leaves were certainly very comfortable now; standing on the bridge with the cool moist breeze wafting over the water from the fields and caressing her body, she must have felt relaxed and satisfied. Relaxation and satisfaction are the elements that make up our happiness and well-being; in those years now past, I understood such things.

After standing up straight, she seemed temporarily to lose consciousness. The dirt on her face was streaked with lines of sweat. She exhaled in repeated bursts through her open mouth. The bridge of her nose was gracefully high and straight. Her complexion was swarthy. Her teeth were pure white. My old home produces many beautiful women, some of them being chosen as palace ladies in every dynasty. A few of them are actresses in Beijing today; I've seen them all and that's just the way they look, none of them are much better looking than she is.

"Nuan!" I called out.

She stared at me with her left eye; it was quite bloodshot and looked terrible.

"Nuan . . . Sis!" I called out as if adding a footnote.

I'm twenty-nine today and she's two years younger, but after a ten-year separation she's changed greatly; if it wasn't for the blemish left on her face from that mishap on the swing, I wouldn't dare have recognized her. The white dog was also examining me intently; he must actually be an old dog of twenty years, I thought. I'd never imagined that he would still be living, and he looked pretty healthy. That year at the Dragon Boat Festival he was only about the size of a basketball when my father carried him over from my great uncle's house in the county seat. Twenty years ago, pure bred white dogs were very nearly extinct, and even ones with slight imperfections like this one, who could still generally be called a "white dog," were very hard to come by. My great uncle raised dogs for a living, and he let my father bring this one home only because of my father's shameless pleading. His introduction into our village full of mongrels led to widespread expressions of admiration; there was even an offer to buy him for thirty dollars, but naturally it was politely refused. Even in the villages of those days, in a desolate place like our Gaomi Dongbei Xiang, there were still quite a few interesting things to do, and raising dogs was no doubt one of them. As long as there were no big natural disasters, most everybody had enough to eat and the dogs were also able to flourish.

That year, when I was nineteen, Nuan was seventeen, and White Dog was four months old, troop after troop of Liberation Army soldiers with their military vehicles crossed over this stone bridge in an endless line from the north. Our high school set up sheds at the end of the bridge and prepared tea for the Liberation Army while the student propaganda brigade stood by beating drums and cymbals, dancing and singing. The bridge is very narrow, and the first big truck went across very carefully with the wheels half over the sides. The back wheels of the second truck broke off a piece of the masonry and toppled over into the river; many pots and pans and cookery of all sorts were smashed up, and the whole river was speckled with gobs of oil. A bunch of soldiers jumped into the river, pulled the driver out of the cab, and dragged him dripping wet up onto the bank. A group of soldiers in long white coats gathered around him. One of them, wearing white gloves with a set of earphones in his hand, began shouting loudly. Nuan and I were stalwarts of the propaganda brigade, but we forgot our drumming and singing for gawking at all the excitement. Later on a number of high-ranking leaders came over, shook hands with our school's poor and lower middle peasant representative, Pockmarked Uncle Guo, and Chairman Liu of the school's Revolutionary Committee, then put on their white gloves and waved to all of us. We just stood there watching the troops cross the river.

Uncle Guo asked me to play the flute, and Chairman Liu asked Nuan to sing. "Sing what?" asked Nuan. Chairman Liu said, "Sing *We Feel So Close to*

You." Thus I played and she sang. Row by row the troops stepped onto the bridge and crossed the river while the trucks drove one by one into and across the water. ("The river water's clear and clean, our crops cover the banks.") The fronts of the trucks whipped up white froth while leaving a trail of roiling mud in their wake. ("The People's Liberation Army enters the mountains, to help us carry out the autumn harvest.") After the big trucks had crossed, two small jeeps slipped dully into the river. One of them went rapidly across the river with frothy waves splashing up five or six meters on both sides; the other one knifed into the water, sputtered a couple of times, died out, and just sat there in the middle of the river belching black smoke. ("We start shooting the breeze, and so many past experiences rush into mind.") "Damn!" said one of the officers. Another said, "The silly sonovabitch! Get Monkey Wang to send some men and pull that jeep out." ("We eat from the same bowl, and share the same oil lamp.") Very quickly a number of soldiers waded into the river to push the stalled jeep out; the soldiers all wore their uniforms into the water, which only came up to their knees, but they were wet up to their chests; after becoming soaked their uniforms grew darker and clung tightly to their bodies, showing their fat or skinny legs and buttocks. ("You are our own flesh and blood, you are our closest friends.") The fellow in the long white coat carried the driver dripping wet into a truck with a red cross painted on the side. ("The party's kindness is beyond expression, we always feel so close to you.")

The officers turned around and looked like they were preparing to cross the bridge; I raised my flute, Nuan opened her mouth, and we stared at the officers in terror. An officer wearing black rimmed glasses nodded his head toward us and said, "You sang pretty well and you played pretty well too." Uncle Guo said to the officers, "You're all working so hard, but these kids can only make a lot of wild noises; please don't laugh too much." He pulled out a pack of cigarettes, opened it, and very respectfully offered them to the officers, but they politely refused. A truck with a lot of wheels pulled up on the other side of the river; several soldiers jumped aboard and threw down a few spools of thick steel cable and some white wooden sticks. The officer with the black rimmed glasses turned to a handsome young officer at his side, "Brigade Leader Cai, have your Propaganda Brigade give them a few musical instruments and so on."

The troops crossed the river and fanned out into the various villages. Division Headquarters was stationed in our village. Those days were just like lunar New Years, everyone in the village was so excited. Dozens of telephone wires stretched out in all directions from the side room of our house. Handsome Brigade Leader Cai took a troop of soldiers who specialized in literary and artistic performances to live in Nuan's house. I went there to fool around every day and became very familiar with Brigade Leader Cai. He let Nuan sing for him. He was a tall, lanky youth with fluffy hair and high, arching eyebrows. As Nuan sang, he hung his head and smoked for all he was worth; I could see his ears twitch slightly. He said that Nuan had a pretty good voice, really very good; too bad she didn't have a famous master to teach her. He said I also had a good future in store for me. He liked our black-pawed white dog very much. Once my father found out, he immediately offered to give it to him, but he declined to take it. The day the troops moved out my father and Nuan's father both turned out and begged Brigade Leader Cai to take me and Nuan with him. Brigade Leader Cai said that he would report back to his commander and come to recruit us both during the end-of-the-year recruiting drive. Just before he left, Brigade Leader Cai gave me a book called *Methods of Playing the Flute* and Nuan one called *How to Sing Revolutionary Songs*.

"Sis," I said with great embarrassment, "Don't you recognize me?"

In our village there are a great variety of surnames from all over the place, including Zhang, Wang, Li, Du, and so on. And the various kinds of generational ranks are all mixed up, too. There have actually been cases where a paternal aunt (*gugu*) married her nephew (*zhizi*) or a nephew ran off with his aunt (*shenshen*), but as long as their ages were about the same nobody sneered at them. I had become accustomed to calling Nuan Sis (*xiaogu*) ever since we were kids, but there wasn't the slightest trace of blood relationship between us.* Ten years ago when I began ambiguously to combine Nuan and Sis together, the term had a very special flavor, but now, after a ten-year separation, when we've both grown up so, even though I still called her that none of the old flavor remained.

"Sis, you mean you really don't recognize me?" As soon as I said that, I immediately regretted my stupidity. She already had a sad expression on her face. Sweat continued to soak through, matting a strand of her dried out hair against the side of her cheek. Her swarthy complexion turned ashen gray. Her left eye was perceptibly moist and shiny. She had no right eye. No tears there, only a jagged line of black eye lashes grew there in the deeply sunken eye socket. My heart grew tight as a knot. I just couldn't stand to look at that hollow socket, so I deliberately diverted my gaze and looked instead at her lovely eyebrows and her wet hair shimmering brightly in the sunlight. The muscles of her left cheek twitched slightly, moving her eye and her eyebrow together into a strangely miserable expression. If anyone else saw her they wouldn't be moved, but I couldn't help being moved by the sight of her. . . .

That night over ten years ago I ran over to your house and said, "Sis, nobody's swinging now, let's go over and really swing." You said, "I'm taking a nap." I said, "Come on! The Cold Food Festival's been over for eight days now; the work team is going to take the swings down and use the wood. The carter was complaining to the team leader this morning about using the cart rope for the swings; said it was about to be worn through." You yawned and said, "O.K.

---

*It is common practice in China to call unrelated people of different generations by kinship terms.

let's go.'' White Dog was half grown up then and, with skinny muscles and thin bones, didn't look as good as when he was little. He walked along behind us, and the moonlight shining on his fur made it glow like silver. The swings were set up on the threshing grounds: two wooden posts up and down, one horizontal cross-beam, two metal rings hanging down, two thick ropes, one flat board to sit on. The swing frame stood there silently in the moonlight, dark and eerie like the gate of hell. Not far behind the swings was the threshing ground ditch and a clump of locust trees with unbroken rows of needles sticking out. The ends of the stiff and sharply pointed needles glowed in the steely gray moonlight.

"I'll sit and you push me," you said.

"I'll push you up to the sky."

"Let White Dog on too."

"Don't try to be too fancy."

You called White Dog over, "White Dog, come on and have some fun too."

You grabbed the rope with one hand and held White Dog in the other while he whimpered worriedly. I stood on the crossboard, squeezed you and White Dog between my legs, and repeatedly exerted a downward force while the swing slowly gained momentum. As we went gradually higher, the moonlight shimmered like water, the wind blew in our ears, and I felt a little dizzy. You just giggled and White Dog barked. Finally we swung even with the crossbeam. The fields, the river, the houses, and the cemetery alternately flashed before my eyes while the cool breeze blew back and forth on my face. I looked down into your eyes and asked, "How do you like it, Sis?"

You replied, "It's great, we're up in the sky."

The rope broke. I fell under the swings; you and White Dog flew into the clump of locust trees and a spike of needles pierced your right eye. White Dog crawled out of the trees and staggered around the base of the swings like a drunkard; the swings had knocked him dizzy. . . .

"You've done all right . . . these past years?" I stammered.

I watched as her shrugged-up shoulders slumped down and her taut facial muscles relaxed as well. Her left eye, which seemed to have grown extremely large due perhaps to hard work or a kind of physiological overcompensation, suddenly fixed me with a hard, cold stare that made me uncomfortable all over.

"How could I go wrong? I've got food, clothes, a man, children; except for missing one eye, nothing else is lacking; isn't that 'pretty good'?" she said heatedly.

I was speechless, thought to myself for some time, and unexpectedly blurted out, "I got a teaching job at my school; they may even make me a lecturer. . . . I felt very homesick, not only for the people here, but I missed the old river, the stone bridge, the fields, the red sorghum in the fields, the clean fresh air, the lovely sound of the birds singing. . . . Since it's summer vacation, I came back."

"What's there to miss in this beat-up place? You missed this broken down bridge? It's like a goddamn rice steamer in the sorghum fields, about to steam me to death.'' As she spoke she walked down the path from the bridge, stood up and took off her blue men's work shirt which was mottled with white patches of brine, tossed it down on a rock, and bent over to wash her face and neck. On her upper body she wore only an oversized round necked tee-shirt that was already so worn out it had little pinholes all over. It used to be white but now it was gray. The tee-shirt was tucked in at the waist, and a strip of rolled-up white cloth cinched up her pants. She didn't look at me again but went on scooping up water and washing her face, neck, and arms. Finally, just as if no one were there, she pulled the ends of her shirt out of her pants and used it to scoop up some water and wash her breasts. The shirt was soon soaked through and clung tightly to her large drooping breasts. Looking at them I thought dryly to myself, well, yes, that's about all there is to that. Just like the song the village kids sing: ''Unmarried she's got golden breasts, married she's got silver breasts, having children she's got bitch's teats.'' So I asked her:

''How many children?''

''Three.'' She brushed back her hair, pulled out her shirt and shook it, then tucked it back in at her waist.

''Aren't we only allowed to have one child?''

''I didn't have two children.'' Seeing my puzzlement, she explained coldly, ''I had three at once, plunk, plunk, plunk, just like having pups.''

I laughed without conviction. She picked up her blue work shirt, dusted it on her knees a few times, put it on, and buttoned it up from bottom to top. White Dog also got up from where he'd been lying next to the bundle of leaves, shook himself all over, and stretched out.

I said, ''You're really something.''

''If I wasn't something, what could I do? All our misfortunes are predestined and there's no way we can avoid them.''

''You have both boys and girls?''

''They're all males.''

''Then you're really lucky: with many sons comes much good fortune.''

''Baloney!''

''Is this the same old dog?''

''He's not long for this world.''

''Ten years went by in a flash.''

''In another flash it'll be time to die.''

''Yes,'' I was gradually becoming annoyed, turned to White Dog sitting next to the bundle of leaves and said, ''This old dog sure knows how to keep on living!''

''Oh, you mean it's all right for *you* to live but not all right for us to live? Those who eat rice want to live and so do those who eat chaff; the big shots want to live and so do the little people.''

"What're you talking about?" I said, "Who's a big shot? And who're the little people?"

"Aren't you high and mighty? A lecturer in a big university!"

I grew red in the face and speechless; for a minute I felt like I couldn't take such abuse and tried to think of something mean to come back with, but I thought better of it and stopped. I picked up my traveling bag and said dryly, "I may be staying at my eighth uncle's house, come on over if you have time."

"Didn't you know I married into Wang's Family Village?"

"If you didn't tell me I wouldn't have known."

"It doesn't make much difference whether you know or not," she said flatly. "If you don't think your little sister lives like an old bitch, then save a little time to come see us; when you get to the village just ask for the home of 'One-eyed Nuan,' everybody knows it."

"Sis, I really didn't imagine things would turn out this way. . . ."

"It was just fate, a person's fate, fixed by Heaven, and it doesn't do any good to worry about it." She walked up slowly from under the bridge, stood in front of the bundle of leaves, and said, "Do me a favor, help me lift these leaves onto my shoulders."

I had a sudden feeling of warmth and spoke up bravely, "Let me help you carry them home!"

"I wouldn't dare!" As she said this, she knelt down in front of the bundle of leaves, put the carrying pole on her shoulders and said, "Lift it up."

I went behind her, grabbed the rope holding the bundle, lifted it up forcefully just as she managed to stand up. Her body bent over once again; in order to make it a little more comfortable, she bounced the bundle up and down on her back a couple of times while the sorghum leaves rustled loudly. A softly muffled voice came up from her deeply stooped position:

"Come over and see us."

White Dog barked at me a few times and ran up in front of her. I stood there on the bridge for a long time watching that bundle of sorghum leaves slowly make its way north. I didn't turn around and head south again until White Dog had become a small white speck and the woman and her bundle had become a black speck a little bigger than the white speck.

It was over three miles from the bridge to Wang's Family Village, and it was six miles from the bridge to our village.

Eighth Uncle told me to ride his bike the nine miles from our village to Wang's Family Village. I said forget it, I could walk the nine miles easy. Eighth Uncle said, "We're well-off now and everybody has a bicycle, not like a few years back when there were only a couple of bikes in the whole village and it wasn't easy to borrow one because nobody wanted to loan out such a scarce commodity." I said, "I know you're well-off, I've seen the bikes tooling around all over the streets, but I don't want to ride a bike. I've been an intellectual so many years

I've got hemorrhoids and it'll be better if I walk.'' Eighth Uncle said, ''I can see that studying's not such a great thing after all; besides all sorts of illnesses and troubles, a person also ends up acting like a lunatic. What'd you say you were going out there to see her for? Out there with the blind and the dumb, aren't you afraid people here will laugh at you? Fish are fish and fowl are fowl; you shouldn't stoop below your station!'' I said, ''Eighth Uncle, I'm not going to argue with you; I'm way past twenty going on thirty, and I know what I'm doing.'' Eighth Uncle went angrily about his own business and didn't bother me again.

I very much wished that I could run into her and White Dog again at the bridge; if she had another big bundle of sorghum leaves, I would carry them home for her if it broke my back. She and White Dog could both act as guides and lead me right up to her house. In the city everybody pays close attention to their clothes, everybody wants to keep up with the latest fads, but the people in my old home kept casting contemptible glances at my blue jeans and making me feel damned awkward. So I explained to them: they're secondhand goods, three dollars and sixty cents a pair—actually I spent twenty-five dollars on them— since they were so cheap, the villagers forgave me. The people of Wang's Family Village didn't know that my pants were cheap, and if I didn't run into her and White Dog all I could do was go on into the village and let them stare at me. Imagining that prospect only redoubled my desire to run into her or even just White Dog, but in the end I didn't. As I crossed over the stone bridge, I saw the bright red sunlight bursting out through the sorghum stalks and a big wide streak of red stretching out over the river, so bright that the whole river seemed to be dyed red. The sun was an unusual shade of red and seemed to be surrounded by darkness; it was probably about to rain.

I held up a collapsible umbrella and entered the village as a light rain came slanting down. A stoop-shouldered old woman was just crossing the street with the wind ruffling up her jacket and making her totter back and forth. I folded my umbrella, held it in my hand, and went up to ask for directions. ''Grandma, where's Nuan's house?'' She stood there at an angle and rolled her dull eyes in confusion. The wind blew through her graying hair, ruffled her clothing, and accented the softness of her body; the rain fell in widely spaced drops as big as copper coins; once in a while a drop hit her in the face. ''Where does Nuan live?'' I asked her again. ''Which Nuan?' she asked. I had to say it, ''One-eyed Nuan.'' The old woman cast a somber glance at me, raised her arm, and pointed toward a row of blue-tiled houses.

Standing on the path I shouted, ''Is Miss Nuan home?''

The first one to answer my call was that black-pawed white dog. He was not at all like those vicious dogs that jump around you barking and carrying on like they're either going to eat you up or at least scare you to death. He just lay there under the eaves on his bed of straw, squinting his eyes and barking rather symbolically, thoroughly expressing the kindly gentility of a pure-bred white dog.

I called out again and Nuan answered in a crisp clear voice from inside, but it was a fierce-looking fellow with a face full of brown whiskers and a pair of brown eyes who came out to meet me. He looked me up and down ferociously with his muddy brown eyes; his gaze coming to rest on my blue jeans, his mouth twitched crookedly to one side with an expression of madness on his face. He took a step forward—I hurriedly stepped back one—he stuck out the little finger of his right hand, waved it around excitedly in front of my face, and uttered a long, unbroken string of indecipherable sounds. Although I'd heard from my eighth uncle that Nuan's husband was a mute, when confronted with the genuinely crazed aspect of the man, I couldn't help feeling immediately depressed. A one-eye marrying a mute—a crooked knife just right for slicing vegetables in a bowl—in principle no one was actually being wronged, but I still couldn't help feeling immediately depressed.

Nuan, we had such high hopes in those days. When Brigade Leader Cai went away he left such high hopes behind with us. The day he left you looked straight at him, and all your tears were shed just for him. Brigade Leader Cai's face was pale when he took out an ox-horn comb and gave it to you. I cried too and said, "Brigade Leader Cai, we'll be waiting for you to come and get us." And he said, "Right, you wait."

In the late autumn when the sorghum was completely red and we heard that the Liberation Army was in the county seat recruiting soldiers, the two of us were so excited we couldn't sleep. One of our high school teachers was going into the county seat on business and we asked him to go to the recruiting office and ask if Brigade Leader Cai was there yet. When the teacher came back he told us that the Liberation Army recruiters this year were all air force orderlies dressed in brown coats and blue pants and not from Brigade Leader Cai's unit. I was disappointed, but you were full of confidence: "Brigade Leader Cai wouldn't lie to us!" "He forgot about us a long time ago." I said. Your dad also said, "Give you a stick and you think it's a rifle. He was just stringing you along like children. Good metal isn't made into nails, and a good man doesn't become a soldier; get through your graduation, come home, and pull a plow; quit dreaming about doing something fancy." You said, "He didn't take *me* for a child. He certainly didn't take *me* for a child." Your face flushed a deep red as you said it. Your dad said, "That's enough!" I looked at your blushing face in astonishment, saw that special expression barely perceptible on your face, and blurted out wildly, "Maybe, if he doesn't come this year he'll come next year, or if he doesn't come next year he'll come the year after."

Brigade Leader Cai certainly was a noble and dignified specimen of a man! He was tall and slender with a cold handsome face that was always cleanly shaven. Later on you frankly admitted to me that the night before he left he held you and kissed you lightly on the forehead. You said that after he kissed you he whispered softly, "Little Sister, you're really pure . . . because of that I've felt so much nameless anger." You said, "After I join up, I'll marry him." I said, "Don't be a dreamer! Even if you gave him two hundred catties of pork into the bargain, Brigade Leader Cai would never want you." "If he doesn't want me, then I'll marry you." "*I* don't want you!" I shouted. You gave me a look and said, "I really got to you!" Thinking about it now, you were quite a looker in those days; those budding little breasts of yours regularly made my heart throb.

The Mute obviously looked down on me; he pointed with his little finger to express his loathing and contempt. I put on a broad smile in an attempt to win his friendship, but he put the fingers of both hands together in a very strange shape and brandished them before my eyes. I recalled the vulgar answer to such a gesture from the accumulated lore of my childhood mischief and suddenly felt as though I were holding a slimy toad in my hands. I even wanted to turn around and run, but then I saw three identically dressed and identical-looking bald-headed little boys come tumbling out of the house, stand in the doorway, and glance furtively over at me with identical muddy brown eyes, their heads all inclined to the right like three irritable but featherless little rooster chicks. The children all looked old, their foreheads were wrinkled, their lower jaws were broad and solid, but they all trembled slightly. I hurriedly pulled out some candy and said, "Have some candy." The Mute immediately waved at them and spat out a few simple sounds. The boys stared longingly at the party-colored pieces of candy in my hand, but they didn't dare move. I wanted to walk over to them, but the Mute stood in my way, flailing wildly with his arms and uttering strange, intimidating sounds through his mouth.

Nuan walked rather haltingly out of the house with her hands crossed in front of her. I understood perfectly why she was so long making an appearance: she had obviously just put on a clean indigo blue blouse and a pair of neatly pressed gray dacron pants. Indanthrene and traditional-style blouses made of indanthrene had not been worn for a long time, and seeing them all of a sudden like that gave me a disturbing feeling of nostalgia. Young women with ample breasts wearing that sort of blouse have their own special charm. Nuan was a woman with a long, straight neck and elegant facial features. She had an artificial eye in her right eye socket and her face had regained its natural symmetry. I felt quite sad for her goodness and her suffering; I generally observe human life in a very low key, my heart strings as fine as silk threads and sensitive to the smallest nuance, so naturally I trembled. I couldn't look closely at that eye; it had no life and it gave off a turbid magnetic glow. She realized that I was watching her and put her head down, walked around the Mute, lifted the bag off my shoulders, and said, "Let's go in the house."

The Mute abruptly pushed her aside with a hot, angry glare in his eyes. He pointed at my pants and stuck up his little finger again, shaking and gurgling at the mouth, his entire face moving, at once pinched up together then suddenly wide open and expansive, his facial expressions were both animated and terrifying. Finally he spit and trampled it into the ground with his heel. The Mute's hatred for me seemed to be directly related to my blue jeans; I regretted wearing these pants home and decided to change into a pair of Eighth Uncle's baggy pants as soon as I got back to the village.

"Look Sis, Big Brother doesn't recognize me." I said with embarrassment.

She gave the Mute a shove, pointed at me, stuck up her thumb, pointed in the direction of our village, pointed at my hand, pointed at my fountain pen and the school insignia on my shirt pocket, made a motion like writing, held her hands in the shape of a book, stuck up her thumb again, and pointed skyward. Her facial expressions were colorful and varied. The Mute was puzzled for a moment, then he suddenly let down all his defenses and stood there with a docile look in his eyes like a big kid. He laughed like a dog barking, opening his mouth wide, and displayed a row of yellow teeth. He gave me a pat on the chest, then skipped and shouted until he was quite red in the face. I understood him completely and was extremely moved. I felt relaxed all over to have won my mute brother's trust. The three little boys came running up around me with their eyes intently fixed on my hand full of candy.

I said, "Go on, take some!"

The boys raised their heads and looked at their father. The Mute chuckled, heh heh, and the boys dashed up quickly and grabbed the candy out of my hand. One piece fell to the ground and those three bald noggins were bumping around together struggling to pick it up. The Mute laughed as he watched them. Nuan heaved a soft sigh and said:

"Now you've seen everything, you probably think we're ridiculous."

"Sis . . . how could I . . . they're all so cute. . . ."

The Mute looked at me sheepishly, laughed, turned around, and kicked the three struggling boys apart with his big foot. The boys stood there panting and looking truculently at each other. I took out all the candy I had, divided it into three equal portions, and handed each boy one. The Mute shouted and made hand signs to the boys. The boys all put their hands behind them and stepped backward. The Mute shouted even louder; the boy's faces twitched; each one took a piece of candy, placed it in their father's big, rough hand, gave a loud shout, and ran off out of sight. The Mute held up the three pieces of candy, looked them over stupidly for a moment, turned toward me, and made "Ah ah" noises while gesturing with his hands. I didn't understand and looked to Nuan for help. She said, "He says he heard of you a long time ago; he wants to taste a piece of this high-quality candy you brought from Beijing." I made a gesture of putting something in my mouth. He smiled, very carefully unwrapped the candy, put it in his mouth, chewed, and bent his head to one side as if he were listening for something. He stuck his thumb up again and this time I understood perfectly that he was praising the quality of the candy. He soon ate the second piece of candy. I told Nuan the next time I come I'll definitely bring some genuine high-quality candy for Big Brother.

Nuan said, "Can you really come again?" I said I'd certainly come.

After the Mute finished the second piece of candy, he thought for a moment and then held the last piece up in front of Nuan. She closed her eyes. "Argh . . . ," the Mute shouted. I felt nervous as I watched him hold the candy up in front of Nuan again. She closed her eyes and shook her head. "Argh . . . Argh . . . ," the Mute shouted angrily, grabbed Nuan by the hair with his left hand, pulled back so that her face was raised up, put the candy in his own mouth with his right hand, tore the wrapper off with his teeth, held the candy, now sticky with his saliva, between two fingers and forced it into Nuan's mouth. Nuan's mouth wasn't small, but it looked very small in contrast to his two cucumber sized fingers. His crude black fingers made her lips seem delicate and tender. Under his huge hand her face became fragile and weak.

Nuan held the candy in her mouth, neither spitting it out nor chewing it, with an expression on her face as unmoved as still water. The Mute smiled triumphantly at me because of his victory.

Ambiguously she said, "Let's go in, we're pretty silly standing here in the wind." I glanced around the yard and she said, "What're you looking at? That big mule kicks and bites so that no human being dares to go near it, but in his hands it's gentle as a lamb. He bought that cow this spring; it just dropped a calf last month."

There was a big open shed in her yard with a mule and a cow. The cow was extremely emaciated. Under its legs a nice fat calf was nursing; it dug in its hind legs, wagged its tail, and repeatedly pushed its head into its mother's udders; the cow arched its back in pain as its eyes glowed pale and blue.

The Mute had an amazing capacity; he drank nine-tenths to my one of a bottle of very powerful "All Cities White Lightning." His expression hadn't change a bit, but my head was reeling. He opened another bottle, filled my glass, and held his up with two hands to me in toast. I was very fearful of hurting this friend's feelings, so I resolved to do the impossible, took my glass, and drank it down. For fear that he'd toast me again, I keeled over on the bed pretending I couldn't hold myself up. He got so excited he was red in the face as he turned and gestured to Nuan. He and Nuan gestured back and forth and then she said softly, "Don't compete with him, ten of you couldn't drink as much as one of him. Whatever you do, don't get drunk." She gave me a long, hard stare. I held up my thumb and pointed at him then held up my little finger and pointed to myself. Then she took away the wine and brought out the dumplings. I said, "Sis, let's all eat together." After Nuan received the Mute's permission, the three boys clambered up onto the *kang** in a bunch and started wolfing down the food. Nuan stood by the side of the *kang* serving the food, pouring water, and waiting on us; asked to eat, she said her stomach didn't feel right and she didn't want to eat.

---

*A northern Chinese brick bed under which a fire can be built in winter.

After we ate, the wind stopped, the clouds scattered, and a murderously hot sun burned down from the south. Nuan took a piece of yellow cloth out of the cupboard, pointed at the three boys, and made some gestures for the Mute in a northeasterly direction. The Mute nodded his head. Nuan said to me, "Rest here for a while; I'm going into town to have some clothes made for the boys. Don't wait for me, you just go on home after a while." She gave me an intense look, picked up her bundle, and walked quickly out of the yard; White Dog followed behind her with his tongue hanging out.

The Mute and I sat there across from each other, and every time he caught my eye he grinned from ear to ear. The three boys played around for a while then lay down sideways on the *kang* and went to sleep; seemed as if they all fell asleep at the same instant. It felt hot as soon as the sun came out; cicadas were buzzing loudly in the trees across the road. The Mute took off his shirt and bared his muscular upper body; I felt both frightened and ridiculous smelling the bestial odor emanating from his body. The Mute blinked his eyes tightly, scratched with both hands at his chest, and scratched off several pieces of gray dust that resembled rat droppings. At the same time he continuously stuck out his quick, lizard-like tongue to lick his thick lips. I felt hot, dry, and nauseous and thought of the green water shimmering under the bridge. The sun came through the window and beat down on my blue jeans. I looked at my wrist watch. "Ah, ah, ah!" the Mute shouted as he jumped down off the *kang* and pulled an electronic wrist watch out of a dresser drawer. I saw the hopeful expression on his face so I insincerely pointed at my watch with my little finger and at his electronic watch with my thumb. As expected he became extremely happy and immediately strapped the electronic watch onto his right wrist; I pointed to his left wrist and he shook his head in confusion. I laughed.

"What a hot day. The crops are growing pretty good this year. You'll have a late harvest this fall. That's a great mule you've got there. The peasants' lot has improved greatly since the Third Plenum.* You've grown prosperous Brother. You should buy a television. All Cities White Lightning is a good old brand, got a real kick."

"Ah, ah . . . , ah, ah . . ." He had a look of complete happiness on his face as he smoothed back his hair with both hands, then he ran his hand back and forth in front of his neck. I wondered in alarm, whose head does he want to cut off? "Ah, ah, ah . . . ah, ah, ah . . . ," his hands trembled and he became very anxious when he saw that I didn't understand. He pointed to his right eye, ran his hand over his scalp again, going all the way down to his neck before stopping. I got it. He was trying to tell me something about Nuan. I nodded. He rubbed his dark black nipples, pointed to the children, then rubbed his stomach. I seemed to understand but not completely and shook my head. He squatted down and ges-

---

*The Third Plenum of the Eleventh Central Committee (November 1978) ushered in the reform policies of Deng Xiaoping.

tured anxiously around like crazy so that nearly every part of his body was sending me a signal; I vigorously nodded my head; I really should learn sign language. At last, with sweat pouring down my face, I bid him good-bye. It was not at all hard to understand when he stood there with a look of childlike naiveté on his face, first patting me over the heart and then patting himself over the heart. I spoke up clearly, "Big Brother, we're good brothers!" He woke the three boys with three quick slaps and had them see me off with sleep still fogging their eyes. In the doorway I took the collapsible umbrella out of my bag, gave it to him, and showed him how to use it. He received it like a rare treasure, held it up, opening it and closing it, closing it and opening it over and over again. The three boys looked up at the rapidly opening and closing umbrella and their lower jaws shook once more. I poked him and pointed toward the road south. "Ah, ah," he shouted, waved his hands, and dashed back into the house. He brought out a five-inch-long knife, removed the ox-horn scabbard, and showed it to me. The cold steel blade gleamed, and it was obviously very valuable. He stretched up on tiptoe and pulled a one-inch-thick branch down off the willow tree in front of the gate; with one slash of the knife the branch fell to the ground.

He stuck the knife into my bag.

As I walked I thought to myself: even though he is a mute that doesn't prevent him from being a man with a genuine personality. Being married to him Nuan probably doesn't suffer too much; he can't talk, but after getting used to relying on hand signals and facial expressions they can break through that physiological barrier. Perhaps all those misgivings I had before were as groundless as the ancient man of Qi's phobia about the sky caving in. By the time I reached the bridge, I'd left off thinking of her problems and all I wanted to do was jump into the water and take a bath. The road was quiet and deserted. The morning's rain had long since dried up and the ground was covered with brownish dust. The oily bright sorghum leaves were rustling on either side of the road, locusts were flying back and forth in the bushes, their pink inner wings flashing and cutting through the air with a buzzing sound. The water was rippling under the bridge; White Dog was squatting at the head of the bridge.

When he saw me he started barking and baring his snow white teeth. I had a premonition of something unusual happening. White Dog stood up and walked toward the sorghum field, looking back over his shoulder and barking at me as if calling to me to follow him. Episodes from many spy novels came into my mind as I resolved to follow the dog; simultaneously I reached my hand into my bag and took a firm grip on the sharp knife the Mute had given me. As I squeezed my way through the thickly growing sorghum, I saw her sitting there on the ground beside her little cloth bundle. She had matted down some sorghum to clear an open space around which the sorghum stood like a tall four-sided screen. As I peered in she took the yellow cloth out of her bundle and spread it out on the matted-down sorghum. Dark, mottled shadows played on her face. White Dog lay down to one side resting his head on his outstretched front paws and panting.

I felt cold and tight all over; with chattering teeth and a stiff jaw I spoke awkwardly: "Didn't you say . . . you were going into town? What're you doing here . . . ?"

"I believe in fate." A stream of glistening tears dripped down her cheeks as she said, "I told the dog, 'Oh dog, dog, if you understand my heart you'll go to the end of the bridge and bring him to me; if he comes with you, then our fates are not yet completely separate.' And he did bring you to me."

"You better go home quick." I took the knife out of my bag. "He even gave me this knife."

"You went away for ten years; I didn't think I'd ever see you again in this life. You aren't married yet? You aren't married. . . . Now you've seen him, that's the way he is, if he feels like it he can kiss you to death or he can beat you to death. . . . He gets suspicious if I talk to any man at all, and then he wants to get a rope and tie me up. I'm so bored that I talk to White Dog all day long. Oh dog, you've been with me ever since I lost my eye; you're getting old even faster than I am. I got pregnant the year after I married him; my belly swelled up like a balloon; just before my time I couldn't walk and I couldn't even see my own feet when I stood up. I had three sons all at once, four and a half pounds each, skinny as a litter of cats. When one cried they all cried, when one was hungry they were all hungry; I only have two breasts, when I fed two of them one of them kept on crying. I almost went crazy in those first two years. I began to worry the moment the kids were born; dear God, don't let them be like their dad, let them all open their mouths and speak. . . . When they were seven or eight months I began to lose heart. Things just didn't look right; they were all deaf and dumb, when they cried it sounded as dull as wood scraping wood. I prayed, God, oh God! Please don't let my whole family be mute; at least let one of them be able to talk and keep me company. . . . In the end they were all mute."

I hung my head very low and mumbled, "Sis . . . Sis, . . . it's all my fault, if I hadn't dragged you out to the swings that time. . . ."

"It wasn't your fault; anyway I think about it, it was my own fault. That time I told you Brigade Leader Cai kissed me on the forehead . . . if I had been brave enough to just go on down to the troops and find him, he would have taken me in; he really did like me. Then came the accident on the swings. When you wrote to me from school, I deliberately refused to answer you. I figured that I was already disfigured and unworthy of you; might as well suffer alone, no point making two people suffer; I was so stupid. Tell me the truth, if I'd asked you to marry me then, would you have wanted me?"

Seeing that look of wild abandon on her face, I was greatly moved: "Of course I would, I certainly would."

"Good, then . . . you should understand now. . . . I was afraid you'd be disgusted, so I bought an artificial eye. It's just the right time of the month. . . . I want a child that can speak. . . . If you agree, you've saved me; if you refuse, you've murdered me. There's thousands of reasons and millions of excuses, but you mustn't use any of them on me."

. . . . . .

The Stream of Life

Hong Feng

Translated by Michael Day

THE HE-WOLF flung itself into the air and fell to the ground with a thud. The she-wolf was motionless for a few moments before lowering her head and surveying her mate. Once again he leveled the rifle barrel. In the early light of dawn he saw the she-wolf's head come clearly into line in the gun's sights. He began to draw his finger back steadily. The she-wolf, too, would be lying on the earth like the he-wolf, the only difference being that this time he wouldn't give her a chance to jump. Just as the firing pin was striking the bullet's detonating cap he saw two wolf pups that had been standing by dumbstruck rush toward their mother, take hold of her tail, and pull it with all their might. For some unknown reason a sudden, powerful surge of sympathy overwhelmed his anger. And then the bullet struck the wolf. He saw her lean to one side, let out a cry, and turn her pointed head toward him. He hadn't been able to kill her.

He stood up from behind the boulder and again leveled the gun. He knew that this bullet would enter the wolf's head. But, instead, he aimed at one of her legs. The wolf watched him. She didn't run.

Once again a new day was becoming visible in the sky. He came out of her hut. He stretched like a tired man, mouth opened wide. A night of indulgence had left his lower abdomen heavy and cold; he walked listlessly. Yet he had to go down into the forest at the bottom of the mountain. He had to bring the trapped roe-deer back.

He glanced at his own hut, as silent as this mountain slope. His son was still sleeping. He didn't want his son to see him come out of her hut.

The tawny-colored mountain drew the life out of his face. The rifle leaned against his shoulder, swaying back and forth. His body was swaying, also. He felt exceedingly bored. That's all it was about between men and women. Just that little bit of happiness, and what followed became of even less interest. He won-

This translation is from *Lianhe wenxue* (Unitas), no. 6 (1987): 162–70.

dered, what does man do it for? For the sake of that, some are even willing to die. He felt then that he was different. But once he entered the mountain or moved into the forest he would think of her, think of doing it with her. His heart would beat wildly, he would run as fast as he could, sending birds fluttering into the air about him. He would run until his muscles were exhausted. In this way he would be left snorting like a bull and forget about her for a good long time. It had been like this ever since that woman had left.

The wolf didn't run, she was watching him with a sad look in her eyes. He didn't walk any farther forward. When the third bullet struck the wolf's hind leg she dropped, but immediately stood up again and continued to stare at him. He decided to shoot once more. This time he wanted the bullet to pass through the injured leg and the other leg, breaking them both. He wanted to capture her. He felt he should capture her.

He saw the wolf use her snout to knock the two pups down. He heard the high-pitched yelps of the wolf pups. He saw the she-wolf take hold of the dead wolf's tail in her mouth and struggle to drag him away. She wanted to carry off her mate.

A rifle report sounded. He saw the wolf fall down. She immediately tried to rise and flee again. Finally, she sat on the earth, one foreleg propping herself up, the other drooping limply. He hadn't been able to break both legs simultaneously—it was embarrassing. He laughed and raised the rifle. He wanted to break that remaining leg. He wanted to see what a wolf that couldn't move would look like.

The snow was heavy, closing off the roads. He thought nothing of it—this was common during the mountain winters. He was walking through the snow and saw a snow drift and a foot protruding from it. It was a woman. She wasn't dead yet. He carried her home on his back. He wanted to fetch his elder brother's wife to come and help, but he quickly turned back after starting out toward their hut.

After the woman had regained consciousness, tears began to wash down her face. That alarmed him. He didn't feel that he had done anything wrong. While she had been unconscious, he had rubbed her entire body with snow. He discovered that women were only different from men in two places, and that was nothing startling. Only when her body began to warm up, to become soft, did he feel that the difference in these two places could really get one going. A strange, suffocating feeling nearly made him pass out. He couldn't bear it any longer and began to knead her large, soft, smooth breasts. After only a very short while he rushed out of the hut and stuck his head in the snow. He felt a bit better after that, his body could move freely again and he was no longer aware of the flow of blood through his veins. This was how he saved her life.

He asked her where she came from, why she was alone, and why she was in such a state. At first she said she was lost and then that she had no home. He asked her where she planned to go. She said there was no place for her to go. He asked her what she wanted to do. She didn't say anything, but only cried. After crying a while, she said, "I'll stay with you here." Flustered, he said, "That's impossible." She began to cry again, and he said, "Please stop." She said, "Come inside." She hadn't put on any clothes yet. He thought of asking, "Go inside and do what?" but he didn't; instead, he lifted a corner of the quilt and crawled in. She let out a shout and said: "You take a bath." He was stunned for a moment, then pealed off his clothes, ran outside, stood in the snow and scrubbed himself all over. As he entered the hut he felt very hot and saw that his body was red all over. So he and she slept together. He was busy in a confused way all night. And she became his woman. That morning the woman cried violently. He felt that something was wrong but dared not to ask what. He had promised the woman not to ask any questions.

The she-wolf released its mate's tail. It looked at the body once more and then lifted its head. Its face bore a grieved look, and traces of blood were visible at the edges of its jaws. When it had been tearing at the roe-deer the blood had clung about its mouth. It tried to move but didn't succeed. And then it ceased all movement, turning its face toward him.

He laughed again. The yellow dawn light made his face look hideous, like the statue of a devil in a temple. He walked two steps forward. A sound rose up out of the wolf's throat. This was meant as a menacing sound; it was not the first time he had heard it. But it was the first time it had made him freeze in his tracks. He suddenly thought of the whimpering sound that the woman had made in the middle of the night before she had left. A great anger filled his chest. The rifle was held level in his hands, grasped so hard that the joints of his fingers could be heard cracking. He caught sight of the roe-deer already torn to pieces. In order to trap roe-deer, every day he had most unwillingly pried apart her arms. For many days now he had not trapped any deer, and that alone was enough to anger him. And now he was even more infuriated by his own split second of fear. He walked forward once more.

Of a sudden, the two wolf pups that had been thrown to the ground sprang up and rushed noiselessly toward him. He sneered. Deftly handling the body of the rifle, with one swipe he smacked it into the head of the wolf pup coming directly at him. He heard the sound of splintering bones, and fresh blood gushed out in a fine spray. He lifted the rifle again and turned it toward the pup coming at him from the left side. The she-wolf called out. It was telling the pup not to waste its life. The wolf pup turned about and scurried to the grown wolf's side. The rifle was left thrusting at thin air.

He grunted and shook his shock-numbed hand. Ketchaa! A bullet into the magazine. He took aim at the courageous little wolf pup. He saw that the she-wolf wanted to shelter the pup but was unable to move. He saw a light flashing in its eyes. He didn't think it could be tears and shot another bullet.

It was a leg of a mountain of the Changbai range. It really looked like the shank of a leg—long, very straight, and there was even a foot. He lived on that foot. On the other side of the foot lived his elder brother, actually his sworn blood brother. Together they had come to the Northeast from southern Shandong and settled on this mountain foot for no particular reason. Somehow his brother came by a girl and she became his old lady. She was pretty, more than ten years younger than his brother, about his age. Eight or nine years had passed and they had no child. That day, he and his brother were sitting in the forest drinking. His brother said, "It's not that your sister-in-law can't have a kid, it's your elder brother that's of no use. There's no child; my ancestors weren't virtuous and I suffer retribution." At that time he hadn't yet found the woman and he laughed loudly when he heard this, firing a shot into the air as he did so.

That night someone crept into his hut. He never latched the door. What could a man, a hunter, fear? That person was his sister-in-law. She covered his mouth with her hand and, trembling, said, "Your brother wants a son." He said, "So what? You creep into my hut late at night, what a spot you've put me in!" She said, "But your brother knows." He didn't wait for sister-in-law to take off her clothes. He grabbed her arms and pushed her out. He didn't sleep well that night because he couldn't stop thinking about his sister-in-law.

The next day, his brother called him out again to go hunting. He stared at his brother, suddenly raised his hand, and slapped him across the face. He swore, "Fuck your mother. We're through!"

That day it snowed heavily, the traps were buried. He needed three bullets before finally felling a roe-deer. The deer was a toothless bag of bones. He felt that it was inauspicious and kicked it into a gully. On his way home he pulled the woman out of the snow drift, and this was how he came by a wife.

He felt that the days had taken on new interest, especially the nights. He was amazed that life held such a good thing in store. On a few occasions he didn't go out during the day, wanting only to stay home and wait on that woman. She was like someone half dead, allowing him to drag her back and forth. Once, he bit her neck so hard that it bled. The woman howled and swore, "You beast!" He became muddled. He felt as if he really were an animal. Then he laid down on the floor and tried to sleep, but he couldn't sleep. He was thinking, thinking until he found himself swallowing down his own saliva, but still he resisted. He wasn't able to swallow down that urge. The woman ignored him and fell into a deep sleep.

He began to hate the woman. Sometimes he would find knit-picking excuses to beat her and she would curse him, "You beast!" He would drink heavily and then think of the woman. The two men turned from each other. From that time onward there were no further dealings between them. But the two women often visited one another. He would solemnly watch these two women. His sister-in-law was not as soft and white as the woman, and her hands were much larger and rougher. He heard his sister-in-law say, "You certainly haven't wasted your

womanhood.'' His woman said, ''That man is just a beast. I can't bear it.''
''That man of mine is just . . .'' He heard his sister-in-law curse and then begin
to cry. His woman cried, too.

He hated his woman even more and decided not to pay any attention to her.
He thought that she wouldn't be able to stand it, that she would soften toward
him in the end, and would plead with him. But the woman certainly didn't plead
with him for anything. In fact, she seemed very contented, very relaxed. He kept
it up for over a month and in the end, he was the one who couldn't stand it and
tried to get back on good terms with the woman. She said, ''No!'' He said,
''You're my woman, what do you mean, no?'' The woman said, ''How did I get
to be your woman?'' He said, ''I saved your life.'' She said, ''You can still beat
me to death.'' Her retort left him feeling greatly ashamed. He pushed her down
and tore at her clothes.

The woman shouted, ''I'm pregnant.'' He asked, ''What does 'pregnant'
mean?'' The woman began to cry, ''There is a child in my belly.'' He was
overjoyed, released the woman, and said, ''Couldn't ya ha' damned well told me
sooner?'' He laughed out loud and shouted, ''Good! The old man's got off-
spring.'' The woman said, ''Who would give you a girl in marriage?'' He said,
''Aren't ya married to me?'' The woman stared blankly out the window.

He couldn't help asking, ''Where did you come from anyway?'' The woman
turned her head and glared at him. His face went red and he laughed awkwardly.
He hadn't kept his word; it was another loss of face.

''You, take a trip down the mountain,'' the woman said.

He didn't like going down the mountain. It was a walk of fifty-five kilometers
before one finally reached the town. The town upset him because people would
look at him with eyes like thieves. He had once seen a crowd herding a group of
trussed-up people on the street, cursing them in every imaginable way. The sight
made him shake in his boots. He would go down every month or two, exchange
skins for money, and use the money to buy oil, salt, soya sauce, vinegar, and
grain. He liked the mountain: no one could interfere with him, and he was no
trouble to anyone. He liked it even more so now that he had a woman, though the
woman was none too willing to sleep with him. But she made meals, clothing,
and even bore a child for him. He didn't want to go, he said.

The woman said, ''Buy cloth to make the child's clothing with.'' He realized
that it was necessary, so he went. He always felt that the journey was too long, as
if it would never end.

He saw the wolf pup's blood spurt onto the she-wolf. It was still able to let out a
few pitiful yelps, still able to burrow its head into the she-wolf's breast. He stood
there waiting for the wolf pup to die. After the pup's last yelp, its body contorted
into a ball, jerked violently out to its full length, and didn't move again.

The she-wolf thrust her snout into the snow and let out a sobbing cry, a cry
that would send chills into the heart of any man. He knew that the wolf was

calling out to others of its kind. He laughed very loudly. He cursed the wolf: "Fuck your ancestral mother! Howl! Howl! Not a one of them will come to save you!" He shouldered the rifle, pulled the tobacco pouch out from his waist, and rolled a cigarette. He struck a match and laughed sneeringly. He saw that the wolf had lifted her head and wasn't howling anymore. She seemed to have heard the summons of death in the hunter's laugh. That little ball of orange flame made her close her eyes. When she opened her eyes, she saw the hunter's mouth puffing out clouds of smoke.

He had killed nearly a hundred wolves. All had looked at him with bloodshot, savage, cruel triangular eyes. Only this wolf stared with a sad expression in its eyes at the barrel of the rifle. He was a bit baffled and even angrier as a result. He liked to watch the last ferocious pounce of the wolf before it died. But this wolf wasn't like that, she just lay there motionless and looked at him sorrowfully. He imagined there was sympathy and derision in that look.

He laughed ferociously. The newly risen sun was as red as his face, puffing out a warm fire. He remembered how it had been that morning. . . . Trees were thick about him, dripping wet. Water was collecting on the ground as the rain fell. Birds flew very slowly, with great effort, just like fish in water swaying back and forth. They chirped to each other—very small sounds the hearing of which made one feel cold on their account.

He wasn't cold. He wanted to shoot some "flying-dragon" birds. His boy was already nine years old. He thought that when he was nine he was not as tall as his son was already, and not as clever either. He first took up a hunting rifle at the age of twenty. But his son at the age of seven had been able to prop the gun up on a mound of earth and shoot a frisking squirrel. His son only liked being with him. His mother had never been close to him and sometimes scolded him. Occasionally the woman would teach the child a few characters, but as soon as he ran into difficulty she would turn on him.

Today he wanted to celebrate his son's birthday. He felt very happy. What made him even happier was that the woman was willing to sleep with him again and had even been attentive to him of her own accord. He felt that now there was something to this family of his.

As he walked, he searched his mind, thinking back over the last ten years. They were like a dream, almost totally forgotten. He only remembered that coming back from the bottom of the mountain a month previously he had been very tired and sat smoking at the side of the brick bed. His woman was outside the hut getting him something to eat and drink. He coughed a few times and said, "Damned strange."

The woman didn't respond and didn't come in. He felt disappointed. His son wasn't in the room. He didn't know his father had returned. The woman had made the boy say, "Daddy" and "Mummy" and wouldn't let their son say "Pa" and "Ma." It didn't sound right to him, but he didn't object. Why put up a fuss about a name? When the woman was with child she had a bad enough time, it almost took her life.

"Damned strange," he said again.

The woman carried in the food and wine. She didn't say a word. He drank a mouthful of wine and watched the woman. She didn't look at him. He couldn't keep it in any longer and finally asked, "I've got somethin tuh say, d'yah wanna listen?"

"Go ahead and talk."

"Damned strange. People all acting like loonies, scratchin those writ big words off the walls." He drank a mouthful of wine and spoke again. "They're making a big fuss about 'households being responsible for production' and such." He shook his head and looked at the woman. She was sitting across from him, listening. Now she topped up his wine cup. He was surprised by her attentiveness and laughed contentedly.

"They're dividing up the mules and horses, too," he added.

The woman pushed the wine cup toward him and asked, "Is the Cultural Revolution over?"

He shook his head. "What revolution? I dunno."

The woman nodded her head, closed her eyes, and suddenly started to cry. He was stunned by this behavior. After a while he sent the wine cup crashing to the floor and berated her, "Cry! Cry! Cry over yer mother's shit! All I e'er get's tears!"

She trembled once and stopped crying.

It was that night, as he was tossing and turning in his sleep, that the woman came under his quilt. She said, "Despite everything, you're still a good person." He was greatly moved. . . .

His heart came into his mouth. Don't think about those days anymore, he told himself. Again he remembered back to that morning. He had been out for a long time and hadn't shot a single flying-dragon. He wasn't happy about it and continued to move deeper into the mountain. He saw a large black object by a stand of pine trees. He thought he had come across some large beast. He roused himself, took hold of his gun, and crept in among some saplings, leaning forward gently.

He was taken aback by what he saw: there was a dead bear, and beside it lay a man. He ran over quickly, muddy water splashing up under his feet. Now he could see clearly that the man was his elder brother. He bent over and took a close look. Half his brother's head was crushed in, brains and blood mixed with rain water and flowed into a small gully. His brother's mouth was open, and there was black blood inside it. He thought that the bear must have done this. The most powerful part of the bear are its paws, they can break trees as thick as soup bowls with them. It would only take a light tap to open a man's head. He couldn't understand: how could his brother go after a hungry bear after its winter hibernation? He looked at the bear again—the white tuft of hair on its chest was stained purple by blood and a knife was still lodged there. Now he understood. It had clubbed his brother to death after it had received that fatal knife. Damn it! He stood motionless, wordless, for a long time. He took his brother's corpse up onto his back and staggered home with it.

The she-wolf suddenly howled and began to back up. She moved with great difficulty, and after only moving about half a foot, she couldn't move anymore. There was a look of desperation in her eyes. He laughed. The cigarette butt dropped from his lips to the ground, making a faint sizzling sound. He walked over, and the wolf didn't try to back off again. He didn't look at the wolf. He gathered up the torn roe-deer and with one motion tossed it into the gully. He kicked at a blackish-red patch of snow, kicking snow onto the wolf. A howl issued from the wolf's throat and her tail churned, whipping snow up into the air. He ignored the wolf.

He raised his head and looked off toward his home. Before him lay the silvery glinting, snow-covered wilderness, the dark forest—he couldn't see his hut, but he knew it was there. He gazed for a while and suddenly took in a deep breath, as if he wasn't certain that he really had a home.

He carried his brother back to the mountain foot. He was already so exhausted his whole body was beginning to lose sensation—he couldn't distinguish between rainwater and sweat. He opened the door to his brother's hut with his head. His sister-in-law was sewing. She saw him, and her hand came away in shock. She stood up, and when she saw the mangled flesh and blood of her husband's face, her mouth fell open. She crumpled to the ground and lay motionless. He hurriedly set down his brother and picked up his sister-in-law, shouting, "What's wrong wid yah! Wake up! Wake up!"

Someone pulled at his sleeve. It was his son. He yelled, "Call your ma . . . mummy, quick!" His son began to cry, "Mummy said, she's gone." He drew his hand back, slapped his son, and swore, "Bastard! Get a move on and call your mum!" The boy, knocked to the ground by the blow, yelled, "Daddy! Mummy said she wasn't comin' back!"

He stared at his son with the eyes of a wolf. His son tried to wriggle away on his bottom. He believed the boy. He sprang up like a tiger and rushed out the door. Again he stood still, shuffling his feet: "Fuck your ancestors!" He went back in, gathered up his sister-in-law, and called out: "Wake up, quick! Damn it!"

Sister-in-law finally started to come around, looked at his brother, and covered her face, wailing loudly. From then on she was alone.

From that day on he and his son were just two. He sometimes remembered that the woman had wanted to go down the mountain but he hadn't let her: if he had let her, maybe she wouldn't have run away. Fuck her mother, that bitch had

never wanted to live here! And he hated the woman even more, hated her enough
to want to kill her.

One day he walked into his sister-in-law's hut and said, "The boy and I're
leaving."

She shuddered once, grabbed the child beside him, and asked, "Where are
you going?"

Looking at the ground, he said, "Who knows? Wherever."

"Going to look for his ma?"

"No! That woman's cold-blooded 'n cruel! We're not gonna look fer her!"

Sister-in-law was watching him, holding the child, and tears began to flow.
She said, "Please don't go."

He didn't say anything, just raised his head and looked at her.

She said, "Please don't go. If you . . . if both of you go, I . . ."

That night he couldn't sleep, his eyes were wide open, staring at the ceiling.
He heard someone enter the hut. He saw that it was his sister-in-law. He got up
noiselessly and followed her into her hut.

That evening, he cried. Holding her, he knew then that she had for a long time
wanted to sleep with him, to live with him. He only then understood that it could
be like this between men and women. That woman had never given him the most
precious thing that a woman can give a man—her heart. He was grateful to his
sister-in-law; he didn't know what to say. For some reason he thought of that
woman again. He said to her, "Good'r bad, that woman gave me a son." This
made sister-in-law very unhappy: "I can also give you children." She said, "I
really am a woman."

"Elder . . . He really never . . . ?" he asked.

"Him?" She snorted and then sighed, saying, "He was so pitiful. In front of
me, he was like a dog."

He also sighed, feeling very uncomfortable for his elder brother and a little
apologetic toward him. He's dead and here I am on his brick bed sleeping with
his wife. What kind of a person am I?

And so on he went, on the one hand taking himself to task, and on the other
doing that thing with her. This made him lose interest, made him want to leave
her. But once he left her, he couldn't think of anything but her.

And so the days went by, one after the other. Almost every day he went to check
the traps for deer. Over the past few days he had lost two deer in a row. They
were not stolen by man, but eaten by wolves. Wolves were rare on the mountainside, so it was really bad luck. Today, if he had come out just that little bit
earlier, he would have been able to bring back a whole deer. But he was late
again. However, he felt better because he had run into the wolves. No matter
what, he wouldn't let them off. He immediately killed the he-wolf with the first
shot. Another three shots and he had broken the she-wolf's four legs. The rifle

butt smashed open the skull of one wolf-pup, and the fourth shot had killed the other cub by its mother's side.

Now only this immobile she-wolf was left. He wanted to torture her for a while, until he grew tired of it, and then give her a taste of the knife, fully releasing the black temper within him. He was paralyzed for a moment, he couldn't understand why he had to do this. He felt as if something was pushing him on to it. He didn't know what.

He was only four or five steps away from the wolf. This was the first time he had ever looked so calmly upon a wolf. He was so close that he could reach out and touch jer. He gazed at the wolf's legs. Her legs weren't completely broken: the hind legs were still in good shape, only bleeding profusely; the forelegs were neatly broken, pressed evenly upon the snow and bleeding so much that the blood was coagulating into so many clots under her body. If he just let her go on bleeding like this, in a short while she would be dead of her wounds. The knife would probably not be necessary. As he thought, he pulled out the knife and tossed it up into the air. The knife described a flashing arc before piercing the snow. He saw the wolf's eyes follow the knife's movements. The knife was sticking in the snow not fully half a foot from the wolf. The wolf's mouth opened and shut a few times. She extended a bright red tongue, running it once around her mouth, licking herself clean of the deer's blood. Her jaws made a sharp clicking sound, and the vicious, cold flame rose again in her eyes.

He laughed grimly. He knew it was the scent of blood that restored the wolf's courage, but now she didn't have the ability to resist. It would be most interesting to send this wolf to a humiliating yet courageous death. He decided to wait and watch her die bit by bit. Anyway, there was nothing to do, and this was as good a way as any to pass the time.

So he rolled another cigarette, smoked, and watched the smoke twisting and turning before his eyes. He blew a puff of smoke at the wolf. The wind dispersed it. He blew several times without success. He was angered and stepped forward two more steps. He could have reached out and touched the wolf's face. The wolf struggled to rise but was once more unable to do so. She lay staring at him ferociously. He inhaled deeply on the cigarette and blew the smoke out as hard as he could. Finally, he saw the wolf shake her head and heard her cough three times.

He laughed heartily. His whole body shook, and he continued laughing. Now he stopped, a sad expression had come over his face. He raised his head and gazed off toward the distant range of mountains. He saw that path—the path he had carried that woman back upon.

He had slipped down the mountain without telling sister-in-law. He still wanted to find the woman. He asked other people if they had seen such a woman. Several people laughed at him heartlessly. He was so angry he pointed his gun, frightening off a large group of people. But some others carted him off into a house. There, two policeman frightened him a lot. He spoke with great effort. In the end, the policemen made sense of what he was saying. The older one said, "You fool, why're you still looking? For sure that woman was running away from trouble. You picked up a woman to sleep with you for ten years for nothing, what more do you want?" And the younger one added, "You didn't even register and lived with a woman, you should be happy you weren't arrested. Go on back home!"

He returned in a daze to the foot of the mountain and entered sister-in-law's hut. His son saw his father had come back and called out, "Daddy." He scolded, "Don't say 'Daddy'! Say 'Pa' "! His son called him "Pa." He stared balefully and asked, "Miss your mother?" His son said, "No, mummy's bad, didn't wan'us." He said, "Good boy." And he began to drink.

Sister-in law put the child to sleep. She asked, "You went to look for her again?" He nodded.

She said, "Don't look for her. If you find her, she won't go with you." She spoke again, "You picked up a woman for nothing, she also gave you a child, isn't that enough?" And again she spoke, "And now I'll be your woman, isn't that enough for you?" And again, "Is it worth the trouble for mountain people to go after city people? Isn't this plenty good enough?"

He was glowering at her with red eyes, thinking, "Isn't this what women are all about?" He knocked her down. She pushed the lamp over with her hand. It was like this with them almost every day.

He discovered that she threw up when she ate and also when she hadn't. He called her useless. She began to cry and shouted, "You've caused me to lose the child, you beast!" He froze, remembering that the woman had also cursed him in such a way. He took her in his arms, saying, "I'm not human! I'm a beast!" and forced her to do it with him again.

On those days he felt extremely exhausted and annoyed. He felt like running off or doing away with himself with his gun. But he still wanted to come out to hunt. It didn't matter to him if he hit or missed, he still wanted to come out. Each time he looked down the mountain he would think: So many people down there, like ants, they're certainly worse off. By comparison, he was pretty much free to do as he pleased. When he thought of this he would feel happier.

And so it went—he was now angry, now happy. He began to fear that he might be crazy.

"Fuck his old man!" He swore and spat the cigarette butt into the wolf's face. The wolf didn't cry out: she bared her fangs and swung her head violently a few times. The cigarette butt had burnt her painfully.

He was watching the wolf. The wolf was watching him too; now her eyes had a very gentle, friendly look in them. He suddenly thought that the wolf was really pitiful, much like himself. He squatted and said to the wolf, "I won't kill you." The wolf was looking at him, her eyes had a very gentle, very grateful look in them. He thought that this wolf really understood his state of mind. Again he spoke, "How would you like it if I took you home?" The wolf shrank away. He said, "Don't be afraid, I won't kill you." The wolf continued to draw back. He said, "I won't kill . . ." Suddenly he noticed that the wolf's eyes were blood-filled and her body had become much thicker. He became aware that he was too close to her. He became flustered, wanted to get up, wanted to move a bit farther off. . . .

The wolf had been waiting for this opportunity. The injured legs would not have let her jump any farther. She could only bear the pain and wait. And now this person was not only squatting two steps away, but was also heedlessly emitting some unintelligible sounds. The sounds didn't seem to carry any hostile intent, but this was the person who had killed all her children, that had killed her mate. She gathered back her body, drawing up her strength. Unexpectedly, stupidly, this person hadn't noticed. She saw the first look of panic appear in the person's eyes. She had been waiting for this moment. She leapt forward, the snow that had been stuck to her body flew into the air in a flurry, forming a white fog. Just as she left the ground, her jaws opened and a cold wind blew into her narrow mouth. Her jaws came together with great force. She felt her teeth sink into his neck. Sweet blood spurted down her throat.

I could have killed her! he thought, as the wolf's sharp teeth sank into his throat.

"Child, we'll go to look for your ma," she said after waiting for him to stop crying.

The nearly ten-year-old child shook his head. He was still looking at his father's corpse. When Auntie had born Pa home, Pa's body had been covered in blood, and only a thin shred of the neck was left. The head was hanging limply on Auntie's shoulder. He had seen dead wolves, dead bears, all had been like this. He knew Pa was dead. He was very frightened and began to cry. He saw Auntie strip the clothes off Pa, use water to scrub the body clean, and put new clothes on it. Crying was tiring him and so he stopped.

"Child, your pa's dead. You still have a ma. I'll take you to look for her."

The child shook his head. He was looking at this aunt who was just about as tall as he and suddenly felt that she was his own mother. He looked at her for a long time. He stared at her so long that she became uncomfortable. "What's wrong with you, Child?" He suddenly called out, "Ma."

She was stunned. Her mouth fell open. Then he hugged her and again called out, "Ma."

She took him in her arms, crying, "My son." And she began to wail, to cry with all the strength in her body. After crying a while, she said, "Son, from now on there's just the two of us."

Her son nodded.

The corpse lay peacefully in the middle of the room. They slept. In the

morning upon waking, she reached out, but her son was not by her side. She
called out several times. There was no answer. She leapt to her feet.

She saw that the rifle that had been leaning against the brick bed was gone.
She was a little frightened, paced around the hut a few times, then took her
husband's rifle down off the wall and ran out. She greatly regretted it. She
shouldn't have told the child. The child had gone out in search of that injured
wolf. The child's too small, what if . . . She dared not continue to think about it.
She scolded herself as she stumbled off in pursuit of her son like a mad woman.

She never caught up to him. When it was nearly dark she returned, crying.
She was in despair and didn't want to go on living. But then she saw her son. He
was standing by the door watching her.

She rushed forward and locked him in her arms, running her trembling hands
over him.

"Ma, I killed it! Ma, one shot and I killed it!"

She had no more tears left to cry.

"Ma, let's leave."

"Where can we go?"

"Ma, I hate this place."

She was looking at her son.

"Ma, let's leave!"

She was looking at her son. The light in her son's eyes amazed and frightened
her a little. She thought it over and agreed.

Two balls of flame rose abruptly into the pitch-black early morning sky. Two
little straw huts on a small foot of a little leg of one of the mountains in the
Changbai range were burning fiercely.

A middle-aged woman and a small child stood by, watching the conflagration.
They waited until all that was left was a pile of ashes and a curtain of smoke and
then went down the mountain. The path was still covered in snow. The pair
moved on with great difficulty.

Lai Suo

Huang Fan

Translated by Eric B. Cohen

MR. HAN'S exhausted, grave countenance came into view on the screen. It was June 24, 1978, a day of no particular significance in a predictably screwed up world, a day as yet without any meaning whatsoever. Lai Suo sat watching the upright television before him with an expression of anger and resignation. To him it was truly the haphazard beginning of a long, confusing chain of events. How does one go about telling this?

After the shock had passed he entered the bedroom weeping and clutching his hair. His wife stood outside the locked door calling his name, but there was no reply so she turned around and went back to her cleaning chores. She loved taking the hose from the tap and washing down everything in sight—to his surprise Lai Suo found himself in the summer of 1968. He was lying naked on a bed in an apartment beside a highway, his wife's big behind pressed up against him, she sleeping there and snoring like a tea kettle. He threw on some clothes as he went out onto the balcony and stood facing the star-filled sky, his empty past, an unknowable future. Not until the first rays of light shone down from the East onto his balding forehead, which stood standing out just like an egg, did he return to the TV screen before him in 1978, for his life a beginning, an ending, and a place of rest.

1

A week out of prison, Lai Suo was already thirty years old. He wore an old gray wool suit, his body thin and emaciated (he was worried about his chronic stomach illness), the corners of his eyes weighted down by wrinkles, his eyes looking steadily down at his feet so that he might avoid anyone's stare. He stood there

The original appeared in the literary section of *Zhongguo shibao* (China times), October 2 and 3, 1979. This translation is from Huang Fan, *Lai suo* (Taibei: Shibao chuban gongsi, 1980), pp. 143–80. The translator wishes to thank professors David Der-wei Wang and Robin Yates for their patient assistance.

before the big office desk of his older brother, a fruit preserve manufacturer.

"I can do any kind of work and I won't cause any problems."

"Don't worry, Ah-suo, I'm your brother."

To date he had not come into contact with any pitying, sympathetic looks on the part of his older brother, looks that would have sent him scurrying away like a rat. And he really was just a little rat, so to speak. Indeed, he had even reported on his fellow inmates, making himself seem that much more rat-like. When he was twenty he had stood before the judge of a military tribunal trying to put on a manly air. He tried to be heroic and passionate, and mumbling to himself, he ended up crying as he spoke. The result was far from ideal, because he was an entirely insignificant person. He'd distributed photocopied pamphlets at the gates of the university and stuttered out the sentences written on them, only to have his ridiculous appearance draw the attention of approaching students who could only laugh. While they laughed, Mr. Han and several of his subordinates stepped down onto Japanese soil and after a few days had rented an apartment among the secluded streets of the Ginza. When all was settled, Mr. Han could then begin to store up quantities of sperm for the four mixed-blood children he would have after going to Japan and gather materials for the speech he would make on TV today upon his return to the embrace of his ancestral homeland.

Mr. Han was the last person whom he had ever idolized: afterward he had felt it best not to worship anybody who was alive. Because everyone will die, he thought to himself; great people die, stupid people die, I will die. . . . And whenever somebody dies, invariably their appearance is unpleasant. Before when Du Ziyi had died it was so unpleasant! He'd farted loudly, his face turning pig-liver red and slowly swelling up more and more, until finally he made an impossibly loud fart. Du's brain was bloated with Communism, and he believed that Marx was some kind of thing in between man and God. Because of this he would say to those who were uneducated, "Divide up the money of the wealthy!" To intellectuals he would say, "Class struggle is the motive force of social progress!" To himself he said, "Don't have any regrets." In spite of all this, Du never once shared with anyone the food that his family members brought to the prison. Du was very fat, his perfectly round face the epitome of a petit bourgeois. At his deathbed he pulled his roommate close, a final suffering witness, and said this: "Never trust anyone."

Lai Suo etched these words in his mind. Now he was lying on the bed thinking about these things, about Mr. Han, about Du, about the Japanese, about the stern-faced judge of the military tribunal, and after this he again began to weep softly.

"Don't wake your father," he heard his wife beyond the door say to his twelve-year-old daughter.

"If he's sleeping, why is he making such strange noises?"

"He doesn't feel too well."

After a while he slipped off the bed and went into the bathroom to wash up a bit. Everything in the bathroom was always very clean. The freshly washed mosaic tiles sparkled, reflecting twisted faces (he stood facing the wall tilting his head this way and that), faces that followed the tile pattern, becoming thoroughly distorted. He bared his teeth, raised his eyebrows, stuck out his chin, and leaned back with his nose sticking up, revealing an Adam's apple the size of a walnut.

"I've definitely gotten thinner," he sighed. He stood up on the scale beside the tub and weighed himself. The needle on the scale jumped to 101 pounds and came to a stop. This was the same weight he had recorded the previous month, except that last month he hadn't worn a stitch of clothing. That time he had taken off his clothes, squatted down on the scale, and hummed to himself ("alone through the night without a companion to watch over this empty house, the icy wind tearing at my face"). He had hummed halfway through the tune when his wife knocked at the door saying, "Ah-suo, what the hell are you doing in there?" He shoved open the door and his wife gave out a shriek, her eyes flashing. "You ought to be ashamed of yourself!" she screamed. So now he took off his pants and squatted down on the scale, forcing the needle up a little bit. After this he got up from the scale and sat down bare-assed on the toilet seat. The seat was covered with water and it sent shivers through him, a cold wave racing up his spine and boring into the deepest recesses of his brain. Immediately he was back again in 1963, the day of his marriage.

2

The bride's face was smeared with a thick layer of makeup and her hair was permed in curls. Her great big rump presaged how in the days to come she would bear so many children for the bridegroom. The wedding banquet that day went along quite smoothly, the large golden "double happiness" signs in the living room adding a great deal of spirit. The bridegroom's parents who had come from the distant countryside and his brothers who were busy chewing on betel nuts spat the juice of the nuts into tissue paper so as to be more courteous. The floor was covered with discarded tissues. Ah-suo's older brother was extremely ex- cited, and, clutching his glass of wine, he made his way between this table and that toasting people, his face completely red from drinking. Suddenly in the middle of all this he made an announcement saying that he was going to divide up the shares of his fruit preserve company and give some to his younger brother, at which the friends and relatives all clapped enthusiastically. This could not be drunken babble, for the wedding banquet only had two tables, and yet there were still two seats unoccupied that had been set out for a pair of important relatives who for some fluke of fate could not attend.

After the guests had all left, Lai Suo hurriedly slipped under the quilt, tearing off his wife's clothing by the handful. He was so preoccupied thus that he forgot to turn off the desk lamp, from which hung the word "happiness." Because of this his bride was squirming about, looking to the left and right.

"Ahh!" she exclaimed, "this room sure is pretty."

"Don't move about so wildly," Lai Sou said, "otherwise this button will never come undone."

Besides undoing buttons, he was also able to thread a needle, to do stitchery, and to do calisthenics, all things which he had picked up in prison. On the morning of this day fifteen years after his marriage, he suddenly bent down from the waist to touch his ankles. He expended a lot of energy in the process, but unfortunately, twenty inches below his knees, his fingers would no longer listen to his orders. All the while he stood there in just his underwear, his spindly legs showing forth, his knee caps like tumors, while his wife looked on unflinchingly.

"When I was young I could reach my hands all the way down to here," he squatted down and tapped the floor, "my entire palm, and now I can't bend at all."

"So what's the use anyway?" his wife said.

Well, if it was useless, then to hell with it! Now he was standing in a daze before the filtering machine in the jam factory. The needle on the pressure indicator was rising, and the motor underneath was making a coughing sound. From one end of a pipe, the syrup entered a filtering machine the shape of a great big bomb. Then it came out the other end, from which it would quickly flow into a condensing vessel hanging in midair. When it finally came out of the condensing vessel, the syrup was no longer syrup but a shiny, paste-like substance. The entire process was a little bit like God's creation of man. Perhaps someone would say something to this effect, that the fetus in the womb is simply composed of condensed blood.

Whatever the case, Lai Suo's mother certainly didn't take it to be this way. When he was only seven months old he had come out from his mother's belly as if there was no tomorrow, screaming at a world that wasn't yet ready to greet him. His mother lay to one side on the bed, her face ash-gray, while his father stood there in his military underwear wringing his hands unceasingly, his entire head drenched in sweat. Suddenly a drop of sweat fell on the infant's nose, mankind's earliest experience of rainfall. Aside from them there were a few people gathered about the bed.

"What should we do? What should we do?" Lai Suo's father mumbled to himself.

"Ai-ya! Why's his skin so green?" The one who said this was his mother's second sister, who in later days had a son who worked for an American military advisory group and for this reason had not attended Lai Suo's wedding banquet.

"My son?" his mother said closing her eyes. "Let me hold him."

"You can't hold him yet," the midwife said. "We must use medicated gauze to wrap him up, otherwise he'll be deformed."

It was probably because of the medicated wrapping that afterward he had grown up more and more ugly and hadn't reached puberty until he was sixteen. Nevertheless, his adolescence did not bring along any headaches for him. He was the shortest one in his class, and he sat on a stool only a meter away from the teacher's desk. The Japanese teacher occasionally reached down secretly to scratch at his crotch, being uptight about his eczema; he thought that no one else saw, but he was mistaken.

"Shina,"* the Japanese said. "Read together with me."

"Ji-Na," Lai Suo said.

"Do you know, you are not people of Zhi-na, you are Taiwanese."

"But teacher," a native asked, "my grandfather says that we all followed Koxinga† here from Zhi-na."

"*Bakayaro!*"‡ the Japanese man cursed. The smell of his breath flew at Lai Suo who lifted his hand to his face, only to find that he had broken out with a number of pimples.

When he started to break out, some of them burst open just as he was walking along the path beside the rice paddies. He walked on alone and at the same time scratched his pimples so that his face was streaked red and white. He was just about to scratch open his fifth when his classmate Xiao Lin (Little Lin) nudged him with his shoulder.

"Hey look!" Xiao Lin said in a lowered voice. "Isn't that Tanaka Ichiro?"

"Which Tanaka Ichiro?"

"The Japanese guy who taught us history two years ago."

The two sides of the road were covered with straw mats, and some Japanese were kneeling on the mats with their heads bowed. The mats were haphazardly covered with things—fake jewelry, fans, knee-high boots, a Japanese doll wearing a kimono. At this time Lai Suo had just turned eighteen, and with the Japanese having surrendered not long before, the native people weren't sure what was best to do. Lai Suo's father had worked for the Japanese, and it was several months before he finally calmed down. Then he rented a room in the central market region and started to run a fruit business. Fruit is a delicious yet difficult type of vegetation. During the day Lai Suo would push a small wooden cart, and he set up several bases along the Tamsui River. Because his voice was not strong enough to attract customers, he was always sitting on the seat cushion, his two feet sticking into the fruit basket, his bare soles unintentionally rubbing against a watermelon the size of a man's head. When night fell he would put his feet into clackity wooden clogs and go wandering all about the streets.

"*Arigato, Arigato . . .*" said the Japanese as they bowed incessantly, their foreheads almost touching the ground.

"Why don't we go say '*arigato*' to Tanaka and see if he still remembers us."

Lai Suo thought about it for a while.

---

*Shina (Zhina in Chinese) is a derogatory Japanese term for China (rightfully Chugoku).
†Koxinga (Zheng Chenggong) is Taiwan's most famous national hero.
‡Fool.

"No, that wouldn't be right."

"Why not?"

Lai Suo thought about it some more.

Still, it was as if there were some force that kept him from thinking further, and what is more, it seemed to transport him back, five, ten, twenty years. . . .

"Mr. Lai, is there something wrong with the machine?" one of the factory workers inquired.

"What did you say? Ehh, it seems like the pressure's gone up a bit."

"There are too many impurities in this batch for proper filtering: listen to the motor."

Not only was it the motor, but the agitator, the pump, and the steam pressurizer all made noises that came together in a great torrent. Lai Suo strained his ears to listen.

3

It was as if he were still listening to something else, his two ears like maple leaves completely exposed to the din of the street—buses, trucks, taxis, motorcycles, an occasional ambulance flying past with siren blaring, all these sounds pounding against his eardrums in droves. As if out of intuition they drove through the deepest recesses of his brain but were stopped midway by something—something like a soundproof bone, on which were inscribed the words, "Lai Suo, a citizen of Taibei, June 1978, a traveler through time and space."

Now he was sitting on a bus returning home. The driver drove the vehicle just as if it were a toy and at the same time had the radio turned up as loud as possible. The speaker was right beside Lai Suo's head. Lai Suo sat shrunk down on the green plastic seat. Beside him sat a great big middle-aged woman with a fierce-looking appearance, her two breasts drooping down like waterfalls, her body bathed in cheap perfume that stung one's nose (his wife usually used Max Factor, and he could tell what it was the minute he got a whiff). On the back of the seat in front of him were a few words scribbled with an eyeliner pencil: "Lonely? Please call 871-3042, Li Meihua." Lai Suo secretly chuckled to himself.

The bus made a stop in front of city hall, and Lai Suo's eyes, watching the retreating landscape, also came to a rest. A few seconds later the scenery was once again retreating, the pedestrians, the gray trees, the filthy houses, the row after row of billboards, it was if they were all being swallowed by an incomparably great mouth. When they went under an overpass Lai Suo closed his eyes momentarily. When he opened them he was standing in the *Pan-Asian Magazine* publisher's reception room facing a full-length mirror. There was a short fellow in the mirror, a listless look in his eyes. Suddenly the door opened and a staff member stuck his head in.

"Mr. Han would like you to come into the conference room."

"What for? I just want to pick up my pay and leave."

"If he called you in then go in."

"If it's okay, I'd just like my pay for the day."

"Enough back talk!"

Besides Mr. Han and the man who had ordered him to go in, he didn't recognize a soul. When Mr. Han saw him and laughed, with a grin Lai Suo ducked his head down embarassedly, glancing at his grimy shoes. As he stepped onto the spotless *tatami* the man who escorted him in shook his head in disgust saying, "Never mind, go ahead."

"Lai Suo!" Mr. Han came over to him and grasped his shoulders, "this is Mr. Chen, Mr. Lin. Here, have a seat, this is Mr. Huang. . . ."

"How long have you been working with us?"

"Four months."

"Where did you work before?"

"I sold fruit down by the Tamsui River."

"How is it that you stopped?" Mr. Han asked as he turned his head to face the gentlemen sitting cross-legged on the *tatami* and said to them, "We're really experiencing an economic downturn."

"I wasn't very good at it," Lai Suo answered. "Sometimes I'd give the wrong change, and my voice is also pretty weak."

"How about this—you've received an education, right? How would you like to be a full-time employee?" The men in the back lifted up their heads and gave him a look, one of them whispering to a second, "He's an honest fellow." Lai Suo heard this.

An "honest man," what does that mean? Thirty years later Lai Suo sat in a bus carefully listening to these sounds. The bus was now passing a stretch of road on which many lengths of pipe were spread out. Both sides of the street were piled up with wooden beams, concrete pipes, and steam shovels. Who knew how many times this street that wound around city hall had been dug up and repaved? In any event, this had absolutely nothing to do with him, and come to think of it, people should do something, if only to keep themselves that much more busy. The big-breasted woman was tugging at the stop-cord, and the whole lower half of her body was pressing down on his shoulder so that Lai Suo raised his head and gave her an angry stare. It seemed as if the ringing of the bell would go on forever before the woman finally got off, her shadow flying past Lai Suo's eyes. He quickly shifted his gaze to the window. The bus was now flying through the fog over a monotonous road. Beyond the windows the scenery receded without stop, throwing itself into a gaping mouth behind. Lai Suo continued his infinitely unbounded meditation.

"What the hell does a full-time employee do?" he heard himself wondering.

"The work is relatively easy, and every month you get an extra hundred dollars."

"Why?" he asked again.

"Here, read this," Mr. Han passed him a thin mimeographed sheet. "Sign your name on the last line and bring your name stamp tomorrow to certify it."

Lai Suo read the first line: "I wish to join the Taiwan Democratic Progressive Alliance, under the leadership of Han Zhiyuan, to struggle for my countrymen. . . . Should I betray my pledges, may I be abandoned by Heaven and Earth."

4

Lai Suo tired himself out over these questions and finally got off the bus and started to walk home. Along the way he stopped off at a bakery and bought a large bag of peanuts and three lollipops. The peanuts were for later that evening when he would sit on the balcony. The lollipops were for the three children, one apiece. This is chocolate, the storekeeper said. These are butterscotch, these are lemon, these are five-spice buttered peanuts. . . . Can I get you anything else, Sir? No, nothing! Perhaps then for your wife? She didn't seem to need anything. She had everything. She had nothing. For a second Lai Suo was confused: How could anyone have a wife with as much energy as his? It was like she was ready to blow up at any moment, and then she would pick up the hose from the faucet and wash everything down. She wanted everyone in the family to switch into a new set of clean clothes every day. She would patiently turn the pockets of their clothes inside out, saying, "You've got all the dirt in the world in here! If it wasn't for my perseverance you would probably have rats in there some day." When she finished she would toss Lai Suo's handkerchief into the washer. She would toss everything in just right, his socks, his tie, the towels, the yellow caps that the children wore to school, and he would stand there shaking his head. Then he would step on the wet floor and go sliding into the living room.

Even though she's like that, Lai Suo thought to himself, he could still put up with such a wife; he could even put up with those nighttime activities.

They would be sleeping soundly when suddenly in the middle of the night she would roll her corpulent body over and press down on him without any warning. Lai Suo would have to summon all his strength to struggle out of his nightmare, on the one hand struggling and on the other hand making strange sputtering noises.

"Ah-suo, I've rolled on top of you again," his wife would say, full of apology.

"Never mind." The first few months after they were married he would always respond in this way.

"Did I hurt you?"

"A little bit," he said. "Every time you do that I have nightmares."

"What kind of nightmares?"

"Strange ones."

Now Lai Suo was sitting on the floor of his prison cell facing the wall and crying. The dreary rays of lights penetrated the small barred window from above and fell on Fat Du's bare feet, reflecting in every direction. Occasionally he grabbed his toes and with a pair of squinting eyes looked on with interest at the weeping Lai Suo. Lai Suo had just gotten word of his mother's death. Once every month she had come to the prison to see him, always bringing something to eat and going off with tear-filled eyes. Sitting behind the wire-mesh partition of the visiting room, he could not help but cry out when he heard the news. He clenched his fists and pounded on the metal divider like some kind of trapped rodent until finally a guard dragged him off, his brother on the other side grudgingly forcing out a few tears. Lai Suo staggered into his cell in a daze. At once Fat Du grabbed the box packed with food that Lai Suo was carrying. Within a few minutes he was happily bloated and decided to say a few consoling words.

"Save your strength!" he said. "You still have six years and four months to cry your heart out."

Lai Suo jumped up angrily and turned around staring at him, his shoulders drawn up.

"What?"

"I said save your strength, there's no use in crying."

"Go fuck yourself!"

A second later the two of them were whirling about on the floor. In no time Fat Du's heavy body was pressing down on top of him. Lai Suo struggled with all his might, his hands and feet flailing about wildly and his spit streaming in every direction and covering Fat Du's face.

"I'll bash you if you start screaming like that again," Fat Du glared at him before he finally calmed down.

"Sometimes I dream about my mother," Lai Suo said to his wife lying beside him.

5

It was already very late, and Lai Suo still sat out on the balcony contentedly shelling peanuts, his feet propped up on the railing. It was the beginning of spring, the horizon sparkling with stars and the highway lit up by a string of headlights. Sitting in his BVDs, this person named Lai Suo was burdened with answering the puzzles of mankind, the gleam in his eyes tender, relentless, bemused, while his two hands were busily shelling peanuts. He grasped them in between his thumb and index finger and then lightly popped them open with his fingertip, the burst-open shells revealing plump white seeds. Thereupon Lai Suo took the shells and tossed them, bouncing, to the road below where, because of a light breeze, they scattered over the street.

"What's the big deal with drinking a little booze?" Lai Suo's father said.

"You'll have a stroke, rheumatism, stomach ulcers, all kinds of illnesses," Lai Suo's mother retorted.

Lai Suo took his two feet off the railing and shifted his position, still listening to the sounds of the dead people arguing.

"I'm not in a good mood."

"Who cares."

Lai Suo's father worked himself to the bone, and though he couldn't read and wasn't very sturdy, still he had raised a family. During the day he worked at a factory that supplied malt sugar to the Japanese army. Stripped to the waist, he would run back and forth to each of the steel drums which were filled with glutinous rice flour and a great deal of water and stir the oar-like wooden paddle with all his strength. Just like rain, the sweat would drip off his body into the vats, and after half an hour he would pour in a bucket of black maltose, the coal underneath still burning away. Lai Suo's father would then run over to another vat, the previous night's malt syrup which had already completely liquefied, and stir it up as well until steam rose up and he could get down. Every day he went up and down like this dozens of times, and as a result his legs became very strong, whereas from the waist up he remained scrawny.

"Ah-yun should go to work right away to help make some money," Lai Suo's mother said as she took his bottle away. "Ah-suo is smarter. Why don't we send him to school?"

"What's the use of studying?" his father asked back.

"You should know how the illiterate suffer."

"Mom, you always want me to study," Lai Suo couldn't help but interrupting from where he sat on the balcony. "Maybe Dad's right."

"How have I suffered?" Lai Suo's father said angrily. "If you don't have money, no one will respect you. I might just as well be dead!"

"I haven't had a single happy day since I married you," Lai Suo's mother also flared up. "All you know how to do is drink, drinking away every good opportunity that comes our way."

"You've been talking with Ah-quan again." Ah-quan was a distant relative of theirs who had brought Lai Suo's father to Taibei and helped him find work. "Has he made any money?"

"Not yet, but that doesn't mean he won't someday."

"Yeah? We'll talk about it 'someday.' " If only Lai Suo's father could see Ah-quan today, wearing a twenty-thousand-dollar suit, driving a Mercedes Benz, his hair dyed jet black, and despite his sixty years still licentiously eyeing the nightclub waitresses' asses.

"Someday Ah-suo is definitely going to have it better than you."

"That's his business."

In the end Lai Suo's father agreed to let his son attend public school for a while and even bought him a pair of cloth-soled shoes for the occasion. It was no small amount of money he had spent, though, and whenever it rained Lai Suo would go barefoot and carry his shoes in his hands.

"Don't think I'm gonna go buy you anything," his father said menacingly.

"If you don't study well, I'll give you a walloping when you get back."

"What the hell are you trying to frighten the child for?"

"I work myself to the bone. I've wasted my whole life just trying to make a living."

What was the point in pursuing this? In the end even Lai Suo became upset and stood up, hurling the remaining peanuts to the street below. He went into the living room where the children were gathered in front of the TV.

"Is your homework done?"

"We finished it a long time ago, Dad."

"Where's your mother?"

"She went to bed."

Lai Suo quietly closed the door, not wanting to wake her up. He was already tired enough for one day, and tomorrow he still had some things to take care of. He was going to take the day off and go see his cousin, who was sick and laid up in Xu Shi Hospital. His cousin's wife had called up and said that he was always trying to slip out (he had an affair going with another woman who must have been very worried not to hear from him for several days), and so she'd come up with a plan—she hid his shoes! If he dared to go out in the streets in his slippers she would have to give in, but what else could she do? At the other end of the phone Lai Suo shook his head without giving any committed response. Why should he get involved in other people's problems, especially when he had to see Mr. Han! His face had shown up in the news some thirty-six hours before, but to him it seemed like years, and because of this he wanted to get everything straight. What was it he wanted to get straight? Who could say? After such a long time he himself had three children, and Mr. Han, he was already seventy. At this age plenty of people were already wearing dentures. Maybe I'll just shake his hand and say, "Mr. Han, it's been a long time."

"Ah-suo, how can you sit alone there on the balcony for half the day?"

His wife wasn't sleeping, she was wearing her pink Triumph underwear and was bathed in perfume from head to toe. These were her little stratagems, the little extras, the resourcefulness that accounted for their three children and the two apartments they had acquired at a court auction. Whenever her relatives from the countryside came to visit she would take them to Taibei to nightclub shows and treat them to a meal out at some nice hotel restaurant. These country folk never ceased to be amazed by the dazzle of the city, their mouths hanging open, unable to utter a syllable. At these times Lai Suo's wife would always be extremely excited, and he would be exceptionally warm and friendly, a look of helplessness showing from the corners of his eyes. On this particular night her passion was uncontrollable, and despite her forty years and rather plump belly she was acting just like a little girl, giggling and pressing her 132-pound body on a totally limp Lai Suo.

"Hey, I'm eating peanuts!"

"Peanuts make you hot," his wife said. "Why have you been acting so strange these past few days?"

"I've been thinking about some things," he said. "That's right, tomorrow I'm not going to the factory. I have to go to the hospital to visit cousin Ahzong."

"Why do you want to go see him? Just a little cold and everyone goes berserk, huh! Who the hell is he?" She didn't like Lai Suo's family. "I'm sure as hell not going. I still have a big load of washing to do."

"Fine," Lai Suo sighed. "I think I'll go to sleep a little early this evening."

But she wasn't about to let him off so easily, and she rolled back on top of him, her heavy perfume wafting all about.

"Do you remember when we had just met?"

"Uh huh."

"You said everyone liked my looks."

"Uhh."

"The first time you kissed me you wanted me to close my eyes, do you remember?"

"Uh hm," he mumbled. "Uh hm, uh hmm, uh, uh . . . , uh . . ."

On the way to Taibei the bus now stopped on the middle of a bridge under which flowed the perpetually filthy Tamsui River. A black and white striped police car was parked at the end. In his best suit, Lai Suo sat crammed in among the throng of passengers with a pained expression on his face.

"Those getting off please move toward the front. Those not getting off please do not crowd around the door," the ticket taker said in a nasty voice. "Why're you always standing here?" he said to Lai Suo. Not until the bus had passed by the Century Restaurant did he answer, mumbling, "I'd like to get off." He got off the bus as usual and bought a basket of apples by the side of the road. It was as if these apples had just come out of a freezer, they were so dark purple. Still, someone staying in the hospital probably would not care about it. Cousin Ahzong would say, "It was so nice of you to come, and you even brought some fruit!" His cousin was a good sixty years old, but still his face was bright red. Every day he would get up around five or six in the morning and go up to the hot springs in Beitou,* after which he would go down the mountain to his mistress's house for breakfast. When he came home his wife would be busily pacing back and forth in the kitchen, and he would sneak up behind her and pinch her behind.

"What delicious food have you made for breakfast today?" he would ask innocently as she jumped with a start.

After a while, Lai Suo got into a phone booth facing Xu Shi General Hospital across the street and put the basket of apples down on the floor. There wasn't the slightest bit of movement at the hospital entrance, however, as if the patients

---

*Beitou is a popular resort area north of Taibei famous for its hot springs and prostitutes.

were all either sleeping or dead. Lai Suo didn't have the time to go investigating things like this: What time did the doctors begin work? What time did the patients get up? Do they eat right after they wake up? He opened the large phone directory and ran his finger back and forth over the lines.

"Excuse me, is this the TV station?"

"That's right," a girl said as she yawned.

"Could you tell me if there is going to be an appearance today by a Mr. Han as reported in the papers?"

"You've got the wrong number; this is the restaurant extension. You should call the information department."

"But surely you know that Mr. Han Zhiyuan is coming to speak?"

"Which Han Zhiyuan? Is he on a variety show or in a soap opera?" she said, beginning to get impatient. "I know all the famous actors and singers here. What's this Han Zhiyuan do? You don't know the information desk's number, right?"

"He, he just came back from Japan."

"That's strange. The only one who's come back from Japan is Teresa Teng (Deng Lijun). I'll tell you the number of the information desk, okay?"

"Thanks!" Lai Suo dropped another dime into the phone and dialed the number.

"Hello, is this the information desk?" he said, a little bit more forcefully.

"Information desk speaking," came a girl's voice.

"Yes, is there a Mr. Han, Han Zhiyuan, appearing tonight?"

"There is—tonight at eight o'clock on 'Contemporary Spotlight.' Don't you have a subscription to *TV Weekly*?"

"No," Lai Suo said, "but I'd like to get one."

"You can dial this number . . . ," the girl went on. "Tell them Miss Ma at the TV station told you about it. Don't forget, that way you won't miss programs like 'Contemporary Spotlight.' Is there anything else I can do for you?"

Now that this was all set, the girl started in on her sales pitch. Holding the receiver and leaning back against the door of the telephone booth, Lai Suo grinned sardonically. This was his way of dealing with salespeople (newspaper, magazines, soy sauce, cosmetics . . .). He listened patiently to the long-winded bombardment of items (to the point that his expression was one of total conviction) and finally brought the whole thing to a halt by coldly interjecting, "What you've said makes perfectly good sense, but my family has already ordered these things, we already have them, and we have always used this brand." "Thank you," he finally concluded. "If I call that number and tell them Miss Ma at the TV station told me about it, can I get a special deal?"

6

Lai Suo left the phone booth; on the other side of the street there now seemed to be some signs of life. Several people came out the front door of the hospital looking back and forth, and a taxi pulled up by the entrance. Two people got out. The first patient of the day? Separated by the congested street, Lai Suo couldn't make out which one of the two was sick. The people who were looking about darted into the cab while the driver looked over his shoulder, and then the car flew away in a puff of smoke. Lai Suo stood by the side of the road and, not finding any break in the traffic through which to cross, went back to the sidewalk and then back toward the stop light fifty meters away. The sidewalk was lined with acacia trees, each encircled by iron fencing. From one of these trees there hung a Taibei municipal trash canister in the shape of a bird on which was printed "I love to eat trash." Lai Suo reached into his pocket but could not find anything to stuff into the bird's mouth. I love to eat fruit peelings and waste paper; everyone loves to eat trash, Lai Suo thought to himself.

The stop light turned green and Lai Suo hurried across the street back onto the red brick sidewalk. The hard rubber soles of his shoes were just right for the streets of Taibei. The streets in Taibei—an official of the municipal government came up with the following suggestion when asked about this problem: Use an atom bomb to blast away every existing structure and start over with a new set of rules. Some joke! Still, the words came back to mind. Lai Suo's hard rubber-soled shoes sparkled in the blinding sun, the color of his shoes matching perfectly with his suit and the red brick sidewalk.

In the end he had to make a big detour before he reached the hospital.

The nurse at the hospital's information desk was wearing glasses and looked as if she had just woken up. She looked at the basket of apples Lai Suo put onto the counter and said, "Patient room number 201. What relation to him are you?"

"Cousin."

"You've got a great pair of shoes," the nurse said as she stuck out her head. "It's too bad they're too small."

"My shoes are too small?"

She shrugged her shoulders.

"Would you like an apple?"

"Thanks," the nurse said, "I've already eaten lunch. You can go up the stairs on your righthand side."

From the doorway of the room he could hear cousin Ah-zong's voice, a great cacophony of imploring, threatening, cursing, his rage just barely contained.

"Okay! So when will I finally be released from the hospital?" his cousin asked.

"When the doctor says you can leave the hospital then you can leave," his wife answered.

"Doctor, hmph!"

Lai Suo pushed open the door, and, as expected, his appearance stopped them in the middle of their fight. Sitting in a Western restaurant not too far from the TV station, Lai Suo vividly recalled the whole affair as he waited for the waiter to bring his food. He pressed his face toward the tinted brown window. What had happened to the world outside? It had taken on a terribly gloomy appearance, the pedestrians, the cars, everything floating by like ghosts. What had happened to the sun behind his back when he had come in the door? Maybe it had died. Lai Suo pulled his face back from the glass, loathing the stupidity of a man outside (a passer-by was looking into the window, but clearly he could not make out anything inside as he stood there in front of Lai Suo fussing with his hair). Wouldn't it be great if the glass became blue or green! Suddenly you'd be standing on an endless golf course and let fly a green golf ball which would fall into a green hole, after which you would open your green eyes and lift up your green legs. . . .

"Ah-suo! How nice of you to come!" Cousin Ah-zong was very excited and danced about barefoot on the blue carpet in his silk pajamas, his face swollen red, his protruding belly and double chin quivering without stop.

"You decide, who is really sick?" he said as he got more and more upset. "You decide."

If no one is sick, then what the hell are you doing in the hospital? Lai Suo laughed to himself as he sat there in the restaurant.

"Ah-suo, your cousin has not only not recovered, but the sickness has gone to his head," his cousin's wife said as she pointed at his head. "Just look at how insane he's acting." The two of them went on at each other this way for so long that Lai Suo finally had to sit down on the sofa, he was so tired, and he put the apples he had brought off to the side.

"Why don't each of you have an apple."

"Sure, Ah-suo, why don't you see if you can plug up his mouth with one."

"What is this suppose to mean?" Cousin Ah-zong was so upset that he flopped down onto the bed. "Not only do you not let me put on my shoes or make a phone call, but you even want to plug up my mouth!"

"Just look at how uptight he's getting," his wife said as she sat down. Lai Suo looked sympathetically at the two of them. He had really wanted to say something to them, but now he was not in the mood. He had an important affair to attend to, and in a while he would go to this restaurant and just sit as long as he wanted.

It was already past lunchtime now, but Lai Suo still sat there, wishing he could find some little thing to keep himself occupied. Perhaps he could call home, but his wife would ask about all kinds of things. She would want to know how much Taibei had changed (she had come into the city just last week). What were all those loose women wearing? Was it true that the supermarket was having a 20 percent discount sale? If it was, could he please pick up something to bring back? What would he take back? Anything would be fine. All of this would be very distressing to Lai Suo, and he didn't want to take any risks. He was going to see Mr. Han and needed to prepare himself. He wanted to be confident and look his best, otherwise why would he have gotten so dressed up?

Come to think of it, when he had gotten married Lai Suo's clothes were not nearly as nice as the ones he wore now. The Lai family had never paid much attention to getting dressed up. "Nothing's more important than eating!" his father always used to remind the family. "Don't go about buying this thing and that. When war comes your way, can you eat all your clothing?" It seemed that Lai Suo's father had spent his entire life fleeing war. He had even gone through American bombing raids. He lived until he was seventy-two years old and then died of a weak heart in the first-class section of the veterans hospital. Before he passed away the room was absolutely still, only the air conditioner outside the window making an almost inaudible hum. Not even the great rumble of the Boeing 747 overhead intruded upon this silence.

7

Maybe he had just dreamed it all, those distressing experiences, his head swimming through so many ups and downs. . . . He was slouched down on the supple vinyl seat, in the soft, ambiguous artificial lighting, all of it seemed entirely lifeless. There were a few gray hairs on Lai Suo's sunken temples (he was completely bald), his face was lined with wrinkles, and his lips were gray, taut. This was the real Lai Suo, the Lai Suo completely sapped of energy, the one who had been proud, had advanced, had cooperated—he was a favorite of heaven, a member of mankind, the one who had awoken, had dozed, was mournful, joyous (he started to laugh like a nervous young girl), the Lai Suo who had so deeply suffered the six desires and seven emotions.

He opened his eyes as the waves of sound poured forth from the microphone.

"Ladies and gentlemen, tonight's program is about to begin." Lai Suo was shocked to discover that the tables about him were fully seated and that the six o'clock program was about to begin. Good heavens! Had he really spent the afternoon sitting here, the entire afternoon, without preparing a thing, just sitting here? He was going to meet with Mr. Han! This was a historic moment and yet he hadn't prepared a thing. At the very least he should have something to say, something like what Mr. Han had said at the airport, something brief, something proper, something with lots of feeling. Certainly he had some kind of speech in mind before he boarded the plane, something that he had polished as he flew over the Pacific, and when finally the instant to open the cabin door arrived, he straightened his tie, cleared his throat. . . .

"Can I get you something to drink, sir?"

"Oh, whatever. Maybe a coffee."

Although there was not a lot of time, to go through the underpass to the TV station across the street would only take five minutes, and with ten minutes left to waste he would spend five in the bathroom. There was plenty of time. He did not need to prepare any long speech; Mr. Han would remember him. In fact he would be so excited that he would grasp his hand and, his face full of tears, he would be so excited that he would tell Lai Suo that he had wronged him and that he wanted to spend the remaining years of his life trying to repay him. All right, since he put it that way, what could Lai Suo say? He could only write the whole thing off as an unlucky break, and in time he would be able to put it behind him.

*"Ladies and gentlemen, I want to sing a song for you."** The spotlight focused in on a young man with long hair and a flat nose, his face a deep yellow. He held a guitar and plucked away at it while he sang a song in English. His expression was full of life, and he sang with abandon, pretending he was drunk toward the end.

"Thank you, thank you, once more? Okay, okay!" the youth said. Lai Suo could not sit there any longer. These people, their fashion, elegance, wealth—this imbecile on stage! Lai Suo was so disgusted with the sounds of laughter and music in his ears, the pretentious gestures, that he felt forced to stand up and hurriedly paid the bill. He pushed through the restaurant's revolving door onto Ren'ai Road stretching out silently into the distance and felt anew the mysterious vitality of a stroll under the setting sun.

It was this powerful feeling that caused him to sit down on the sidewalk bench with a totally blank stare as he faced the towering TV station across the street.

"What the hell was I thinking of doing?"

For a moment Lai Suo could not help but have some pangs of regret. Perhaps he shouldn't always be running away. By now his wife had certainly cleaned up the kitchen table and they were all happily sitting around the TV, the children all in a circle. In the center was the empty sofa where Lai Suo usually sat. He was the head of the family, the father of the three children, and so that was where he usually sat, his feet propped up on the coffee table as he laughed at the sitcom, his wife and kids laughing along. This was Lai Suo's family's routine, their evening entertainment.

He really should not have come out here. He should be sitting in front of the TV drinking tea and eating soda crackers. He should be stretching out and yawning, going into his room, taking off his clothes, and in the darkness crawling into bed, whether in distress, joy, or total indifference, bringing this day to an end.

8

The sky gradually darkened while the mercury lamps on the two sides of the road suddenly flashed on like silent strings of burning firecrackers. Following the glare of the car lights Lai Suo stared off toward the end of the street. There was not much time! He would have to decide quickly. He drew his eyes back to the magnificently illuminated building across the street. He thought of his child-

---

*This line and the next one in italics are in English in the original.

hood, his adolescence, and the incomprehensible years after his marriage. His entire life, it was an abysmal failure! He had lost face for the entire family while his older brother Lai Yun became wealthy, took care of his younger brother who was off at school, arranged his marriage, and gave him shares in his company. The day before he had died Lai Suo's father still had looked at them in sorrow saying, "Ah-yun, you must look after your brother." Lai Yun was fifty years old, his stomach filled out. He laughed, his eyes squinting. His face was covered with tears, his nose red from crying.

"Dad, you'll get better," Lai Suo said as he clutched his father's mottled hands, his nails all gray. "Next month we'll take you shopping at the Southeast Asia department store."

"I'm afraid not," his father said. "Ah-suo, come here." He was fonder of the older son, while Lai Suo's mother liked her more refined younger son. When Lai Suo was released from prison he stood crying before his father. His father looked at him, tears running down his face, and sighed, "Ahh! Ahh!" He "ahhed" for half the day, unable to say a word. After a long time had passed he brought out an old gray wool suit from another room (when Ah-yun had been married, their father had made it for him). "Put this on," he said, "we're going to see your brother."

"Dad," Lai Suo said hesitating, "is it all right if we go to see Mom's grave first?"

It was not until the first week he started to work in the fruit preserve factory that they went out to the Mu Zha municipal graveyard. In all there were eight of them, four grownups and four children, the entire three generations of Lai Suo's family. Lai Yun was busy pacing about, taking responsibility for getting everything in order, his wife hopelessly entangled with the four children. Lai Suo's father looked on angrily from the car window without saying a word while, on the verge of tears, Lai Suo wrung his hands without stop. The two cars were parked one in the front and one behind, and the children stuck their hands out the windows and yelled over to the other car, "Grandpa! Grandpa!"

After an hour they stood before the tombstone bowing solemnly amidst the weeds that were growing all about.

"In a few years we won't even be able to get over here," Lai Suo's father said. He was mistaken, though; seven years later he was buried in a spot just a little ways off. By then there was no road to get through, and so Lai Suo's family had to skip from grave to grave to get through to his father's.

"Ah-suo," Lai Suo's father said, turning around, "before your mother died she was still calling for you." Lai Suo told himself absolutely not to cry, but just when the children were about to come up he had already started wailing. Lai Yun was holding the youngest son, and before he even had time to sigh he started to sob uncontrollably. When the caretaker of the graveyard saw this scene he shook his head and said, "Why don't we burn some paper money." It was not until then that the sobbing of Lai Suo's family gradually abated.

"How is it that the inscription has faded so badly?" Lai Suo said as he felt the tombstone.

—Mrs. Lai of the Xu family from the province of Honan,
Yanshan county . . . —

"We should have someone come and redo it and plant some more flowers on the grave. What do you say, Dad?" Lai Yun added.

"That wouldn't do," the caretaker interrupted, "not only would that interfere with the *feng-shui*,* but sheep would come and eat them up." The sheep that belonged to the people in this area grazed freely over the mountain, trampling over and defecating on Lai Suo's parents' graves.

"How could this be!" Lai Suo said, angrily bolting up from the bench.

God is the shepherd of mankind, at least that is what Christianity teaches. Far off in the distance there stood a church, and on its steeple there was a blinding cross of neon. Lai Suo went into the underpass. When he came out he could no longer make out the church.

9

Lai Suo arrived at the TV station half an hour before the interview was to take place. Before the guard at the entrance even had time to consider who he was, Lai Suo confidently charged in, his head held high. The guard stared at this lively man of short stature and his receding shadow, wondering where he had seen him before.

And so Lai Suo had recklessly gotten himself into this labyrinth of a building. It was a modern-age blend of fantasy and reality, art and beauty, hypocrisy and exaggeration, all synthesized in a single building. He went from one studio to another, one era to the next. He spent five minutes in the Ming dynasty, looked around the Qing for awhile, and then at quarter to eight he stumbled into his own show.

Wearing a well-tailored sky-blue suit, and a Thai silk shirt turned out at the collar, Mr. Han walked out from the dressing room, his gait firm and steady, his face beaming. He looked as if he were about to take the stage.

"Please take a seat in the middle, Mr. Han," the director said, full of respect. "Mr. Zhang, Chen, and Yang, you sit over here."

"Are we going to begin now?" Mr. Han asked calmly.

"Everybody get ready!" the director called out.

Lai Suo stood behind the glass of the control booth. To his side there was a row of TVs, all flashing the same image. The control-room technician put on a

---

Feng-shui (wind and water) refers to the geomantic configuration of a grave, home, or any architectural structure.

pair of earphones and put out his cigarette. The show was about to begin, and everyone was holding their breath. Lai Suo was fascinated as he stood watching people running back and forth moving stage lights and props and testing microphones, the director all the while gesticulating wildly.

"Roll'em!" the director cried out.

"First let me say that on behalf of the seventeen million compatriots of our free nation, we welcome you, Mr. Han, on your return home and welcome your participation in the Anti-Communist League," said Mr. Yang of the Overseas Chinese Advisory Board.

"Thank you," Mr. Han said, facing the camera, his eyes transfixed. "I am sincerely moved by the government's magnanimous benevolence. In the past few decades that I've been in Japan, not a second passed when I didn't feel remorse. I let down the fatherland. I let down all my fellow countrymen." By now he was clenching his fists and pounding the table. "The Communist bandits tricked me!"

In the same way the sound of Mr. Han's fist pounding on the table had shaken Lai Suo out of his doze thirty years before as he sat in the last row in charge of opening the door.

"What have the Nationalists relied upon for their legitimacy? Someone take a guess!" Mr. Han was becoming more and more excited, his clenched fists flashing back and forth. He stood there before the thirty-five members of the Taiwan Democratic Progressive Alliance shouting himself hoarse while the petrified Lai Suo looked on with unending admiration. Just a while before, Mr. Han had asked how his family and friends felt. Feeling rather embarrassed, Lai Suo had answered that they had no opinion, seeing as how they couldn't read. Then how did he feel? Did Lai Suo like his work? It wasn't a matter of liking or not liking the work: Whatever Mr. Han wants me to do I'll do. That's just fine, just fine. At this point Mr. Han turned around and asked Mr. Ji, "How are you doing?" Mr. Ji lowered his voice (Lai Suo overheard) and said, "Where the hell did you find this idiot? He's gone and passed out the pamphlets at the market! They were only good for wrapping up pieces of meat!"

"Good Heavens!" Mr. Han exclaimed, slapping himself on the forehead. "Just when we're, when we're . . ."

"And so, Mr. Han, can you describe to us your feelings when you first stepped back down onto your homeland?"

The cameraman removed the lens, handed it to an assistant by his side, then pushed open the door and walked over beside Lai Suo, whom he offered a cigarette. He enjoyed programs like "Contemporary Spotlight." One didn't have to go running back and forth with the camera to do this kind of work. He did not like music shows or trying to focus on the singers swinging their asses about.

"How did you get in? This program is off limits," he said without looking at Lai Suo.

"The door wasn't locked so I just came in."

"The guard must be sleeping," the cameraman said. "You should go check out studio two; there's some exciting stuff there. There isn't anything very interesting about this show." Lai Suo no longer bothered to answer back. He didn't come here to answer other people's questions.

"The fatherland's progress is really just too incredible to believe," Mr. Han said. "The minute I disembarked I was totally shocked. I said to myself, this is a modernized city! In Japan I had seen reports on TV about Taiwan's prosperity, but I never really believed . . ."

Lai Suo listened patiently. The cameraman finished his cigarette and exclaimed, "Oh God!" as he went over to his assistant.

"You've been to the mainland. How do you feel about it?"

"I know a few people over there—the ones who tricked me. Sun Qimin, Zhang Wansheng, and a few others all came to Taiwan that year to create a united front. If they're not dead yet then they're still in detention camps. Ai! The mainland authorities will always turn their backs on an old friend. Never once have they acted out of morality. But our government is different. Although I committed a grave mistake," he paused for a moment before going on, "and was temporarily confused . . ."

Lai Suo had seen Sun Qimin and Zhang Wansheng a long, long time ago. The two of them both spoke Taiwanese beautifully. In the conference room of the magazine publisher's building Mr. Han had wanted everyone to stand up and welcome them with a round of applause. The second Mr. Sun took the stage he made a full 90-degree bow as if he was Japanese, saying, "Elders, brothers . . ." Having received special training, his speech was extremely colorful. At first Mr. Han was extremely excited, but the more he heard, the more he became disenchanted.

The young Lai Suo noticed that several times he had made as if he were about to get up but then in the end would always sit back and shake his head. Sun was now saying things like "in our relations with the Tibetans, the Mongols, and the Miao, we have always allowed for self-government. To be honest, we have more than enough manpower to govern this giant tract of land, not to mention such a remote little place like Taiwan, but today our only desire is to assist our local compatriots to establish democracy, progress, and equality, a society free of greed and hatred"—then what about the tens of millions of mainlanders who were the victims of persecutions, what was that? From the corner of studio three Lai Suo saw through these unending lies, he saw through the Communists' deceits, and he felt very proud.

"Our Communist party loves peace foremost," Sun said, stopping for a moment to take a sip from his glass of tea. Mr. Han took advantage of the opportunity to jump on stage and say, "A big round of applause please, everyone! Thank you for your talk, Mr. Sun!"

"Could you tell us how you first discovered the Communist scheme?"

"I always had some suspicion that they intended to use me for their goal of 'liberating' Taiwan. . . ."

The young Mr. Han told them that after Taiwan was liberated, each of them would assume important positions. And Lai Suo? Perhaps he would be head of a district. Which district? Whichever district he wanted, of course the districts in the north were the best. Whenever he would go home, people would call out, "Hey! Magistrate Lai Suo! Venerable Magistrate! Hey! Hey! Hey!"

"When they went to Japan, many of our compatriots from this province arranged to see me, and I would tell them of the importance of Taiwanese independence."

"What was their reaction?"

"When I had just started I got some response, but these past few years there hasn't been any interest. It was then that I began to ask myself . . ."

At this point Fat Du came to Lai Suo's mind. Du said condescendingly, "We've got Marxism, the Nationalists have the Three Principles of the People, and you? You haven't got anything!"

"We have Mr. Han."

"What Mr. Han? Who's ever heard of him?"

Lai Suo was so busy he didn't have time to think. He was caught up talking with a large group of people, some friends of his, others total strangers. Because of this he could not find the time to listen to Mr. Han's speech. The situation was entirely different from thirty years ago. Lai Suo was now using a sensibility informed by the eighties to judge events that had taken place in the forties. This was decidedly advantageous. These reporters should have focused their cameras on him, these young reporters! When he was in vogue they hadn't even been born yet. Had they ever seen the Japanese? Had they seen the Communists? No. Had they endured American bombing raids? Been imprisoned? God! What the hell do you know! If someone pointed a camera at you, you probably couldn't even fart! Lai Suo was listening, thinking.

"Once again, on behalf of all our fellow countrymen I would like to say, in all sincerity, welcome home. And finally, we hope, Mr. Han, that you can say something to those of our nation who have been hoodwinked by the Communists."

"Certainly . . ."

The program was just about over, and the director made some gestures while one of the technicians squatted down and began to gather up electrical cables. Lai Suo began to leave the control room, thinking that once the show was over he would head straight over to see Mr. Han.

"Oh, so this is where you are," a young man in a white shirt said to him as he blocked his path.

"What the hell are you doing?" Lai Suo said in a rather unhappy tone.

"I'm the security guard," he said. "Since you don't have an invitation badge and you're unescorted, maybe you could tell me how you got in?"

The program had already been over for a while and Lai Suo was still standing on the steps of the entrance. No matter what anyone said, he was waiting for someone. The automatic door suddenly opened and a crowd of people totally oblivious to Lai Suo hurried down the steps.

"Mr. Han Zhiyuan!"

"Yes, what is it?"

"It's me, Lai Suo."

"Lai Suo?"

"The *Pan-Asian Magazine* publishers . . ."

"What?"

"The one who sold fruit. . . ."

"I don't know you!"

A fellow in a well-trimmed suit patted Lai Suo on the shoulder and broke off his questioning. Afterward the crowd all got into two black sedans and sped away, leaving a trail of smoke drifting over the street that was lit from above by the street lamps.

The immense shadow of the TV station, as if part of some interminable nightmare, stretched across the street to the other side. Suddenly Lai Suo was the only person left in the world.

"It's me, Lai Suo, Lai Suo," he stammered out, "I only wanted to say, to say, it's, it's been a long time."

10

When he got home it was almost midnight. He quietly opened the door and flicked on the light, putting the things he brought back from Taibei on the sofa—his wife's pajamas, a coloring book for the children, a box of chocolates.

The Dutch clock on the wall now struck several times, the two hands overlapping. This was a conclusion and an outset, a beginning and an ending.

Lai Suo became perfectly still, and slowly, slowly, he lifted up his head.

Mountain Road

Chen Yingzhen

Translated by Rosemary Haddon

"PROFESSOR Yang, the lady in Room 3 of intensive care . . . ?"

Trailing behind the supervising physician, who had just completed his rounds of the unit, he found himself at the nurses' station. On either side of the tall, elderly physician with the shock of curly, iron-gray hair were two young doctors, Chen and Wang. Reverentially, they listened to "Professor Yang" as he theorized about the case, thumbing methodically through the thick medical history.

For the moment he was obliged to stand mutely in one corner of the station. He watched the nurses who hurried to and fro at his side, images of white with white shoes and white socks, and began to feel shame for his obviously superfluous presence and for barging in where he didn't belong. Raising his head, by a stroke of good luck, his eyes happened to meet the two weary eyes of Professor Yang behind the black, broad-rimmed tortoise-shell glasses.

"Dr. Yang. Professor Yang!" he called.

Calmly, Professor Yang and the two young doctors turned to stare at him. The phone rang. "Endocrinology," a nurse spoke into the receiver.

"Professor Yang, excuse me but can you tell me what's wrong with the elderly lady in Room 3 of the intensive care unit?"

He walked forward. Dr. Chen extracted a new sheet of data from the medical history.

Professor Yang began to thumb through the case history again; at the same time, he queried Wang about something in a low voice. The junior doctor raised his head and inquired:

"Professor Yang asks, you are . . . what relation are you to the patient?"

"Younger brother," he said, then hastily amended: "No . . . brother-in-law." He smiled. "She's my older sister-in-law."

Written in 1983. Translated from Liu Shaoming and Ma Hanmao, eds., *Shijie zhongwen xiaoshuo xuan* (The commonwealth of modern Chinese fiction) (Taibei: Shijie ribao wenhua chuban gongsi, 1987), 1:69–99.

He extracted a name card from the pocket of his suit jacket and politely presented it to Professor Yang:

LI GUOMU
Chengxin Accounting Firm

Professor Yang read the name card and passed it over to Dr. Chen on his right to staple to the patient's file.

"We, I'm afraid we must do some more tests." Then, weighing every word, he added, "Tell me, please, about the onset of the old lady's illness."

"Onset of illness?" he echoed. "Uh, she just became weaker and weaker. One day she was perfectly fine, and the next she suddenly went into a slump."

Professor Yang was quiet; he crossed his arms in front of his chest. He looked at Yang's left hand—it was large and fleshy and had the sterile look of his profession. A gold, expensive-looking watch adorned the left wrist. Professor Yang sighed and looked over at Dr. Chen who explained:

"Professor Yang means, that is, was there any particular cause, for instance, excessive worry or anger . . . ?"

"Oh."

Prior to switching to this well-known instructional hospital in Taibei, they had gone to several private clinics and joint-run hospitals, but not one had asked such a question as this. Here, before these people, his lie arose almost from instinct.

"Hmm, no, none . . ."

"Go home and think it over carefully," Professor Yang spoke to him as he walked out of the nurses' station. "I'm afraid we must do some more tests."

He returned to Room 3. His sister-in-law had gone to sleep, and he gazed at her profile resting lightly on the immaculate, soft hospital pillow; she had grown visibly emaciated during the past one and one half months. The best rooms in the hospital came equipped with carpeting, telephone, fridge, kitchenette, television, and separate bathroom, and while she waited for him to relieve her to go home and fix something nutritious, his wife had cleaned this room so it sparkled. The heater emitted warm air. He took off his overcoat and walked lightly over to the window. Outside was a wide, classic pond, planted all round the periphery with various broad-leaved tropical plants. From this fourth-floor window, he could see a white, veil-like haze—the misty emanation of a lofty garden fountain—that moved lightly in the breeze. It swayed gently above the thick fleshy leaves, the irregular-sized rocks, and the large red and white carp in the pond.

Though it was late spring, they had been taken unawares by a cold-weather system, and the sky was a heavy leaden color. They had switched hospitals several times, unable from one to the next to find the cause of Lao Dasao's illness,* and during these past few days, his one preoccupation was whether her illness was somehow connected with that news. "Oh, for instance, excessive

---

Dasao means sister-in-law. Adding *Lao*, "old," makes it more intimate.

worry or anger . . .'' The doctor's words echoed in his brain. He reminded himself that what had happened did not involve anxiety or anger, and he gazed back outside at the carp swimming languid and stately in the waters of the pond, heedless of the cold current of late spring. He brooded uneasily.

One day about two months ago, Lao Dasao got up just after four o'clock as usual, and after making congee for Li Guomu and his family, she went for a walk along the dike with some elderly neighbors. Returning after six to get the children ready for school, she settled down to read the newspaper. It was then that it happened. His only child, a daughter who was in first year of middle school, banged loudly on the bedroom door: "Pa! Pa!" Cuiyu yelled hysterically. "Pa! Get up quick . . . Auntie . . . !" Li Guomu and his wife rushed in a panic to the living room where they were met with his sister-in-law's tear-stained face and the newspaper, which lay on the floor, spread out at the foot of the sofa.

"Ah-sao!!" cried Li Guomu's wife, Yuexiang. Circling the coffee table, she rushed forward and sat down on the armrest of the sofa where Lao Dasao was sitting. Yuexiang put one arm around the old lady's shoulder, and with the other, she used a corner of her housecoat to wipe the tears flooding her cheeks. "Sao, what's wrong? Where are you feeling bad?" she asked, also beginning to sob.

Silently, he stood before the coffee table. It was a full thirty years since Lao Dasao had come to the Li family, and of these thirty years, the most difficult were in the past. Yet not once during this time had he seen this sister-in-law, whom he respected more than his natural mother, cry so grievously. He knit his brows and searched for an answer.

Lao Dasao buried her face in her hands and attempted to restrain the waves of grief swelling forward like a tide. "Sao, say something. What's wrong?" Yuexiang inquired tearfully. Li Guomu put both hands on the shoulders of his daughter who was standing, stunned, to one side.

"Go to school," he said softly. "When you get back, Auntie will be better."

Silently, in the clear dawn of the living room, Li Guomu and his wife sat and listened to Lao Dasao's sobs gradually subside.

That day he told Yuexiang to go to work, and he himself remained at home to watch over his elderly relative. He walked into her bedroom. His sister-in-law was lying alone; her eyes, swollen from crying, were staring up at the newly painted ceiling. Her hands were lying on top of the quilt, tightly clutched around the morning paper which she had rolled up, club-like.

"Sao," he called out, sitting down on a rattan chair beside the bed.

"Go to work," she said.

" . . . "

"There's nothing wrong with me." She had switched to Japanese, adding: "please don't worry."

"I didn't feel like working anyway," he said. "It's just that, Sao, if there's something on your mind, why not tell me?"

Lao Dasao was silent. Her longish face, which had seen fifty years of living, was paler than usual. Time had etched deep traces in her forehead, around her eyes, and at the corners of her mouth. "What were those years all about?" he wondered to himself.

"For these thirty years, you've been like a mother to me. . . ." Moved by emotion, his voice quavered.

She inclined her head toward him and looked at his moist, reddened eyes. She smiled and put out her hand for him to take.

"You're more than forty now," she said. "You've made it, both in business and in establishing a family for yourself. Others don't need to worry about you."

He stroked her hand and with both of his laid it back on top of the quilt. Groping for his cigarettes, he lit one.

"You should smoke less," she gently chided.

"Yes, Onesan."

He addressed her with the Japanese term he was accustomed to using since childhood: in Japanese, the sound for "older sister" and "sister-in-law" is the same. Observing the expression in his eyes, which demanded a full explanation of the incident of the morning, she sighed. He had always been a compliant child, she thought to herself. Once he had his heart stubbornly set on something, some demand or other, he never made a fuss even when he was a little boy. Instead, he just used that insistent expression to achieve his goal. She mused over this and, in the end, handed him the club-like newspaper.

"I saw it in the paper," she said cheerlessly. "They've finally come back."

He opened the paper. The news circled with red in the society section was about the size of a cake of beancurd: "After more than thirty years' imprisonment, evidence of reform has led to the release of four prisoners convicted of sedition. These prisoners were transferred yesterday to the district police by appointed units wherein they regained citizenship."

"Uh," was all he could find to say.

"Huang Zhenbo was your older brother's best friend."

Lao Dasao began to sob. Li Guomu reread the news carefully. Huang Zhenbo had been sent back to Thotin where he tearfully embraced his blind old mother of over eighty years of age. "Those are tears of remorse, tears of rebirth and joy," the paper declared.

Li Guomu suddenly relaxed. All that had happened, he concluded, was that Saosao had associated this life convict called Huang Zhenbo with his older brother and had been overcome with weeping. Or else, if not this, she had been moved to tears by those who had returned alive after assuming they must have died of melancholy and exhaustion in the prison on that barren, lonely island.

"That's terrific," he laughed. "In a few days I ought to go visit this good friend of my brother."

"Eh?"

"Ask him to talk about my older brother!" he said happily.

"No, that's no good," she replied.

"Oh. Why not?"

Lao Dasao looked out the window, saying nothing. Outside, where at some time it had begun to drizzle, there was a rusty iron shelf hung with a few pots of his sister-in-law's beloved orchids.

"No," she repeated, "that's no good."

From that day on, Li Guomu and his family perceived a change in Lao Dasao: she became quiet and somewhat troubled. Gradually, she ate less, and after two weeks she took to her bed. Almost overnight, it seemed, Dasao had become old. During that period, Li Guomu and Yuexiang returned home from work every day and drove all over town seeking medical help, hauling the elderly sister-in-law on their backs. If she was coaxed, she would docilely swallow dose after dose of the medication they brought back. If no one coaxed her, she would set the unopened medication on a little stand by the head of her bed. Day by day, she faded away. ". . . For instance, excessive worry or anger . . ." Once more Li Guomu recalled the words of Dr. Chen as the latter strained laboriously to conceal his deep-seated contempt. He undid his tie and threw it carelessly on the easy chair at the side of the sickbed that he and Yuexiang took turns using when they spent the nights there.

How can I confide in these doctors and nurses about what happened that morning? Or about my older brother and Huang Zhenbo?

He sat down on a coffee-colored chair set to the left of the sickbed and, distraught, tried to think things through.

Just then the inner door of the room opened and a pregnant nurse came in. Her object was the patient's temperature and blood pressure. Lao Dasao opened her eyes and held the thermometer compliantly in her mouth; she then let the nurse measure her blood pressure. Li Guomu stood up to allow the nurse more room to work.

"Thank you," he uttered when the nurse left.

He sat back down in the chair and put out his hand to clasp her rough, dry one.

"Did you sleep a while?" he asked with a smile.

"Go to work," she responded weakly. "You shouldn't stay with me, this useless person. Isn't your job more important?"

"It doesn't matter," he said.

"I had a dream," she suddenly announced.

"Oh?"

"I dreamt of the trolley track," she said in Japanese. "I had a dream about the trolley track."

"Oh." He smiled and recalled the winding trolley track of long ago in his old home of Engtin. The tracks began from the shaft of the coal mine in the valley, followed the winding mountain slope, passed beneath famous Oriole Rock, and headed out toward the colliery beside the train station. His home was the lonely mud brick cottage in the valley beyond Oriole Rock.

"When I married into your family I was on my own. I came treading the ties of the trolley track and found my way to your home," she recalled.

Inside himself, Li Guomu uttered a startled cry. He could not tear his eyes away from the woman on this sickbed—Lao Dasao who would be fifty this birthday. During this period of more than a month, her body had shrunk as though it had dried out. She was lying on her side, her face toward him, and he extracted the glucose tube that had become flattened under her right shoulder. He noticed that the pale, wrinkled, and emaciated face was oozing delicate drops of perspiration.

"At that time you were sitting alone on the doorsill, staring off into space . . . ," she smiled wearily.

These were past events of which she often spoke, and spoke without tiring. The year was 1953, exactly thirty years ago today. It was a windy, dry morning of early summer. Hauling a little bundle, the girl by the name of Cai Qianhui took the train alone the one stop from Thotin to Engtin. "Once I walked out of the station, do you think I dared ask the way?" While she was reminiscing, Dasao would ask this of Li Guomu, who would be listening attentively at her side. "Who would dare say how to get to the home of someone who had been taken away and shot?" At this point she would sigh and would always start talking about those dreadful days. "During that time in Thotin, friends would go out every day and roam about incommunicado on the streets," she would recall. "Off in the distance you would see someone or other and know that he or she was still unharmed. If several days had passed without seeing so-and-so, you could be sure that person had been taken away."

It was during those terrible days that the young Li Guomu on the doorsill watched Cai Qianhui as she walked over from the distance, treading the ties of the trolley track. Both sides of the track were thick with lush, green groves of acacia trees. A black butterfly, each wing etched with a design of bright blue, danced and flitted in the groves. He remembered, too, that the young girl occasionally raised her head to look at the lonely mud brick cottage that was his home, and while she continued along the ties of the trolley track, she looked at him, just as lonely, where he sat on the cool doorsill. They gazed at each other wordlessly and fearlessly. A flock of gray starlings made a clamor somewhere in the acacia, and now and then the sound of a coal trolley reverberated as it rolled down the hill: "Clack clack clack!" From the distance it gradually drew closer, and from nearby it moved off again. He, the young and sickly Li Guomu, watched her without once turning away his eyes as she jumped away from the trolley tracks and, selecting a little pathway full of pampas and other grasses, walked toward him.

"Excuse me, does . . . does Mr. Li Qishi live here?" she asked.

He would never forget it. He remembered raising his head to look at her, feeling not the slightest curiosity or shyness. Her eyes were swollen, unfamiliar. In that instant he said nothing, only nodded his head lightly, aware of a creeping lethargy he felt whenever he was hungry. The moment he nodded, he discerned a smile that spread over the corners of her thin-lipped mouth, a smile that told of boundless love, and from those puffy, single-lidded eyes that gazed at him so intently, a stream of crystal tears fell. A wood pigeon cooed in the nearby acacia, and the little family dog who had run off into the mountains somewhere to seek food suddenly came forward from behind the house. It barked fiercely, but at the same time, it wagged its brown tail vigorously.

"Hey! Don't bark!" he snapped.

When he turned back to look at her, she had freed a corner of the cloth tied round her bundle and was wiping her tears. A smile was on her face. Then they heard his mother's voice from inside the house.

"Ah-mu, who's that?"

Silently, he led her inside the dark house. His mother lay on the bed; the bitter smell of herbal medicine, simmering in the kitchen, permeated the entire house. Laboriously propping up the upper half of her body, his mother said, "Who is that? Ah-mu, who is this person you've brought in?"

The young girl, Cai Qianhui, sat down quietly at the edge of the bed. She announced:

"I'm Guokun's . . . wife."

At that moment, though little Li Guomu distinctly heard every word she said, he did not fully understand the meaning. After a moment of stunned silence, his mother began to weep: "My son, my beloved son . . ." She sobbed, choking back the sounds that swelled like a chant. He looked out the window, realizing only then that the sky had largely darkened. Muted thunder sounded in the distance. The little brown dog was agilely chasing some iridescent grasshoppers.

More than a year previously, his older brother, Li Guokun, who was then a laborer in a coke plant on the outskirts of Engtin, was arrested in broad daylight and taken away with several other workers. His father, a coal trolley operator in the mines, had gone to Taibei only two months previously with the letter of notification. He had brought back a bundle of old clothes tied up with fine hemp string, a pair of old worn running shoes, and a fountain pen with a rusted nib. That night, his mother had also cried in this manner:

"My son, my beloved son . . ."

"Lower your voice . . . ," his father enjoined her. That evening, the crickets in the hills had competed noisily with the sound.

"My son, my beloved son, my son . . ."

His mother cupped her hand over her mouth. Snot, saliva, and tears seeped through the cracks between her fingers and dripped down onto that old, worn bed.

"Sao." He cleared his throat, which had become obstructed during his reminiscences. "Sao!"

"Huh?"

Just then the door of the hospital room was cautiously opened and Yuexiang walked in carrying fruit and a lunch box.

"Sao, I've brought you some perch soup," Yuexiang said.

"At the time, I was sitting on the doorsill," he interjected. "Do you still remember that?"

"A little boy sat there," his older sister-in-law recalled, and she closed her eyes. On her wrinkled face, a wan smile floated up. "He was a little too thin," she added.

"Uh huh."

"But I remember the events of that evening the best."

Lao Dasao suddenly opened her eyes. Her line of vision looked past Li Guomu's right shoulder as though focusing on some point in the far distance. "Pa said, why is it that we never heard Ah-kun speak of it before?" she said. "I said I . . ."

"You said your family was opposed to it," he interjected with a smile. From the time he was a child to the year he turned forty he had heard Lao Dasao tell these stories so many times he had lost count.

"I said that in our house there were some people who didn't approve." After a pause she continued: "I said that Ah-kun and I had already made the decision, and now that he's gone you must take me in. That's what I said."

Yuexiang came out of the kitchen. She had ladled the perch soup into a large porcelain bowl and was carrying it gingerly.

"Have some soup, Sao. Let it cool a minute first."

"I've really put you to a lot of trouble," Lao Dasao replied.

"After Ma died, the family was really lucky to have you," Li Guomu remarked pensively. "Why not get Yuexiang to put some noodles in the soup?"

"No." Little by little she closed her eyes. "Your father said that the family is very poor, that I must be able to bear hardship. 'I can see you're not someone who can work.' Pa said this, he did."

He thought of his father of that time: his average-size physique had been made lean and strong by many years of hard labor. Every morning at the crack of dawn, he would tie a large lunch box to his belt, put on a pair of shoes made of tire rubber in the manner of the sandals of today, and walk to the Xingnan Mine in the valley. Many times a day his father went down that slope outside the front door; releasing the coal trolley, he would take off flying like a shuttle. When Lao Dasao came, he adored her in his own quiet way. Every day at dusk, his father would return home black with coal dust, now and then a few pieces of dried beancurd or salted fish dangling from his hand.

"Ah-ba, you're back."

Every evening upon hearing the excited barking of the dog, Dasao would put aside her work and welcome him at the entrance way, wiping her hands as she called out.

"Uh," his father would respond.

After drawing the water for his bath, she would put the clean, neatly folded clothes before him:

"Ah-ba, take a bath."

"Uh," came his father's reply.

After eating dinner, she would steep a fresh pot of guava tea and bring it to the side of the easy chair where his father was sitting.

"Ah-ba, drink some tea," she would say.

"Uh," Ah-ba would reply.

He remembered the luminous, exquisite patterns formed by the swarms of fireflies suspended over the clumps of grass beneath the acacia, and everywhere in the mountains the disorderly, delightful singing of the night insects.

Yuexiang was sitting beside the sickbed. With a dainty spoon, she was feeding mouthful after mouthful of perch soup to the patient.

"Is it good?" she asked in a low voice.

Lao Dasao made no response. Docilely, mouthful after mouthful, she ate what Yuexiang fed her, chewing conscientiously.

All this suddenly made him remember his mother.

When his older brother disappeared, and especially when his father brought back Guokun's belongings from Taibei, his frail, sickly mother violently coughed up blood on a number of occasions, then finally took to her bed. When Lao Dasao came to the family in early summer, Qishi Shen was better for a while, but as soon as autumn arrived—when pale yellow cotton flowers began to bloom on the pampas grass at the sides of the trolley track—it became obvious that Qishi Shen would not be long for this world. During that time, Lao Dasao was like Yuexiang now, mouthful after mouthful spooning nourishment into his mother. The difference was that Lao Dasao was lying in this expensive hospital room while his mother lay in that dark, damp room which a large nightsoil bucket had contaminated with the stench of urine. Moreover, after his mother's illness became serious, her personality changed: she became irritable and easily flew into a rage. He still remembered one time when Lao Dasao had fed her the last half spoonful of congee how his mother had willfully thrown it all up, dirtying the quilt and one corner of the bed. "This wretched existence, don't make me take any more of it," she wailed, dry-eyed. "Die . . . ! Let . . . me . . . die . . . !" Then she cried for his older brother, the sounds rising like a groan: "My son, my son, my beloved son . . ." It made the tears course down Dasao's face.

His mother had not made it through that autumn. She was buried in Engtin's Niupu Mountain cemetery.

"Ah-mu, we ought to go to Niupu Mountain," Lao Dasao suddenly remarked.

"Huh?"

Startled, he raised his head to look at her. Yuexiang was carefully wiping away the traces of soup from the corners of her mouth. Soon it would be the Festival of Tombs, and in previous years at this time, Lao Dasao, Yuexiang, and he would always take the train back to Engtin and climb to the top of Niupu Mountain. There they would clear the site and worship at the gravesides of his parents. It was only three years ago that they had formally erected a tombstone for his brother. Lao Dasao had also planted a pair of cypress in his grave plot, which had begun to put out leaves.

"Since the Gaoxiong Incident,* people no longer fear prisoners of conscience."

Lao Dasao had said this, and thus it was decided that when they formally interred his father they would erect a tombstone for Li Guokun.

"She's eaten a whole bowl of perch soup," Yuexiang remarked happily.

"This year I won't go with you," she observed sadly.

She lay back on the pillow. Outside the window, the clouds had gradually thickened and the sky was dark.

"Sao, are you tired? Go to sleep for a while," Yuexiang coaxed.

Unconsciously, he groped in his pocket for a cigarette, then immediately took his hand back. Lao Dasao had never been like Yuexiang, forever grumbling and nagging at him for not kicking the habit. In the hospital, however, he had had to suppress the desire to smoke more than once. He could go out to smoke, but he didn't like to take the trouble. Lost in silence, he thought of the rank, stubborn weeds carpeting Niupu Mountain and the site of the old and new tombs. From the shrine to the God of Earth one walked along a pathway, and there, halfway up the slope of a hill in the shape of a steamed bun, was a new grave with the red earth exposed. Having finished the job of erecting the tombstone, the worker had said:

"You can bring out the offering and worship now."

He and Yuexiang each received three sticks of incense from Lao Dasao, and the three of them stood together and worshipped before the new tomb. His thoughts turned to his brother's bundle of clothing and pair of running shoes, which had been carefully guarded by Lao Dasao for more than twenty years and were now buried in the tomb. Having completed his devotion, he handed his incense to Yuexiang, who inserted it into the holder before the tomb. At one side, she and Lao Dasao began to burn a big pile of silver paper. Suddenly, a photograph of his older brother flashed into his mind, one that Lao Dasao had recently taken to be enlarged. With his hair cut in the style of the fifties, ragged and shaggy, and standing somewhere under the skies of Taiwan, his brother was gazing resolutely into the distance, a look of boundless confidence on his slightly

---

*The Gaoxiong [Kaohsiung] Incident occurred on December 10, 1979. In the wake of this disturbance, fifty-two persons connected with the Dangwai opposition movement and the journal *Meili dao* (Formosa) were arrested and sentenced with offenses ranging from sedition to obstruction of public order.

elongated face. The body of this young man was once alive, but where was it now? he wondered. When he was attending university, he happened to hear a friend say that the cadavers of those who had been executed bore wounds that gaped like split pomegranates. Silently they floated in the formalin troughs of the hospitals. As before, he puzzled over the question of where his brother's body lay.

At the summit of that wild, uncultivated mountain, Dasao had gazed at that new black tombstone with something like a contented expression.

Born March 17, 1928

Died September, 1952

Tomb of Li Guokun erected by his descendants

Lao Dasao had said that although his brother had disappeared early in the 1950s, his father had brought back his possessions in September 1952, though the exact day of the month was beyond her recall. "Why not use the traditional *ganzhi** system to indicate the year and month?" he had asked. "Your older brother was a progressive type!" Lao Dasao had responded. As for his older brother's descendants, she had intoned, "Your descendants are his descendants." He still remembered that at the time Yuexiang had lowered her head. Ever since Cuiyu had been born they had awaited the birth of a boy, but he had never come.

"Time's really flown." The old worker stood beside his brother's new grave and smoked a cigarette stub so short that it burned his finger. "It's been more than twenty years for Ah-kun. . . ."

"That's right," replied Lao Dasao.

The old worker, Wang Fan, was his father's friend. When Engtin's coal mining industry declined due to the gradual ascendancy of oil as the main resource, he and Li Guokun's father were among the first workers to lose their jobs. Initially, his father had done form and cement work in town, and afterward, he had gone to Taibei to work as a casual laborer on construction sites. Up to now, Ah-fan Bo† had always regarded tomb building as an auxiliary line of work; now he turned to it as his main profession. That winter when Li Guomu began university, his father fell off some scaffolding at a site on the periphery of Taibei's bustling metropolis. He was killed instantly, and it was Ah-fan Bo who constructed the tomb. He remembered standing beside the grave, watching shovelful after shovelful of earth being scooped up and thrown inside. It emitted a dull, heavy sound as it hit the planking of his father's flimsy coffin. Ah-fan Bo stood beside him watching; with his dirty fingers he wiped the tears from his

---

*The *ganzhi* (Heavenly Stems and Earthly Branches) is the traditional Chinese sixty-year cycle for recording time.

†The term *Bo* means uncle older than one's father and is politely applied to unrelated men of that age.

cheeks and exclaimed softly, "Goddammit! I told you to build tombs with me, but you wouldn't listen. Instead you had to rush off by yourself to Taibei . . . !"

Lao Dasao, whom he had assumed was asleep, opened her eyes.

"Where's Cuiyu?" she asked with a smile.

"She's still in school," Yuexiang replied, looking at her watch. "I'll bring her by this evening."

"I can feel easy about this family now."

"Uh huh," he replied.

"It was hard all around. I wanted you to study and you succeeded," she continued.

He laughed bitterly.

That year when he finished elementary school, his father and Ah-fan Bo wanted to arrange a position for him as coal washer in the colliery. Dasao wouldn't hear of it.

"Ah-ba," she said, "Ah-mu's a good student. Let him study."

His father, however, stubbornly refused to allow him to continue his schooling. All day long, whether she was washing vegetables, cooking rice, or washing clothes, and even when she was at the pithead eating from her lunch box with his father, Dasao would weep silently. One time at the dinner table his father sighed and said:

"After all is said and done, it's a matter of whether or not one can afford . . ."

" . . . "

"As a worker, you just have to accept fate," his father declared angrily. "Kun-ah, he . . . my mistake was to let him attend Normal School."

" . . . "

"He said that going to Normal School wouldn't cost anything." Father shook his head, lost in thought.

"Ah-kun said we should let Ah-mu go on studying, and at a better school," Dasao put in.

He watched his father lay down his bowl and chopsticks and raise his aging, grizzled face. Whisker stubs cast a shadow over the length of his jaw.

"He . . . when did he say that?" he asked.

"In . . . Thotin."

For many years, Thotin had been a mysterious name for Li Guomu, one that he associated with sorrow. His brother had been arrested at a river that coursed between Engtin and Thotin, implicated in a big case in Thotin. When he was little, he had gone to the edge of that river more than once, but all he could see was a stretch of white pebbles, extending in a long line into the distance. In the river bed an expanse of cloudy pampas swayed in the breeze.

"So many years ago and you still believe in him," father said faintly. Groping in his pocket, he lit a cigarette.

"I believe in him," she affirmed. "That's why I came to this family."

Dasao gathered up the bowls and chopsticks without saying a word. In the dim forty-watt light he clearly remembered seeing tears course silently down his sister-in-law's face, which was still firm and young at that time.

Father said no more, but he did consent to his sitting for the entrance exam to middle school. He passed with one try and entered Taibei Provincial "C" Middle School.

"I've come to your home expecting hardship," she recounted.

The heater had brought a faint blush to her thin face. Pulling the quilt down from her neck toward her chest, she repeated:

"I've come to your home . . ."

Yuexiang straightened the quilt for her.

"I've come to your home expecting to endure hardship," she finally reiterated. "Our life is so much easier now. . . ."

He listened quietly with Yuexiang, but neither of them was able to establish any meaning in what she was saying.

"This, this life of ours . . . is it acceptable?" The elderly sister-in-law asked the question with a note of grief in her voice, and in her dry eyes tears gradually welled up.

"Sao."

He put out his hand to feel her forehead: there was no fever.

"Sao," he repeated.

The patient quietly closed her eyes. Yuexiang sat a while longer, then she stealthily went back into the kitchen and brought out a second small bowl of perch soup.

"There's a little left. How about if you have it?" she suggested pleasantly.

He took the soup and ate it by the bedside, careful not to make a sound. Perhaps she is beginning to get confused, he reflected, and pondered over what his sister-in-law had said, groping for an explanation. The fine rain falling outside the window gave rise in him to an endless, meaningless depression.

"Professor Yang!" Yuexiang called out softly from the kitchen where she was washing dishes.

Tall, thin Professor Yang accompanied by Dr. Wang pushed open the door and came in.

"Is she eating all right?" Professor Yang took up the chart hanging at the head of the bed where the patient's meals and excretion were recorded. He seemed to be soliloquizing.

"Not at all bad," Wang informed his senior respectfully.

"And sleeping?" Professor Yang continued, looking at the soundly sleeping patient. "She's asleep."

"Yes," said Yuexiang, "she just went to sleep a moment ago."

"Hmm," came Yang's response.

"Professor Yang," Li Guomu addressed the physician.

"That's right." The professor turned and looked right at him through his black tortoise-shell glasses. "Have you thought of it? About what happened when she first became sick?"

For one instant he recalled the man by the name of Huang Zhenbo; he recalled, too, the shock that his sister-in-law had sustained because of this prisoner of conscience who had recently been released after serving life imprisonment.

"No," he replied and looked over at his peacefully sleeping sister-in-law. He felt sick at heart, as though forgoing something: "No, I can't think of anything special."

"Uh," the doctor muttered.

He accompanied Professor Yang to the doorway where he inquired earnestly about his sister-in-law's illness. Yang opened the door leading to the hall. The cool breeze in the hallway blew toward him, caressing his face.

"I'm still not clear," the physician knit his brows and said. "My feeling is that the patient has absolutely no will to go on living."

"Ah," he replied.

"I'm not at all sure about it," he resumed, a look of perplexity on his face. "I've been practicing for nearly twenty years, and it's not often that I've seen a patient who has lost the will to live to the extent that she has."

He watched Dr. Yang walk into the hospital room next door, his curly gray hair vibrating nervously in the breeze of the hallway.

"No," he reflected to himself absent-mindedly. "It really couldn't be that."

He returned to the bedside. The chair he was sitting in a moment previously was now occupied by Yuexiang. Smiling at the elderly invalid, his wife put her hand inside the quilt and took hold of her dry, yet warm, hand.

"Did you sleep?" Yuexiang asked genially.

"No," Lao Dasao replied.

Recalling the sleeping face of just a moment before and how the old lady knew nothing of Professor Yang's visit, Yuexiang smiled.

"You slept, Sao," Yuexiang said. "Not long, but you did sleep."

"No, I didn't," the patient insisted, "I was only dreaming."

"Do you want some water?" Yuexiang inquired. "Let me get you a glass of juice."

"That long trolley track," Lao Dasao murmured. "That long track of the coal trolley."

Yuexiang turned her head toward Li Guomu, who had been standing for some time intently watching the old lady. She stood up.

"Sit here."

His wife went back to the kitchen to prepare a glass of fresh juice, and he sat back down at the bedside. ". . . it's not often that I've seen a patient who has lost the will to live to the extent that she has." Professor Yang's words rang in his ears.

"Sao," he called softly.

"Uh."

"I also dream often of that trolley track," he said in Japanese. "I often see that road in my dreams."

". . ."

"It's not easy to forget it," he said and gazed at her pale profile. "That year, Sao, you began to work, to push the coal cart with father. . . ."

"Uh huh," she smiled.

"I don't always dream this at night. During the day if I happen to be daydreaming I can call up the events of that time scene by scene." He spoke in Japanese. "Sao, for the sake of that trolley track, isn't it worth the struggle to keep on living?"

Slowly she turned her head to gaze at him. One little teardrop hung at the corner of her eye where there was also the trace of a smile. Then she closed her eyes once more.

Outside it had gotten darker; the rain fell ceaselessly. He called to mind that long, narrow, and very worn trolley track, which originated in the mountain of the mine and circled round Oriole Rock before heading out to the shipping yard of the train station. The track often made the trolley cars derail and become stuck. In the third year after Dasao had come to their home, she had found employment pushing the coal cart deep in the mine. "Other women can do it, so why can't I?" Dasao had countered when his father voiced his opposition to her working. At the time, he was in grade five and often saw Dasao straining, step by step, under the burning sun with another female worker to push a full cart up the hill to the station. Her arms and calves were swaddled in protective wrapping like other female mine workers, and a coolie hat was on her head. Her clothes were soaked in sweat. When there were no classes, he dearly loved to go out with Dasao on the coal trolley. When the track ran uphill he would jump out and help her push; when the ground was even, Dasao would get off and push for a while before jumping back on. The trolley's inertia would take them forward, rolling on for a stretch, and he would always sit inside enjoying the ride. When they came to a downhill section, he and Dasao would stay on board, Dasao applying the brakes as she chatted to him, taking care not to shoot off the tracks as they went round corners.

In the summers, the "clack-clack" of the trolley rolling down that winding, downward incline would invariably rouse the cicadas in the narrow passageway between the dense thicket of acacia; at other times, their chirping roared to a crescendo. On midslope of the mountain and under huge Oriole Rock, the cart would roll forward on the trolley tracks, lost in the din of the "clack clack" and the clamor of the cicadas. At these times, he would always be reminded of the legend about Zheng Chenggong. When Zheng led his military officers to bivouac under the outcrop of Oriole Rock, they found that a large number of soldiers disappeared every day. Later they discovered that a giant monster, Yingge, lived on the mountain and came out every night to feast on the soldiers. Zheng Chenggong became enraged and knocked off the monster's head with a cannon, and instantly Yingge was transformed into a giant rock. From that time on, the monster never again harassed either the military or civilian populations. Each time the coal trolley passed beneath Oriole Rock, the young Guomu would visualize a misty cloud issuing from it, swallowing up him and his Dasao.

The terminal for the trolleys transporting coal was located in the shipping yard behind the Engtin train station. The shipping yard was a broad, empty space cooperatively used by several mines. After a transaction had taken place, and prior to shipping to the central or southern parts of the island, coal was transported by trolley to the storehouses on these grounds. The piles of pitch-black coal towered high on the grounds, waiting to be loaded onto freight trains and shipped to various destinations.

There were many times when he and Dasao, together with another female worker, pushed the coal cart up the steep cliff access and emptied the contents onto the mountain of coal. Looking down from the lofty access, he saw many children of poor families clustered about the storehouses that were built around the worn trolley ties. Equipped with little bamboo baskets and brooms, these children were sweeping up the chunks of coal that had fallen outside the storehouses as the carts were being unloaded. When the supervisor wasn't looking, Dasao would always avail herself of the opportunity to throw down large chunks for the children to sweep up and take back for fuel.

"We're all poor," Dasao would say. "We must help each other."

Returning in the empty trolley, Dasao softly chanted:

> The folks back home, the workers . . .
> Dwell in broken shacks with broken doors and windows;
> Three meals a day there's shredded sweet potato,
> Every meal there's beans, dried and salted . . .

He turned his head, startled, to look at her. The sun was setting on the far side of Kamahng—the orange grove—and the sky of Engtin was washed in a russet red. From the groves of acacia the breeze blew over toward them, greeting the trolley car rushing down the incline and ruffling Dasao's hair.

"Sao, what are you singing?" he said with a laugh. Dasao stuck out her tongue. He raised his head to scrutinize her. The day's labor had suffused her cheeks with pink, and her eyes flashed with an excitement rarely seen.

"No," she grinned. "I can't sing. I really can't sing now."

"Why not?"

She did not answer. Going round a fast curve, she manipulated the brakes and leaned expertly in the opposite direction to maintain the balance of the swiftly moving trolley. The brakes squealed. In the distance they heard the sound of turtle doves.

"Your older brother taught me that."

Dasao suddenly said this after they had slid round the corner. A mass of black scurried adroitly into the soft branches of the acacia.

"Sao, look!" he called excitedly. "Look, a squirrel! A squirrel!"

"Your older brother taught me." As she spoke, Dasao looked intently at the trolley track before them, her eyes gleaming with a warm light. "It's a three-character opera from thirty years ago called *Three-Character Miscellany*. Your older brother said that in the Japanese period a Taiwanese activist in the labor movement taught it to the workers and farmers to get them to resist the Japanese. That's what your older brother said."

"Oh," he said blankly.

"In that year, your older brother was revising the original *Three-Character Miscellany*. He said there were some things that were different from the Japanese period." Dasao spoke as though conversing with herself. "Later, the situation became tense, and your brother brought the manuscript to me to hide. When things eased up a bit, he would come back and get it, he said. . . ."

" . . . "

The trolley was slowing down. Passing Lamah, there was a stretch of road that went from flat to a slight uphill climb. Dasao jumped off and began to push the trolley gently uphill. He remained inside, slipping into a silence that was unusual for his years.

And later? Later what happened to my older brother? There were many times when the young Guomu wanted to ask this question, but he would always swallow it back. Even now as he sat beside the sickbed where Lao Dasao was deep in sleep he felt a yearning to get to the bottom of what had happened to his brother. In the wake of years of personal growth and education he had gradually gained some insight into his brother's death on the execution grounds, but despite this, he still experienced this deep questioning, and the more insight he gained, the more he itched to clarify everything. For several decades, his brother had come to symbolize the longing, the fear, and the taboo of his entire family, becoming the wound that not only he and his father and mother but the whole of society could not bear to touch. After Dasao's selfless sacrifice for this indigent, broken family, this hidden, secret wound became a compelling force that unconsciously coerced Li Guomu into avoiding politics and into striving to succeed. It drove him—the child of a nakedly poor, penniless family—to complete university and, after undergoing a few years of practical labor, to obtain his qualifications as accountant, which he had done just three years before. Although not large, the office space he rented in the eastern section of Taibei had a trim and very tasteful decor. There he single-handedly ran a prosperous accounting firm. Taking Dasao, they left their old home in Engtin and moved into an apartment in a high-class residential area of Taibei. All this had happened in that year too.

Three months passed. Lao Dasao died in the hospital from some inexplicable, gradual debilitation.

On the evening of the day when Li Guomu took Lao Dasao's body to the funeral home, he went alone into the old lady's room to arrange her effects. There, in a black lacquered box housing a few pieces of simple jewelry, he found a thick envelope. On the outside "Mr. Huang Zhenbo" was written in his sister-in-law's attractive hand. Without realizing what he was doing, Li Guomu opened the unsealed envelope and began to read. The letter was written in a refined Japanese, very different from what he had learned at university.

Dear Huang Zhenbo,

I am Cai Qianhui whom you once cared for so lovingly.

Do you still remember how you first took my hand that evening so long ago in the little village of Kamding in Thotin? You said to me that for the sake of the masses of workers you risked your life every day, and so you had decided temporarily to suspend our engagement arranged by our families. Writing today, I still remember your profile under the mass of bright stars in Thotin when you said that I must understand your feelings.

Six months after that evening you at last introduced me to Li Guokun, whom you had talked of often and with so much feeling.

That was more than thirty years ago today. Consequently, when I read about your release and return home in the newspaper two days ago, I felt I had to speak out, whether it was from a sense of morality or just from feeling. At the time, you told me to address Guokun as "Guokun Dage"—Older Brother—and I felt woefully happy. "She's a good girl, Zhenbo." I remember at the time Guokun laughed brightly and said this to you. Then, with those crystal-clear eyes shaded by those thick brows, he looked at me keenly, my face blushing: "Zhenbo wants only to die for others. There could be nothing more difficult than to be the wife of that rascal." After we left Guokun Dage, we walked toward Thotin along a twisty, winding mountain road. On that road you talked a lot—about the work that you and Guokun Dage were engaged in, and about your ideals. You talked about the bright and hopeful future of China. "Hey, Qianhui, why aren't you talking today?" you asked me, do you remember? "I'm thinking about what you're saying. It's hard to understand," I replied, then allowed the tears to fall unheeded.

You didn't notice, of course. There on that mountain road, Zhenbo, my heart was filled with nothing but the image of Guokun Dage—his intimacy and warmth, his bright laugh, his thick, black brows so determined and brave, and his passionate, straightforward gaze. Because all that is in the past, and because it is the present of more than thirty years later and you and Guokun Dage are still those peerless, upright men, I recall myself as a young girl on that stretch of mountain road, and with the heart of a woman who has passed more than fifty years, I realize that there was a young woman who had fallen desperately in love.*

Zhenbo, if we could turn back the clock and narrate history anew, I would still be willing to be your wife. All along the length of that twisty mountain road I listened silently as you opened up and talked freely. At the same time, I made up my mind that I would be the wife whom you could trust, and that for you and someone like Guokun Dage I would eat life's bitterness and never feel regret.

Then, mercilessly, disaster struck. I had gone back to Tainan to go to school, and it wasn't until October that I found out about your arrest. My second brother, Hanting, was also arrested, causing my parents to suffer a near breakdown. Not long after this, however, I discovered that that quietly escalating mass arrest in Thotin was the cause of my parents' distress, and that they who had suffered personal experience of the terror of the KMT's purge on the mainland had secretly negotiated the terms of Hanting's surrender. As for Hanting—that useless second brother of mine—he went out several nights with them, returning only at dawn. He deceived his good friends and his comrades—you and Guokun Dage—but in the end he was still arrested.

Zhenbo, I hope you will restrain the shock and anger you must feel. No matter what, you must continue reading this letter written by the younger sister of a traitor.

Half a year later, Hanting came back, pale and weakened. He had always adored me, as you know, and unable to endure the berating of his conscience, this drink-besotted brother of mine told me by bits and pieces about the arrest in which so many people were implicated.

Hanting had sent to their doom many brave and selfless young men like you and Guokun Dage. This, in turn, pained and depressed me. I could never get over it.

I felt I had to redeem my family's wrongdoing, Zhenbo. This was my conviction after much tortuous soul-searching.

Over a year later, I read in the paper that Guokun Dage and many young people I had never heard you speak of were shot. (Among these were two open and candid young men whom I remember meeting at Kamding in Thotin with you.) I also knew that you had been sentenced to life imprisonment.

Finally, I decided that I would pretend to be the girl whom Guokun Dage had married and throw myself upon his family. Based as this was on my hidden love for Guokun, my actions were not done out of disinterest.

Why did I do this? Because I remember your telling me more than once that Guokun Dage's family was very poor. You told me his mother was frail, he had an old father who was a laborer in the mines, and he had a little brother. As for you and your family of three brothers, you possessed but scant property, and I

---

*The Japanese words *setsunai otome no koigokoro* (the love of a suffering young maiden) are written in parentheses at the end of this sentence.

felt I ought not to be a source of anxieties for you. In view of the expression of friendship between you and Guokun Dage, which was so intimate, bright, self-less, and honest, I made my decision fearlessly. Thinking that I would never again see you alive, I persuaded myself to go to Guokun Dage's home, there to exhaust my energy and the strength of my muscles for the one who had gone bravely to death for the sake of the happiness of workers.

Zhenbo, equipped with the trust that I imagined you had in me, I entered Guokun Dage's dark and broken home. I worked hard, abusing my body and spirit. I worked in the mine shaft as a laborer pushing the coal cart and loading coal in the storehouse. Each time I felt physically and mentally exhausted, I would remember those who had gone to their death with Guokun Dage, and those, like you, who were shipped off to that distant island where rumor says not one blade of grass grows, and where torture is meted out without end. Every time I bathed and saw my body that was once as youthful as a flower become marred by heavy labor, I thought of Guokun Dage, who had long since fallen in the execution grounds and rotted to dust, and I thought of you suffering life imprisonment, forgotten by the world, alone and slowly growing old, and my heart would be glad.

Because of you and Guokun, a dream has lain hidden in the deepest recesses of my heart—a dream that you often had. Whenever I feel lost, this daydream that the flag of your hopes is waving in the skies of the town brings the hot tears flooding to my eyes, whether from joy or sorrow I can't tell. I don't understand politics, but because of the two of you I have never relinquished my habit of reading the newspaper. In the past few years I have worn reading glasses, and I have read all about the changes on the China mainland, and occasionally, I entertain the doubts and anxieties of a woman. I feel concern for nothing other than this: if the revolution on the China mainland founders, won't your long incarceration and Guokun Dage's death be in vain, more cruelly in vain than death itself and half a lifetime's incarceration?

Two days ago, like a bolt from the blue, I found out that you had come home safely. Zhenbo, how happy I am! You have endured more than thirty years of detention and as many years of suffering. In the thirty years that you were away, others have gotten married, had feasts, and completely forgotten about those who sit and chafe on that lonely, deserted island. As I thought this, it suddenly occurred to me that in the wake of Guomu's business and marriage, our life has undergone great improvement. Seventeen years ago, we moved away from the mud brick cottage beside the tracks of the coal trolley. Seven years ago, we moved to Taibei where I received the filial care of Guomu's family and lived a life of luxury and ease.

As I think about it, Zhenbo, for the last seven or eight years I have completely forgotten about you and Guokun Dage. My degeneracy has taken me unawares, and now I am stunned.

These last few days, the house, carpet, heater and air conditioner, sofa, color television, stereo, and car that Guomu has built up inch by inch have given me a stabbing sense of shame. This is the predictable result of my having constantly urged Guomu to avoid politics and to strive to transcend worldliness. The bitterness and the tribulations that I imposed on myself, not to mention the desire to redeem the wrongdoing of my family—all these things that I embraced at the beginning have become forgotten in the last seven years.

I feel hopeless, forlorn. For a long time I entertained the delusion that in abandoning my own home and making myself suffer in order to offer my life to others, I would receive praise from you and Guokun on the day when I went to the underworld. At times, I daydream that I am dressed in white and adorned with red flowers. I am standing between you and Guokun as though we were advancing to receive our reward from the saints of the workers.

Today your release from prison has startled me into awareness. I who have been tamed by the products of capitalism and fed like a domestic fowl recall with horror that forest—a forest of hardship, yet at the same time so filled with life. For the moment, I am awakened, but yet, I am a lamp whose oil is exhausted.

You will likely find many drastic changes when you go back to the home you have been away from for thirty long years. You once struggled for the life people by rights ought to have, but after your release, I fear you will encounter yet another difficult beginning. In facing this tame, domesticated world, I fear your struggle will be more bitter than before. I'm so anxious on your behalf.

Please fight on strongly.

As for me, my life of defeat ought to come to an end. If you are still willing, though, please don't ever forget that young girl on the winding mountain road of Thotin.

Qianhui

He put the thick letter written in the fluid, attractive characters back into the envelope, his cheeks wet with tears.

"Guomu! What's wrong?"

Yuexiang was carrying a bowl of iced lotus seed soup. She had come into Lao Dasao's room and cried out in alarm.

"It's nothing." He silently took out a handkerchief and wiped his tears.

"It's nothing," he repeated. "I'm only thinking of Dasao. . . ."

He began to sob. Raising his head, he looked at the picture of his older brother: he was standing somewhere under the clear skies of Taiwan, gazing off into the distance.

Dream Scenario

Shi Tiesheng

Translated by Michael S. Duke

WHEN Almighty God wanted to accomplish anything He could accomplish it immediately, and for that reason He alone was incapable of dreaming. Because we are only able to dream when we are unable to fulfill our aspirations.

God Himself was fully aware, however, that in order to be worthy of the title Almighty God, He simply had to be able to dream. But what should he dream about? God knew that, since the only thing he could not do was to dream, then the only thing he could dream of was Himself having a dream.

But if He were able to dream, would He still dream a dream of dreaming? And if He were still unable to dream, how could He dream of Himself having a dream? Even supposing this sort of problem was easy to solve, God Himself knew that the problems that followed upon this one would be well nigh fatal for Him: what would the dream inside of His dream be dreaming about? He could not always be dreaming about dreaming about dreaming about dreaming about dreaming . . . could He? Would that not be tantamount to His still being unable to dream at all? God Himself knew that He had to dream of a nondream before He could have a genuine dream and thus become truly deserving of the title Almighty God. Once an ontological entity became His dream, however, poor God Himself knew, He would of necessity no longer be that Almighty God who could immediately accomplish anything he wanted to accomplish. God once found Himself bogged down in just such a predicament.

A life devoid of dreams is the most unbearable kind of life. Living without dreams made Him feel lonely, wretched, and bored. Living without dreams made it impossible for Him to fantasize or to theorize, made it impossible for Him to understand His own aspirations, and almost caused Him to lose His passion for creation and His physical and spiritual vitality. He walked listlessly around His vast and lusterless Heaven, a solitary form with a lonely shadow, His divine countenance wan and sickly like a perennial somnambulant. But He understood

The original appeared in *Dongfang jishi* (Eastern report), no. 2 (1989): 62–63, as part of a trilogy of short stories.

in His heart that the life to come was eternally unending. He understood in His heart that without the seduction of dreams, an eternally unending life could only imply an utterly incomparable ennui. Fortunately, He also understood that He might just as soon destroy everything including Himself, but He absolutely could not tolerate this dreamless prison. Fortunately, His longing to dream had not yet withered away, still refused to give up, and thus His passion for creation was not completely extinguished. This allowed Him one last, slim breath of vitality. As it came to pass He finally realized that, although He was unable to dream, aside from this one inability to dream He was still in every other way omnipotent; He could not see the real world in a dream, but He could create a dream in the real world; He Himself could not dream, but He could cause the ten thousand things to fall into the dream state, and that would become His dream-like game. Thus, He could participate in a game similar to dreaming and, as He enjoyed watching the dreams of the ten thousand things (if there are melon seeds in Heaven, He could eat them as He watched), even though He could not dream He could experience the same illusive fascination and elation of dreams. Having imagined this much, God became thoroughly exhilarated. He fully appreciated that this was His only way out. He vowed to employ the entire range of His divine wisdom to carry through this project, otherwise He might go mad from the power of ennui or turn into a walking zombie from the weight of apathy.

God had made up His mind. He sat there calmly for a moment to let his heart and mind settle down. First He decided on a name for His dream-like game: He called it a play. After that He began to ponder the scenario.

Of course, none of the performers in this play could be omnipotent like Himself; if they were, they too would be unable to dream, in which case it would be impossible for this play to go on, and He would then be unable to enjoy watching the dream process and having His senses aroused by the effects of dreaming. Thus, God understood quite clearly what He had to do first: He had to establish a perpetual distance in front of these performers. This was without doubt very wise, but how was He to set it up? If He dangled a bundle of straw in front of a jackass, the jackass would chase the straw when it moved; when the straw moved, the jackass would chase it, but this sort of low comedy was only suitable to be acted out like a skit on the edge of the stage. The dream world of a jackass was too prosaic and lifeless; it was insufficient to fill up the vast emptiness in God's heart. God thought the performers on center stage ought to be more intelligent and more clever; they ought to have very rich powers of imagination, and their desires should be hard to satisfy; for things to go well, they ought to be able to have an infinitely changeable variety of bizarre, fantastic, and multicolored dreams. He could not and should not treat them in the same way He handled the jackass.

Nevertheless, His ruminations on the jackass had given Him an inspiration: God firmly believed that a perpetual distance must necessarily be established between the abilities and the desires of these performers. God further thought if

this perpetual distance is to be established through the mechanism of their desires never being fulfilled, then perhaps it would not be possible to trick these
intelligent performers. In that case, sooner or later they too would lose the ability
to dream; total incompetence would lead to the same ultimate despair as omnipo-
tence. It seemed that He ought to allow them the ability to fulfill their desires,
but He must set limits to that ability. Fine. But then the question arose: limits?
How extensive should these limits be? No matter how extensive these limits are,
as long as they are limits, the day will definitely arrive when this play is too
tiresome to perform and is performed for the last time. (When these limits are
reached, the performers will once again become totally incompetent, and then,
the dream being over, could the play still continue? If the same play continued to
be performed over and over again, wouldn't that be tiresome?) God thought
again how His life was eternally unending; in order to be able to enjoy the
limitless effects of dreams in such a life, this play cannot be allowed to become
tiresome or come to an end. What was to be done, then? Did He have to grant
these performers an unlimited ability to fulfill their desires? That would not do;
in that case would they not be omnipotent also?

God actually had to ponder this question for a long time; in the end He
suddenly realized the truth and even laughed at Himself for being so muddleheaded. This so-called limited ability did not refer to either time or space; it only
referred to their desires. Their limited ability would produce unlimited desires;
unlimited desires would then tempt them to venture forth in unceasing explora-
tion and expansion, causing space to become infinite, and in unceasing movement and change, causing time to become infinite as well; a play of this sort
could never become tiresome to perform nor reach its final curtain. At this point
God had a wonderful idea: rather than not allowing them to fulfill their desires,
He would cause the fulfillment of each desire to give rise to from one to many
thousands of new desires! That is to say, He would not prevent them from
finding the solution to any mystery, but He would make any solution, any truth,
produce from one to many thousands of additional mysteries. Right, God
thought, in this manner a perpetual distance will be ingeniously established
between their ability and their desires.

God breathed a sigh of relief and relaxed for a short while. He was silently
deliberating something in His mind: that jackass was so dull because it could not
have any bigger dreams; but why couldn't it have any bigger dreams?

The method of making one mystery spawn many more mysteries is as follows: suppose that one performer amounts to one mystery (A), two performers
make not merely two mysteries (A and B), however, but rather three mysteries
(A, B, and AB). What about three performers? They make not four but rather
seven mysteries (A, B, C, AB, BC, CA, and ABC). Then what about ten thousand performers? Five billion performers? God had only to insure that these
performers take an interest in each other and everything would be fine: they
would have an infinitely changeable variety of dreams, and God could enjoy

watching a rich and colorful array of plays. The jackass would not do. The jackass is simply too dim-witted; jackasses are too indifferent to each other, with the result that a million jackasses together still amount to only one jackass, one repeatedly and tiresomely solved "mystery." Therefore, God concluded, let the jackass remain a jackass; let it serve as a warning.

In actual practice, this method of making one mystery spawn many more mysteries is also the method of transforming several mysteries into an infinite number of mysteries. If each single performer carries in his or her body the information contained in the bodies of all the other performers, that is to say, if each single performer is created from all of the other performers, then each solution will give rise not only to several further mysteries, but to an infinite number of mysteries. This is because if you want to solve any single mystery, you always have to solve all of the mysteries, but if you want to solve all of the mysteries, you always have to solve this one mystery; this one single mystery contains all of the mysteries, and all of the mysteries contain this one mystery; all of the mysteries are also solutions or truths, and all of the solutions or truths are also mysteries. How wonderful!

Having imagined this much, God laughed heartily; He knew that He was on the verge of crafting an outstanding play. He knew that given the intelligence of these performers, they would be unable to resist infatuation with this game; but given their intelligence also, they would definitely not be able to discover the flaws in this game; they would go on playing it and playing it and playing it and playing it . . . for all eternity. They would be as if crazed and intoxicated. God was beside Himself with happiness.

What remained to be done would be rather simple.

Three things, in general, remained to be done.

The first was to see that the performers always maintained a sense of novelty and wonder about this scenario; to put it more precisely, He must always preserve a certain number of performers who feel a sense of novelty and wonder about this scenario. When one group of performers becomes bored, jaded, and old, and actually comes to realize that this is a play with no purpose, He must quickly replace them, make them disappear, and let another group of performers who don't understand things take the stage, or make them cross some river where they will forget everything in their past and return once again as young, tender, fresh, and lively performers complacently proud of their abilities and bursting with unbounded passion.

In the second instance, what was to be done if God was careless and forgot to replace a few performers who had actually seen through His plans? This really presented no great difficulty. While they were waiting for God to replace them, they could be allowed two other choices (only these two choices, of course): they could retire to the wings and be turned into jackasses for the time being, or they could remain at the center of the stage singing and dancing to their hearts' content in an ever more flamboyant manner until they gradually experienced the difficulties that originally drove God to compose this scenario. Both of these choices would be fine; they could wait for God to replace them in either state. But what was to be done if these few performers whom God forgot to replace started publicizing the things they had seen through all over the world? That would lead this scenario to be altogether too clear and obvious and make it lose its fascination for any of the performers. To prevent such an event from occurring, God would make all of the other performers absolutely refuse to believe this small group of performers.

The third thing was also the final thing. Once everything had been neatly arranged, God still had one last thing He wanted to do, and that was to close His eyes and give this stage that He had created a good shaking to confuse the positions of all of the performers, just as one would shake up the lot box before drawing lots or shuffle the cards before beginning to play, to make the position that every performer occupies the result of chance, and the relative ranking between them purely random. God Himself knew that a play without suspense is not enjoyable, a play the ending of which can be immediately deduced from the opening is not enjoyable, and a play that gives away all its plot details in advance is not enjoyable; an unenjoyable play could not produce the effects of dreams.

God's work was now finished. It remained for the performers to go into action.

Perhaps the performers would not believe this was the way things stood. That's right: to achieve the most esthetically pleasing dream effects, God made certain they would not believe it.

The Conquerors

Zhang Xiguo

Translated by Ross Lonergan

"LET ME be on top, okay?"

He lay back flat, both hands caressing her tender breasts. She sighed and closed her eyes.

"Don't force it. Let it go in by itself. Not so hard, you hurt me again."

He felt as if his flesh were burning. She was tired so he dared not use too much force; he stroked her delicate skin. Without her clothes on she did not appear at all thin; his hands moved to her rounded buttocks. She gradually relaxed and he pressed hard on her tailbone, letting himself enter her completely. She collapsed panting on top of him. He hugged her tightly, enjoying his fill of her perfect, sumptuous flesh.

The road had come to an end.

The three of them happened to look back at the same time. The small path that twisted its way up to the mountain ridge resembled a dead snake, the skin of its white belly turned upward to be baked by the blistering sun. Whiskers irritably drew out his handkerchief and wiped off the perspiration. Fatty lit a cigarette and then threw it down impatiently. Spectacles opened his briefcase and took out a stack of paper money, spreading it out carefully on the ground. Fatty handed him his lighter, and Spectacles pulled a piece of yellow paper from the stack and lit it. The black border around the paper extended its sphere of influence until, within a few seconds, it had devoured the golden circle in the center. Clutching the lighter, Spectacles looked around uncertainly.

"It's all burned?"

"Yes, yes." Whiskers said, "That's right, it was right here."

The half-burned paper money danced in the air in all directions like dead

This story originally appeared in the literary section of *Zhongguo shibao* (China times), January 4, 5, and 6, 1982. Translated from Zhang Xiguo, *Buxiuzhe* (The immortals) (Taibei: Hongfan, 1983), pp. 113–45.

leaves. The air on the mountain ridge had grown drier and hotter. Wiping the perspiration from his forehead, Fatty suddenly burst forth:

"My sword drawn, I laugh at Heaven / My life in the balance, two rare friends."*

Spectacles fixed his gaze on the curling, struggling paper money on the ground; he could not keep his eyes from tearing. Fifteen years, he silently calculated, fifteen years and they had finally come up the mountain again. But what had been the use?

When he was young he had been a bed wetter, right up until the time he was eleven or twelve years old. At first it was something he had no control over; later on, however, it was because he just didn't feel like getting up and facing the cold. He liked the brief feeling of warmth on the mattress after he wet the bed; afterward he would roll over onto the other side of the bed, the farther away from the trouble spot the better. He would wrap himself tightly in the bedcovers, feeling slightly guilty, but also somewhat pleased with himself. The worst thing was when he would forget what he had done and thoughtlessly run his hand over the clammy patch, thus being forced to get up to wash his hands. The toilet was behind the kitchen; it was an old-fashioned one in which one squatted over a hole in the ground; the only light came from a small lamp in the doorway. Behind the house, on the other side of the rice paddy, was the railroad. Sometimes he would get up in the middle of the night and he would see in the distance a fiery dragon hurtling forward in the darkness. Sometimes that fiery dragon would also come steaming into his dreams and carry him off to some faraway, nameless country. In the daytime, the blue train would appear small and insignificant. But the fiery dragon that appeared in the deep of the night would always make his heart pound. He would stand outside the toilet, often forgetting the cold, waiting for the fiery dragon to make another appearance.

When she was sucking him she would sometimes take it out and lightly rub her cheek against it. When he was about to ejaculate, she would squeeze it tightly at the base, briefly causing him to groan with pain; then she would interrogate him: "Feel good? Do you love me?" He would respond vaguely. Quite unwilling to give up, she would ask him again. He would say in a loud voice that he loved her. All argument would at this point be superfluous and extremely ridiculous. She enjoyed, at the most intense moments of their lovemaking, pressing him to tell her whether or not he loved her. His declarations and her interrogations were equally futile, yet they never tired of the game just the same. Her skill could

---

*The last two lines of a quatrain, entitled "Inscribed on Prison Wall," written by the late-Qing reformer Tan Sitong (1865–98) shortly before his execution. The first two lines are: "In flight to refuge think of Zhong Jian / In submission to brief death expect Du Gen."

undoubtedly conquer all men. Her fair, naked image would often appear afterward in his memory, calling to him with open arms.

"It's all yours. We'll do it whatever way you like, okay?"

She would then close her eyes and lie languidly in his embrace as if she were indeed prepared to surrender him everything. When he became aroused, she would hug the pillow and laugh maliciously at his excited member. This was always when he felt the most uncomfortable; it was only at such times that he might wonder who was actually playing with whom. If she were ever to stop loving him, would she drop him without the slightest hesitation just like she would treat some other boyfriend? Perhaps he ought to be the first one to make a move and let her have a taste of rejection for once.

"How come it shrank?" Flinging the pillow aside, she came over and grabbed him. "What are you thinking about now? One spy to another, you tell me a secret and I'll tell you one."

"I don't have any secrets. I told you all of them."

"Don't give me that." She was massaging him, her other hand slowly caressing his glistening chest. "I'm the spy that you love who lives in the little house. Tell me, what other secrets do you have?"

Anaïs Nin, he thought, even when she was making love she didn't forget to show off. He began to get hard again and pushed her down on the bed; she didn't offer any further resistance.

"Tell me, what other secrets do you have?"

"It was Sunday."

"Huh?"

"Yes, it was on Sunday."

It was Sunday; he had laid his cards on the table with Anna Chu. The affair with Lily had long been out in the open; there was no way that Anna Chu did not know about it. This woman really must have loved him if she could put up with it to the very end without getting angry. Although he was somewhat reluctant, he nevertheless had to harden his heart and say everything that needed to be said. They had been together for three long years, or three short years, depending upon which way one looked at it, and had gradually come to understand clearly each other's temperament. He could not possibly marry her; this had been said he didn't know how many times, and it was repeated once more today. If they could not get married, then it was best to separate as soon as possible; this had also been said he didn't know how many times, but today was the first time it had been said in earnest like this. Anna Chu sat on the side of the bed weeping silently as she listened to him. Finally, she said softly, "She could destroy you, Xin; I feel sorry for you."

She was sleeping now, her soft breasts pressed against the mattress, her face half-covered by her long, dishevelled hair. Gazing at her milky white flesh, he became excited again. He never ceased longing to possess her, and his desire was becoming more and more feverish. She was Salomé; she was the Whore of Babylon; she was Ianthe;* she was Pan Jinlian;† she was lust incarnate; he had to have her. If one could destroy oneself in the flames of desire, then let those flames burn him up! Let the ashes from his bones be sprinkled all over her naked flesh, forever to lightly kiss her soft breasts, her supple skin, and the soft down between her buttocks . . . he would never regret it.

Who was it who wanted to scatter his ashes throughout the land of China? Who was it that pledged to fertilize the fields of the motherland with the ashes of his last remains? Who was it? Who was it?‡

Spectacles finished burning the last stack of paper money and stood up, his legs aching. Fatty tapped him on the shoulder and said, "Let's go, Zhixin."

"You go ahead. I'm going to have another look around."

Fatty and Whiskers walked down from the mountain ridge together. Spectacles stamped out the last burning embers of the paper money. A black leaf stuck to the leg of his trousers; he brushed it with his hand and it turned into black soot, still clinging stubbornly to the trouser leg. He thought of something *Long Long*§ had said just before he died: if a man loses his faith, what then is left?

But he had lost his faith, and what did he have left?

He wanted to have a good cry. When Ruan Ji** died, it was a long time before the sound of weeping could be heard in the quiet hills. But he could not cry; he had long since forgotten how to cry.

Her softly crying figure was beautiful, especially when she was naked. Her tender breasts were lightly resting upon her exquisite knees; he had a tremendous urge to reach out and pinch them.

"You're not listening to what I'm saying at all."

"I'm listening, of course I'm listening. Let's go to bed, okay?"

She glared at him and went on: "My mother and my aunt don't like me. My aunt was a heroine; she could fire a gun with either hand. She was really famous in the guerrilla attacks in the Taihang Mountains during the Anti-Japanese War of Resistance."

"I know," he said with patience. "After the victory she served a term as

*A name used by Byron, Langdon, and Shelley for real women they had known.

†Well-known femme fatale and a principal character in the vernacular novel *Jin ping mei* (The golden lotus).

‡It was Premier Zhou Enlai.—Ed.

§This name appears in English throughout the original and thus in italics in this translation.

**(A.D. 210–63). An eccentric scholar in the Three Kingdoms Period. One of the Seven Sages of the Bamboo Grove.

provincial commissioner. It was only after old Yan from Shanxi* fell from power that she went to America, right?''

"My uncle was also a celebrity. When Li Zongren was president he wanted for a time to use him for some important job, but my uncle refused. According to my mother, my uncle was an important player in political circles at that time. I don't really understand what it was that he was doing, but anyway, I do know that at that time he was pulled every which way by all kinds of groups.''

"The Democratic Alliance.'' He lay back, exposing the naked lower half of his body to her. Apparently ignoring him, she hugged her knees, seeming to have once again become a girl of fourteen or fifteen. It was no use; he covered himself with the bedclothes.

"Later on, Uncle had some psychological problems and my aunt left him. Uncle stayed in New York and my aunt came back to Taiwan to live for a short time. She went to Hong Kong later on and ran a school. My mother adores her more than anyone else. It's really strange: my mom loathed my dad so much, yet she treats my aunt just like her own sister. Whenever my aunt comes to Taiwan she always comes to stay at our place. But neither one of them likes me.''

"How can they not like you when you're the only daughter?'' He put out his hand, wanting to pull her over to him. "I like you baby, even if nobody else does.''

She pushed him away.

"My mother is a fine pianist, and my aunt is musical too. My mom forced me to play the piano ever since I was a child. We went through I don't know how many teachers, but I just couldn't learn how to play. I couldn't help it, I just hated the piano more than anything. As soon as I sat in front of the piano my hands would go numb.''

Wiping the tears from her face, she suddenly asked him:

"Do you really think I sing well?''

"Of course, yours is the only singing I like to listen to,'' he lied.

"But I know I don't sing well. Helen Ning sings much better than I do. My mom has never really wanted to come and hear me sing. Once when Auntie had just come back to Taiwan, they showed up all of a sudden. I sang terribly that night. I wanted so badly to sing well, but I don't know what happened—it just wasn't right. . . .''

She was crying again and he hugged her close; this time she didn't push him away.

"Don't you feel sorry for your baby?''

---

*Yan Xishan. Military governor of Shanxi Province after the 1911 Republican Revolution, Yan remained in control of that province throughout the Republican era (1911–49). He instituted a number of important reforms in Shanxi throughout this period but was forced out of the province under Communist pressure in April 1949.

He kissed her lightly. "It's all right, I'm here."

"She could destroy you, Xin; I feel sorry for you."

Spectacles pulled open the bottom drawer of the desk and took out several batches of old letters. Some of the letter paper had already yellowed. Already he was unable to remember clearly how many among them he had conquered. The manuscript paper laid out on the table was still blank. After he had read through the old letters, he retied all the bundles and returned them to the drawer. The smell of fried fish wafted in from the neighboring flat. The few pots of flowers and plants on the window sill appeared to be half-withered already. He had never had the patience to look after them; Anna had always watered them and kept them nice for him. There were two pots that Anna had bought, the other few having been brought over, one after another, by Mrs. Song when she brought Fenfen to see him—Mrs. Song complained that his living quarters were too dull and empty, that there was nothing there except books. Fenfen had drawn a few crayon pictures for him; it was anyone's guess where he might have stuck them. Of the ornaments that Anna had bought, Lily had given some away and thrown some out. Women are always like that: right after they move in, they single-mindedly root out all traces of their predecessor, as if they could assume control from that point on. The manuscript paper was, as ever, blank; his mind numb, he opened the drawer once more; the letters were still lying there neatly, storing how many dried and withered teardrops? He closed the drawer and locked it with a key. The smell of frying fish still hung in the air; it wasn't until he went over to close the window that he realized that the stain on his trouser leg had still not disappeared.

Her breasts were certainly the softest part of her body. He could suck her breasts forever and never tire of it. Anna's breasts were small and elegantly erect, and their first night, when she had been moved to tears, he whispered solemn promises of love in her ear, holding her firm breasts tightly in his hands. He once thought he would never be want to part with Anna's breasts; he now knew that what he worshipped with his whole heart and soul was in fact Lily's soft, serpentine body, and above all her tender white bosom. His entire being was submerged within it, never wanting to come to the surface.

But each time he finished, he could not bear her persistent asking whether or not he really loved her. She would wrap herself around him like a grapevine, not letting him get out of bed.

"That's enough now, I have to get up and do some writing."

She continued to tease him. Sometimes he would become aroused again and the tension would be temporarily relieved. Sometimes he would suddenly feel an immeasurable exasperation; she would unfortunately sense this and choose the occasion to attack his weak point.

"You don't have to put on an act for me, you can't even write good poetry anyway."

He simply could not understand why she was being so cruel. Five minutes before he had been inside her and she had been crying out his name in ecstasy. Now she was sitting at the head of the bed, teasing him like a hunting dog guarding its prey, affording him no chance of escape. At least he had never criticized her poor singing. Magnanimity was not one of her virtues.

"All you know how to do is play around. There are lots of men around the West Gate area, why don't you just go and grab one?"

She shrugged her small shoulders.

"Actually, I couldn't care less. I was doing you a favor. What's wrong with coming up with another excuse for your inability to write poems?"

He fled to the study. Half an hour later she came in, her face covered in tears, and kissed him.

"We mustn't fight anymore, okay? You don't know how much I'm suffering. If you don't care for me, who else will?"

She opened her night clothes and pressed her milk-white breasts tightly against him. He was compelled to open his mouth and to bite down hard on the cherry-like nipples swaying in front of him, knowing full well that it would do no good. In spite of this fact, as long as he could still do it he was secure.

Long Long. Where is your faith? You were only twenty-six when you died; they all said you were gifted. Where is your faith?

When she was willing to listen respectfully and patiently, he would relate to her events from his childhood. He talked about the morning after the explosion at the munitions recycling factory, when he and his classmates ran over to take a look. The warehouse on the riverbank was still spewing out clouds of smoke, and planks and spent cartridges that had been burned black were scattered all over the cobblestones. A light rain had fallen in the early morning, and the smell of sulphur still hung in the air. As they were picking up the empty cartridges, they eventually discovered, in front of the warehouse, a bent, squatting, half-burnt human figure.

"Late at night . . ." He hesitated, uncertain if he should continue. "Late at night, I would sometimes run outside and watch the fiery dragon come charging out of the darkness."

She was of course no longer willing to listen. She interrupted him and talked about her performance two days hence. She was always concerned only for herself; sometimes he would become extremely angry over this surprising lack of self-confidence of hers. She was constantly asking him about which songs she should sing, or if she should sign the contract Lao Jin* wanted her to sign. Anna had never bothered him with such things. But she sensed when he was about to

*"Old" Jin: an affectionate term of address for friends, co-workers, classmates, etc., who are generally older than oneself.

explode and, kicking off the covers, she stood naked in front of him.

"I'll try on my new clothes for you."

She hid behind the door of the clothes closet and seconds later came out wearing a light yellow dress. "Your own private fashion show. Do you like this one?"

He stared greedily at her softly trembling breasts. She flashed him a professional smile and disappeared again. When she again closed the closet door, she had changed into a black *qipao** splashed with bits of flowers. "How about this one?"

"It's split too high up the side."

"You don't like it?" She pouted her small mouth. "If you don't, your baby isn't going to perform any more. Tell me the truth, do you like it or not?"

"Yes, of course I like it."

"My uncle's coming to Taibei." She was sitting in front of the dressing table, carefully applying her eye-shadow. "I'm sure you two will get along. Just be careful what you say. Don't upset him."

"How can I avoid upsetting him?"

"Just don't bring up my aunt." She smiled winsomely in the mirror. "Is your baby beautiful?"

He was deeply attracted by the delicate beauty in the mirror. Admiring her from this distance was like appreciating a painting. Not allowing him a moment's respite, she suddenly threw herself into his arms. "Don't go out. Wait for me to come back, okay?"

"What kind of wicked ideas are rolling around in that head of yours now?"

"Look who's talking. Who was it that was finished before he even got it in this morning? Should he be punished or not?" She thought for a moment, then, inclining her head to one side, asked "Does it bother you when I pester you like this?"

"No, of course it doesn't bother me."

Spectacles squeezed his way wearily in and out of the crowds outside the airport. Even his shirt was drenched in perspiration when he finally located the old man beside the road. The latter, however, appeared totally unconcerned and was casually looking around, his hands behind his back. Spectacles rushed up, respectfully calling out, "Uncle Ren." The old man narrowed his eyes, saying coldly:

"You're late. Do you know what time the plane got into Taibei?"

"I got to the airport some time ago, but I couldn't find you. Didn't we decide on the phone to meet at the entrance to the terminal?"

---

*A long, close-fitting woman's dress with high neck and slit skirt, sometimes referred to as a *cheongsam.*

"How was I to know which entrance you were talking about? You're so dense. Couldn't you have taken a look on both sides? Why didn't you come around the corner?"

"No way, I just now looked for you on both sides. Have you been standing here waiting the whole time?"

"Pretty much." The old man sniffed, not a trace of guilt in his expression.

"Pretty much?"

"People do have to go to the bathroom, you know. Lily went on in her letters about how clever you are, but I certainly don't see it myself. All right, all right, hurry up and fetch my luggage. Surely you don't want me to stand here all night. It's those two yellow suitcases. There's also a scroll painting. Be careful you don't bend it, it's a gift for someone."

In fact it wasn't just two suitcases at all. Spectacles called a taxi over and, after pleading with the driver, finally managed with great difficulty to stuff the luggage into the car. There were altogether five pieces of varying sizes.

"Five pieces! Are there any more?"

"Of course not." The old man shot him a look. "I'm not moving after all. What would I be bringing so much luggage for?"

By the time Spectacles got into the car he was so tired he wanted to close his eyes. The old man, who was sitting in the back, was not at all ready to let him off the hook.

"Lily says you're doing history of thought? And you like to write poetry?"

"I haven't accomplished anything. I'm just interested, that's all."

"You'll certainly have no future that way," the old man grunted. "If you're going to do research, you'd be better off researching me."

"Yes." Spectacles turned around to discover the old man sizing him up through squinting eyes. "Uncle Ren, after you've had a few days' rest, I'll bring my tape recorder over and ask you some questions." There was no reply from the old man. They had almost reached Taibei, and Spectacles turned around once more, wanting to point out for him the magnificent Grand Hotel, when he discovered that the old man had lain back in the seat and fallen asleep.

In October, Germany launched the war in Europe and blitzkrieged across Western Europe; the French army was defeated. In September, Japan's Fifth Division occupied Vietnam; the Headquarters Division and the Taiwanese Brigade were still tenaciously defending Yongning and Qinzhou in Guangxi. In our Fourth Theater of Operations, as the lines of communication behind enemy lines were stretched thin, their strength had diminished, and I ordered all armies to launch an offensive. The Thirty-first Army lay siege to Longjin; the Forty-sixth Army mopped up the enemy at Mingjiang. On October 26 the enemy in Longzhou began retreating toward Vietnam and my troops retook Longzhou. The Fourth Theater ordered the Sixteenth Group Army to carry out mop-up operations against the remaining enemy at the eastern end of the Yong-Qin road and to carry out a joint attack on Nanning. It also ordered the Thirty-fifth Group Army to carry out, from the Yong-Bin and Yong-Wu roads, separate sudden attacks on the enemy in Nanning. Another unit was to cross the Yong River, cut off the Yong-Qin road, and carry out a joint attack on the enemy at the north end of the road. Every one of my units attacked bravely; the Sixty-fourth Army took Gaofeng'ai and Santang in Binyang and pressed on to Nanning. The 155th Division crossed the Yong River from Yongheng and attacked the enemy. At the same time the enemy on the north bank of the Yong River retreated toward the Yong-Qin road and on the 30th, our Thirty-fifth Group Army retook Nanning. At this time the total strength of the enemy was around thirty thousand men. Each of our units continued to press their attack, and up to November 17 the enemy suffered flank attacks and rear attacks on all sides until, with naval air cover, they moved out along the Yong-Qin road and beat a retreat by sea; there was already no trace of the enemy in Nanning.*

She was crying in her sleep again. He woke up with a start; she didn't wake up at all. He wiped the tears from the corners of her eyes. She looked like a child when she was in a deep sleep, completely without guile, her face half-buried in the pillow. He would prefer that she remain in a deep sleep forever; it seemed that this was the only way he could fully possess her. He took her once while she was sound asleep. She woke up, and with her eyes still closed and a smile on her face, she wrapped her legs tightly around him. In that instant he knew he was finished, already beyond salvation.

"She could destroy you, Xin; I feel sorry for you."

The old man sat, arms folded, on the sofa in front of the window. His wrinkled face had no discernible angles; his eyes, on the other hand, appeared to be extraordinarily clear, the gray pupils following Spectacles' movements, their expression belying his mistrust of Spectacles. Spectacles turned on the tape recorder, fixing his attention on the revolving spools.

"Can we talk about your political ideals?"

"You go ahead."

"What?"

"You go ahead." The old man was watching him cunningly. Suddenly feeling uncomfortable all over, Spectacles managed to force himself to reply:

"I don't have anything to say. Uncle Ren, how can we compare with you?

---

*On November 24, 1939, the Japanese captured Yongning in Guangxi where they remained for some time. In October 1940 the Chinese Guinan Army counterattacked, forcing the Japanese to withdraw their troops completely to Vietnam on November 30. Zhang Yufa, *Zhongguo xiandaishi* (Contemporary Chinese history) (Taibei: Donghua shuju, 1977), 2: 610–11.—Ed.

Any casual comments you happen to make, they're all oral history, they're all of value. . . ."

"You go ahead. I'll talk after you."

Spectacles could only turn off the tape recorder. He thought of Lily's milk-white, soft breasts swaying in front of him; he opened his mouth, wanting to bite down hard on the cherry-like nipples.

> There was already no trace of the enemy in Nanning.
> There was already no trace of the enemy in Nanning.
> There was already no trace of the enemy in Nanning.

Long Long, where is your faith? Tell me, *please* tell me, where *is* your faith? Or are you just like me, letting maggots breed inside your skull? Please tell me, where is your faith?

When he got back home, Lily had already left. She had left a note on the desk: "Gone to Gaoxiong to do a show. Back on the 17th." He found a package of frozen *jiaozi* in the refrigerator and, heating up some water, one by one dropped in the frozen lumps of dough; the water, which had been boiling, immediately became calm. He stirred it with chopsticks to keep the *jiaozi* from sticking to the bottom of the pot. Lily should already be backstage getting made up, hiding her fear under layers of cosmetics. She had said so many times that she did not want to go on singing, but he couldn't think of any other way for her to go either; they both needed the applause of others. The *jiaozi* in the pot suddenly rose to the surface and he rushed to turn off the gas. After the white foam had disappeared, the half-black, half-white *jiaozi* lay on their sides on the surface of the water like so many floating corpses. His appetite completely gone, he forced himself to ladle out a few and, dipping them in soya sauce, ate them. He took out some manuscript paper and spread it out on the dining table. He turned on the tape recorder, and from the machine came the muffled sound of his own voice.

"Can we talk about your political ideals?"

The old man took off his leather shoes and stood on the sofa, regarding Spectacles with a dignified air.

"Do you know what I came to Taibei for this time?"

"Didn't you come back for a meeting?"

The old man laughed contemptuously.

"You young people are really shortsighted. Who do you think I am that somebody could win me over just by inviting me to a meeting? I'll tell you the truth, even if they offer me a special assignment, I won't do it. Take a look, you just take a look for yourself."

The old man pulled out his pocketbook and with great care drew out a letter that had been cut into small squares, handing it to Spectacles.

"Take a look. Whose handwriting is it?"

"Too bad!" Spectacles gave an involuntary gasp of alarm. "Why cut off only the signature? If the letter had been preserved intact, it would be even more valuable."

The old man gave him a scornful look, delicately putting away the square pieces of the letter.

"Lily tells me that you have quite a varied group of friends. I suppose you do have some talent, but isn't it a shame that if a hero doesn't act then he's really just a coward? It would be much better if you were to get a hold of that bunch of friends of yours and join me in a great undertaking. You young people have no prospects at all. If you're going to do something, then you have to do something great."

"Just tell me what you want me to do, Uncle Ren."

His eyes darting every which way, the old man jumped down from the sofa and went to the hotel room door where he listened carefully for a moment before running back up onto the sofa.

"Go and get together a group of people—it doesn't matter what kind of people they are as long as they have guts. We'll fix a code word and you'll move on my order. We are going to carry out a momentous undertaking on a grand scale! When I've gathered my forces, I'll announce it to the world and advance on Southeast Asia. I'll attack Malaya first, because Malaya has always treated its Chinese population poorly. All of Singapore is Chinese so they'll support me for sure. Thailand will support me as well because they want a share in the spoils too. But it has never occurred to them that when I've beaten Malaya, I'll form an alliance with Burma, catch the Thais unawares, and wipe them out. After I've wiped out Thailand, I'll take advantage of the momentum and wipe out Burma. Then I'll lead an army to the south and march on Indonesia. Of course Indonesia will collapse with the first blow. Once I've finished mopping up in Indonesia, I'll launch a major offensive on the Philippines. When all of Southeast Asia is in my grasp, I'll openly declare war on Japan and exact revenge for the millions upon millions of my countrymen, soldiers and civilians, who were sacrificed in the eight-year War of Resistance! After I've conquered Japan I'll broadcast to the whole of China from the Tokyo Tower, telling everyone that the national shame has been wiped away. At that time all of China will naturally be unified. I want no official position; I'll voluntarily 'remove my armor and return to the fields.' Later generations will respect and admire my great contribution. This is an undertaking worthy of real men! I've been planning it for decades, and now the time is ripe. It's time to act!"

Standing on the hotel sofa, the gray-haired old man, stomach bulging, gesticulating wildly, delivered his speech to the imaginary multitudes. As wave after wave of cheering erupted from the rapt crowd, an expression of satisfaction appeared on his face.

He shut off the tape recorder. The aroma of leeks wafted over from the kitchen next door, making him feel suddenly hungry. Unable to sit still, he walked restlessly into the study. The letters were still lying neatly in the locked drawer; the top layer was Anna's letters. Not only did he not have to reread them, he could even recite the contents from memory. The best thing was that she had been able to find a new boyfriend. He never thought she would be getting married so soon. All his worries had been unnecessary. Their separation had been without rancor; this was a rare woman. He had never done anything for her, but she did not reproach him. He had never done anything for Lily either, apart from interviewing her slightly mad uncle. A magniloquent megalomaniac, he actually wanted to conquer Southeast Asia and Japan. But there was already no trace of the enemy in Nanning.

Fenfen's report card was on the table. At the end of each term, Mrs. Song would always remember to bring around his daughter's report card for him to look at. All her grades were quite good: an "A" in conduct, "B–" in physical education. He had never done anything for Fenfen. He had never done anything for anyone. But there was already no trace of the enemy in Nanning.

Long Long, it's not my fault that I've become like this; they forced me to become like this. They really owe me so much. *Long Long*, it's lucky for you that you went early; it was the only way that you could keep your faith. It's not my fault, *Long Long*, can you forgive me? I haven't forgotten our pledge; look, the scar from the knife is still there on my wrist. Whiskers, Fatty, and I even went up the mountain to hold a memorial for you and for our old alliance. *Long Long*, can you still forgive me?

Lily's voice on the long-distance call was so weak that it seemed that it could float away at any moment.

"Come and get me, okay? I really can't go on. I'm so upset. Please come and get me?"

"Isn't Xiao Chen* with you? What about Lao Jin?"

"They're both here, but when I'm upset you're the only person I think about. It doesn't matter how many people I have around me, they're no help. Come and get me please. I can't live a minute longer if you don't come."

He kept silent, waiting for her to plead once more before he blew up.

"You know very well I have to go to work first thing in the morning. What kind of spoiled brat are you, calling at 4:30 in the morning!"

"Don't yell at me, I haven't slept all night. Don't be mad, okay?"

He maintained his silence, the sound of her intermittent sobs coming over the line. Finally, she said:

---

*"Little" Chen.

"I'm taking the first Far Eastern flight back to Taibei. You can at least meet me at Songshan airport, can't you? Just how do I have to beg you?"

The train sped along in the blackened distance. The world was gradually changing shape; the limitless darkness was being transformed into a delimited vastness. The violet plain was slowly coming into view; the outline of the mountains was becoming distinct; the power lines beyond the window rose and fell, resembling the vibrating strings of a zither. As the train rounded the base of the mountain, a cluster of golden rays was reflected from the surface of a small square pond into the carriage. Moaning in pain, he turned around; the carriage was full of deathly pale, unsympathetic faces.

Spectacles waited at the airport until 8:30 and Lily still had not appeared. He wasn't particularly angry, as this was not the first time she had changed her mind at the last moment. When he arrived home, the old man, who had been there for some time, was standing in the hall outside the door waiting for him. The old man's shirt was not tucked in properly—half of it was hanging outside his trousers, and his stomach was protruding. As soon as he saw Spectacles, the old man grabbed his arm.

"It's terrible, they're coming to kill me."

Spectacles used all his strength but was still unable to break free of the old man's grip.

"Who's coming to kill you? Don't worry, no one wants to kill you."

"It's true. They all sold me out, every one of them . . . every one of them. They know all about my plan. Someone informed on me, everyone I know informed on me. I know, they all want to kill me. Every one of them wants to do me in. Where's Lily? Where's Lily?"

"Lily's not here!" Spectacles struggled with the old man for a few moments, finally unable to restrain himself from slapping him across the face. "Who's coming to kill you? Who would want to sell you out? Are you worth selling out?"

Having been struck, the old man was momentarily dumfounded, his gray pupils betraying a look of fear.

"Now I see. It was you who sold me out. I told you everything and you sold me out. You're damned ruthless!"

Spectacles slapped him across the face again.

"You're right, somebody did sell you out. It was nobody else but yourself. You hear me? You sold yourself out. You brought everything down on yourself, and this is the punishment you deserve. You hear me?"

The old man sobbed briefly but then immediately settled down. Spectacles tucked his shirt in for him; the old man's abdomen was extraordinarily soft, like a baby's belly. He allowed himself to be ordered about by Spectacles, the corners of his mouth turned down, the light in his gray pupils completely extinguished.

Spectacles could not believe that this was the same man who had just yesterday been standing on the sofa in his hotel room delivering an impassioned address on how he was going to conquer Southeast Asia. He called a taxi and took the old man back to his hotel, having no difficulty whatsoever duping him into returning to his room. When he was leaving, the old man looked at him expectantly, the corners of his mouth twitching, but in the end said nothing more.

Lily did not call until the late afternoon of the next day. She sounded very cheerful.

"Can you believe it? Somebody's asked me to go to Singapore and Malaysia. All I have to do is perform for a week and they'll give me a house. That's on top of the other benefits."

"Have you decided to go?"

"Of course." After a short pause she said, "That's okay with you, isn't it? The day before yesterday was my fault. I shouldn't have called so early and disturbed you. I realized that afterward and called you again, but you'd already left."

"It doesn't matter. We should bring this to an end, shouldn't we?"

As he expected she would, she started to cry.

"You're really cruel. I had a tough time getting this chance, so why do you have to treat me like this? I'll come back to Taibei right now if you want me to."

"I don't want you to come back. Okay, baby, you go ahead and go to Singapore. We'll talk about it when you get back."

"I'll be back in a week." She said, "Say something sweet."

"Hmm."

"Miss me?"

"Yeah."

"Love me?"

"Yeah."

"Will you wait for your baby to come back?"

"Of course I'll wait."

He was about to hang up when she continued:

"Thanks for taking care of Uncle. Auntie came back yesterday too. His old disorder probably flared up again as soon as he heard Auntie was coming back. It's beyond me why the two of them get along so badly."

"He said somebody sold him out, leaked his plan for conquering Southeast Asia."

"That story's old as the hills. Uncle always wants to become some heroic figure like the Curly-bearded Stranger.* I'll call you again when I get to Singapore. Do you know who asked me?"

He thought for a moment and said, "It's okay, I don't want to know."

---

*The hero of the Tang dynasty romance *Qiu-ran ke zhuan* (The curly-bearded stranger).

He boiled the remaining half package of *jiaozi*. Who would Lily be sleeping with right now? And who would she be allowing to caress her soft breasts? He could almost hear the sound of her moaning and was overcome by a powerful jealousy. He heard a roaring sound in his ears: he had let the liquid from the *jiaozi* spill all over the gas stove. He hated her weakness and had every right to refuse to marry her for that reason. When they were first together she had said, "If you really love me, don't let me be away from you for very long." She completely understood her own weakness, but they were both powerless to do anything about it. Anna had never cheated on him; she had even written him a letter when she was about to get married. He knew it was Anna's final hint, but there was no possibility that he would change his mind. In spite of the recriminations, he actually loved Lily. He hated her weakness; he loved her weakness; he loved her soft flesh and her weak soul—if man still had a soul. He could never forgive her; he could always forgive her. Where was she at this moment?

Long Long, I'm just a third-rate poet, so you can't expect anything of me. You don't know how fortunate you are. You'll always be remembered as you were at twenty-six, your crewcut, a copy of *Leaves of Grass* under your arm, so insistent about life it made my heart ache. *Long Long*, it's a wonderful thing to be cherished forever in people's memories. Lily has told me she regrets not meeting me when she was nineteen. She was still a virgin then; maybe she hopes that would make me always remember her, never leave her. *Long Long*, it's not my fault I've become like this. Can you still forgive me?

There was already no trace of the enemy in Nanning.
There was already no trace of the enemy in Nanning.

Whiskers and Fatty were animatedly discussing their plans for publishing the poetry collection. Spectacles made every effort to concentrate on dealing with the pork chop on his plate. Whiskers was saying something to him, but he had not really heard him clearly; when Whiskers repeated what he had said, he couldn't help smiling. They had been at it for so many years, yet Whiskers had not lost his enthusiasm. Yes, this type of cover design is quite good. Romantic black flag, romantic anarchists. Spectacles carefully cut the pork chop into small pieces, slowly putting them into his mouth and chewing them. Across from him, Fatty wore a slightly mournful expression.

"Zhixin, I met Anna Chu the day before yesterday, and she asked how you'd been recently. Did you know she's getting married?"

With few customers about after lunch, the Old Gentleman had a certain peculiarly bleak atmosphere. Spectacles remembered that some years back, when the poetry society was first established, they had also had a dinner party here. Whiskers' and Fatty's present fascination with the poetry collection was nothing more than an attempt to recapture the past.

"Reconsider very carefully, Zhixin. This Anna Chu is pretty good, and it was your good fortune to run into her. That's all I'm going to say, old friend. You think it over."

"You people don't understand," Spectacles said. "You can't possibly imagine what I've been through, so where do you get off criticizing me?"

"I don't understand, I really don't understand. If you were indecisive about other girls I could see it, but to be like that with Anna Chu, I really can't let you get away with it."

As Fatty went on talking, he eventually began getting worked up, Whiskers exhorting him from the sidelines. Listening to them squabble over him—Fatty berating him, Whiskers defending him—he had actually become a spectator. He found this amusing and hoped that they really could struggle on to some kind of resolution. They finally stopped fighting and both looked at him. Spectacles again thought of Lily's body. They needn't have bothered; there was no possibility that he would change his mind.

He collapsed, limp, beside her, the perspiration running off him. With surprising tenderness, she dried his sweat-soaked body with a towel.

"Miss me?"

"Yeah . . . but now I don't."

"Rat!" She punched him lightly. "Were you bad while I was away?"

"Of course not." He hesitated a moment before asking, "What about you?"

"Silly, I love you."

It would never be clear to him whether or not she was being sincere. Every time he thought of what she might be doing behind his back he became extremely jealous.

"We should split up."

"You said it first." She jumped out of bed and quickly put on her nightgown; sitting down on the edge of the bed, she looked at him coldly. "There's somebody that wants me to marry him and be his third concubine."

"Have you agreed?"

"We're still negotiating."

"What about us?"

"It's never going to come to anything anyway."

"That's not fair. I love you."

She suddenly started to cry. "It's no use. What do you want me to do? I can't go on singing my whole life. I know I'm not a good singer."

"I know I'm a third-rate poet, so we make a good pair."

She stopped crying as quickly as she had started and again regarded him coldly.

"Well I can't help you. You should be taking care of me, yet you force me to make all the decisions. Why didn't you stop me from going to Singapore?"

"It was you who wanted to go."

"Forget it. You only know about looking after yourself. Whatever comes up you can always say it wasn't your fault. You can never let go of the past. Your bloody poetry society, all you are is a bunch of hacks. Has any one of you actually written any good poetry?"

"*Long Long* wasn't like that. He was different."

"If he was still alive, he'd probably be just like the rest of you."

He had no reply. She burst out laughing.

"You look so upset. Get a bit critical of *Long Long* and it's like somebody insulted your highest ideal. I'm not going to force you. Anyway, we still have some time together. You want to?"

"Yeah."

But there was already no trace of the enemy in Nanning.

The old problem of headaches and sleeplessness had returned. A weariness that penetrated deep into his bones prevented him from falling asleep. He had never hated the compilation work at the publishing company more than he did now. A totally futile undertaking, it interfered with his creative thought processes. He often sat the whole day in boredom; he had no feeling whatsoever. His sense of touch had lost its keenness; the words and phrases in his memories were like a broken phonograph, playing the same tune over and over. He often thought of Lily's uncle. It was, after all, a wonderful thing for an old man of seventy to be able to dream of conquering Southeast Asia. He was stronger than Lily's uncle in only one respect: he could still make love.

Even though this was the case, it in fact guaranteed nothing. Since she had come back from Singapore, Lily had rarely initiated overtures. And often when he was in the mood, she would plead some excuse. He had always considered her to have a powerful sex drive, but the present situation had proven this to be a great misconception. In spite of this, she was even more lovely. He could not help creeping onto all fours while she was asleep and admiring the soft glow of her flesh. She was so frail yet tremendously powerful. She was thoroughly degenerate, yet it was he who was the real degenerate. She no longer needed him; he would always need her.

"Auntie and Uncle are both leaving on Sunday. I'm going home for a few days so I can spend some time with them. After that I have to go to Hong Kong again. My aunt is inviting us all to Emerald Lake on Friday, so why don't you come too? Auntie does want to thank you for looking after Uncle that time."

He knew this was only a pretext: all her bags had long since been packed. Standing there in front of him, she looked so delicate, so alluring. Perhaps she may have prepared her lines beforehand, but coming from her lips, they still moved him.

"I can never be apart from you. Even though we are separating, I'll always have a part of you within me, and you'll always keep a part of me."

But there was already no trace of the enemy in Nanning.

The roller coaster rumbled up to the highest point and the roar momentarily abated; it suddenly increased several times, becoming even louder than before, as the roller coaster flew screaming by over their heads. Lily's mother and her aunt both wrinkled their brows, while her uncle appeared to be totally oblivious to the roar; hands behind his back, he was completely absorbed in his own measured pace. It was actually the first time Spectacles had seen Lily's aunt. Half a head taller than Lily, she was completely gray while not appearing at all old, her back ramrod straight. In his imagination Spectacles could see her heroic bearing as she fought those guerrilla battles during her years in the Taihang Mountains. Standing side by side, Lily's mother and aunt looked much like twin sisters—the latter was typical of the southerner with northern features. A heroic spirit flowed from her square face. There was actually not the slightest similarity between Lily and her mother. The roller coaster made a brief stop at the end of the line before roaring off once more. Covering her ears, Lily said:

"It's awfully noisy. Let's take the tour bus down the mountain and get something to eat. There really isn't anything here at Emerald Lake Amusement Park—it's all kids' stuff."

"Come and take a look at the view. It's pretty nice." Spectacles pointed down the mountain. The water in the New Market River sparkled, and Taibei, in the distance, was shrouded in mist. The tiny point of a transmission tower poked out of the gray fog. Spectacles could not determine which television or radio station the transmitter belonged to. Lily's aunt and mother walked side by side to the edge of the little mountaintop park and stood tall and erect under the phoenix tree; it seemed so natural for them to be standing there. The roller coaster was circling above them, but they never once turned their heads to look. Lily suddenly cried out: "He's taken off up there. Uncle!" Spectacles looked up and saw Lily's uncle standing behind the railing at the end of the line, muttering to himself. Thinking of the scene that day when the old man stood on the sofa and delivered his speech, he raced in the direction of the roller coaster. When he climbed onto the platform, the roller coaster was just coming to the end of the line. Spectacles grabbed the old man, saying:

"Uncle Ren, let's go back down."

The old man shook his head firmly and struggled free, stepping by himself onto the roller coaster. Spectacles could only pay for the old man's ticket and take the seat behind him. The roller coaster moved out slowly, making a clicking sound. They were the only two people in the cars. The old man looked up toward the sky and raised his arms high in the air. Afraid he was going to stand up, Spectacles hugged the old man around the waist. Laughing wildly, the old man shouted:

"Don't be afraid, the time is fully ripe. It's time to go into action!"

The roller coaster climbed to the highest point, seemed to pause for a second, then shot like an arrow toward the foot of the mountain. Spectacles instinctively wrapped his arms tightly around the old man's soft belly. He managed, amidst the uproar, to glance in the direction the phoenix tree ahead of the roller coaster. Lily's aunt and her mother were still standing under it, straight as ramrods. As the roller coaster hurtled toward them, Spectacles heard the old man shout:

"Advance! Advance! The time has come!"

The old man's windblown hair momentarily obscured Spectacles' line of vision. Below, Lily seemed to be calling out his name, and Spectacles heard himself yelling too. Just as the roller coaster was about to careen into the phoenix tree, it made a sudden ninety-degree turn. As the old man's head shifted to one side, Spectacles' field of vision became clear, and he saw an expanse of deep blue sky.

A Love Letter Never Sent

Li Ang

Translated by Howard Goldblatt

> *In modern society, language is affected by the clichés of daily life, a variety of ideologies, and the pollution of empty slogans, until its real meaning is ultimately lost.*

DEAR G. L.:

It's now three o'clock in the morning, and I'm lying in bed as the rain falls outside my window. We've had a wet spring this year, starting way back in January, when the weather was still cold, and not only did the rains continue through February, but they didn't even let up in March, when the days should be getting warm. Everywhere you look there's a layer of damp moss. It's like tears of sadness, which can give the same feeling of pervading dampness if they flow long enough.

It's the weather and the lateness of the hour that compel me to write this letter. You probably don't even know who I am. I'm just someone who touched your life for a fleeting moment, without leaving a trace. Some might describe it as a ''hands-off love affair.'' And that's what it was. I'm not going to sign this letter, and if you can't recall who I am when you've finished reading it, then I'll just have to deal with an unspeakable sadness. If what I want to say to you doesn't come through clearly, then what good is language? Besides, you and I are separated by the vast Pacific Ocean and more than ten years in time, so even if I wanted to tell you what's in my heart, I wouldn't know where to begin.

Actually, I've been meaning to write this letter for a long time, but I kept putting it off. The desire to write always comes to me at night when I'm alone, but up till now I've always kept the impulse under control, knowing that when I woke up the next morning, with the sun shining brightly, the emotions of the night before would be forgotten, and that would be the end of it. I'd sit back and laugh at myself for what I'd been thinking.

Translated from Li Ang, *Yi feng wei ji de qingshu* (A love letter never sent) (Taibei: Hongfan, 1986), pp. 3–37.

Naturally, I'm amazed and frightened by the tenacity of that impulse. My love for you made me a laughingstock in the past, and I wonder whether writing to you like this will bring me troubles that could be avoided, particularly since my situation has changed since then, and those kinds of troubles are the last thing in the world I want now.

Taiwan is a changing society, one that's making the transition from agriculture to industry; during this transition, pronounced changes in society's values are evolving at the same time, particularly where relations between the sexes are concerned. The dual moral standards of men and women have become a matter of serious debate.

And yet, I've retained my faith in you, which is how I'm able to write to you on this late, rainy March night. But before I tell you why I'm writing, G. L., I want you to know what a tremendous and lasting impact you once had on my life.

When I met you I wasn't yet twenty years old, an age when most girls are in the bloom of their youth. They fancy pretty clothes, look forward to going out on dates, secretly read love letters at home or wait anxiously for telephone calls as they stare in their mirrors at their radiant faces and dazzling eyes, or just sit there combing their hair over and over, dreaming of all the lovely things that have happened to them.

I was cursed (I use this word with full knowledge of its significance—it truly is a curse) with youthful intelligence for which I was praised by others, but which made it impossible for me to enjoy the direct, simple pleasures of youth, falling instead under the spell of something far more profound, something people call the spiritual realm. But what I want to emphasize is that I never wanted that. Driven on by some inexplicable force, I didn't find happiness; in fact, I cursed my fate of never knowing the pleasures of youth.

When most other girls were going out on dates, I could only look on, eventually losing myself in one novel after another. That's right, I read novels, all kinds of them, from the so-called classics by women novelists to best-sellers that are available in the bookstalls. There's one type of book that still moves me, funny as this sounds, and which always leads to cheap tears and pleasures. I'm talking about popular best-sellers, both Chinese and Western.

In these novels, I see stars and sparks and all manner of beautiful, fantastic things. The heroes and heroines in these novels have but one reason for living, one function in life—love. How beautiful that is! Love, especially a love that's fortified by adversity and filled with countless embraces, warm tears, and love and hate, moved my young-girl's heart like nothing else in the world could. Never in my wildest dreams would I have believed that this kind of love story could have taken hold of my heart and become such an important part of my life.

G. L., can you possibly understand the heart of a young girl that has been polluted by love like that? You see, I used the word "polluted." But it's true. I, and many girls like me of my generation, have been polluted, not just by those romantic novels, but by all sorts of things that have promoted romantic love. The reason is simple: as we were growing up, everything we knew about love we learned from our reading, things that we'd try out later when it was time to fall in love. Instead of spending time with boys, and letting nature take its course in matters of love, all our concepts of love came from the pages of a book, and these were the foundation on which our later loves were to be built.

The direct, natural, necessary relation of human creatures is the relation of man to woman. The case could not be better stated.

That's how it was when I met you. What a glorious year that was! When I recall that year I see a beautiful, clear autumn day, with you standing on a Taibei street, bright golden sunlight covering your back like a screen and lighting up your face. You had just returned from America, a talented student who at the age of thirty had completed a Ph.D. in comparative literature, a man with the airs of someone who had made great sacrifices for his country, but who now announced that he wanted to return to Taiwan to live in his hometown in the south.

"No matter what I've done, so long as it was overseas, it was a lie, because it belonged to them."

That's what you said in public speeches and on television, a look of despondency on your face.

"But now that I'm back, whatever I do is mine."

How could I have been unmoved by this? Back in the late 1960s, many of us who considered ourselves young people of insight and intelligence entertained ourselves mainly by staying up all night getting drunk, engaging in idle talk, and singing, occasionally taking in a movie or watching a performance at City Hall (that was before cultural performances were held at the Sun Yat-sen Memorial Hall, if you'll recall). By then existentialism and psychoanalysis were considered passé, but we were still discussing Sartre, Camus, Jung, and that progressive woman who vowed never to marry, Simone de Beauvoir.

Even though we spent so much time together, boys and girls, even staying out all night, our relationships were strictly platonic. We hadn't begun playing sexual games by then, and we were keeping a tight rein on our emotions. In any case, I'm sure you still remember that girl whom everyone called progressive, but who was actually nothing more than a youngster in long black hair that covered half her face, who used to sit in The Barbarian or The Genius Café making a big show out of smoking cigarettes and drinking most of the day.

We really had no idea what was going on. We had no hopes to speak of and weren't particularly happy, although we never indulged ourselves to the point of becoming maudlin. Back then we were at the bottom of a valley, intellectually and spiritually, unable to have spirited discussions about "being" like the intellectuals of the 1960s, or commit suicide over nihilism, for these were dead issues that led nowhere. Nor could we be like the young people in the West, who, let's face it, just retreated into a dream world of drugs. So all we could do was pass the time sitting in Taibei's coffee shops talking about nothing.

We knew we were spending the days with our heads in the clouds. And it was then that I saw you at one of your speeches at the United States Information Service office on Nan-hai Road. That was before the literary scene had become engulfed in the tide of "nativist" writing, at a time when the United States still exerted the greatest influence on our literature and art; in order to be accepted into certain social circles—circles in which the conversation was dotted with English phrases, where the members knew which wines went with which entrées and were even willing to eat any and all kinds of cheese—a student returning from studies overseas had to make the obligatory speech at USIS.

Not only did these kinds of social circles exist in Taibei, but my friends and I got a kick out of making friends with Americans who had come to Taiwan, most of whom had interrupted their studies at home to come here to live or study Chinese. My reaction to American culture and many of the things that happened in the United States was a mixture of curiosity and envy.

G. L., there's something I want to tell you at this point, and even though you'll think it's funny, I don't care. As a young girl I was always terribly envious of the lifestyles of people my age in other countries, particularly the hippies. I never had the courage to be like them, but I envied the way they rebelled against their society, their culture, even their own families.

Then I saw you, someone who had come back from the States, that progressive country where people had the courage to try new things and seek new adventures, and when I gazed up at you as you stood behind the speaker's podium at the USIS office on Nan-hai Road in Taibei, Taiwan, dressed in an informal Western herringbone suit, a blue dress shirt, and maroon tie, I was completely enchanted.

I listened with rapt attention to your speech, pouncing on every word and phrase you spoke, and when you had finished I was in such a daze I remained sitting where I was and watched people from the audience walk up to the podium to ask you some questions. I didn't get up and leave the by-then empty USIS lecture hall until you had walked out with a group of your friends.

It was beautiful that autumn night on Nan-hai Road, even though the winds were pretty cold. I bundled my wool sweater and coat around me and, for no particular reason, walked toward the botanical gardens, my head filled with the speech you had just given.

I'm not afraid to admit that I was astonished at the time. Not only was I totally ignorant of the Latin American literature you had spoken about, but even the way you treated your topic came as a surprise to me. You analyzed Latin American politics, economics, society, and culture, bringing into your talk such topics as imperialism in Latin America, as well as foreign aggression and pillaging. But I couldn't help feeling that you were holding something back. Something in your flashing eyes behind those horn-rimmed glasses, a look of pain or distress, seemed to get in the way of every word you spoke, held back what was really on your mind, and gave you a look of tortured melancholy.

Yes, that was the look that moved me so much and made me so conscious of being a woman. I experienced something I had never before known existed— tender affection. That was what I was feeling so strongly. There's no doubt about it, I was experiencing a rush of tender affection.

I felt sorry for you for being so unhappy, for the pathetic look in your eyes whenever you spoke about the people suffering under oppression, and for your anxieties regarding the course of development of Taiwan culture. Oh, how I wanted to stroke your worried face as I became aware of my maternalistic feelings for the first time in my life, how I wanted to console you and make you happy! I would have paid any price, even for a moment or two.

According to Margaret Mead's research and deductions regarding gender relations among South Pacific islanders, male dominance and female pliability are roles created by society and culture and are not necessarily innate characteristics.

From then on you had no more loyal a listener than I. I never missed one of your speeches, as long as it was open to the public. I always sat somewhere in the middle, where I could gaze at you attentively without fear of your spotting me. And as I sat in a crowd some distance away from you in the brightly lit lecture hall, my heart overflowing with emotion, a hidden ache in my breast filled me with pleasure.

It continued like this from autumn through late winter. I enjoyed watching you leave the halls after finishing your speeches, then walking home all by myself. Since you spoke in places all over town, there weren't many spots in Taibei I didn't see at night. I walked all the way down what used to be the canal on Hsin-sheng South Road, whose waters kept shrinking between the peony-covered banks until it was converted into an eight-lane highway; and I walked through the Qing-tian and Li-shui Street district, where the rows of Japanese-style houses, with their stately trees, had been replaced by expensive five-story apartment buildings.

G. L., what I was seeing back then was the city of Taibei, or maybe I should say the changes of Taibei, although at the time I wasn't aware of it, for there was no room in my vision for anything but you, for that sad face of yours.

The things you spoke about didn't seem so earth-shattering after I had heard several of your talks. Besides, Latin America was so far away, and for a college student like me, who had grown up in Taiwan, where the economy was developing so rapidly and the standard of living kept getting better and better, it would have been impossible to relate in a concrete way to oppressed or exploited people. Even though I knew there was something hidden in your words, the signs weren't clear enough for me to figure out just what it was.

From the way you talked, I could tell that you knew exactly what you were doing, and even though it was all beyond me, I could sense how different you were from me and my friends. You were steady and deep, calm and level-headed, clearly willing to translate your words into actions, unlike us, who just went from one coffee shop to another after work or school, busying ourselves with nothing but shallow conversations.

How I loved and respected you! You were the center of my universe, the foundation of my frame of mind. And so I followed you: from autumn through winter, all the way to the beginning of spring; from the USIS offices to one college and university after another, even to high school lecture halls. I was always there in the audience, gazing up at you from a distance as you stood behind the podium, always so close and yet so far.

I was much too young and innocent then to take precautions against the possibility of falling in love, so I just let myself be swept away by the image of you standing behind the podium, thinking only of you, wanting desperately to see only you. Following winter vacation, while the endless rains carried into late spring, I learned that you were cutting back on your speaking engagements in order to become the editor of a general-readership magazine.

I realized that I would no longer be able to see you as often, no longer be able to listen to you speak in downcast tones about black literature or Latin American literature, no longer look at the tortured, melancholic look in your eyes as you spoke of matters so relevant to contemporary Taiwan. As this sunk in, I was inundated with a sense of longing that made me feel unbearably lonely, and I suddenly realized how much you filled my heart, and how permanently.

That's when the hurt began.

I guess I was so inexperienced in matters of love that I couldn't have put you out of my mind even if I'd tried. In fact, I actually put my innocent heart and intelligence to work in the task of finding ways to keep seeing you.

My friends, who knew I occasionally went to hear you speak, held you in high esteem. (Naturally, none of them knew that I was head over heels in love with you. I'd never been one to wear my heart on my sleeve, which made it easy for me to conceal my true feelings for you. Besides, I got a thrill out of holding this sentimental secret inside me.) My friends, who knew only that I was keenly interested in the subjects of your talks, often called me your "fan." One of them, a writer who heard that you were the editor of the magazine *Gazing Back, Looking Ahead*, promised me that someday he'd take me along to meet you.

That was how I found myself face-to-face with you one day, so close I could see your flashing eyes behind the horn-rimmed glasses and the range of expressions on your face that kept changing as you spoke. How could there be such a man, someone whose eyes expressed every feeling in his heart, that were the windows to his very soul? I was right there in front of you, overwhelmed by the changes I saw in your expression.

It was March then, and the late spring rains were still falling, soaking the kapok flowers that were beginning to bloom on Ren-ai Road. As I looked from the third-floor window of the magazine office down onto Ren-ai Road, which had been planned as a tree-lined boulevard, but whose recently planted saplings could not yet provide the desired green awning, my eyes were drawn to the kapok flowers that adorned both sides of the street with fiery oranges and reds as far as the eye could see.

True love is built upon the mutual understanding and knowledge of two free people, both of whom should strive to discover the similarities and differences between them, and neither of whom should abandon what makes him or her unique, in order to avoid the destruction of either party.

That afternoon, as the sound of the rain came in through the window, I listened to you talk about indigenous culture, the decline of village life, and the profound changes in society. It was the first time I had ever heard you speak without a microphone, and what caught my attention was the soft, low quality of your voice; it was fascinating.

Of course, G. L., I can't remember every word you said, but even after all these years I haven't forgotten some of your favorite comments:

"As long as we are slaves to the West in art and literature, no matter how hard we try, we'll always be in their shadow, always the student." You were fond of saying, "If you try to introduce this kind of creative work to the West, it will be lost in the shuffle. Western readers don't want imitations, they want things that are uniquely Chinese."

You usually concluded by making the same point:

"Why is it that we can't create literature and art out of our own culture? Why must we always follow in the footsteps of the West?"

And now, G. L., ten years later, in the mid-1980s, I can see that even you lacked confidence in what you were advocating. In today's Taiwan there are many people who state confidently that the value of the existence of Third World literature and art is no longer determined by acceptance by the powerful nations, because we all have different sets of values. But at the time, even though you stressed the importance of one's own culture, your goal was still to gain approval from the West, and depicting your own country's national characteristics was, in large part, intended to draw the attention of Western readers to the exotic East. It's as simple as that.

It was the same when you spoke about Latin American literature at the USIS office without being aware of the ironies in what you were doing; you were trying to promote the spread of our unique national characteristics to the West in order to gain their approval before trying to convince your fellow countrymen of the fine qualities of their own culture.

I know, G. L., that what I've just written won't make you happy, especially when you reflect on all you tried to do. And I know that I don't have the right to criticize you like that. But I'm really not criticizing you, just recalling something that happened a long time ago. We all have to function within the limits of our age, and even you, whom I once worshipped, whom I loved beyond reason, have your own limitations.

Back then, what passions you stirred in our starved hearts! Maybe for me that passion was built upon my love for you (I'm not afraid to admit it), and I was happy to go out and cover some stories for your magazine. G. L., do you remember how the nativist movement was just building up steam then, and how you covered one story after another for the magazine in order to make your readers aware of the beauty of their own cultural heritage? It was you who made us aware that many old gravesites were about to be excavated, that the ancient craft of making dough figurines for children was dying out, and that local opera was on its last legs. Even though the news reports back then were filled with emotionally charged terms like "the end of an era" and "glories of the past," you nonetheless succeeded in getting us out of Taibei's coffee shops, and that was no easy task.

You often encouraged me to write articles, and I always responded bashfully that I lacked the talent. You would smile gently and tell me you weren't looking for poetry or short stories, just news stories. That, you reminded me, shouldn't be so hard.

But I could never get up the nerve to do it and was content with merely having the courage to busy myself around the office with proofreading and other odd jobs. At a time when there were never enough people around, I wanted so badly to make things easier for you and help smooth out some of the worry lines that always creased your brow. I didn't care how difficult the work was; as long as it was for you, I was willing to do it.

There at the magazine office I was given the opportunity to see you often, allowing my secret love for you to settle in my heart, at least for a while. Just seeing you regularly was enough for me. But, G. L., while I was there I began to learn a great deal about you.

I learned, for example, that you were married and that you were devoted to your wife, who, for a variety of reasons, found it necessary to stay in the States for the time being without you. You'll never know what heart-rending pain this knowledge brought me! It was summertime, I recall, and we had been blessed with several months of good weather and clear skies. The streets of Taibei were sweltering, but there in the magazine office, with no air conditioning, I was shivering.

G. L., back then my heart was filled with the need to preserve my girlish virtue, and when I learned that you had a wife, my first reaction was that it would be impossible for you to ever love me (I won't deny that I had stayed close to you in the vague hope that someday you would learn of my love for you and return that love). The news that you were already married convinced me that the loving relationship I had hoped for was only a dream.

> *Montaigne considered marriage to be a sacred union, and any happiness derived from it should be temperate and managed with an attitude of solemn earnestness.*
>
> *Kierkegaard once pointed out that love is a natural emotion that emanates from the bottom of one's heart, but that marriage is a commitment; love does not necessarily lead to marriage, for it is no easy task to turn love into responsibility.*

Oh, how I believed that marriage was the only means of making love eternal! It never occurred to me that marriage could undergo changes, or that true love could exist outside of it. So, at the time, I knew only that even if someday you were willing to return my love, I would never allow myself to become "the other woman."

For the first time in my life I knew what painful feelings love was capable of producing, and I knew also that my love was doomed. And yet that love was as strong as ever. For several days I was unable and unwilling to get out of bed, and not a second went by that my heart wasn't stabbed by the pangs of a love that could never be. I wanted to die. I didn't get out of bed until my family grew frantic, thinking that I had some mysterious and serious disease, and were about to take me to the hospital.

The moment I got out of bed I was faced with a new dilemma, for I couldn't get rid of the crazy thought that was running through my mind: I wanted to see you, I had to see you, I wanted only to see you.

I struggled all that day and night with the desire to see you, but it was simply too strong to be pushed aside. Finally I managed to convince myself (even though I must have known that I was deceiving myself) that all I needed was to see you one last time.

I tried to make myself presentable, but when I looked into the mirror I was shocked to see how much I had changed. I had never been a raving beauty, but all that crying and unrelieved distress had robbed me of even the glow of youth. I was pale and drawn, but I didn't have the strength to do anything about it, since all I could think of was seeing you again.

You weren't in the office. When the editorial staff told me that you had gone out for a cup of coffee with a friend, I felt the last ounce of strength in me ebb completely away. I sat down unsteadily, managing somehow to tell the people in the office that I just had a bad cold, and that my family had threatened to take me to the hospital, but I'd refused and sneaked out of the house.

I managed to drag myself home from the office before really falling ill. I hoped that I'd never get better, just like the heroines in those romantic novels, but unfortunately I only had a slight fever and some mild cold symptoms, and was back on my feet in a few days.

By then I knew that I had to force myself to forget you.

When I finally went back to the magazine office I told you I'd been sick. I could see that you were concerned when you told me to take care of myself, but then you coughed lightly, and all of a sudden it dawned on me how much you'd changed in the year you'd been back. Your fiery spirit had been eroded by life in Taibei, your zeal and your incisive views on things and events had begun to fade. You no longer demanded the reform of unreasonable policies and measures, as you had shortly after your return. Weariness was written all over your face.

"I'm so tired. I need a rest," you said to me on several occasions. "I really want to return to my hometown down south to teach in a middle or elementary school, where I can live a peaceful life and not have to worry about anything."

"Do you think you can?"

You'd gaze at me then, a mysterious look suddenly filling your eyes, and answer slowly with a sigh:

"I doubt it."

I treasured the understanding we shared, and I knew it wasn't going to be easy to forget you. My hopeless love hurt like knives cutting into my flesh, but I didn't know how to remove them without destroying the healthy tissue that surrounded the wounds.

Autumn came and went, then winter, and before I knew it the rains of late spring were falling all around me. The image of you standing on a Taibei street, your back illuminated by the golden rays of the sun, had been replaced by weariness and exhaustion.

I don't know how I could ever have freed myself from the love that held me in its grip if it hadn't been for that one incident. G. L., throughout all these years, every time I recall that incident, I'm struck by how unexpected and chaotic it was! I realize that dredging up the past like this might bring you unpleasant memories, but I can't help thinking that, having gone down this road yourself, you have plenty of tolerance and understanding.

I still remember clearly how, after one of the magazine issues had been put to bed, I'd stayed away from the magazine office for several days. Then late one night I received a telephone call from one of the assistant editors, who told me that you'd been arrested a few days earlier, and that the magazine office had been searched that very afternoon.

A class of people can be under the total control of another class simply because of a difference in numbers; a majority always oppresses a minority. But it is not the same with women as it is with, say, minorities like the Jews or blacks of America, for there are as many women on earth as there are men—more, in fact.

Generally speaking, the status of women today is lower than that of men, and their environment offers them few opportunities for development. Many men are content to maintain the status quo, and the conservative bourgeoisie consider the liberation of women as a threat to their moral position and thus not in their best interests.

I couldn't get back to sleep that night, and the next morning, as soon as I figured there'd be someone at the office, I rushed over to look around. The place had been ransacked and the office was empty, except for a woman sitting at your desk, slowly straightening up some of the scattered manuscripts.

She raised her head when she heard the door open, the haggard look on her face showing through her makeup under the strong light of the fluorescent lamp. No one had to tell me that she was your wife.

I stood there on the other side of the ransacked office, looking straight into the face of your wife and not knowing what was happening to you at that very moment, or even where you were. The rain had died down a little, suddenly allowing the pale light of dawn to peek through, making the time seem all wrong.

She greeted me first. As she stood up, I saw how slim and very tall she was. Then I noticed her even features and neatly trimmed, shoulder-length hair. She appeared to be an attractive and unpretentious woman.

In the midst of all that confusion I anxiously asked her what was happening to you. She calmly told me that no one knew for sure. Her voice was soft and mild, sort of tranquil, except for a slight hoarseness at the end of her words. I hurriedly explained that I'd gotten to know you by helping around the office. She just nodded slightly as she calmly heard me out. Not knowing what else to say, I told her I'd better be going since there was nothing I could do. Although she didn't move from where she was, she nodded more deeply than the first time and said in measured tones:

Thank you for coming.

After walking out of the office, at first I didn't know where to go. My heart was pounding, my cheeks were burning, and my limbs felt like rubber. I walked aimlessly for a while, dragging my feet listlessly, then sat down on a bench beside the fountain on Ren-ai Road.

Now that the rain had stopped, a pale light shone down, even though the sky was still gray and gloomy. I sat there for a while, as cars zoomed up and down the tree-lined street, making wet, depressing sounds as their tires passed over the slickened asphalt. I don't know how long I sat there before I looked up and noticed how disorderly the kapok flowers were up and down the street. The trees that had lost nearly all of their blossoms in the rain stood there with fresh green leaves on their branches; some of the nearly bare trees were holding on to a few dead flowers; on other trees the kapoks were just beginning to bloom. My thoughts drifted vaguely to the spring rains that seemed heavier than usual, and to how the sky never seemed to clear; no wonder the kapok flowers, deprived of the sort of weather they needed to blossom, never had a chance.

It had only been a year earlier, on this very street, that I was looking at row upon row of kapoks in bloom, and in the midst of these thoughts my mood began to clear. I started to realize that you were moving further and further out of my life, allowing peace and order to return to my confused heart.

But that didn't make me happy. All I felt was a vast emptiness.

At the very instant I spotted your wife sitting at your desk I understood that my love for you had ceased to exist. Only she, your lawfully wedded wife, could sit in your chair when your whereabouts were unknown and straighten up the manuscripts on your desk, one page at a time. And in the future, no matter what happened to you, only your lawfully wedded wife could stand up in court and speak on your behalf; even if you were convicted and put away, only she, your wife, could visit you and bring you food and clothing.

For the first time in my life I understood that the institution of marriage was greater than everything else, that it embraced a love that was irreplaceable, especially during times of difficulty. That knowledge was exactly what I needed to free myself from the intense emotions that had entangled me for more than a year.

But, G. L., that doesn't mean I stopped loving you, you must believe that. For it was then that I knew just how deep my love for you really was. As time passed, the depressing emptiness in my heart gradually disappeared, while my understanding of my love for you increased. The love I felt then was greater than any hopes of being with you, purged of that chaotic, confining infatuation, which had been transformed into a profound emotion that clearly and painlessly filled my heart, with no more waves of agitation.

And so, at a time when you had been abandoned by others who were afraid of getting involved in your troubles, I had no such misgivings. I went from place to place trying to find news of you, hoping to learn what had happened to you, perhaps even coming to your aid in some insignificant way. The funniest thing of all was that just when I had freed myself from what had been a destructive love, people suddenly began talking derisively about how I had fallen in love with you!

But I had no time to worry about rumors, for I was too concerned about your safety. Eventually, what you had been doing in Taiwan became known, and the cloud of suspicion hanging over the magazine began to lift. They recommended publication, with no apparent changes, except that you were no longer the chief editor.

The late-spring rainy season passed, and it was summer. As the days grew warmer, it was no longer off-limits to talk about you and your affairs. At last the news surfaced that you hadn't been arrested after all, merely interrogated about the suspicious actions of a friend of yours in the States. They wanted you to tell them everything you knew.

From the rumors flying around I learned that you had gone back home, and that your wife, an American citizen, had gotten you an exit permit. In late May I heard that you had returned to the States.

I never went to see you, although I was delighted to know that you weren't in any trouble. I had put everything behind me, and no good would have been served by seeing you again.

I graduated from college in early June. The following spring I agreed to marry a man my family had picked out for me.

> Most people live in a typical nuclear family: the father is the bread-winner, the mother takes care of the home and the children. But there's no longer such a thing as a standard family.
> There are so many family types in the 1980s that it is like a Rubik's Cube, and trying to change things back to the way they used to be would be the same as trying to get a Rubik's Cube back to its original design.

My agreeing to the arranged marriage was not like the stories in novels or in the movies, where the disheartened heroine gives herself up. Quite the opposite; I based my decision on my reverence for the institutions of marriage and family. When I saw your wife sitting at your desk performing her wifely duty of straightening up the manuscripts, I was moved beyond words and was sure that after my crazy infatuation with you, no one but a lifelong companion could ever love you like I did.

My husband is a decent man, progressive and possessed of many husbandly virtues. And I've been the best wife I could possibly be, except for my wedding night, when all I could see as I accepted the first man in my life was your melancholic face and the ever-changing expression in your eyes.

Married life has been calm and uneventful for me. My husband and some of his friends formed a trade company, at a time when the import-export business was a sure-fire way to get ahead in Taiwan, particularly in dealing with the so-called underdeveloped regions. After six years of marriage we had everything a family could want: a car, a house, a servant; and I was able to put my foreign-language college degree to good use by writing some documents in English and doing some translations for my husband's company. Then, as my husband began working later and later at night, I started to do some writing.

That's right, G. L., I started to write, just as you had urged me to do: not short stories or poems, but reportage. Owing to what I had learned at the magazine, I had plenty of opportunities to take up freelance assignments. At the time, the slogan "Back to the roots" was sweeping across Taiwan, and feature items on past lifestyles, forgotten occupations, and relics of all types were being fought over by newspapers.

My experience in working with you had taught me how to separate the wheat from the chaff among the nativist topics that were all the rage with everyone else: I did a report on the origins of blackfoot disease in the Northgate District; I went up into the mountains with an aborigine service team to observe the devastation of the minority culture there; I went to psychiatric hospitals, where I learned firsthand what it meant to live under truly inhuman conditions. G. L., while I was working on these stories I realized that I understood you better and better, that I knew why it had been so important to you to talk about Latin American literature and black literature, and why you had thrown yourself so completely into what you were doing.

But I also began to realize that my marriage was in trouble.

After leaving the service team up in the impoverished mountain area, I wanted to get home as quickly as possible, so I took an airplane back to Taibei from the south. But when I reached my home on Dun-hua South Road, where a maid was waiting for me, I found it impossible abruptly to change my mood or fit into another role. I also discovered that my husband and I had virtually nothing in common to talk about. I wasn't remotely interested in how to promote the exportation of Taiwan products to Africa, while he was so wrapped up in his work that all my talk of orphans and child prostitutes fell on deaf ears.

I tried to figure out a way to improve the relationship, but apparently I didn't try hard enough, because soon after that I discovered that my husband was involved with another woman, a nightclub hostess—young, I was told, and sexy. Ironically, in a story I did on sex I had made a strong plea for my readers to be concerned about and come to the aid of girls forced into prostitution.

But none of that was important, G. L. I'm sure you can understand that the sheer fright of coming suddenly to my senses hit me the hardest. The profoundly intimate institution of marriage, in which I had placed so much faith and which was so sacred to me, and that idealized love I held so dearly, proved to be nothing but a deception. My world was crumbling around me.

My husband tried to explain how meaningless the affair was, just an innocent game that all his business friends played. A nightclub was a good place to make business deals, and this woman was nothing more than his regular companion at the nightclub. He could end the relationship anytime he wanted to.

I was in a terrible dilemma, but after some hard thinking, I made up my mind: against the advice of family and friends, I told him I wanted us to separate for a while. At first he opposed the idea, but eventually he gave in.

I moved into a small apartment he rented for me, but whenever he came by to see me, which was often, we were like man and wife, which was something I hadn't anticipated. And when we were together like that, my enjoyment was ruined by the thought that this is what he did with other women. But I didn't know how to refuse him. And so, after all those years of marriage, I finally understood the important role that sex played in love.

Living apart like that did seem to improve things between us after a while, and we began to talk again about many things, just as we had done during our courtship. By listening to his evasive comments, I got a pretty good idea of what marriage meant to him. He hated the idea of divorce, not just because he loved me, but also because, like all his friends, he believed that marriage was a way of life, that the family was inviolable, and that playing around was okay as long as it wasn't taken too seriously. Not long after that, my decent, progressive husband had given up his vow where extramarital affairs were concerned, although I can't say whether that was caused by his character, his work environment, or was a result of evolving social mores. How could he have changed so dramatically in just a few short years? It was truly mind-boggling.

> *Generally speaking, only a woman can question whether or not the consciousness of women is leading toward the proposition that their liberation is inevitable, and whether or not they must cease to accept the view that their fate is determined solely by biological, psychological, and economic conditions. Only when women begin to doubt the portrayal in traditional religion, in philosophy, and even in myth, of "the eternal nature of women" or "true womanhood," and attempt to identify the origins of these declarations, will they have taken their first step forward.*

And so, in large part to avoid having to face all these problems, I once again threw myself into my investigative work. After years of writing in Taiwan, where someone can be called a ''writer'' with the publication of a single work, I began to acquire a bit of a reputation, and by working hard after our separation, my accomplishments gained even greater recognition. And that's how I met Xia.

Xia was the publisher of a business and economics magazine who, like so many young people with vision who start out right after college at a time when the market is just right, made quite a name for himself with the overnight success of his magazine. By the time I met him, he had become a wealthy man through a number of shrewd investments.

I met him through my work. He had come to ask me to write a piece for his magazine on the environmental impact of constructing a cement factory in the mountains. To be honest, I was flattered to be given an opportunity to write for such a prestigious magazine, and I threw myself into the project, for which it was necessary to spend a lot of time with Xia. We went together to look over the proposed construction site, where we met with several experts, and it didn't take me long to discover how much alike you and he were.

Like you, he had keen insight, which allowed him to sense the slightest change in my mood; and like you, he had to be the center of attention. He never felt that he got as much love and attention as he needed, which made him want it all the more, just like a child. Again, just like you, he invariably caught cold after periods of intense activity, which always frustrated him. Then, as though his own well-being were his only concern, he would say to me, I think I'd better stay put for a few days and do my best to get good and sick, since that's about the only way I can get any rest.

I'm sure, G. L., that you can imagine what all this meant to me. At first I felt giddy, then frightened, as I discovered that I was falling head over heels in love with him *because* he was so like you; and, to make matters worse, I discovered that I wasn't alone in feeling the way I did.

I knew I was in love with him, as madly as when I fell for you way back when. The difference was that after eight years of marriage, I knew what was in store for me this time. Not only was he married and the father of two children, but I was no longer the infatuated little girl of before, and there was still the unresolved situation between me and my husband.

By this time I knew what love was all about, and I was aware that if I let my emotional relationship with Xia continue to develop, one day just talking and trying to understand each other would not be enough, and we'd need to take the relationship a step further. Then it would no longer be just a matter of two people but would involve both of our families, and whether I would be the one to suffer was something I couldn't be sure of.

I was frightened.

Everyone could tell that something was bothering me, but most people thought it was a result of the separation. Several friends advised me to take a vacation abroad. That was when the relaxation of restrictions on tourist visas had just begun, and foreign travel was becoming a favorite pastime of the idle rich. Before long, it also became the preferred excuse for people who wanted out. Since I was looking for a means of escape, I made up my mind to go to the States.

I didn't choose the States because I wanted to see you again, G. L. It had been years since I'd received any news of you, and the last I'd heard you were teaching in an East Coast university somewhere. Besides, since I was happily married during much of that time, the desire to see you again had faded. That's why running into you so unexpectedly on that cold, snowy night in New York caused me to burst into tears.

It happened at the American Association for Asian Studies meeting. While in New York I'd gone to see a famous scholar I'd once interviewed in Taiwan, who dragged me off to the meeting to "see where the action was." Since I didn't know any of the people there, I stood off to the side of the lecture hall, which was packed with Chinese and Americans, and glanced around the room.

Walking through the heavy snowfall that cold night had given me a real lift, and when I entered the heated room with all those people I couldn't get my bearings right away. Then, suddenly, I was caught completely off guard when there in the midst of that crowd I saw you.

At first it seemed like déjà vu, but it was so far, far away, and I began to tremble, as though my heart were in a vise. It soon began to pass, and I knew that my eyes weren't deceiving me—it was you, all right. You had changed a great deal, although you were wearing an American-tailored suit, just like the first time I saw you, and nearly identical horn-rimmed glasses. No gray hair, no wrinkles; it was almost as though time had not touched you during all those years. And yet, to me you were a completely different person, not just because the spirited expression was gone, nor because you didn't have that exhausted look that always came after a period of intense activity, but because of your forlorn expression, the look of loneliness that comes when one's heyday is behind him, the loneliness of someone in decline.

I stood there and watched you for several minutes. Then, as the tears welled up, I walked quickly out of the hall and into the snow flurries. Feathery snow-flakes fell on my face, still and silent, and as they melted, the icy water mixed with my warm tears and ran down my cheeks, until I could no longer tell whether it was the snow or my tears that was stinging my face.

Through my tear-filled eyes I watched the snowflakes disappear without a trace into the snow on the ground. I knew for a certainty that my youth and everything that had occurred between us were now completely behind me.

I won't deny that I still thought of you from time to time after that. My unrealized love was like dreamy moonlight at the foot of the bed late at night, cold and clear, and eternal. It was especially hard to put you out of my mind after I met Xia, who had so much in common with you. Seeing you again like that on that snowy night in a foreign land after the passage of so many years, and being separated from you by the freezing ice and snow, brought an end to everything; you lost the hold you had on my heart, the thread was broken.

At that very moment, a strange thought purged my heart of all its confusion, and I couldn't help but think back to that day when I was stunned by the news that you were a married man, and how I knew I had to leave you. And how, too, several years later, myself a married woman, I threw caution to the wind and fell in love with Xia, a married man with children. How things had changed!

People are always giving up something. When I was standing there on the snow-covered ground, thinking tearfully about my lost youth and emotions, I realized for the first time how very much I had lost.

> *The infinite degradation in which man exists for himself is expressed in this relation to "the woman" (man's oppression of women based perhaps on his misunderstanding of "the woman"). . . . The direct, natural, necessary relationship of man to man is the relationship of man to woman.*

One day, after returning to Taibei, I was walking down Ren-ai Road when suddenly I noticed that the trees planted so many years before had grown into tall shade trees, that both sides of the streets were lined with high-rises, and that there were far more cars and pedestrians on the street than I remembered. And me, I was no longer the little girl who had fallen head over heels in love with you way back then.

So now you know why I've written you this letter, G. L. Finally, after all these years, I'm able to deal with my past, and I find no need to keep you ignorant of the path I've taken. I'm confident that you'll understand and treasure the enormous impact, which time itself cannot erase, that you've had on my life. I'm also writing to let you know that even though my love for you back then brought me pain and ridicule, I can state unequivocally that I have no regrets.

And so, G. L., if someday I accept Xia, you must believe me when I say that I will not be using him finally to attain the love that was denied me so many years before, but that I truly love him. On that snowy night when I saw you again, saw that loneliness that I recognized, but which failed to move me, I knew that the passage of ten years and the differences between us had made it possible for me finally to put my past behind me, without bitterness or sorrow.

Maybe Xia is a lot like you, but that doesn't matter. For every one of us there is an ideal type of lover, and it has been my luck—good or bad—that both you and Xia fit that ideal, that both of you have been able to stir my heart. But that doesn't mean I'll ever forget or belittle my husband, with whom I shared my life for so many years, or the emotions I nurtured over such a long period of time, and which I esteem so highly.

I know that someday I'll have to make a choice, and that I still have a long road to walk down. And yet, G. L., no matter what choice I make, as I walk the road ahead I'll never regret in the slightest the love I once felt for you. Of that I'm absolutely sure.

I hope you can recall who I am,

C. T.

A Woman Like Me

Xi Xi

Translated by Howard Goldblatt

A WOMAN like me is actually unsuitable for any man's love. So the fact that the emotional involvement between Xia and me has reached this point fills even me with wonder. I feel that the blame for my having fallen into this trap, from which there is no escape, rests solely with Fate, which has played a cruel trick on me. I am totally powerless to resist Fate. I've heard others say that when you truly like someone, what may be nothing more than an innocent smile directed your way as you sit quietly in a corner can cause your very soul to take wing. That's exactly how I feel about Xia. So when he asked me: Do you like me? I expressed my feelings toward him without holding back a thing. I'm a person who has no concept of self-protection, and my words and deeds will always conspire to make me a laughing stock in the eyes of others. Sitting in a coffee shop with Xia, I had the appearance of a happy person, but my heart was filled with a hidden sorrow; I was so terribly unhappy because I knew where Fate was about to take me, and now the fault would be mine alone. I made a mistake at the very beginning by agreeing to accompany Xia on a trip to visit a schoolmate he hadn't seen for a long time, then later on, by not declining any of his invitations to go to the movies. It's too late for regret now, and, besides, the difference between regretting and not regretting is too slight to be important, since at this very moment I am sitting in the corner of a coffee shop waiting for him. I agreed to show him where I work, and that will be the final chapter. I had already been out of school for a long time when I first met Xia, so when he asked me if I had a job, I told him that I had been working for several years.

What sort of job do you have?

He asked.

I'm a cosmetician.

I said.

The original appeared in the literary section of the *Lianhebao* (United daily news), September 6–7, 1982. The translation first appeared in *The Chinese PEN* (Spring 1984) and is reprinted here by permission.

Oh, a cosmetician.

He remarked.

But your face is so natural.

He said.

He said that he didn't like women who used cosmetics, and preferred the natural look. I think that the reason his attention had been drawn to my face, on which I never use makeup, was not my response to his question, but because my face is paler than most people's. My hands too. Both my hands and my face are paler than most people's because of my job. I knew that as soon as I divulged my occupation to him, he would jump to the same erroneous conclusion that all my former friends had. He has already assumed that my job is to beautify the appearance of girls in general, such as adding just the right touch of color to the face of a bride-to-be on her wedding day. And so when I told him that there were no days off in my job, that I was often busy Sundays, he was more convinced than ever that his assumption was correct. There were always so many brides on Sundays and holidays. But making brides-to-be beautiful is not what I do; my job is to apply the final cosmetic touches to people whose lives have already come to an end, to make them appear gentle and at peace during their final moments before leaving the world of man. In days past I had brought up the subject of my occupation to friends, and I always immediately corrected their momentary misconception, so that they would know exactly what sort of person I am. But all my honesty ever brought me was the loss of virtually all my friends. I frightened them all off; it was as though the me who was sitting across from them drinking coffee was actually the ghost of their own inner fears. And I never blamed them, for we all have an inborn, primitive timidity where the unknown mysteries of life are concerned. The main reason I didn't give a fuller answer to Xia's question was my concern that the truth would frighten him; I could no longer allow my unusual occupation to unsettle the friends around me, something for which I could never forgive myself. The other reason was my natural inability to express what I think and feel, which, over a long period of time, has led to my habit of being uncommunicative.

But your face is so natural.

He said.

When Xia said that, I knew that it was a bad omen for the emotional road he and I were taking; but at that moment he was so happy—happy because I was a woman who didn't use makeup on herself. Yet my heart was filled with sadness.

I don't know who will someday be applying makeup to my face—will it be Aunt Yifen? Aunt Yifen and I have one hope in common: that in our lifetimes we will never have to make up the face of a loved one. I don't know why, after the appearance of this unlucky omen, I continued going on pleasure excursions with Xia, but maybe, since I'm only human, I lack self-control and merely go where Fate takes me, one ordained step after another. I have no logical explanation for my behavior, and I think that this might just be what humans are all about: much of our behavior is inexplicable, even to ourselves.

Can I come and see you work?

Xia asked.

That shouldn't be a problem.

I said.

Will they mind?

He asked.

I don't imagine any of them will.

I said.

The reason Xia asked if he could see how I worked was that every Sunday morning I have to go to my workplace, and on those days he never has anything else to do. He offered to walk me to work, and since he'd be there already, he might as well hang around and take a look. He said he wanted to look at the brides-to-be and their maids-of-honor and all the hustle and bustle; he also wanted to watch me as I made the pretty ones prettier or the attractive ones plain. I agreed without a second's thought. I knew that Fate had already led me up to the starting line, and what was about to happen was a foregone conclusion. So here I am, sitting in a small coffee shop waiting for Xia, and from here we'll go together to my workplace. As soon as we get there he'll understand everything. Xia will know then that the perfume he thought I was wearing for him actually serves to mask the smell of formaldehyde on my body. He'll also know then that the reason I wear white so often is not a conscious effort to produce an appearance of purity, but merely a convenience in going to and coming from work. The strange medicinal odor that clings to my body has already penetrated my bones, and all of my attempts to wash it off have failed. Eventually, I gave up trying, and I even got to the point where I no longer even notice the smell. Xia knows nothing of all this, and he once even commented to me: That's a very unusual perfume you wear. But everything will soon become crystal clear. I've always been a technician who can fashion elegant hairdos and tie a bow tie with the very best. But so what? Look at these hands of mine; how many haircuts and trims have they completed on people who could no longer speak, and how many bow ties have they tied around the necks of totally solemn people? Would Xia allow me to cut his hair with them? Would he allow me carefully to tie his tie for him? In the eyes of others, these soft, warm hands have become cold; in the eyes of others, these hands, which were made to cradle a newborn infant, have already become the hands for touching the white bones of skeletons.

There may have been many reasons why Aunt Yifen passed her skills on to me, and they can be clearly perceived through her normal daily remarks. Sure, with these skills no one would ever have to worry about being out of work and would be assured of a good living. So how can a woman like me, with little schooling and not much knowledge, compete with others in this greed-consumed, dog-eat-dog world? Aunt Yifen was willing to pass the consummate knowledge of her lifework on to me solely because I was her niece. She had never let anyone watch her when she was working until the day she took me on as her apprentice, when she kept me by her side instructing me in every detail, until I lost my fear of being alone with the cold, naked corpses. I even learned how to sew up the sundered bodies and split skulls as though they were nothing more than theatrical costumes. I lost my parents when I was very young and was reared by Aunt Yifen. The strange thing is that I began to resemble her more and more, even becoming as taciturn as she, as pale of hand and face as she, and as slow in my movements as she. There were times when I couldn't shake my doubts that instead of being me, I had become another Aunt Yifen; the two of us were, in fact, one person—I had become a continuation of Aunt Yifen.

From today on, you'll not have to worry about your livelihood.

Aunt Yifen had said.

And you'll never have to rely upon anyone else to get through life, like other women do.

She had said.

I really didn't understand what she had meant by that. I couldn't figure out why I wouldn't have to worry about my livelihood if I learned what she had to teach me, or why I wouldn't have to rely upon anyone else to get through life, like other women do. Was it possible that no other profession in the world could free me from worrying about my livelihood or let me avoid having to rely upon others to get through life? But I was only a woman with little knowledge, so of course I would not be able to compete with other women. Therefore, it was strictly for my own good that Aunt Yifen had taken such pains to pass her special skills on to me. Actually, there is not a single person in this city who doesn't need help from someone in our profession. No matter who they are—rich or poor, high or low—once Fate has brought them to us, we are their final consolation; it is we who will give them a calm, good-natured appearance and make them seem incomparably gentle. Both Aunt Yifen and I have our individual hopes, but in addition to these, we share the common hope that in our lifetimes we will never have to make up the face of a loved one. That's why I was so sorrowful last week: I had a nagging feeling that something terrible had happened, and that it had happened to my own younger brother. From what I had heard, my younger brother had met a young woman whose appearance and temperament made her the envy of all, a woman of talent and beauty. They were so happy together, and to me it was a stroke of joyous good fortune. But the happiness was all too short-lived, for I soon learned that for no apparent reason, that delightful young woman had married a man she didn't love. Why is it that two people who are in love cannot marry, but wind up spending the rest of their lives as bitter victims of unrequited love? My younger brother changed into a different person; he even said to me: I don't want to live any more. I didn't know what to do. Would I someday be making up the face of my own younger brother?

I don't want to live any more.

My younger brother had said.

I couldn't understand how things could have reached that stage. Neither could my younger brother. If she had merely said: I don't like you anymore. He would have had nothing more to say. But the two of them were clearly in love. It was not to pay a debt of gratitude, nor was it due to economic hardships, so could it be that in this modern, civilized society of ours there are still parents who arrange their daughters' marriages? A lifetime covers many long years, why must one bow to Fate? *Ai*, I only hope that during my lifetime I will never have to make up the face of a loved one. But who can say for sure? When Aunt Yifen formally took me on as an apprentice and began passing her consummate skills on to me, she said: You must follow my wishes in one respect before I will take you on as my apprentice. I didn't know why she was being so solemn about it. But she continued with extreme seriousness: when it is my turn to lie down, you must personally make up my face; you are not to permit any stranger to so much as touch my body. I didn't feel that this would present any problems, but I was surprised by her inflexibility in the matter. Take me, for example: when it is my turn to lie down, what will the body I leave behind have to do with me? But that was Aunt Yifen's one and only personal wish, and it is up to me to help her fulfill it, if I am still around when that day comes. On this long road of life, Aunt Yifen and I are alike in that we harbor no grandiose wishes; Aunt Yifen hopes that I will be her cosmetician, and I only hope to use my talents to create the "most perfectly serene cadaver," one that will be gentler and calmer than all others, just as though death were truly the most beautiful sleep of all. Actually, even if I am successful, it will be nothing more than a game to kill a little time amidst the boredom of life; isn't the entirety of human existence meaningless anyway? All my efforts constitute nothing more than an exercise in futility; if I someday manage to create the "most perfectly serene cadaver," will I gain any rewards from it? The dead know nothing, and all my efforts will surely go unnoticed by the family of the deceased. Clearly, I will not hold an exhibition to display to the public my cosmetic skills and innovations. Even less likely is the prospect that anyone will debate, compare, analyze, or hold a forum to discuss my cosmetic job on the deceased; and even if they did, so what? It would cause as much of a stir as the buzzing of insects. My work is purely and simply a game played for the benefit of myself in my workroom. Why then have I bothered to form this hope in the first place? More than likely to provide a stimulus for me to go on working, because mine is a lonely profession: no peers, no audience, and, naturally, no applause. When I'm working, I can only hear the faint sound of my own breathing; in a room filled with supine bodies—male and female—I alone am breathing softly. It's gotten to the point where I imagine I can hear the sounds of my own heart grieving and sighing, and when the hearts of others cease producing sounds of lament, the sounds of my own heart intensify. Yesterday I decided to do the cosmetic work on a young couple who had died in a love-inspired suicide pact, and as I gazed into the sleeping face of the young man, I realized that this was my chance to create the "most perfectly serene cadaver." His eyes were closed, his lips were pressed lightly together, and there was a pale scar on his left temple. He truly looked as though he were only sleeping very peacefully. In all my years of working on thousands of faces, many of which had fretful, distressed looks on them, the majority appearing quite hideous, I had done what I felt was most appropriate to improve their looks, using needle and thread or makeup to give them an appearance of unlimited gentleness. But words cannot describe the peaceful look on the face of the boy I saw yesterday, and I wondered if his suicide should be viewed as an act of joy. But then I felt that I was being deceived by appearances, and I believed instead that his had been an act of extreme weakness; I knew that, considering my position, I should have nothing to do with anyone who lacked the courage to resist the forces of Fate. So not only did I abandon all thoughts of using him to create the "most perfectly serene cadaver," I refused to even work on him, turning both him and the girl who had joined him in stupidly resigning themselves to Fate's whims over to Aunt Yifen to let her carefully repair the cheeks that had been scalded by the force of the powerful poison they had ingested.

Everyone is familiar with Aunt Yifen's past, because there are some around who personally witnessed it. Aunt Yifen was still young at the time, and she not only liked to sing as she worked, but she talked to the cadavers who lay in front of her, as though they were her friends. It wasn't until later that she became so uncommunicative. Aunt Yifen was in the habit of telling her sleeping friends everything that was in her heart—she never kept a diary—letting her monologues stand as a daily record of her life. The people who slept in her presence were mankind's finest audience: they listened to her voluble outpourings for the longest time, yet her secrets were always completely safe with them. She told them how she had met a young man and how they had shared the happiness of all young lovers whenever they were together, even though there were times when they had occasional ups and downs. In those days Aunt Yifen went to a school of cosmetics once a week, rain or shine, fifty weeks a year, to learn new techniques, until she had mastered all that the instructor could teach her. But even when the school informed her that there was nothing left for her to study, she persisted in asking if there weren't some new techniques that they could pass on to her. Her interest in cosmetology was that keen, almost as though it were inborn, and her friends were sure that someday she would open a grand salon somewhere. But no, she merely applied this knowledge of hers to the bodies of the people who slept in front of her. Her young lover knew nothing of any of this, for he was convinced that physical beauty was a natural desire of all girls, and that this particular one was simply fonder of cosmetics than most. That is, until that fateful day when she brought him along and showed him where she worked, pointing out the bodies that lay in the room and telling him that although hers was a lonely profession, in a place like this one encountered no worldly bickerings, and that no petty jealousies, hatreds, or disputes over personal fame or gain existed; when these people entered the world of darkness, peace and gentleness settled over each and every one of them. He was shocked beyond belief; never in his wildest dreams had he thought that she could be a woman like this, one engaged in this sort of occupation. He had loved her, had been willing to do anything for her, vowing that he would never leave her, no matter what, and that they would grow old together, their mutual love enduring until death. But his courage failed him, his nerve abandoned him there among the bodies of people who could no longer speak and who had lost the ability to breathe. He let out a loud yell, turned on his heel, and ran, flinging open every door that stood in his way. Many people saw him in a state of complete shock as he fled down the street. Aunt Yifen never saw him again. People sometimes overheard her talking to her silent friends in her workroom: Didn't he say he loved me? Didn't he say he would never leave me? What was it that suddenly frightened him so? Later on, Aunt Yifen grew more and more uncommunicative. Maybe she had already said everything she wanted to say, or maybe since her silent friends already knew all about her, there was no need to say anymore—there truly are many things that never need to be spoken. When Aunt Yifen was teaching me her consummate skills, she told me what had happened. It was I whom she had chosen as her apprentice, not my younger brother, and although there were other factors involved, the major reason had been that I was not a timid person.

Are you afraid?

She asked.

Not at all.

I said.

Are you timid?

She asked.

Not at all.

I said.

Aunt Yifen selected me as her successor because I was not afraid. She had a premonition that my fate would be the same as hers, and neither of us could explain how we grew to be so much alike, although it may have had its origins in the fact that neither of us was afraid. There was no fear in either one of us. When Aunt Yifen was telling me about what had happened to her, she said: I will always believe that there have to be others somewhere who are like us, people who are unafraid. This was before she had become so uncommunicative; she told me to stand by her side and watch how she reddened lips that had already become rigid, and how she worked gently on a pair of long-staring eyes until she had coaxed them into restful sleep. At the time she still talked now and then to her sleeping friends: And you, why were you afraid? Why do people who are falling in love have so little faith in love? Why do they not have courage in their love? Among Aunt Yifen's sleeping friends were many who had been timid and cowardly, and they were even quieter than the others. She knew certain things about her sleeping friends, and sometimes, as she powdered the face of a girl with bangs on her forehead, she would say to me: *Ai! Ai!* What a weak girl she was. She gave up the man she loved just so she could be considered a filial daughter. Aunt Yifen knew that this girl over here had placed herself into Fate's hands, of her own accord, out of a sense of gratitude, while that one over there had done the same by meekly accepting her lot. She talked about them not as though they had been living, feeling, thinking human beings, but merely pieces of merchandise.

What a horrible job!

My friends said.

Making up the faces of dead people! My God!

My friends said.

I wasn't the least bit afraid, but my friends were. They disliked my eyes because I often used them to look into the eyes of the dead, and they disliked my hands because I often used them to touch the hands of the dead. At first it was just dislike, but it gradually evolved into fear, pure and simple; not only that, the dislike and fear that at first involved only my eyes and hands later on included everything about me. I watched every one of them drift away from me, like wild animals before a forest fire or farmers before a swarm of locusts. Why are you afraid? I asked them. It's a job that someone has to do. Is it that I'm not good enough at what I do, or that I'm not professional enough? But I gradually grew to accept my situation—I got used to being lonely. So many people search for jobs that promise sweetness and warmth, wanting their lives to be filled with flowers and stars. But how does a life of flowers and stars give one the chance to take firm strides in life? I have virtually no friends left today; a touch of my hands reminds them of a deep and distant land of ice and cold, while a look into my eyes produces innumerable images of silent floating spirits, and so they have become afraid. There is nothing that can make them look back, not even the possibility that there is warmth in my hands, that my eyes can shed tears, or that I am warmhearted. And so I began to be more and more like Aunt Yifen, my only remaining friends being the bodies of the deceased lying in front of me. I surprised myself by breaking the silence around me as I said to them: Have I told you that tomorrow I'm going to bring someone named Xia here to meet you? He asked me if you would object, and I told him you wouldn't. Was I right in saying that? So tomorrow Xia will be here, and I think I know how it's all going to end, because my fate and Aunt Yifen's are one and the same. I expect to see Xia as his very soul will take wing the moment he steps foot in here. *Ai!* We cause each other's souls to take wing, but in different ways. I will not be startled by what happens, because the outcome has already been clear to me by a variety of omens. Xia once said to me: Your face is so natural. Yes, my face is natural, and a natural face lacks the power to remove someone else's fear of things.

I once entertained the thought of changing my occupation; is it possible that I am incapable of doing the kinds of work that other women do? Granted that I'm not qualified to be a teacher, a nurse, or a secretary or clerk in an office building, but does that mean I can't work as a saleswoman in a shop, or sell bakery products, or even be a maid in someone's home? A woman like me needs only a roof over her head and three square meals a day, so there must be someplace I could fit in. Honestly speaking, with my skills I could easily find work as a cosmetician for brides-to-be, but the very thought that lips I was applying color to could open to reveal a smile stops me cold. What would be going through my mind at a time like that? Too many memories keep me from working at that occupation, which is so similar to the one I have now. I wonder, if I did change jobs, would the color return to my pale face and hands? Would the smell of formaldehyde that has penetrated to my very bones completely disappear? And what about the job I have now, should I keep Xia completely in the dark about it? Hiding the past from a loved one is dishonest, even though there are countless girls in the world who will do anything to cover up their loss of chastity and the authentic number of years they have lived. But I find people like that despicable. I would have to tell Xia that for a long time I had done cosmetic work on the sleeping bodies of the deceased. Then he would know and would have to acknowledge what sort of woman I am. He'd know that the unusual odor on my body is not perfume, but formaldehyde, and that the reason I wear white so often is not symbolic of purity, but a means of making it more convenient for going to and coming from work. But all of this is as significant as a few drops of water in a vast ocean. Once Xia learns that my hands often touch the bodies of the deceased, will he still be willing to hold my hand as we cross a fast-flowing stream? Will he let me cut his hair for him, or tie his tie? Will he be able to bear my gazing intently at him? Will he be able to lie down in my presence without fear? I think he will be afraid, extremely afraid, and like all my friends, his initial shock will turn into dislike and then fear, and he will turn away from me. Aunt Yifen once said: There can be no fear where love is concerned. But I know that although what many people call love is unyielding and indomitable on the surface, it is actually extraordinarily fragile and pliable; puffed up courage is really nothing but a layer of sugar-coating. Aunt Yifen said to me: Maybe Xia is not a timid person. That's one of the reasons why I never went into detail with him about my occupation. Naturally, another reason was that I'm not very good at expressing myself, and maybe I'd botch what I wanted to say, or I'd distort what I hoped to express to him by choosing the wrong place or time or mood. My not making it clear to Xia that it is not brides-to-be whom I make up is, in actuality, a sort of test: I want to observe his reaction when he sees the subjects I work on. If he is afraid, then he'll just have to be afraid. If he turns and flees, then I'll just tell my sleeping friends: Nothing ever really happened at all.

Can I see how you work?

He asked.

That shouldn't be a problem.

I said.

So here I am, sitting in the corner of a coffee shop waiting for Xia to arrive.

I spent some of this time carefully thinking things over: Maybe I'm not being fair to Xia by doing it this way: If he feels frightened by the work I do, is that his fault? Why should he be more courageous than the others? Why does there have to be any relationship between a fear of the dead and timidity where love is concerned? The two may be totally unrelated. My parents died while I was still young, and I was reared by Aunt Yifen. Both my younger brother and I were orphans. I don't know very much about my parents, and the few things I have learned were told to me later by Aunt Yifen. I remember her telling me that my father was a cosmetician for the deceased before he married my mother. When they were making their plans to get married, he asked her: Are you afraid? No, I'm not, she said. I believe that the reason I'm not afraid is that I take after my mother—her blood flows in my veins. Aunt Yifen said to me that my mother lives on in her memory because of what she had once said: I'm not afraid, and love is the reason. Perhaps that's why my mother lives on in my memory too, however faintly, even though I can no longer recall what she looked or sounded like. But I believe that just because she was my mother and that she said that love had kept her from being afraid does not mean that I have the right to demand the same attitude of everyone else. Maybe I ought to be hardest on myself for accepting my fate from the time I was a child, and for making this occupation that others find so hard to accept my life's work. Men everywhere like women who are gentle, warm, and sweet, and such women are expected to work at jobs that are intimate, graceful, and elegant. But my job is cold and ghostly dark, and I'm sure that my entire body has long been tainted by that sort of shadowy cast. Why would a man who exists in a world of brightness want to be friendly with a woman surrounded by darkness? When he lies down beside her, could he avoid thinking that this is a person who regularly comes into contact with cadavers, and when her hands brush up against his skin, would that remind him that these are hands that for a long time have rubbed the hands of the dead? *Ai! Ai!* A woman like me is actually unsuitable for any man's love. I think that I myself am to blame for all that has happened, so why don't I just get up and leave and return to my workplace; I have never know anyone by the name of Xia, and he will forget that he once had such a woman for a friend, a cosmetician who made up the faces of brides-to-be. But it's probably too late for that now. I see him there through the window, crossing the street and walking this way. What's that in his hand? What a large bouquet of flowers! What's the occasion? Is it someone's birthday? I see him enter the coffee shop; he spots me sitting in this shadowy corner. The sun is shining brightly outside, and he has brought some of it in with him, for the sun's rays are reflected off of his white shirt. He is just like his name, Xia—eternal summer.

Hey, happy Sunday!

He says.

These flowers are for you.

He says.

He is so happy. He sits down and has a cup of coffee. We have had so many happy days together. But what is happiness, after all? Happiness is fleeting. There is such sadness in my heart. From here it is only a walk of three hundred paces before we arrive at my workplace. After that the same thing will happen that happened years ago. A man will come flying through that door as though his very soul had taken leave of him, and he will be followed by the eyes of the curious until he disappears from view. Aunt Yifen said: Maybe somewhere there is a man of true courage who is unafraid. But I know that this is just an assumption, and when I saw Xia crossing the street heading this way, a huge bouquet of flowers in his hand, I already knew, for this was truly a bad omen. *Ai! Ai!* A woman like me is actually unsuitable for any man's love; perhaps I should say to my sleeping friends: Aren't we all the same, you and I? The decades fly by in the blink of an eye, and no matter what the reason, there's no need for anyone to shock anyone else out of their senses. The bouquet of flowers Xia brought into the coffee shop with him is so very, very beautiful; he is happy, but I am laden with grief. He doesn't know that in our profession flowers symbolize eternal parting.

Reunion

Shi Shuqing

Translated by Jeanne Larsen

BY THE TIME she rushes across the harbor to the Regent Hotel, Zhang Jing is already forty minutes late. But Qiu Cuiping answers the door in her bathrobe.

"So you've come after all, Zhang Jing," she says. "I thought maybe you were avoiding your old college friends now that you're a Hong Kong lady."

"Things were really hectic this afternoon—I couldn't get away. And there was a traffic jam in the Harbor Tunnel."

At noon, a group from a "Hainan Island in Seven Days" tour rushed to Zhang Jing's travel agency to complain the minute they got off their plane: the hotels hadn't had enough hot water for baths, the meals were cold, and they wanted their money back. After they wrangled all afternoon—with no results— some reporters arrived, having heard that something was up. The complainers crowded around to give a full account to the press.

". . . even the TV reporters came. I snuck out by the back stairs, leaving Wu, my manager, to answer their questions."

Tossing her purse aside, Zhang Jing collapses, slouching on the sofa in front of the window. "And then I ran into the afternoon rush hour, and had to fight my way across the harbor."

"Look at you! A regular superwoman!" Qiu Cuiping is surprised. "I thought you just worked to keep from getting bored. I didn't realize you really *did* things!"

Some time back, when Qiu Cuiping was elbow-deep in her first baby's diapers, she heard that Zhang Jing had met the son of a prominent overseas Chinese at the Citibank in Taibei and had married him and moved off to be a Hong Kong lady. Right up until this afternoon when Cuiping got off the plane and pried Zhang Jing's office phone number out of her Filipina housekeeper, she still had the impression that this old classmate who'd risen in society was definitely a celebrity type, a local star who'd raised the capital to start up a nouvelle cuisine

---

The original appeared in *Jiushi niandai* (The nineties) (December 1986).

Cantonese restaurant or open a jewelry store in the shopping district, flourishing her scissors before cutting a satin ribbon in front of the press on opening day.

"That woman in your office is a real terror. I called five or six times, but she refused to put me through to you. Said you were in a meeting."

Zhang Jing rubs her temples as hard as she can with both hands. "That tour group was an incredible hassle. It was a little foggy the day they left, and the equipment at Haikou Airport on Hainan isn't exactly up-to-date. One clump of fog didn't disperse, so they couldn't take a chance on landing. No radar."

"No kidding? It's that bad on the mainland? How rotten! Forget about a little fog, last year when I did my big Europe trip, there was a blizzard in Munich and the snow was piled up really high on both sides of the runway, but everybody flew just the same—"

"All in all, more than a hundred people got stuck that day, and now they've charged into my agency, pounding on the counter and demanding that each one of them be refunded a hundred dollars to make up for the loss of the day—"

Qiu Cuiping's little eyes widen. "You were dealing with those people over fifty or a hundred Hong Kong dollars?! I can't believe it. Zhang Jing, what's the good of money if you don't enjoy it? You brought all this on yourself. And just look at how tired you are!"

"Oh, I was born to be a workhorse. And whose fault is that?" Zhang Jing looks around the room. "Let's not talk about that mess. Your coming to Hong Kong is a rare treat, Cuiping. And this room's not bad at all. The Regent's certainly first class."

"It's nothing special. My husband's secretary sent a telex reserving me a suite, but they were all booked." Qiu Cuiping's features have had a pinched look since the day she was born, but when she thinks about this particular grievance, even her eyebrows squeeze together. "If I'd known earlier that you ran a travel agency, I could have called on you. You've got good connections—it would have been easy for you to get a reservation!"

"A suite at the Regent for one night runs—" Zhang Jing swallows the rest of the sentence and revises her estimate of the college classmate she hasn't seen for so long.

"How much? Ten thousand H.K.?" Crossing her legs, Qiu Cuiping sits on the bed like a hill of flesh and waves one plump little hand in a spendthrift gesture. "My Shiming makes money like he was printing it. It's a sin not to help him spend it."

"Really!" Zhang Jing responds without thinking. "Taiwan's economy has sprung back to life this past couple years. It's easy to make money."

"Shiming just opened another factory. With the ones in Taoyuan and Zhongli, that makes five altogether!" She spreads her fingers, counting as she speaks, and waving her hand for emphasis.

Zhang Jing's expression reveals nothing.

"Congratulations, Cuiping. You've come a long way in the seven or eight years since we saw each other."

"You haven't seen the way Shiming works all the time. He barely stops to eat. If you ask me, he acts like we haven't got a cent!"

"I forget just now what Shiming manufactures."

"Plastic toys, for export."

"Every year, Hong Kong's the world's biggest exporter of plastic toys. Think you can beat us?"

"You've got your turf and we've got ours. Last year our sales ran to two hundred million N.T."* Cuiping pauses, then adds casually, "Not including the new factory."

In her heart, Zhang Jing doubts this offhand reckoning, but what she says is, "That's terrific!"

"These days, whenever I go out, I treat myself to the best. Food, clothes, places to stay—first class all the way."

Head high, Qiu Cuiping declaims this as if to spite herself. Only Zhang Jing understands why she's like this; she knows better than anyone about Qiu Cuiping's past.

"You're with an old friend, Cuiping, so save your breath. You absolutely reek of money. No one's going to put up with this kind of talk."

At first Zhang Jing thinks Cuiping has taken offense, but—to Zhang Jing's surprise—she laughs and sets her hands on her hips, saying in an ostentatious voice, "So I'm nouveau riche! Who cares? Zhang Jing, you're a travel agent. Use your connections to help me out a little. Get me a suite by tomorrow."

Zhang Jing resents Cuiping's dictatorial manner. "I'll have my secretary ask for you in the morning," she says.

"Hong Kong visas are harder than hell to get. I've made up my mind to have a good time for once. Zhang Jing, suggest something new to do for fun. Let me expand my horizons. A person could die of boredom in Taibei!"

Leafing through some *This Week in Hong Kong* magazines on the table, she continues. "There's a lot more going on here than in Taibei. One social event after another—a fashion show by a European designer, a charity ball for the Benevolent Association. . . . Oh, that champagne party after David Bowie's concert—some magazine said all the guests had to dress completely in white. Is that really true?"

"I don't know. I wasn't there."

"Huh," she says in a slightly disappointed tone. "You didn't go. But didn't you hear? Aren't the wives here like in Taibei? News spreads like wildfire there."

"Young lady, look at me. When am I going to have the free time to notice whether people wore white or black?"

---

*About U.S. $7.4 million.

"I suppose there's always someplace fun to go?" Qiu Cuiping is unwilling to drop the subject.

Zhang Jing feels she really ought to be hospitable. "The French restaurant on the first floor is the best in Hong Kong. I'll try to reserve us a table by the window."

With the efficiency she displays at the travel agency, Zhang Jing first calls home, running through a clear list of instructions for the Filipina servant: get dinner, bathe the two little girls, and put them to bed. Then she makes reservations at La Plume, insisting on a window table with a good view of the harbor.

"I've got a guest from out of town," she says. Hanging up the phone, she turns toward Qiu Cuiping. "I made the reservation for eight-thirty so you'd have plenty of time to fix yourself up."

"Looks like I've got a chance of getting into that suite tomorrow." Cuiping bounces up from the bed. "Zhang Jing, come stay with me for a couple of nights. We'll be happy as a couple of crazies."

"We'll see."

Zhang Jing opens the door of the bathroom and calls out in surprise. Behind the translucent plastic curtain, suds have piled up in the tub like clouds; she can see that they are just about to overflow. The faucet roars like surf and shows no sign of stopping. Qiu Cuiping rushes in barefoot, groping around until she gets the water shut off. The roaring stops, but steam still floats upward.

"Practically a flood!" Qiu Cuiping pats her chest in a self-congratulatory manner, then points to the jars and bottles on the rim of the tub. "Before you got here I was doing an experiment. I bought a bottle of every brand. When I know which one I like best, I'm going to buy a whole lot to take back with me."

Zhang Jing doubles over with laughter. "So how many bubble baths have you taken this afternoon?"

"I'm not sure. If you hadn't shown up I was going to try this kind, the lime-scented one."

"Cuiping, do you remember our landlady on Greenfield Street? The one with legs like a crane's?"

Their junior year in college, the two moved from the women's dormitory in the hills to a district in the city, renting rooms in the same house. The landlady lived alone except for her German shepherd, and her thin legs really were straight and long, just like a crane's. In the winter she heated bath water for them on a stove in the yard where her green pomegranates grew. Qiu Cuiping, who'd grown up in a village in Jiayi County, would stay curled up in bed with a novel and let the water on the stove boil over with a hissing sound. Finally the landlady, having finished her own bath, would haul the kettle of boiling water to the bathroom herself, yelling as she went, "Hot water, pouring out like rain. What a waste!"

Zhang Jing used to think the whole thing was pretty funny, but Qiu Cuiping would raise her face from her novel and say, "Whenever my old grannie back in the country saw a scrap of paper in the road, she'd always bend over and pick it up.''

Now, in the bathroom of the Regent Hotel in Hong Kong, when Zhang Jing brings up the events of more than ten years ago, Qiu Cuiping's whole face goes vague.

"Huh. Is that what we used to do?''

A feeling of loneliness comes over Zhang Jing.

"Whenever you come back to Taibei, come see me in my new place in Tianmu. We just finished decorating last month. All the bathroom fixtures are imported from the United States, a kidney-shaped tub, lots of black marble. . . .'' Stretching out her polished toenails to poke at a heap of foam, Qiu Cuiping says dreamily, "From now on, my bubble-baths in Tianmu will be like in a Hollywood movie. . . .''

"When did you turn into the kind of person who likes to take baths?''

"Miss Guo, my beautician, is always telling me that when I'm feeling stressed I should soak in a hot tub. Once I close my eyes I couldn't care less if the sky falls. She says I'm too high strung; even when she massages me one muscle at a time, they don't relax. . . .''

"Cut it out! If someone like you isn't happy with life, other people might as well have thrown themselves out the window five hundred times already!''

"Zhang Jing, there're a lot of things I could tell you. . . .''

"Such as? Oh, Cuiping, your nail polish is chipped!''

Qiu Cuiping cradles one hand in the other. "Damn it,'' she says in a broken-hearted voice, "I chipped it on the faucet.''

"Look at your eyebrows—they're all squinched up! Now I know the real reason you're unhappy!''

Cuiping doesn't catch Zhang Jing's sarcasm. "I got bored, waiting for you, so I went down for a shampoo, pedicure, the works. I guess I tipped too much—the whole way out people were holding doors for me, and pressing the elevator button. Now it's all ruined.''

"You rich women from Taiwan think Hong Kong dollars are play money. It's crazy, the way you spend. You break all the rules. The next time I go for a shampoo will be a disaster!''

"You go to that stylist? The place was full of foreigners sashaying around.''

Zhang Jing falters. She strokes her ear-length bob self-consciously.

"The one who combed me out had green eyes, like a cat's,'' Qiu Cuiping continues. "He didn't blink the whole time. His shirt was unbuttoned and beneath the gold chain he wore, his whole chest was covered with hair creeping downward. . . .'' Her neck shrinks back as she speaks.

Her arm, too, is starting to relax; Zhang Jing slaps at it. "Don't be naughty!'' she says. "Besides, they're all gay.''

"You're kidding! A waste of heaven's gifts.''

The two women squeeze together in the bathroom, laughing wildly at the top of their voices. It's as if they're back in the old days, talking about boyfriends again.

From their seats by the window at La Plume, they can see small lights glimmering here and there on the distant black surface of the sea. Every time a boat sails past, Qiu Cuiping lets out a sound of surprise. "They're just like a cartoon movie," she says. "Slipping by without even a whisper—"

Sipping at her half-glass of white wine, Zhang Jing feels the collar of her blue pantsuit; it is stiff and rubs uncomfortably against her neck. She wishes she'd had time to go back and change into a dinner dress that would fit the restaurant's elegant atmosphere.

Just now she took advantage of the time while Qiu Cuiping was getting dressed to close herself up in the bathroom. She took out the cosmetics she carries with her and put on fresh makeup, making sure to apply a thick layer of undereye concealer. As a career woman, she often has to rush straight to social engagements after getting off work; her purse is full of emergency accessories. This evening, she tied on a white Dior silk scarf patterned with violets, in an attempt to add a dash of charm to her pantsuit, which is much too plain for the occasion.

But when Zhang Jing emerged from the bathroom, Qiu Cuiping's outfit made her stare stupidly in surprise. Cuiping wore a sequined evening gown of the sort that has just come into fashion; it flashed red and blue in the lamplight.

"Why on earth are you so dressed up, Cuiping?" she said. "It's just the restaurant downstairs—"

"Didn't you say it was the best in Hong Kong?"

That one sentence shut Zhang Jing up.

"You think I'm a tourist—fine," Cuiping continued. "I'm not afraid to step out in front of people." Wrapping one arm around Zhang Jing, Cuiping grabbed her matching beaded purse and dragged her old roommate downstairs to admire this new world.

For half the evening now, Zhang Jing has felt a sense of defeat. But the minute she thinks about making her escape, she decides she has to stick with it. Cuiping's stagey sequined get-up reminds Zhang Jing of the Taiwanese opera stars the two of them saw down south once when they were young: flashing crystal-bright and gaudy from head to toe.

The atmosphere tonight is soft and easy. On the dance floor a number of bodies, their armpits shaved bare, their ivory arms draped around their male companions' necks, cuddle close in response to the urging of the music. The redhead sitting sideways at the next table laughs wildly; her back is bare, and her black evening dress so low-cut that you can nearly see her buttocks.

Qiu Cuiping sticks out her tongue.

"If you're still afraid that I'm overdressed, Zhang Jing, take a look at that!"

"She's like you—a tourist!"

"How can you tell?"

"You forget what I do for a living."

A sampan slowly wavers past; even at night, the woman in old-style shirt and trousers standing at the bow wears her bamboo hat. Zhang Jing recalls Mrs. Andersen, who left just yesterday, a society woman from the eastern United States traveling around the world with her husband, a recently retired judge. She fell in love with sampans like this one at first sight.

"Buy one for me and send it back to Pennsylvania!" Mrs. Andersen said, stroking her chin. "It could be my little souvenir of Hong Kong." Then she told Zhang Jing that she'd decided to donate a sampan to her hometown, an old city in Pennsylvania.

"Think of it, Nancy." She used Zhang Jing's English name. "A little boat with its sail spread, floating on the river back home. It'll have such an air about it—"

"Simply impossible," Zhang Jing laughs now, telling the story to Cuiping, "But she still handed me the job with absolute seriousness. American ladies!"

"Huh! So you don't think it's a good idea?" Qiu Cuiping points at the sampan that is sailing by just then. "One exactly like that one, with a brown sail—buy it and send it back to Taiwan. It would positively create a sensation!" But then she sighs regretfully. "The pity is, there's no river near Tianmu. Waishuang Stream's too far away—"

Zhang Jing assumes she is joking, so she plays along, adding, "Great. If you do buy one, you can save yourself a lot of trouble. You won't even have to take the plane, just hop on board your sampan and make your way back through the Taiwan Strait. I hope you have favorable winds—"

"No problem with that. My father used to take a fishing boat—just about that size, I guess—from Lugang over to Quanzhou on the mainland. When the wind and waves picked up, the crew would get seasick and throw up, leaving a trail of noodles—"

The brown-sailed sampan swings about, fading away in the darkness.

"The two sides of the Strait . . ." Zhang Jing is moved. "Have you kept in touch with Jingwen? She is arriving sometime in the next couple of days. Couldn't get a Hong Kong visa, so the best she can do is stop over on the way back from Bangkok to meet her father."

"He's coming out from the mainland?"

"Uh-huh. From Lanzhou up in Gansu, on the Yellow River."

"The Yellow River . . ."

Zhang Jing stares out at the black waters beyond the window for quite some time before she hears Qiu Cuiping's voice say, "Taiwan and the United States are still better. You're free to get ahead."

Cuiping mentions several old school friends and is surprised to learn that Zhang Jing knows nothing of them. ". . . Li Wenwen's husband gave up on literature and went into business. He's opened up a chain of motels in the States, twenty or thirty maybe. He's really made it big! Wang Lan switched over to computer science. Her husband has an electronics factory in San Jose with more than a thousand workers. Pretty good, huh? And the ones who've stayed in Taiwan haven't done badly either. Guo Hualing really knows what to do with money. Last year she founded a hospital.''

"I didn't realize everyone had done so well.''

"Zhang Jing, I'm gong to be frank with you. You didn't know it, but back then, when we heard that you were marrying a guy from an aristocratic family and moving here to Hong Kong, we could have died of jealousy. When we saw your engagement ring we—Oh, young people are so funny!''

The diamond ring on Zhang Jing's finger glitters somberly in the candlelight; it has been dull for a long time now. Qiu Cuiping glances at it carelessly, giving no sign of recognition. "And your husband? You're not going to keep him hidden away, are you? Get him to come over and go out for a good time with us. It's still early, anyway. He must know where to go for some fun.''

"He . . . he's out of town on business. In Sydney. He's really busy these days. He may be getting back tomorrow. . . .''

The crowd is thinning; disappointed, Qiu Cuiping leaves the restaurant. Taking the marble staircase, she steps into the mirror-bright lobby.

A group of young men and women carrying an assortment of canvas bags parades past, holding their heads high and stepping with dancers' steps. At the head of the column, a young woman in a white skirt carries a bowl of purple orchids in both hands; she greets the world as if taking a curtain call, her neck erect, her manner relaxed. With a proud smile, she crosses the lobby.

The young woman's walk catches Zhang Jing's attention. She can't help staring at the white skirt and its youthful flutter. "Come to my place tomorrow afternoon, Cuiping,'' she says. "I want you to meet my little girls. The older one's already nearly up to my shoulder.''

The next day is Saturday. Zhang Jing goes off to the travel agency in the morning. Manager Wu, who fielded the complaining tourists' questions, hasn't come in to work. Jenny, who took the group to Hainan, grabs Zhang Jing and starts to air her grievances.

"They were a gang of wild men! That fat guy who was leading them threatened Manager Wu. He said if we didn't give them the compensation they were demanding, they'd break the place up. But their accusations were a bunch of damn lies! And all we got for supper was hamburgers. We were here dealing with them till eleven-thirty.''

"So how did things turn out?''

"Manager Wu wouldn't give in. Said it wasn't our fault. Eventually things got so rowdy that the security guard came up a couple of times to see what was going on. Manager Wu tried to get hold of you, but no luck. It was completely—''

"What happened?''

"We had to promise to refund each of them a hundred bucks. Twenty or thirty have already come by this morning."

Zhang Jing pats her chest and goes into her private office. She can still hear Jenny's whiny voice complaining to the others in the office. "That fat guy's family was the worst. They wanted me to wake them up every morning at five. Said it took their two girls that much time to get dressed. . . ."

"They were making trouble for you on purpose, not letting you get a good night's sleep."

Zhang Jing stands for a moment in front of her desk. She planned to have her secretary call the reservations desk at the Regent Hotel and see about getting a suite for Cuiping. But what she actually says is: "Jenny, after you finish your overtime, take a couple of days off."

Grabbing the car keys from the desktop, Zhang Jing leaves the agency and drives her Mitsubishi across the harbor.

As usual on weekend afternoons, the driveway in front of the Regent is crowded with cars. Qiu Cuiping waits under the portico, squinting hard at the line of Rolls Royces beside the fountain. The hood ornaments, so redolent of luxury, seem to have dazzled her vision.

Every stitch she has on today is new. On her feet, she wears three-inch heels of red and blue patent leather. The skirt of her crimson-flowered silk dress doesn't have a single wrinkle; it has obviously just been put on. She carries a Nina Ricci shopping bag. Zhang Jing feels a protest rise inside her. Having learned her lesson last night in the French restaurant, she put extra effort into today's outfit. When she finally stood in front of her mirror, she wore a designer t-shirt and an Yves Saint-Laurent skirt of checked linen. Her cream-colored flats, she decided, would be good for walking around on a shopping expedition.

She hadn't thought Qiu Cuiping would wear a garden-party outfit like this one. Zhang Jing waves to Cuiping from inside the car, but her friend doesn't respond. This irritates Zhang Jing; heatedly, she blows the horn, and Qiu Cuiping turns her head toward the sound. After recognizing Zhang Jing, she takes a look at the car. She hesitates a moment before running over.

"The hotel uses Rolls Royces to transport its guests." Zhang Jing waits until Cuiping is inside the car before speaking lightly. "When you go back home, you can reserve one of the newer ones to take you to the airport, to show your good taste—if you want to waste the money!"

Bobbing her head, Qiu Cuiping takes careful note of what Zhang Jing has said.

Zhang Jing takes a quick glance at the shopping bag by Cuiping's feet and adds, "The day's barely started, and you've already got a harvest!"

"It's my old dress and shoes in a bag. I'm just too lazy to take them back to my room."

"No time to lose." Zhang Jing smiles slightly. "You put them on as soon as you bought them?"

"Even the saleswoman laughed at my impatience. She could tell I'm from Taiwan!"

Whenever there is a sale at the Ricci boutique, the salesclerks take on a completely different manner, wiping the mocking look off their faces. After Christmas last year, Zhang Jing bought an apricot knit dress at 90 percent off. The sleeves and neck have black pleated borders, and the tight belt bears the maker's mark in exquisite embroidery. When Zhang Jing wears it to social events, she loves to brush the belt accidentally on purpose. Her chief concern is that other people won't recognize the thing for what it is, an authentic designer piece.

"You came too early," Zhang Jing says. "You should have waited for the big sales in July. I always—"

The look Qiu Cuiping gives her is surprised, uncomprehending.

"What I mean is—" Zhang Jing quickly changes what she has to say. "Whenever there are big sales here, the news gets around fast in Taiwan and everyone comes over to pick out what they like. Then they send back box after box and resell them at huge profits. That's what I've heard, anyway. . . ." As she speaks, her mouth goes dry. She feels a kind of contempt at her own insincerity.

Before her husband's success, Qiu Cuiping's two hands were roughened by housework. Now they rest one atop the other on her knees while she looks out the window as if the subject has nothing to do with her. "Huh," she says. "If people want to do a little petty smuggling, that's their business. But I'm just not willing to fight the mob!"

"I'll take you to The Landmark. They've got every famous maker in the world under one roof. There should be enough for you to buy there!" Then Zhang Jing adds, "I go to some of the shops all the time, so I'm pretty familiar with the place."

After crossing the harbor, as she is parking the car, she can't control herself any longer. "Cuiping," she says. "Why don't you take off your new shoes? Walking around shopping can be exhausting. I feel sorry for you, traipsing about on stilts like that!" The minute the words are out of her mouth, she regrets them.

Qiu Cuiping bends down and pulls the clothes she wore downstairs that morning from the paper bag. Tossing them into the back seat, she takes out the shoes. "Wait till I've gotten tired. I can change then."

"You're just asking for trouble. Well, it'll serve you right!"

Zhang Jing deliberately steps out in long strides. Qiu Cuiping follows, waddling behind her like a goose.

Although it's the weekend, the designer boutiques in The Landmark are deserted. People crowd around the fountain instead, listening to the musicians on the red-carpeted stage play "The Last Rose of Summer" without the slightest touch of melancholy. The faces above the performers' Scottish tartans are all yellow.

Qiu Cuiping pushes her way up to the front of the crowd to see what's so interesting. But when she gets there, she discovers that the crowd of listeners around her are petit bourgeois types in distinctly common clothes. Feeling that she has done something beneath her dignity, she turns back and pulls Zhang Jing through the door of a high-fashion clothing shop.

"Huh. Armani. My husband's brand." Thereupon, Qiu Cuiping buys everything: handkerchiefs, socks, shorts, neckties, a belt, shirts, and an overcoat. She carelessly adds two pairs of baggy pantaloons and winks at Zhang Jing. "Let him be in style for once!" With a forced sigh, she adds, "The only name Shiming recognizes is Giorgio Armani. Last year, with the best of intentions, I went to Paris and bought him silk shirts from Yves Saint-Laurent. People say you have to buy them at the main store in Paris if you want to get the real French-made ones. But he never wore them, not even once. I was so angry! He just doesn't know about anyone but Armani. . . ."

When it comes time to pay the bill, Zhang Jing turns over a perfectly ordinary-looking shirt. The price is more than six thousand Hong Kong dollars.*

"Cuiping, am I right in thinking that there are a lot of people like your husband in Taiwan who choose their clothes by the brand name?"

Qiu Cuiping signs the bill without really looking at it. "Not necessarily. It depends on the brand. Someone who doesn't recognize anything but Pierre Cardin is obviously hopelessly unsophisticated. But only people who know quality wear Armani. They say it's really top notch."

"I wonder why Taiwan is always behind Hong Kong?" Zhang Jing sees her opportunity. "Armani's been out of style for ages. Nowadays, the world belongs to the Japanese designers. You've really got to wear Miyake Issei if you want to keep up with fashion!"

"Can you buy his things in Hong Kong?" Qiu Cuiping sounds dubious.

Eventually she rejects the Japanese designs as too extreme. "If you wore this stuff in Taiwan, everyone would be convinced you'd lost your mind!"

As she speaks, she strolls into the neighboring shop, an Italian women's clothing store. She shows no inclination to leave. Zhang Jing sits on the store's rattan sofa leafing through fashion magazines, from time to time advising Qiu Cuiping by commenting on her appearance when she emerges from the dressing room.

The saleswomen know from experience that another extravagant customer has arrived from Taiwan and vie with one another in politeness, waiting on Qiu Cuiping as if she were an empress.

In the freshman women's dorm in college, the two of them were assigned to the same room. Back then, Zhang Jing's aunt sent her a white satin floor-length negligee from the United States. In the eyes of college women in Taiwan in the mid-1960s, it was a rare luxury indeed, and Qiu Cuiping begged and begged to be allowed to try it on.

---

*About U.S. $1,000.

Later, the business college moved downtown, and the two of them turned out to be neighbors again. Qiu Cuiping was wild about dancing in those days; she said it was because on the dance floor she could forget everything. The word was that her mother, who had been widowed for years, had finally taken up with men, and that lately there'd been a lot of talk about her in Jiayi.

Zhang Jing saw her once, shortly before New Year's, when she came to Taibei to see her daughter. Her face was far too bright with makeup, but it was her hands, big-knuckled as a man's, that made a real impression on Zhang Jing.

Qiu Cuiping complained volubly about her mother until the money she sent came, whereupon Cuiping spent the best part of her living allowance at the little tailor shop on the corner. She started going to more dances and came up with the idea of borrowing the landlady's sewing machine to avoid being seen in the same two outfits every time she glided across the floor.

She told Zhang Jing about the days when her mother was young: "She used to change a piece of clothing whenever she wore it. I especially remember a lavender silk dress with lotus leaves embroidered on the puff sleeves and around the neckline. Later she tore them all out and I squatted next to the sewing machine and picked up a long ruffled collar. . . ."

"Cuiping, don't borrow the landlady's sewing machine. Let your mother alter your things and mail them back to you—then you'll have plenty of clothes to show off in."

When Qiu Cuiping heard this, her mouth shut without a sound and she went back into her own room.

Later, she met an intern from the Medical College of Taibei who did the tango remarkably well. She spent the whole day first thinking that things might work out with him, then that they couldn't possibly. She complained that the tailor shop on the corner had no sense of style; she simply couldn't go out in their things. She conceived a greater interest than ever before in the negligee Zhang Jing's aunt had sent from the States, and finally she badgered Zhang Jing into lending it to her so she could shine at a party.

Back then Qiu Cuiping had been slender and quite short. Zhang Jing would see her late at night, hovering close by a lamp to take a deep hem in a borrowed skirt. As soon as the dance was over, she'd be busy again, ripping out the hem and fixing the skirt back the way it used to be. A whole semester passed this way—sewing and ripping, sewing and ripping. Zhang Jing couldn't see the worth of it.

When they go to buy makeup, Qiu Cuiping snatches up a silver-gray eyebrow pencil and squints at the price. "Huh. Cheap! At the Sesame Department Store back in Taibei, one of these costs more than a thousand N.T.*—for the same brand. This is unbelievably cheap!"

Holding the eyebrow pencil, she faces the mirror and makes the motions of

---

*Around U.S. $40.

penciling in her brows. "Too bad I can't use it. Zhang Jing, I suppose you've noticed? I've had my eyebrows done. It's quite the thing in Taibei these days. It's like getting a tattoo—once you've made the effort, you never have to mess with them again!"

Yesterday when they first saw each other, Zhang Jing felt that there was something different about Qiu Cuiping, but she couldn't quite say what it was. Tilting her head to one side, Zhang Jing examines her closely. Her chin used to be a little lopsided, and she's gained weight, but those changes aren't so obvious. No, it's the messing around with her eyebrows.

"These days, even false fingernails are nothing unusual," says Qiu Cuiping. "Any style that women can think up, Taibei's got it!"

"Really? People here in Hong Kong laugh and say when women from Taiwan go to Japan for cosmetic surgery, they evidently go to the same doctor, because they all look alike, as if they'd been cast in the same mold!"

"Honestly, Zhang Jing, you talk like you're not from Taiwan yourself!"

After taking all the packages, large and small, to the car, they are driving up Garden Road when Qiu Cuiping suddenly calls out, "Stop a minute, Zhang Jing! I've forgotten to bring presents. If I'm empty-handed when I meet your daughters, their 'auntie' will look like a fool!"

At first Zhang Jing intends to give her a word or two of comfort, but she can see the hill of packages piled up in the back seat. Qiu Cuiping's only concern has been spending money on herself; she hasn't given a thought to the little girls. Seeing her sit there calmly with folded hands, showing no sign of embarrassment, confirms Zhang Jing's assessment: Cuiping said what she did just to say it and figures that's enough. So Zhang Jing decides to keep quiet and not help her extricate herself from her predicament.

Zhang Jing used to know a businessman from Taiwan who traded with the People's Republic through Hong Kong. He insisted on meeting her daughters, and she finally had to give in and promise he could. He asked her over and over what would be a good present to take when he met them. Zhang Jing, feeling like she'd gotten in over her head, said the first thing that came to mind, "Here's a suggestion for you—bring a couple of lollipops!"

In the end, when he came he pinched the little girls' tender faces until they were black and blue, and he showed up completely empty-handed.

"Zhang Jing, what about your husband? When can I meet him?"

"I'll have to ask him. He knows you're here."

"Oh. Didn't you say he was gone?"

"He . . . got back ahead of schedule. Last night just after I got home, he rang the entrance buzzer and scared me silly!"

"Zhang Jing, you two aren't—having problems, are you?"

The light up ahead turns red. Zhang Jing grasps the steering wheel firmly with both hands. As she stares in front of her, a bit of brightness disappears from her eyes. "When you've been married as long as we have, all the rough spots are worn away. Not like the two of you. . . ."

"You have no idea. . . ."

Last night when Zhang Jing got home, the lights in the living room were on. Her husband, hearing the door shut, said in a preoccupied voice, "Is that you?" and then went back to his television show.

Zhang Jing pulled her silk scarf from around her neck, kicked off her shoes, and, turning her back to her husband, sat at the head of the bed to remove her stockings. How long has it been that she's resisted letting Mingzhi see her naked? When she puts on her nightgown, if he's there she shuts herself in the bathroom and buttons every single button. Afterward, she holds the skirt of her nightgown close around her and lies down on the edge of the bed, staring wide-eyed into the darkness. If her husband moves the least bit or rolls over toward her, she jumps up as if startled.

Once again last night she sketched out a plan in the dark: recently, her back has been aching, probably because the bed is too soft. Surely it would help to get a new mattress.

Her husband probably wouldn't object to her plan, so later Zhang Jing rehearsed once again: "Two days ago at the Ocean Terminal I saw a pair of brass twin beds." She would stress the words *a pair of* to test her husband's response. Eventually, she'd gather her courage and say, "I always toss around so. Maybe if we had separate beds—" But in the end, she was so tired she fell asleep after all, and though she moved her lips, she didn't utter a sound.

"Do you remember Qiu Cuiping?" Sitting there at the head of the bed, she continued to keep her back to her husband as usual. "The one who always used to borrow my clothes to go dancing? Her husband was a high school teacher, but he's opened some toy factories and has done quite well for himself. Cuiping's come on a shopping trip and wants to stay in a suite at the Regent!"

She could feel no response from the person behind her.

"I never would have imagined that people would be jealous of me. Cuiping said my travel agency was just something I did to keep busy."

The mirror on the dresser reflected the haircut she'd gotten at the little neighborhood beauty salon. She turned and faced her husband. "I invited her to lunch tomorrow. She really wants to meet you." Then, unaware that she was making mischief, she added, "She's really curious about you!"

"Then let her come and see!"

Her husband's easy-going manner somehow disturbed Zhang Jing. "Actually, I told her you might not be home—"

Ever since her husband's partner had decided to retake the Canadian test for an architect's license and emigrate to Vancouver, their architectural firm near the Happy Valley Racecourse has existed in name only. Every day, Lin Mingzhi shuts himself up in the office, covering the floor with crumpled sketches, and ignoring the telephone. No one knows what he does in there.

Can this be the same person who appeared at the Taibei Citibank on Double-Ten Day?* Back then, he'd just received his architect's diploma in Australia and was getting ready to go back to Hong Kong and enter the fray. He was accompanying his father, who used to amuse himself by writing old-style poetry in his spare time; they'd been invited to come for the national holiday on account of their status as patriotic overseas Chinese. His father had published a collection of poems in Taibei at his own expense with a photo of himself and Chiang Kai-shek as the frontispiece. It was because of this that he'd been mistaken for a leader of the overseas Chinese community.

Zhang Jing was on her way to a date, wearing a dress her aunt had sent from the States; the skirt was as good as new except for the needle marks where Qiu Cuiping had temporarily shortened the hem. Cuiping's intern had married into a rich family, becoming the husband of a woman whose dowry included a nice place uptown on Zhongshan North Road as well as a three-story clinic with all the latest equipment. Qiu Cuiping had stormed off to become the bookkeeper at the Jiayi Farmers' Association and was living as hard a life as her mother's.

Since Lin Mingzhi's stay in Taibei was to be brief, Zhang Jing—who had never let herself be rushed into anything before—hurried to pour out all she had to say. The time they had to get to know one another sped by, and often after they talked, she didn't really know what they'd said. She would hold her face in both hands, smiling without self-confidence.

She'd come to Hong Kong wearing this same uncertain smile.

Thanks to the financial assistance of his father, the part-time poet, part-time real estate speculator, her new husband fixed up an architect's office for himself in the Happy Valley district; everyone who came into the place was surprised and pleased at the way it looked. The architecture magazines predicted that Lin Mingzhi's new concepts in the use of space would lead to real breakthroughs in the population density problem.

Then as if in the course of a single night, construction leapt to unseen heights. The building contractors cast aside Lin Mingzhi's exuberant new ideas, along with his equally promising blueprints. Taking advantage of the buying frenzy, they put up skyscrapers built like cardboard boxes.

Even before the shock of Hong Kong's 1997 change of government hit, her husband was trapped in a forest of cement, with no way out.

Circling the little plaza in front of the bank, the car climbs a steep slope where the slightest inattention means an accident. Zhang Jing mercilessly steps on the gas, ascending a narrow lane. The coarse, weathered wall alongside makes the hillside especially desolate. A sharp left turn: Qiu Cuiping exaggeratedly pats her chest. ''Oh! Slow down a little. I'm getting dizzy.''

''The taxis from Kowloon side don't dare come to the Mid-levels. It's like a maze. Once you come in, you can't get out.''

---

*October 10 is National Day in the Republic of China (Taiwan).

Facing them, a pale blue high-rise built against the soaring cliff overshadows the old-fashioned buildings on either side.

"Are we there?" Qiu Cuiping doesn't understand. "Lucky thing your husband's an architect. Building a new high-rise in a spot like this, aren't you afraid of a price drop? I really don't understand. . . ."

"Isn't Taibei the same? The nice modern houses with yards are hidden away on the back streets surrounded by shanties and noodle stands—"

"It's different now. The residential district out in Tianmu where we live— Oh! We're not there yet?"

The car stops at the end of a gray, colonial-style building. A swing, a see-saw, and toy cars are scattered around the little yard.

"There's a school here?"

"A kindergarten for the neighborhood kids." Zhang Jing opens the iron gate. "My younger daughter goes here. Every day I hear her reading 'The rooster says *cock-a-doodle-do*' in Cantonese."

"She's not learning Mandarin?"

Zhang Jing shakes her head as if it were nothing and climbs the spiral stairs. She hasn't gone far when she hears Qiu Cuiping panting behind her.

"I told you it'd be better walking if you changed your shoes, but you wouldn't listen. We live on the top floor. That should be enough of a climb for you!"

"I'm a guest!" Qiu Cuiping protests loudly, her face flushed.

Sliding her hand along the slick stair-rail, Zhang Jing says, "Mingzhi's partial to these older houses. He likes high ceilings and wide hallways. . . ." She's surprised by her own self-justifying tone.

She wonders if that other exquisite two-story building in another wooded cove on Victoria Peak still has the romantic air it used to. That was where they'd had the home they were so proud of, before the bottom dropped out of the real estate market. In remodeling, her husband had brought all his special skills into play, not overlooking an inch of space. After supper, Zhang Jing would glide down from the dining room, following the guests to the sunken fireplace. There she'd smile and listen quietly to children of high-ranking cadres from the mainland, who guzzled brandy and bragged about how they were going to make use of their positions to force the clearing out of the Eastern Chambers in the old imperial palace in Beijing and convert them into a modern restaurant for foreign tourists.

That wing of the imperial palace is still locked up in darkness, but Zhang Jing and her family had to move. Her husband restored a perfect little archway between the entrance and the living room of their new home. But since then he hasn't had any enthusiasm for working on the place.

Qiu Cuiping accepts a cup a tea from the hands of the dark-skinned Filipina housekeeper, feeling a quiver of nausea at the servant's cheap perfume. Right up until she stood in front of this ordinary living room, Cuiping thought that Zhang

Jing surely lives in a villa up at the Peak, driven around by a crisp-uniformed driver, and that certainly whenever her two precious daughters go out a nurse or an amah in a white shirt and black trousers follows them, taking her place in that eye-catching line of servants when they go to afternoon tea at the Peninsula. . . .

And on Sundays and holidays, Zhang Jing, wearing sunglasses that cover half her face, stands in the breeze aboard a white yacht, sipping the champagne she holds in her hand. . . . A picture like this one used to float before Qiu Cuiping's eyes as she washed her first child's diapers, her own hands immersed in water bone-chillingly cold.

Now she has met each of the two girls. Qiu Cuiping can see their father in the little faces; the rest is purely Zhang Jing. She is hurrying back and forth between the kitchen and the little dining room, an ordinary working mother who comes home from the office, puts on her slippers, and rushes into the kitchen to scold the housekeeper for making too simple a supper. Qiu Cuiping's gaze follows her uncertainly. Finally she decides that the only things worth envying Zhang Jing for are her slender waist, her stomach—flat as if it had been pared with a knife—and her ability to eat whatever she wants without gaining weight.

"From now on, I'll take the stairs," Cuiping tells herself. Then, sitting complacently at the dining table, she says to the two girls, "Tonight Aunt Cuiping's taking you out to the Fulin Gate restaurant for shark's fin and sugared abalone." She adds, "Now, I want you to help me get Daddy to come along. Don't forget!"

The phone rings. The dark-skinned servant charges out of the kitchen, listens for what seems like hours, and turns in Zhang Jing's direction. "One of your Chinese friends!" Dropping the receiver, she struts away.

"Jingwen! You're here early. I'll be there right away. And you'll never guess who I'm bringing along."

"Mommy! Is Auntie Jingwen here?" the little girls ask with concern. "What about old Mister Luo? Did he get out?"

"Jingwen has just flown in from Bangkok, two days early. Her travel agent in Taiwan made arrangements for her to stay at the Fudu, but Jingwen says the room's too expensive. Besides, now she'll have to pay for two extra nights, so she wants to move to the YWCA."

"What about her father? Is he all right?" Qiu Cuiping interrupts, changing the subject. "Did he get out?"

"She got a telegram. He's waiting in Canton. As soon as he gets word from Jingwen, he'll come straight out."

"So you single-handedly arranged for Jingwen and her father to get together?"

Because the travel agency was developing a new tour called "Along the Silk Road," Zhang Jing went to Lanzhou. At a banquet given by the China Travel Service featuring camel's hump, *fat choi, danggui,** and other exotic dishes, she

---

*Fat choi (hair-vegetable) is a homophone for "become rich" in Cantonese; danggui is a medicinal root used to flavor duck and other dishes.

heard that there were ten or more Taiwanese living near Wuxian mountain there in Northwest China.

The next night, an old man came to the Golden Wall Hotel, where she was staying, and stood timidly in the darkness outside the doorway, afraid to come in. He stared with sunken eyes, stammering questions in half-forgotten Taiwanese dialect about the village of Hengchun in southern Taiwan. The old man was none other than Luo Jingwen's father, who long ago had abandoned his four-year-old daughter and never returned. From Manchuria he'd made his way to take up residence in Lanzhou, marrying a local woman who spoke in the rising inflections of the Lanzhou dialect.

Zhang Jing stood beside the first steel bridge across the Yellow River; the roiling waters of the river somehow made her decide to help this father-daughter reunion along.

"Jingwen teaches high school down in southern Taiwan," Qiu Cuiping says. "She rarely gets up to Taibei. We've been out of touch for ages."

"Cut it out, Cuiping! Of course she's not one of the old school friends you'd have kept up with."

"Zhang Jing, you only see the surface of my life. You think I get whatever I want in Taibei, nothing but luxury. But the truth is, my Shiming has been keeping a—"

Zhang Jing cuts her off in a self-righteous tone. "Let's go! We don't want to keep Jingwen waiting!"

Backing her little Japanese car out of the garage, Zhang Jing holds her head high, undisturbed by the sight of the designer clothes piled in the back seat. The inexpressible psychological threat of the past two days has been wiped clean away.

After worming her way through the Cross-Harbor Tunnel, she turns first to the Regent Hotel. Qiu Cuiping unloads her purchases, filling her arms with them. "Wait a minute," she says. "I'll be right back."

When Qiu Cuiping reappears, she's holding a big stack of cardboard boxes in both hands. Opening the car door, she puts them in the seat she was just sitting in and stretches her head into the car. "Fresh fruit from Taiwan for your daughters! And Zhang Jing, give these two boxes of hothouse grapes to Jingwen's father for me, as a little token of my esteem. He's come so far to get out of the mainland. . . ."

"You're not going with me to see Jingwen?"

"No. Shiming's planning to run for a seat in the Legislative Yuan at the end of the year, so I have to be extra careful. Reds, Taiwan Independence types, non-KMT politicians, they're all the same, really. Nothing you want to play around with!"

The head withdraws itself from the car's interior. "You go on, Zhang Jing. Don't worry about me. I've got plenty to keep me occupied this evening. It's going to take time to cut all those Made in the PRC labels out of the silk dresses and padded jackets I picked up at China Arts and Crafts."

That evening, when Zhang Jing gets home, the lights are still on in the living room. When her husband hears the sound of the door closing, he says in a preoccupied voice, "Is that you?"

Zhang Jing can't help herself. She tells him everything that happened that afternoon. Her husband stares at the television screen. Zhang Jing thinks he isn't listening, until she mentions that Jingwen is getting ready to move into the YWCA. Then he speaks.

"Tell her not to move. We'll help her out with the price of a couple extra nights at the Fudu. It'll be easier for you to get together with her that way. . . ."

Hearing this, Zhang Jing remains standing where she is for a moment. Then she turns off the television and walks over to her husband.

A Place of One's Own

Yuan Qiongqiong

Translated by Jane Parish Yang

SHE suddenly began to cry.

Lips pressed tightly shut, Liangsan sat there in silence and said nothing more. Tears streamed down her face as she looked at him, and her cheeks burned. She didn't know why, but all she could think about was that burning, itching sensation. She didn't know how Liangsan felt facing a crying woman, or how Liangsi and Liangqi felt. The three large men sat around the table watching her cry. Tears blurred her vision. All she saw before her were three heads held high, but she couldn't make out their expressions.

"Sister-in-law," Liangqi said. The blur in his direction moved. Jingmin looked down and tried to find her handkerchief in her purse. She heard Liangqi repeat "Sister-in-law" as she dried her eyes.

"Uh," she answered. Her vision cleared. Liangsan and Liangsi both looked down to avoid her eyes, their faces expressionless. Liangqi was still a youth and unable to control his feelings. He sat there red-faced.

Jingmin looked at him and he suddenly stood up. "Why'd you make me come here anyway!" His voice broke.

Liangsi tugged at him. "Sit down."

Liangqi sat down. Jingmin saw his eyes were red. When she first married, he had still been in elementary school. Up until he entered high school, he had gotten along best with her, his sister-in-law. Now it seemed that he was the only one sympathetic to her. Heartbroken, she began to cry again.

"Didn't you already agree that you wouldn't cry?" Liangsan said slowly. He paused, then continued speaking in the tone of a superior to an inferior. "This isn't home, you know."

The original was written in August 1980 and published in Yuan Qiongqiong, *Ziji de tiankong* (A place of one's own) (Taibei: Hongfan, 1981), pp. 133–51. This translation first appeared in *The Chinese PEN* (Summer 1982) and is reprinted by permission.

The brothers in this story have been given names according to their seniority. Liangsan is third brother; Liangsi, fourth brother; and Liangqi, seventh brother.

Jingmin wiped her eyes.

Liangsi played the role of meditator between them. He chimed in, "Don't cry, Sister-in-law. Liangsan didn't say he didn't want you."

Liangsan said, "That's right." He spoke without a trace of shame. "It's only a temporary arrangement. She's making a big fuss right now. It's just a cover-up to calm her down." "She" referred to that dance hall girl.

When he mentioned that woman, a faint smile crept over his face, but just for an instant. Jingmin saw it clearly but couldn't understand how he could be so heartless. After all, they had been husband and wife for seven years. If other men had mistresses, their wives would have raised the roof. Only he could have arranged everything so neatly. He didn't take her seriously at all. And now he even wanted her to move out so that other woman could move in. He took it for granted that she'd obey.

Liangsi said, "That apartment Liangsan's rented for you is an efficiency. It's a little small, but it's got everything."

Liangsan said, "It's a nice place to stay." He frowned, but not out of vexation. It was an expression of solemnity and resolution. "I'll visit you every week."

Silence. Jingmin wiped her eyes with facial tissue, the slight rustling sound blended with her breathing. She inhaled and exhaled heavily, as if having caught a cold.

Liangqi hugged his arms in front of his body and stared at her gloomily, as if he had suddenly turned into her enemy. Liangsi was the slickest operator in the family, and now his face was arranged in a solemn expression. Liangsan's face was a blank, as if about to doze off. He rarely looked so friendly. Perhaps he, too, had a conscience and felt he might be going a bit too far.

Jingmin finally spoke up. "Why?"

The three men stared at her. She fell silent, bowing her head to think. Strangely, she discovered her mind was a blank.

This was an important matter for a woman. Her husband was having an affair and now wanted to separate. But she couldn't think of anything else, not even of crying. Then why had she just cried? Maybe because she had always cried easily, or because she had been taken by surprise. She hadn't thought this kind of thing could happen to her. Perhaps it was because she felt unhappy that they hadn't talked it over at home but had brought her here, the four of them sitting around a large round table like they were waiting to be served. It was absurd. By coincidence all the booths were full, so the brothers sat at one side of the table and she sat alone across from them as if they had nothing to do with each other.

She ought to have given a more appropriate response, such as rebuking Liangsan's ingratitude: *What have I done wrong that you'd treat me this way?* There was a lot of that shown on television. The least I should do is faint, she thought. But she merely sat there, painlessly healthy, her hands gripping her handkerchief under the table. She crumbled it up then released it. She noticed a cigarette burn in the carpet. The carpet was a deep red with a black pattern. Unless one looked closely, the hole didn't show. She wiped her face with the handkerchief again, guessing that her face looked terrible. She was afraid her nose was all puffy. She suddenly felt ashamed to appear this ugly at the time he wanted to leave her.

Liangsan said, "She'll give birth in June. She needs a bigger place."

Jingmin became despondent. She replied, "Oh." She felt stricken when he mentioned the child. She and Liangsan didn't have any children, but she hadn't known he wanted a child so badly. He had never said anything about it. She suddenly felt like crying again, and the tears came flowing down her cheeks. The men were silent. She clearly saw a tear drop onto her skirt, the sound seeming horribly loud, like rain beating on the pavement.

The door to the elegant private dining room opened. The waiter had finally shown up. The restaurant was very busy. Jingmin sat with her head bowed.

Liangsan said, "Let's eat something! This place is famous." He looked over the menu quietly, calmly soliciting the others' opinions. "How about an order of shrimp balls?"

The waiter scribbled it down on his notepad.

Liangsi said, "Let's order something a little less rich. Liangsan, this won't do. You'd better be careful about high blood pressure."

"This dish is their specialty, understand?" Liangsan ordered four dishes and a soup.

The waiter departed.

"I think I'll go to the ladies' room," Jingmin said, her head still bowed.

"Go on then," Liangsan said.

Getting up, Jingmin fumbled in her purse for something, then finally decided to take it along. The three men sat there politely in silence. Liangsi even smiled faintly.

Jingmin closed the door. On the other side was that family of three brothers who called her wife and sister-in-law. But at this moment she was shut out and felt at a loss for what to do. She just stood there in a daze. Warm, pungent fragrances from the restaurant kitchen came floating over to her as she walked along the hall. At the end was the kitchen where she could see the chef's white hat and apron and the stainless steel cabinets. Around the corner was the restaurant, and beyond the many tables and chairs crowded with people was the automatic door. It was of brown glass, which made the outside seem dark like evening. Jingmin looked, wanting to walk right out. The hum of voices buzzed in her ears. But if she left, what would she do next? She felt frustrated. For all seven years of her marriage she had always depended on Liangsan. She'd never even gone out alone on her own. She didn't even know where this place was. Besides, she hadn't brought much money because she was always with him. And now he had brought her here to tell her this. She had believed in him, but he didn't take her seriously at all.

She was angry at herself for not being more competent. Why hadn't she even brought some money? There were too many things she wasn't up to doing. Before, when she went out, it had always been Liangsan who picked her up and took her home. She doubted whether she could even direct a taxi in the right direction. She was really incompetent. No wonder he wanted to get rid of her. To him it was just as easy as throwing out an old newspaper.

All she could do was head for the ladies' room. She looked in the mirror and saw in fact that her face was a mess. She washed her face and looked in the mirror to put on her makeup. After crying, her eyes sparkled. She looked closely at her reflection in the mirror, feeling she looked quite spirited, not like a woman who had just received a crushing blow. But why take this as a crushing blow anyway? She didn't feel she loved Liangsan that much. They had been introduced to each other by a matchmaker. It was a quiet marriage that hadn't required any effort. Perhaps Liangsan felt deeper toward that other woman. When he mentioned her, his whole expression changed.

But she had cried so much just now. Liangsan probably thought she had had a mental breakdown. His whole idea had been first to shock her, then pacify her. He didn't want her to entangle herself around him and make a fool of herself. He didn't know she didn't care one way or the other. She had kept on crying because she was scared. Besides, she remembered she was almost thirty years old and was suddenly an outcast woman. If this had happened several years earlier, she would still have been considered young. She couldn't quite think how being a bit younger when cast out was an advantage, but everything seemed better when one was young. She began to hate Liangsan, as if he had dumped a bucket of cold water over her as she lay soaking in a hot bath. She began to make her face up very carefully. It was for Liangsan. She had always made herself up on account of him. But, having just put her eyeliner on, she wiped it off again. This too, was on account of Liangsan. If she looked too stunning, he'd probably feel unhappy. He had always thought that he was everything to her.

When she returned to the private dining room, the three had already begun to eat. Liangsan looked up at her and said, "How about eating a little something!"

This was just like at home, the family sitting around and eating. Liangqi didn't look at her at all. Jingmin didn't know why, but she sensed a strong sense of shame in him, as if he were the only one here in the family who had done something wrong. She knew he sympathized with her. Maybe Liangsi did, too, but he didn't have such a strong moral sense. He picked out a lotus-leaf-wrapped steamed meat and gingerly spread the leaf apart with his chopsticks. Liangsan was always in a good mood when he ate. He slowly related how he had discovered this restaurant and directed Jingmin's attention to the dishes as he always had done in the past. "Jingmin, you should really study how they did this. They really know how to cook here."

Liangsi asked, "She's not very good at things like that, is she?" He didn't look at Jingmin. He wasn't referring to her. "With her background."

Liangsan looked a bit regretful. "That's true!"

Jingmin sat in silence, a bit unhappy that they would talk about that woman right in front of her like this.

Liangsan seemed to want to pacify her. "Jingmin really is a good cook. That's really hard to find."

His praise for her was probably limited to just these words. Liangsan was a real connoisseur. Actually, all the men in his family were. She sympathized with him at the thought that that woman of his didn't know how to cook. In that instant she thought of him as just another man and sympathized with him that his wife was no good. She forgot he was her own husband.

Jingmin said, "Too bad you won't get to taste it anymore."

Liangsan laid his chopsticks down and looked at her. "What?"

"My cooking!" Jingmin replied slowly. She suddenly felt a sense of release. "I don't want to separate."

Liangsan looked up and blanched. "Didn't we just agree to it?"

"Let's get a divorce."

Jingmin felt a sense of satisfaction when the three brothers all stared at her at once. Their expressions differed, though. Besides, Liangqi was thin and Liangsan had a round face. But all the men in the family looked a lot alike.

This was how Jingmin got divorced. When she told people, they reprimanded her: "How could you have been so stupid?"

Liu Fen reprimanded her as well: "How could anybody be so foolish? Why'd you lay it out so clearly? No one will even sympathize with you."

Liu Fen was two years younger than she was and a divorcée as well. Hers was another kind of marriage. She had gotten pregnant in high school. Forced to get married, she never adjusted to married life and had gotten a divorce. Before turning twenty, all the important events in a woman's life had already happened to her. Her mother raised the child. She took good care of herself, not looking at all as if she had had a child already. She saw her former husband often, too. She said, "As long as he's not my husband, I think he's really adorable."

Jingmin used the money Liangsan gave her when they divorced to open a handicraft shop. It was small and she didn't hire any help so it usually had more business than she could attend to. Liu Fen would come over at those times to help out. She was a seamstress in a shop across the street. When not busy, she liked to go over and chat with Jingmin. The two would sit on the step in front of the store like grade school kids. In the afternoon when there was a breeze, it was a cool spot.

Liu Fen was used to plopping right down and crossing her legs. When it was hot out, she'd even wear shorts. She leaned over and patted Jingmin. "How come you're so ladylike? At first I thought you were some cultured lady!"

Jingmin sat with her legs together and feet tucked under her. She was used to sitting in a constrained manner and couldn't loosen up all at once.

Liu Fen looked absently toward the entrance to the lane. Her son would be getting out of school soon. He was in fourth grade and already grown tall and sturdy. Liu Fen went on chatting about the news in the paper about Cui Taiqing. "You're already divorced, so why hate him so much? As soon as Xiaobing and I were divorced I didn't hate him anymore. We weren't fighting or hitting each other anymore."

Xiaobing was only a year older than she was. They both had fiery tempers. They were no longer husband and wife, but when Xiaobing came to stay overnight they'd still quarrel with each other upstairs. The next day the garbage pail would be full of broken objects. "Xiaobing is coming today," she said slowly, thinking of something.

"Really?" Jingmin replied. "You haven't been fighting much lately."

"Eh?" Liu Fen said, startled. "That's not fighting. You don't know what it was like before. It was as if I were a guy. He'd beat me up!" She concluded, "Xiaobing has matured a lot."

Someone came into the lane. Liu Fen had sharp eyes. "Hey, Little Brother Xie's here again." She mocked Liangqi by calling him "Little." She raised her voice listlessly from the step in front of the store. "Hey, Little—Brother—Xie!"

Liangqi came over to them, his face rigid. Liu Fen didn't pay any attention. She grabbed him and made him sit down on the step. "You haven't been here for a long time."

Liangqi looked past Liu Fen to greet Jingmin. "Big Sister Jingmin." She had forgotten when he had begun calling her "Big Sister Jingmin."

Jingmin replied, "I'll get you a glass of cold water."

She brought out two glasses of cold water. She looked at Liangqi from behind. He had lost weight. His shirt hung on him.

She sat down and asked, "How come you've lost so much weight?"

Liu Fen answered for him. "He's been taking tests and staying up late."

She finished off the cold water and went back to her store.

Jingmin sat on the steps with Liangqi. Between them was the empty space where Liu Fen had been sitting. She had a funny feeling when the wind blew. It was as if they were sitting so close but there was still a distance between them.

Liangqi often came to see her. He was the only one in the Xie family to feel bad. He always had something on his mind. He sounded like he was angry with himself. "It's the baby's one-month anniversary."

Liangsan had had a daughter. Liangqi looked down at his feet. "Liangsan wanted a son."

"Oh," Jingmin answered gently. "Men are always like that."

Liangqi protested, "I'm not." He looked away from her as he spoke.

"Well, it's too early for you anyway." Jingmin smiled at him. She looked over at the back of his head. His hair as always too long, thick and disheveled. She reached over as she spoke and tugged at his hair. "Your hair's really long."

Liangqi was startled and replied recklessly, "Who's to cut it for me?"

"Let me do it, all right? I'm not bad with my hands." She had learned how from a magazine, but she had actually done it only on Liu Fen and herself. She turned her head to show Liangqi. "Look at my hair. I did it myself."

Liangqi turned around and stared at her awkwardly, his eyes soft and liquid. Jingmin couldn't help flirting with him. She leaned closer. "Well, how about it?" She felt astonished when she blurted it out. Liangqi had always been a younger brother-in-law to her. She had watched him grow up. But just then she treated him just like any ordinary man.

She looked around for a sheet and wrapped him up in it. He didn't like the heat so she placed an electric fan in front of him. She first dampened his hair with a water sprayer. His wet hair plastered against his skull made his head look a lot smaller. Liangqi sat there obediently, his whole body encased in the sheet, only his head sticking out for her to work on. Jingmin first pinned his hair up and said to him, "You look like a coed." She smiled down on him. Liangqi looked up at her without moving his head.

She said, "Do you remember I used to wash your hair for you when you were little?"

Liangqi said, "Yes." She didn't know why he answered so formally. Jingmin felt like laughing. When she had contact with him before, he had been a mischievous little boy. Now he was really grown up. He hadn't even shaved his mustache, probably because he'd been busy with finals. A visible dark streak lined his upper lip. Young men's skins were smooth and looked so clean. Liangqi sat with his lips pursed. He always looked like that.

The hair she cut off smelled of tobacco smoke. Jingmin sighed, "How long has it been since you washed your hair?"

Liangqi replied, "No one to wash it for me!"

"How about your own hands?"

"You've got them tied up." He moved his hands under the sheet.

They were silent for a moment, then Jingmin said, "Well, I'm not going to do it for you." She added, "Lazy."

School had just let out, and the lane gradually filled with students. Some of them came to buy thread. Some girl students crowded around the counter. Jingmin went over to wait on them. Her business was always like this. It came in spurts. The girls knew her well. They burst out laughing. "Mistress, you can cut hair!"

Liangqi sat stonily on the counter, the clips still in his hair. He shut his eyes as if angry. He was probably embarrassed. Jingmin ordered him, "Liangqi, go sit inside." Inside was her bedroom. Liangqi went inside the back room. She explained to the others, "My little brother." She turned to another girl and said, "That's my younger brother." Actually, no one paid any attention to what she was saying. She taught several of them some embroidery stitches. She took out the colors and background with printed borders to show them. She finally finished waiting on them and hurriedly went into the back room. The store and back room were separated only by a curtain. She pushed it aside and went in, calling out, "Liangqi."

He had already taken off the sheet. He was sitting on the bed leafing through the *TV Weekly*. The curtain clacked together behind her. She had made it herself out of wooden beads. Bits and pieces of the world outside were visible between the beads.

In the room were a vanity table, a single bed, and a chair, with cardboard boxes and materials in the corner. With Liangqi in the room, she suddenly felt it had gotten a lot smaller. She stood awkwardly with her back against the curtain. "Liangqi, are you angry?"

"No." He put the magazine down. "Big Sister Jingmin, you've changed. You're so capable." He gestured and added mischievously, "I don't mean you weren't capable before, though."

"Let me cut your hair again."

This time she had him sit in front of the vanity table. After cutting for a while, she discovered that Liangqi was watching her in the mirror. She stopped and asked, "What's the matter?"

"What do you mean, what's the matter?"

"You keep staring at me." She made a face like a shrew. She had watched him grow up. She wasn't embarrassed in front of him.

He said, "Then who should I watch?"

"Look at yourself!"

Liangqi replied, "All right," and the two of them burst into laughter. Jingmin asked cautiously, "Do you have a girlfriend?"

"Not yet." He pursed his lips when he laughed, and looked even more mischievous. Jingmin looked at him in the mirror and suddenly felt a bit shaky. Perhaps Liangqi's clean-cut features seemed especially bright in the mirror's reflection. His face narrowed to his chin, its smooth outline very handsome. The clumps of hair in her hand were wet and glossy as silk. She felt as if she couldn't stop herself from sinking into his arms. Her head felt heavy. Body odor from Liangqi floated up toward her, the faint smell of cigarette smoke and perspiration. She had never had a man in here before.

Jingmin was afraid of herself.

She said, "I'm going to watch the store for a minute." She lifted the curtain and went out.

Liangqi followed her, taking the sheet off as he went. The hair clips were still in his hair. Jingmin felt like laughing. She lifted the curtain and went back inside. Liangqi followed again.

He suddenly spoke up. "Big Sister Jingmin. I really like you." He stood with his back to the curtain, the world shut away beyond him. On his crazy, damp, unfinished hair, the gray hair clips rested on his head like giant moths. He was scared, too, and having spoken, pursed his lips tightly as he stood there. He was a grown-up, but his slender, frail frame seemed to invite one to embrace him like a child.

Perhaps he had been thinking about this too long. Once having spoken up, he was like a taut string that suddenly snapped. He wasn't smiling. His expression was determined.

They didn't know what to do. They just stood there. At last Jingmin said, "Come over and let me finish cutting your hair." Liangqi went over and sat quietly in front of the mirror.

She began to cry. She'd probably never be able to change this part of her. Liangqi tried to get up but she pushed him down. Tears fell onto his hair as she proceeded to cut it. She wiped the tears away as she cut. Liangqi anxiously apologized, "Big Sister Jingmin, I'm sorry."

"Never mind. I just like to cry."

Liangqi was dumbstruck. Jingmin sensed something frightening in herself. She wasn't weeping hysterically, just sobbing silently, her eyes welling with tears as if she were finding release from daily injustices. Actually, that wasn't true. Having left Liangsan, she felt she had gotten along quite well on her own. Men just weren't that important. Whenever she was in a foul mood she'd cry. She'd cry when she read novels or watched movies on TV, too. Thinking of this, she laughed again and Liangqi, watching her in the mirror, was reassured. He smiled back sheepishly.

Jingmin said, "It's just that I like to cry. It has nothing to do with you."

She cut his hair with care. She did like Liangqi somewhat but not to that degree. He was still young; just look at the way he stopped worrying right away. She was angry with herself. She had been divorced less than a year but still cried when a man said he liked her!

"Liangqi, that's nonsense." Jingmin said, but sensed her tone wasn't quite right. She took the scissors and rapped him on the head. "I'm your Third Sister-in-law!"

Having finished cutting his hair, she washed his hair for him. The two squeezed into the narrow little bathroom. Liangqi bent over and lowered his head into the sink. Jingmin reached over and gripped his head with her left hand. A man this intimate with her was like a younger brother, lover, or son.

The cool water splashed out of the faucet and flowed over her fingers. Between her fingers were his long locks, like small black snakes curled on the back of her hand. The hair in the water floated up like strands of silk, in an orderly and beautiful fashion. She'd probably remember this for the rest of her life. In the afternoon there wasn't a sound outside. The old electric fan buzzed noisily in the front room, sputtering from right to left as it turned back and forth. The apartment was not new, and the bathroom smelled of mildew. The fragrant scent of the shampoo seemed to cover the mildew smell as well as the acrid perspiration from Liangqi. He lowered his head to let the water wet his hair. The parts she touched were all cool. He was quiet and obedient but breathed heavily. She knew he was in an awkward position. She felt the same way. She breathed carefully, inhaling only a little each time, then when she could no longer hold back, she exhaled deeply as if sighing. The two of them were pressed tightly together. Liangqi's breathing came rapidly as if they were committing an indiscretion, but they weren't.

After this she became restless and was always on edge. She finally got rid of the store and began selling policies for an insurance company. This was the only work she could find.

She carried big packets of information wherever she went and greeted people wreathed in smiles. She couldn't believe that she could do this. She wasn't particularly eloquent, but she looked sincere. She didn't force the policies on people. She just sat there and spread the information out for them to see and read the pertinent portions to the prospective customers in a candid manner. Whatever they said she'd only reply slowly with a "yes." Her stretching the word out over several seconds made people think she had something to say but didn't dare. Prospective customers found it hard not to sympathize with her. If they turned her down, they would always call her back sometime later. Her sales record was excellent, and she began to move up in the organization, becoming section manager.

She was darker and thinner now. She wore jeans because they were convenient. She wasn't as shy as before. Her eyes sparkled, and she had learned to cross her legs up high when she sat down. Her smile was warm and bright without any trace of slyness. When people saw her this way, they let down most of their defenses.

She met Qu Shaojie when she was out selling insurance. They began living together soon afterward. This time it was she who was the "other woman." She knew he was married, but she liked that tough-guy appearance of his. A spoiled man over forty, he hadn't yet learned how to live. He was manager of an import-export company when Jingmin came bursting into his luminous office all of glass, stainless steel, acrylic, plastic, aluminum, and steel.

Qu Shaojie sat behind his desk, clean face and hair, wearing a freshly pressed suit. He listened to her impatiently, his face in a scowl, tough and stubborn looking. He had insurance. He didn't need to take out any more. He didn't want to discuss it. Sorry. He had other things to take care of.

He was still polite and escorted her to the door. He wore aftershave lotion, the scent of green olives.

Jingmin decided she wanted him. She was thirty-three then, having been out on her own in society for four years. She had begun changing into a confident woman. Besides learning how to dress and make herself up, she had learned how to use people, learned how to deal with different kinds of people and what words were most effective to get what she wanted. She paid attention to detail and was willing to sit quietly listening to others talk, with the result that she learned how to sympathize with others' feelings and imagine their way of thinking.

She understood what kind of person Qu Shaojie was.

The second time she went, she dressed in a very feminine manner—a thin silk dress, her hair neatly combed close to her face. She only took up ten minutes of his time and didn't talk about insurance.

After that she went there often, and her visits increased in length. Sometimes they went out to eat together. She fell in love with him then, and it was as if her mind was suddenly a blank and she didn't take anything into consideration. All she could think of was him. Her confidence disappeared. She dressed up every day and went floating gracefully into his office. She would sit in a very dignified manner, her legs tucked underneath the chair, and watch him closely. Her whole person was fluent and elegant. Anyone could tell she was brimming over like a vase filled with water. Anyone except him, that is. He would knit his thick handsome brows obstinately. He was intractable. Whenever she came he'd raise his eyebrows. "You're back to sell insurance?"

Jingmin couldn't stand it anymore. She was frightened when she discovered she was in love. She couldn't take this kind of seriousness. She loved him so much she felt her whole body was transparent. In front of him she was as sensitive as a fragile grass that retracted at the slightest touch. She was already grown up. Wasn't she a little too old to play this game? She stopped going to see him, as if she had forgotten all about him. But she couldn't give him up. She finally went back again and decided to come to terms with this affair. She didn't even know how he felt about her.

Qu Shaojie hadn't changed a bit, as if after all this time he had been nailed to his chair at his office desk without having left once. He looked up and arched his thick black eyebrows. "You're back to sell insurance?"

He hadn't even changed those words.

Jingmin cried once more.

She finally got him to buy some insurance. Shortly afterward, they began living together.

When she told Liu Fen about all of these happenings, it sounded relatively simple. She recounted it in two or three sentences: "I tried to get him to buy insurance, but he kept on refusing. I went there every day to pester him." She held Liu Fen's new son in one arm. He was plump and heavy, and holding him made her arm ache. She switched arms. Lui Fen reached over. "Let me hold him!"

"And then?"

Jingmin said, "Later we got acquainted, and he finally bought some insurance!"

Liu Fen looked at her and passed judgment, "It looks to me like you're doing OK." She explained, "You really look beautiful."

"Oh," Jingmin giggled.

Liu Fen married Xiaobing again. They opened a restaurant in the city with Liu Fen as cashier behind the counter. She had grown heavier. Sitting at the counter, she looked plump and white like a roll of steamed bread just out of the bamboo steamer. She put the baby on the counter and wiped the saliva from his mouth.

Jingmin played with him: "Let's not eat anything but this little piglet!" She nipped at him. "Take a bite. Take a bite."

Some customers entered. The waitresses were busy, so Liu Fen went over to wait on them herself. She called out, "Sit over here! What can I bring you?"

Jingmin had become the child's godmother the moment he was born, and they got along famously. She wondered if she really could get pregnant or not. Maybe she was just too old. She really wanted a child—by Shaojie.

Liu Fen came over and patted her on the back. "Jingmin, the people at that table asked about you."

"Which table?" This happened a lot. She had met many people while selling insurance.

"Come with me." Jingmin smiled, picked the child up, and squeezed past the tables. A couple was sitting at the table with two children. The wife stared at her from afar, very cautiously. The man was wiping one of the children's hands, his face to one side. When Jingmin came closer, he finally looked up.

It was Liangsan.

Jingmin called out, "Why it's Liangsan." She really was a little pleased. Both sides introduced themselves. Liu Fen took the child back with her. Jingmin said enthusiastically, "I haven't seen you in ages!"

All these years of experience had trained her in this kind of greeting. Liangsan looked startled, then smiled and said politely, "You've changed a lot." The two at this moment had no common past. Liangsan seemed like a new acquaintance. Jingmin felt that though she had forgotten many things, she didn't think he had been like this. She couldn't remember what he had been like, though.

She stood holding onto the back of a chair. Their family of four filled the four chairs at the table and didn't make any move to let her sit down. Jingmin therefore squeezed into the seat with the older daughter. This was something she wouldn't have done in the past. She saw Liangsan's strange expression. He repeated, "You've changed a lot!"

"Everyone changes!" She smiled. She had a strange feeling that she had become two different persons. She rarely thought about what she had been like in the past, but facing Liangsan, her former self reappeared. She suddenly experienced a powerful realization of the great change between her past and present self. She smiled, holding her chin lazily in her hand. She knew she was making that woman uneasy.

"Liangsan, you've changed a lot, too!"

"No, I haven't." Liangsan denied hurriedly.

"You're fatter."

"I'm not either!" He still denied it. He suddenly seemed so pitifully disingenuous.

They chatted a bit about what they were doing now. Liangqi had gone to study abroad. And his little sister was married. Jingmin lied and said she was married too in order to save face.

Liangsan stared at her and asked, "That's your son?"

"Yes," replied Jingmin, half in jest.

Liangsan looked pained and, after a struggle, said regretfully, "Who'd have thought you could give birth to a son!"

The three other women at the table, Liangsan's wife and daughters, sat there quietly in a daze. Jingmin understood what it was like to be Liangsan's wife. She felt sorry for that woman. Wearing a plain, neutral-colored dress, she sat there quietly and obediently. When she met Liangsan she had been the most popular taxi dancer in the music hall. One could still tell she was beautiful, but she looked a bit faded. It was as if that woman had taken Jingmin's place at Liangsan's side and gone on living in a quiet, faded, contented manner. Maybe she was also happy that way. Jingmin hadn't had such a bad life before. But because of that woman she was now living a different kind of life. She felt she was better off now than before. She smiled at his wife good-naturedly but couldn't help joking, "Does he still hate to brush his teeth before going to bed?"

Liangsan and his wife blanched. He laughed, but she became angry. Maybe she wasn't as gentle as she seemed on the surface. This time she was herself, not like the former Jingmin. And she didn't feel like she was going to cry. Maybe she'd pick a fight with Liangsan when they went back home.

Jingmin went back to Liu Fen at the counter and had the kitchen make a special dish for Liangsan and his wife. As she headed for the kitchen, a cloud of steam came floating toward her. The chef in his white apron, the shiny stainless steel cabinets—perhaps this was the same impression from many years ago. Why were restaurant kitchens always the same? But she was not the same. She was an independent, confident woman.

Green Sleeves

Zhong Xiaoyang

Translated by Michael S. Duke

CHEN CUIXIU (Green Sleeves) walked out gracefully. She was wearing a leaf-green knee-length dress with a broadly pleated skirt, a short-sleeved blouse with embroidered hems, and a row of round buttons down the front. With one voice Mr. and Mrs. Chen introduced her to Wo Gengyun. She nodded slightly, greeted him with a smile, and sat down to one side.

Gengyun looked her over carefully out of the corner of his eye and liked what he saw. As, in the course of further idle conversation, he came to know that she taught elementary school and was not without a certain level of culture, he grew even more enthusiastic about her. Gengyun listened respectfully without speaking while Auntie Yao enumerated all of Cuixiu's good points for him; at the same time he watched Cuixiu shake her head slightly so that the short hair that had fallen over the side of her face was whisked back behind her neck to reveal a dimple the shape of a crescent moon on her ripe round cheek. Her skin was extremely fair and, set off by the leaf-green dress, gave one altogether the impression of pure white jade inlaid on an emerald background. A silk thread dangled lightly over one arm from the embroidered hem of her sleeve like a thread of green jade seeping out of a white jade pendant—a fulsome intimation of springtime in a snowscape.

Gengyun continued to discuss various things with Mr. Chen. He had wanted to talk further with Cuixiu to get to know her better but was hard put to find anything appropriate to talk about. He would feel too embarrassed to enquire about her age, and he already knew about her work; it seemed as though there was really nothing to ask her. Cuixiu, seeming to sense this, soon moved her chair around to face him and asked: "Do you come to Shanghai often, Mr. Wo?"

"At least two times a year, I suppose." Gengyun answered.

"That's wonderful." As Cuixiu smiled, the dimple on her right cheek

Translated from Zhong Xiaoyang, *Liu nian* (Passing years) (Taibei: Hongfan, 1983), pp. 1–21.

blossomed forth. "From now on, Mr. Wo, you should come to our house more often; that will give you another place to visit in Shanghai." She went on to ask: "Are you here on business, Mr. Wo, or visiting relatives?"

"I'm visiting relatives, my elder brother lives in XXX district."

"I heard Auntie Yao say you're in the import-export business; what sort of import-export is that?"

Gengyun replied, "I'm in chemical supplies . . ."

After they'd gotten started back and forth, the two of them went on talking most agreeably. Cuixiu was quite a fine conversationalist; she had a clear, crisp voice that made the whole room ring as if to the notes of an oriole's song. Several times while they were talking she felt her arm itch, and, looking down, she discovered it was that green silk thread dangling loose. "It itches so," she muttered and tried to tear it off, but it wouldn't break and she only succeeded in pulling her sleeve over to one side. It would have been too impolite to bite it off in front of everyone, so she had no choice but to get up and look for the scissors. She could not find them right away, and as she bustled about, a blur of bright greens and lustrous whites, opening and closing all the drawers in that little house, Gengyun felt somewhat mesmerized.

Cuixiu mumbled as she searched: "Where'd they go to?"

At this juncture Cuixiu's younger brother, twenty-two years of age, came home from work, greeted Gengyun, and then Cuixiu asked him if he had taken the scissors. He fetched the scissors from another room and cut the offending thread off for her. She smiled at Gengyun and explained, "We used to have quite a few pairs of scissors, but all of them but one were carelessly misplaced by my younger brother." At that moment a bright light from the window showered down over her shoulder and illuminated her lovely face.

Gengyun was so captivated that he stayed to dinner. As he was leaving, Auntie Yao urged him to make a final decision quickly if he was interested in Cuixiu.

Gengyun was a native of Shanghai. He went to Hong Kong in his early years and tried his hand at many things before making a success of it in his current business. He originally had a wife who bore him two sons, but she had taken ill and died. He was now nearing fifty, his sons had grown up and married, and his youngest son helped him out with the business. When he considered his situation, having no one at his side, he knew his later years would be pretty lonely; thus he announced publicly that he was going to look for a second wife. Considering his family's financial state, there was no reason for him to worry about finding a wife in Hong Kong, but the women there who were after his money were all young working girls who worried that he was not old enough and that he might still live for a long time to come; besides, he wasn't interested in that sort of young woman anyway. Of those women who were a little older and a little more bearable, most of them didn't care for him; the ones that did like him, he felt, were too old and ugly; so his attempts to take a second wife continued without success. At that time it was common practice for bachelors who found themselves in difficult straits in Hong Kong to return home, marry themselves a wife, and then apply to bring her out. Gengyun thought it over to himself and decided it would be a good idea to marry a young lady from Shanghai who would suit his temperament. Thus he joined in the popular trend to go home and find a wife. All of his friends and relatives came fawning around him when they learned why he was back. Auntie Yao was a member of his lineage; she set her sights on the Chen family and arranged everything for Gengyun. Gengyun just went along to try his luck, knowing that it would be very difficult to accomplish anything, and never expected that he would actually like the girl. Cuixiu was around thirty years old, just right for him, her parents were both educated people, and her own speech and deportment were natural, graceful, and in every way attractive.

Mr. and Mrs. Chen were retired and living at home so that Gengyun was given a warm reception every time he came to visit. As it was summertime and Cuixiu didn't have to work, sometimes she was home but sometimes she had gone out; they were not able to meet very often. One day when Gengyun was visiting the Chen home, Mrs. Chen handed him a cup of tea and said, "While you're in Shanghai, Mr. Wo, you don't have anyone to accompany you. Cuixiu doesn't have to teach now, someday she could show you around." Gengyun was a native of Shanghai and didn't need anyone to "show him around"; Mrs. Chen's real intention was obviously to bring them together.

Gengyun understood the suggestion and began to ask Cuixiu out. For the most part they went to the Bund to stroll on the Baidu Bridge. It was quite a long way from Cuixiu's house, so they took the bus. There are so many people in Shanghai, everywhere they went there was a great crush, and they could not walk side by side on the street. Cuixiu walked very fast, but, due to his age, Gengyun was rather slow and could never keep up with her. He could only glimpse her sleeves and the back of her dress appearing and disappearing amid the crowds. He also felt that Cuixiu's attitude toward him was growing more indifferent than it had been at first. He understood quite well the psychology of such a young woman: once she had latched onto someone whose situation was as good as his, she would not easily let him go; but having him confidently in tow as she did now, she was acting cold and reserved. Nevertheless, he wanted very much to marry Cuixiu.

That day the sky was gray and the wind was blowing; they had dinner and went for a walk on Baidu Bridge. The wind blew even more fiercely on the bridge, and the hair and clothing of the couples walking by flapped loudly and unrestrainedly in the wind as though they were hurrying to keep an appointment. Cuixiu asked Gengyun a great deal about the customs and conventions of Hong Kong society, and when she heard something amusing off and on she laughed crisply; her dimples were more apparent and her sparkling laughter seemed to waft over to form part of the bustling night scene by the Suzhou River. They stood by the railing, Cuixiu propped herself up with her elbows leaning on the railing and her hands holding back her short hair that was blowing wildly into her face and looked out over the billowing water. She suddenly glanced over at him, held onto the railing with two hands, pushed against it, and kicked her heels up behind her in the air; her breasts were thrust forward so prominently that Gengyun just stood there gaping in astonishment. In that instant his heart jumped completely into his throat, and at the same time she reined herself in against the railing. Her behavior was rather more than he could bear. Cuixiu slipped quickly down from the railing, looked at him with a mischievous smile, and turned to gaze at the enchantingly melancholy night scene: yellow and green lights spread out along the bank, the green ones were peppermint-green and melted coldly into the water as if dissolving in one's mouth. "Kachew!" she felt a rush of goose flesh rippling up her spine as she sneezed loudly; then she quickly removed the handkerchief from her sleeve, dabbed her nose, and stuffed it back in her sleeve. At that moment Gengyun was just thinking to himself that he had already remained in Shanghai a week more than planned, that many important affairs were waiting for his attention in Hong Kong, and that he could not delay any longer. He had originally intended to send Auntie Yao around to the Chen's to propose marriage, but after some consideration he decided it would be more sincere if he asked Cuixiu himself. The way Cuixiu moved a moment ago, the more he looked at her the more enchanting he found her, and the more he could not let her get away; he took advantage of her momentary stillness to come right out and ask, "Cuixiu, let's get married, how about it?"

A strong gust of wind came up just then; Cuixiu hurriedly grabbed at her hair; the handkerchief in her sleeve, probably not having been tucked in properly, dropped out as she moved and was born fluttering upon the wind down toward the river. The two of them both grabbed at it at the same time, trying to catch the last bit of it, but they were too late and could only stand there staring helplessly as it drifted slowly down into the water.

After this momentary interruption, the two of them seemed too embarrassed to resume their original discussion; after a few moments Gengyun continued, "You go home and think it over. Give me your answer in a couple of days."

Cuixiu brushed the blowing hair off of her lips, glanced up at him, lowered her eyes, and said, "There's no need for that. I accept your proposal."

Gengyun smiled slightly as he nodded his head, then walked back beside her. She expected his reaction to be one of great enthusiasm, but it was surprisingly devoid of passion. When people grow old they become apathetic about everything. She turned and looked down at her handkerchief; on the surface of the black water, it looked like a white sea gull with a broken wing.

The following spring Gengyun came back to Shanghai to arrange the wedding. Since he had few friends and relatives left in Shanghai and did not associate with most of them any more, it wasn't a very elaborate affair. After the wedding he took Cuixiu to Suzhou and Hangzhou for their honeymoon.

Suzhou is a small town, but since most travelers only stay there for a brief period like dragonflies skimming over the water without alighting, one doesn't feel it too crowded. The day they arrived a chilly spring rain was falling softly, quietly, and continuously, so they had to buy themselves a big black umbrella. Suzhou city in the rain was at once elegant, refined, and beautiful in its simplicity. Many people carrying umbrellas were splashing up and down the big streets and the little lanes in their high-topped wet boots; the boats were tied up along the banks of the canals with their oars pulled up, the boatmen's songs silent for the moment. Gengyun and Cuixiu were walking under a single umbrella, the first time they had walked so close together; looking at Gengyun's hand holding the umbrella, wrinkled and covered all over with brown spots, Cuixiu felt a strange sensation of marital affection.

In the morning they hired a car and visited a whole series of famous spots— the Hospitality Gardens, the Garden of Contentment, the Western Garden, and the Lion Park—all in one round. They had lunch at the Pine and Crane. Because it was raining so heavily, the ground was covered with mud, and everything was cold and damp; both of them were quite uncomfortable and felt their interest waning slightly. Their driver accompanied them and told them when the Qianlong Emperor visited southern China he bestowed the name of "finest under Heaven" to one of the dishes at this very Pine and Crane restaurant, but it was nothing more inspiring than *guoba*—rice burned crisp on the bottom of the pot. After lunch their driver took them to the famous Caizhi Zhai candy shop nearby. Cuixiu jumped for joy as she pushed her way into the crowd of customers. Gengyun was so happy that he bought her a large bag full of candies.

In the afternoon they went to the Garden of Ingenuous Government. Relaxing in the Broad View Pavilion they gazed out on a veritable panorama of green piled upon green as the clouds brushed the tops of the distant trees and the rain washed the willows by the embankment. Cuixiu unwrapped a piece of candy, sucked it for a while, and asked Gengyun, "I hear it's very difficult to get an exit permit right now."

"Don't worry, I'll find a way." replied Gengyun.

Cuixiu smiled and thought his words quite agreeable. Gengyun watched her cheeks billow out as she smiled and her dimples purse up so roundly that they looked like another pair of lips sipping wine. He couldn't help blurting out, "I've always thought it very strange that a young woman like you would not have a man by now."

"By now? Don't I have one now?"

Gengyun laughed out loud. Cuixiu picked a bit of candy from between her teeth and said, "I had a boyfriend, but we separated two years ago."

"Oh," he said and continued, "You probably knew each other a long time."

"Uhn. But later on . . . I didn't feel like marrying him."

He nodded, reached his hand out, and took a piece of candy. She quickly scrutinized him. His looks could still be considered young, and, most significantly, he was not bald; it did not turn one's stomach to look at him, and that was enough. She was already thirty and had no right to be choosy. Besides, his qualifications were pretty good, he was quite honest and sincere and a fellow townsman to boot. The more she thought of his good qualities, the more confused she became. Teardrops trickled down her cheeks, and she hid her face behind a pillar as she took a handkerchief out of her sleeve and dabbed her eyes. Fortunately, Gengyun had not noticed a thing.

Gengyun and Cuixiu's feelings for each other increased quite a bit during their trip to Suzhou and Hangzhou. Afterward whenever Gengyun came to Shanghai at three-month intervals he no longer stayed in his older brother's cramped quarters, but took a hotel room and received Cuixiu to live there with him for a few days.

After Gengyun arranged things in various places for a little over a year, Cuixiu received permission to move to Hong Kong. She moved into Gengyun's place in a Western-style house on Waterloo Road. This building had three floors and they lived on the top one. The interior of the apartment was designed by a famous Hong Kong architect. The living room was done primarily in a light burgundy fitted out with a cream-colored sofa in the middle and a small bar in one corner. Just off of the entrance to the master bedroom was a small room of unfinished wood; Cuixiu opened the door, peered in, and asked, "What's this for?" "That's a Finnish sauna; I spend ten minutes in there every night before I go to bed." answered Gengyun.

Cuixiu shrugged her shoulders and went into the bedroom. She examined everything one by one: soft, thick gray-green carpet, white curtains with green bamboo patterns, white wallpaper with light green designs, gray-green bedspread, even the lamp hanging from the ceiling was green, ink-green like an empty Coca-Cola bottle. Gengyun said, "I redecorated this room myself, it used to be chocolate brown."

"Autumn turned into spring." Cuixiu said smiling. Gengyun smiled too. She went on, "Such a big place, how do you keep it clean?"

"We have maids who work by the hour in Hong Kong; one comes in every day for a couple of hours to clean up the place and wash the clothes. All we have to do is cook our meals."

"Oh." Cuixiu walked around to the dressing table, sat down in front of the mirror, looked at her image in the mirror, and then looked at Gengyun's. The images in the mirror composed a complete portrait of their life together.

The Cuixiu in the mirror changed very rapidly. Her hair had a permanent wave, her eyebrows were plucked into long thin lines that flared up at an odd angle; her eyes were outlined with eye liner, her lips were painted bright red, and the nails of her fingers and toes were polished in the same hue. She could wear three-inch high-heeled shoes and walk as steady as an ox. It was only on suitable occasions, however, that she would make herself up so stunningly; most of the time she maintained her usual delicate refinement. She knew the value of refinement.

Gengyun soon had the confidence to take his wife to various and sundry kinds of social gatherings; everyone always said that he had made an exceptional choice.

It's always better to go to school than to teach oneself, and Cuixiu could be said to have graduated after following the other wives' curriculum. She was perfectly clear now about such things as which restaurants had the first-class cooks, which theaters had the most comfortable seats, which cosmetics were imitations of famous brands, and which movie starlet had just given birth to a baby girl and at exactly how many ounces.

Whenever Gengyun came home after work, there to greet him was the loud noise of either the tape recorder or the television; there were no cordial words of human kindness; it was as if his home was only a tape recorder or a television set that he just walked right into. After a while Cuixiu frequently commented on other people to him—people they had social relations with and people they had nothing to do with—she critically examined and passed judgment on all manner of gossipy anecdotes and scandalous rumors, and her conclusions were always phrased in terms of banal and all-encompassing moral platitudes. Gengyun grimly concluded that she had already been hopelessly corrupted into a vulgar urban housewife. He had originally imagined her laughter to be the chirping of orioles; now it was more like an electric current; it withered everything it touched. He continued to be tolerant toward her, however; he could hardly avoid taking her with him when he went out into society.

Their disagreements were about household expenses. For Cuixiu it was the more the better, but for Gengyun every little bit was too much. On top of this, Cuixiu always wanted him to send some money to her family, but he did not want to.

If Gengyun had a little extra money he wanted to invest it in stocks and bonds. Cuixiu did not understand at first, but after hearing him on the phone several times a day talking about buying in, selling off, going up today, falling off tomorrow, and so on, she realized he was talking about stocks. On the other end of the line was his stockbroker, Huang; she had seen him a couple of times at Gengyun's birthday parties. He must not have made very much money for Gengyun, because recently he had changed to a man named Lu. From then on the telephone calls grew longer and were punctuated with a good deal more laughter; they must get on much better. Many an evening Gengyun sat beside her talking animatedly away while she curled up in bed watching a martial arts TV series. When he finished talking, he went into the Finnish sauna, came out, took a bath, and went to sleep. She just went on lying there, enjoying her best-loved idols on the television.

She met that Mr. Lu at Gengyun's fifty-third birthday party. It was early autumn and she wore a specially made floor-length red velvet *qipao** encrusted with silver sequins and a silver-gray mink stole. The banquet was held in the VIP room of a big restaurant. Gengyun's two sons were welcoming the guests at the door for a short while when a young man in a light blue suit came in; he seemed to be well acquainted with the eldest son, shook his hand, and chatted for some time. Cuixiu had never seen him before, but, seeing that he was quite handsome, she couldn't help taking a careful look at him. A short time later Gengyun led her over and introduced him: "This is Lu Zhichong." Turning, he said, "This is my wife."

Cuixiu jokingly remarked, "Your God of Wealth."

Gengyun smiled at Zhichong, "You see, even my wife has long wanted to meet such a famous personage."

"Sit down anywhere, Mr. Lu, don't stand on ceremony." Having said that, Cuixiu took a look at him: a little over thirty, she consoled herself with the thought. A little more realistically, he looked to be no more than twenty-seven or twenty-eight.

She moved off to talk to her other guests but felt rather unsettled, glancing over at him out of the corner of her eye and then back again to her guests. She was aware when he was looking at her, and her gestures and poses became particularly alluring; all the while she chatted and smiled in the most naturally sociable manner.

Lu Zhichong watched her mingling with that room full of guests, the sequins on her *qipao* sparkling brightly, with the high slits up the side revealing her long, round legs; they must be very white, too bad they were at that moment enveloped in dark brown pantyhose that robbed them of their luster. That night Cuixiu had coiled her long hair up in a chignon held down with a diamond tiara that shone with flaming brilliance. The high chignon revealed her long round neck, but Zhichong thought she should be wearing a bare-shouldered dress; her full, round milk-white shoulders covered with that mink stole made one feel an excitement compounded of fire and ice. When the dinner was over and the guest seated beside Cuixiu had moved away to chat with someone else, Zhichong seized the opportunity to slip over and sit there. Cuixiu knew that he was moving closer to her and felt slightly flustered, as if his every step was treading on her heartstrings.

"Mrs. Wo, you're from Shanghai?" asked Zhichong.

"Yes." Cuixiu smiled.

"How long have you been in Hong Kong?"

"A little over two years."

"Gotten used to it, I suppose?"

---

*A long, close-fitting woman's dress with high neck and slit skirt, sometimes referred to as a *cheongsam*.

"More or less."

"Do you like it?"

Cuixiu was momentarily at a loss, didn't know how to answer, then shook her head and smiled resignedly. Zhichong chatted with her about other things. He spoke Mandarin in order to accommodate her; his Mandarin was not very good, but he spoke quite naturally. All the time he deliberately stared straight at her; his eyes seemed to be able to penetrate and understand everything and also to attract and absorb everything. He also stirred up Cuixiu's enthusiasm and she became very talkative. Zhichong suddenly leaned his head over and said, "Say, why do you put a handkerchief up your sleeve? That's gone out of fashion now."

"I'm used to it." Cuixiu said smiling and went on, "It's perfumed, smell it." She pulled the handkerchief out and waved it under his nose. Zhichong was not prepared for such a display, and his whole body lurched backward. Then Cuixiu pulled herself back, laughed, and looked askance at him. He would never have imagined her to be so uninhibited, not the least bit frightened; fortunately, she was already a married woman or else he really wouldn't dare trifle with her. At that point, her friend returned and Zhichong had to get up and move away.

When Cuixiu and Zhichong shook hands and said good-bye as she was seeing off her guests, he gave her hand a good squeeze, and the sweat of his palm seeped onto hers.

One morning when Cuixiu had just finished washing her face and had not yet combed her hair, the doorbell rang. She thought that Gengyun had probably forgotten something and sent someone around for it. Opening the door, she was surprised to see Zhichong standing there, smiling broadly. Cuixiu took a step back and said with a smile of surprise, "It's you? What're you doing here? Come in and sit down."

Zhichong stepped through the door onto the thick carpet and asked apprehensively, "Do I have to take my shoes off?"

"It's best if you do," Cuixiu said with a smile as she kicked a pair of slippers over to him.

He bent over to put them on and joked, "When I take my shoes off all the cockroaches in the room will be done for; you won't have to buy any more insecticide."

Cuixiu thought it over a bit before she understood; then she laughed out loud, "It'll suit that miser just fine." She combed her hair as she talked, pulling on it in long, straight handfuls.

"Have you had breakfast?" she asked.

"Yes."

"Can I make you a cup of coffee?"

"OK." Zhichong slumped down onto the sofa after he answered her. He was wearing a sort of hunting outfit that fit his tall and well-proportioned body perfectly and gave him a dashing look whether standing or sitting.

Cuixiu went into the kitchen and started clattering around to make the coffee. Zhichong spoke up over the noise of the cups and saucers: "Mr. Wo's not home?"

Cuixiu's voice came from the kitchen, "Did you just now notice?" She paused a moment and then shouted, "Don't you have to go to work today?"

"I'm taking the day off."

"You must have plenty of free time, to drop in here at my house."

"I came to see you; what's wrong with that?"

The two of them teased back and forth, hot and heavy, without tiring. Zhichong walked over toward the window; the breeze had the chill bite of autumn to it; as he passed the window he stepped up silently and drew the curtains back slightly. The house was directly facing a busy overpass, so close that one felt small by a head standing in front of the window. He shouted out in his usual manner, "Your house is right in front of an overpass; isn't it noisy?" He really didn't expect Cuixiu to answer him. When he turned around, she was standing there suddenly very close to him, carefully balancing a tray on top of which were two cups of coffee. Zhichong had intended to look into the kitchen, but at this point his line of sight was completely cut off by Cuixiu.

Cuixiu smiled winsomely and said, "I'm used to it, just like you're used to shouting." She held the tray up a little higher, "It's instant. I didn't perk any."

"It doesn't matter," Zhichong said, but then he sat down and continued, "Why didn't you perk it?"

"It takes too long and I was in a hurry to drink it." She stirred her coffee with a teaspoon.

"In a hurry to come out here?" Zhichong teased her mischievously.

Cuixiu gave him a look, picked up her dripping teaspoon, and tapped a couple of times on the back of his hand, leaving a small drop of coffee. He raised his hand to his lips, licked off the coffee, and smacked his lips as though it was delicious, all the time staring suggestively into her eyes. Her heart beat rapidly and she hurriedly lowered her head to sip her coffee, but she carelessly spilled a little on her robe; Zhichong took out a handkerchief and wiped it off for her, brushing her breast in the process. She got up as if she had felt nothing and said, "I'll go in and change clothes."

She changed into a sleeveless black and white dress. Zhichong teased that she looked like a zebra, and, seeing that she had not put a handkerchief under her arm, he held his out to her and said, "Wouldn't you like to hold this under your arm?" As he said it he tucked his handkerchief under her arm pit and began tickling her at the same time. He tickled her so badly that she fell laughing into his embrace; she laughed so hard that saliva splashed out from between her lips and she writhed around in his arms like a water snake. He took advantage of the situation to fondle her ample breasts, fondling them with great ardor and enjoyment while all the time continuing to tickle her. Cuixiu struggled a moment and, while still in his embrace, finally fell to the floor. Laughing until she was quite out of breath, she just lay there on the floor squinting up at him. Just as he was about to kneel down to embrace her, the doorbell rang. Cuixiu looked at her watch, cried out "Ai ya!" and pulled herself up by hanging onto him, saying, "The maid's here!" Then she straightened out her dress, smoothed back her hair, and went over to open the door.

The maid came in, nodded to her, and went quickly to her work. Cuixiu stared over at him and pursed her lips into a surreptitious smile. Zhichong sat there with his feet up, his ardor totally blunted, and thought to himself that his planning had certainly been on the weak side to have overlooked this possibility. The maid having arrived, naturally the two of them could not do anything further; full of frustration and disappointment, Zhichong made a few more perfunctory remarks and then took his leave.

Having learned his lesson, from then on Zhichong always came over after the maid had gone, but he hadn't many days off, and, Gengyun being at home at night, his moments together with Cuixiu were severely limited.

As usual he phoned Gengyun in the evenings. Sometimes Cuixiu would answer the phone and Zhichong would speak up in his most foreign-sounding manner: "*Hi! Honey!** Drag that old miser over to the phone." Cuixiu would laugh out loud and go call Gengyun. That whole night she would not be able to watch her TV serials in peace for thinking of him, thinking of him on the other end of the line. One night she heard Gengyun say into the receiver, "You can certainly come over for dinner, this Sunday, how about it?"

Cuixiu waited for him to hang up and then asked, "What happened?"

Gengyun answered, "Lu Zhichong made three hundred thousand dollars for me so I've invited him to dinner on Sunday to thank him. You can make a few special dishes, can't you?"

Cuixiu pouted and said, "What a cheapskate, three hundred thousand and you don't even take him out to a restaurant," but in her heart she was quite excited.

Zhichong had told Gengyun six o'clock, but he arrived at four and put on a pair of slippers in his customary manner. Cuixiu wore a long-sleeved Southeast Asian–style sarong on which the straw-yellow and yellowish green colors blended together to form a luxuriant forest tableau. She was sitting at the dinner table picking the roots off of bean sprouts. Zhichong sat down beside her, watching her work, and asked, "Where's the old man?"

"Taking a nap." She just kept on working without even glancing over at him. Although her eyes were lowered, her lashes still fluttered slightly upward.

The dinner table being inside and far from the windows, the sunlight not able to reach it, and the lights not turned on, the air was filled with evening colors much earlier than outside. Cuixiu's hair hung down one side, slicing off part of her face. Zhichong did not pay any attention to that; he was concentrating his

---

*In English in the original.

gaze on her ample backside as she bent over her work: the long, yellowish green sleeves hung down loosely, revealing two plump round arms. A truly vibrant woman!

The two of them were silent. Zhichong could not quite stand it; nervously he rapidly stamped his left foot, the slipper hung loosely off his toes and finally fell to the ground with a "plop." He put out his foot to scoop it on, but the more he scooped at it the farther off it slipped; at last he had to bend over to get it. Cuixiu was not wearing nylons but had put on slippers as a matter of course. Her legs were extremely white even in the dark under the table and had round calves and round ankles; Zhichong put his hand around her ankle and said smiling: "Tch, tch, such a round ankle; if my hand wasn't so large, I probably wouldn't be able to get around it!" With her other free foot, slipper and all, she kicked him hard right in the face. He scrambled up quickly, furiously wiping off his face, and said angrily, "What the hell are you doing?" Then he marched off to the kitchen to wash his face.

Cuixiu said, "You be careful; the old man's slept about an hour; he's about to wake up; if he caught you, you'd be in for it."

"You're afraid of him?"

"Who said?"

He came out of the kitchen, but Cuixiu was coming in with the finished bean sprouts. He blocked her way momentarily but then allowed her to slip into the room. He understood perfectly the feelings and actions of young women who were married to older businessmen—they were all of them penned up and seething with resentment. Cuixiu came out, and Zhichong tried once again to push up close to her, but she pulled in her shoulder, turned about, slipped off to one side, crossed her hands in front of her body, and stood there gracefully, smiling and looking at him enchantingly. He couldn't help feeling attracted to her; growing quite tender, he said, "A woman like you being married to that old man is certainly a terrible shame."

Cuixiu shrugged her shoulders and said, "I don't think so. At least the benefits I've gained are countless, but it's easy to add up what I've lost."

Zhichong leaned close to her ear and said with a tone of great significance, "One of the things you've lost might be your entire self."

She stared at him, visibly shaken by his words; he also trembled slightly as he faced her. He had really gone too far in saying that; if by chance she believed him and wanted to go with him, that would be a mess.

Cuixiu forced a smile and said, "It's really too bad when I think about it, the old man used to go to Japan and Taiwan quite often on business, but now he leaves it all to his youngest son; otherwise you could come around at night."

Zhichong did not dare say anything to further excite her and just sat down on the sofa farthest away from her. He certainly didn't have any intention of sleeping with her. After one night together in bed, women too easily get the mistaken impression that you have established a marital relationship; then you can never get rid of them. What's more, he had no intention whatever of staying with her for very long. Now she was several years older than he was, but in a couple of years she'd be several times older than he would be.

He reined in his feelings and just sat there flipping through some picture magazines until Gengyun woke up.

Zhichong's sense of timing was exceptionally good, and his self-control was quite strong; he came as he was called but left as soon as he was asked to; if Gengyun were to suspect anything, his suspicion would have to come from Cuixiu. After Zhichong left, her whole body was filled with a provocative and unbridled seductiveness which she could not restrain for some time; even Gengyun sensed her leftover warmth, but she herself was completely unaware of it. She hated Gengyun for being too stupid to see what was happening after such a long time. She would prefer that he find out, make a big scene, and divorce her so she could go and marry Zhichong. She believed their love to be faithful and unchangeable.

In bed that night, Cuixiu weighed Zhichong's words over and over in her mind, and the more she weighed them, the heavier they became, pressing down on her so hard she couldn't breath and she began to weep profusely; Gengyun, sound asleep beside her, went on snoring without hearing a thing. She turned over in bed and began to cry even louder; she cried a little too hard, actually choking on her tears. Finally Gengyun emitted a very weak "Huh?" Cuixiu opened her eyes wide and stared at him. In marrying him she was greatly wronged; she felt an overwhelming sense of injustice. She pushed him a little and he opened his eyes slightly and mumbled, "What is it?" Cuixiu just wept silently. Gengyun saw her tears glistening, more or less woke up, and pretty well guessed what was going on. He felt that the atmosphere between Cuixiu and Zhichong had been rather peculiar at the dinner table. When a man and a woman have a particular relationship, even the atmosphere around them is of a different nature, and they cannot deceive other people nearby because those other people also breathe in the same atmosphere. He ambiguously rolled over the other way. He did not want to face it, did not want to face it at all. He only wished that he could wake up in the morning and it would all be over.

There was nothing Cuixiu could do about it. She sat up and threw on her robe, thought to herself, and began to cry again, one great sob after another without stopping. She dragged a leather suitcase out from under the bed, hurriedly tossed a few clothes into it, dressed in the dark, picked up the suitcase, opened the door, and left. Zhichong had given her his address; she could go look for him.

Gengyun woke up and realized that there was no one in bed beside him; he stared blankly at the lamp hanging from the ceiling; it looked like an eye with the bulb for an eyeball staring right back at him. He recalled those glistening tears and the expression behind the tears he'd dimly seen the night before; at first he could not fathom what had happened; it seemed as if he was stuck back in that moment, but slowly he began to understand. At dinner last night he had drunk some wine, became extremely tired, and had a number of dreams; he could not imagine that this morning she would be gone without giving him any time at all. He pulled back the covers, got out of bed, went in to wash up, fixed some breakfast in a state of distraction, and could not help thinking of Cuixiu's kindness. He should have known this would happen, but how did she want him to treat her? The way she treated him was merely a matter of handling all of his daily necessities with careful consideration; and as a husband he gave her some extra money to spend; even though she was sometimes too extravagant and he hated to give it to her, in the end he always gave in. He gave her everything! Women today are never satisfied. Despondently he finished his breakfast and, as was his daily custom, took his morning paper into the toilet for half an hour.

He dozed off on the bus, his seemingly boneless neck drooping softly down into his paper, his glasses bobbing up and down on the bridge of his nose with every bump and jostle of the bus, slipping lower and lower until they almost fell off. A considerate fellow passenger caught his glasses and called out, "Old man." He woke with a start, hurriedly took back his glasses, said thank you, but did not go on with his paper; he simply put on his glasses and looked all around him with a feeling of limitless misery. He ate dinner alone in a restaurant and did not want to go home after, so he went to a seven-thirty movie. When he came out a light rain had started to fall.

He had a home, and in the end he had to go back. When he arrived home it was almost ten o'clock. As he went in he saw the light from the kitchen shining warmly, and he heard a clatter of bowls and dishes from that direction. Cuixiu came out looking relaxed and self-possessed with her hair tied back in a pony tail. She didn't even look directly at him but went straight into the living room, took up last night's ash tray to wash it, and said, "You didn't even call to say you weren't coming home for dinner. I waited all night and only just now finished eating."

When she walked past Gengyun, she stopped suddenly, looked at his pant legs, and said, "So, it's raining out?"

Gengyun nodded, "Yea, a very light rain."

At that point Cuixiu finally looked at him and said, "Take them off and I'll soak them for you." Then she went into the kitchen to wash the ash tray.

Gengyun followed her in, saying, "It's not necessary, it's late, the maid'll be here tomorrow, and besides they're not too wet anyway."

"No, I don't trust that maid. She ruined our sofa covers by washing them, and besides they'll be cleaner if I soak them first."

Gengyun had to do as she said. He remembered the first time he met her how she had searched furiously for a pair of scissors to cut a piece of thread off her sleeve. She was the kind of person who if she noticed anything out of place had to put it back just right before she could let it be.

He was too tired for his Finnish sauna and went directly to his bath. Cuixiu took up the pants he'd left on the bed and set them to soak; when she came back he was still splashing away in the bath so she got into bed first. Last night was certainly absurd. She had climbed up seven flights of stairs in the dark and finally found the door to Zhichong's apartment; inside the little narrow room his entire family of eight people all got out of bed to see who was at the door. Zhichong looked very angry as he brusquely installed her in his younger sister's room and secretly scolded her for being so rashly indiscreet and not calling to warn him first so they could talk things over. Suddenly she understood everything clearly. His family was so poor and he had so many family obligations, she could not possibly wrong him and ruin herself. Thus she came home early that morning.

Gengyun finished bathing and came out smelling of soap and fresh steamy water. He lay down carefully by her side. Neither of them said a word. After a few minutes he finally whispered slowly, "In a little while after I retire I can stay home with you every day."

She didn't say a word. He turned on his side and looked at her; she was staring blankly at the ceiling; because she was not smiling, her dimple had disappeared and her face seemed strangely devoid of enchantment. Gengyun's hand, which was outside the blanket, started to itch; looking down, he noticed that it was a thread from Cuixiu's mint-green nightgown. He picked it up, twisted it a bit, and said softly, "It's frayed." He said it so very softly, almost like a hint. Cuixiu took a pair of scissors out of a drawer in the headboard and cut it off.

Everything was quiet again. Cuixiu turned over with her back to him, then, suddenly remembering something, she said, "Mrs. Liu phoned tonight to talk about Mrs. Fan's son; you remember him? The one we ran into last week at Fragrance Gardens, very skinny fellow with gold-rimmed glasses; remember he said he was getting married? The invitations have already been sent out. Now he says he's changed his mind and doesn't want to marry the girl. Says he's fallen for a rich man's daughter who seems to be engaged already too, but she's actually willing to break it off for the sake of Mrs. Fan's son. The two of them want to marry, and Mrs. Fan is ready to explode. If it were me, I'd blow up too. Young people today have no sense of shame carrying on any way they feel like. Really! Anything can happen in this sort of a world."

She finished speaking in a single breath and then switched off the lamp with a loud "click."

The Window

Zhong Ling

Translated by Wendy Larson

LUO XIAONI was standing on the hydrofoil on her way to Macao, staring at the waves cut by the stern. The white bubbles, turning and swirling turbulently, were like layers of clouds that had exploded, noiselessly cracking apart in her body. Ever since that afternoon, when she had seen Hongyu with that girl, her heart and mind had been in great turmoil. She had escaped from Hong Kong, escaped into Macao.

She had seen them in Kowloon this afternoon. Seldom did she come over to Kowloon, but on hearing that a good friend had had a traffic accident and was in the hospital, she quickly asked leave from the publishing company and came across the bay for a visit. When she came out of the subway, she ran right into a group of people surging out in front of her from a movie house that had just let out, a theater that specialized in pornographic shows.

The street was full of men emitting the stench of sweat, a look of unsatisfied perplexity hanging on each face. In the waving sea of heads, she suddenly spotted him ten feet away, him and her. In an instant, Xiaoni felt as if the blood had been drained from her body, and she lost all feeling. After a few seconds the two of them walked out of her range of sight, and only then did she realize what she had just seen—his hand, his hand resting on her shoulder. The woman's face was turned away from her and she could not see what she looked like, but she was sure she had clearly seen him squinting to talk to her, his head pressed against her ear, and the glance of his brilliant eyes that seemed to have seen Xiaoni herself.

How was this possible? This morning he was still so gentle and attentive, like the rays of the sun blanketing the green grass, his whole body covering hers, his two hands holding her head, his teeth softly biting her earlobe, wave after wave

The original appeared in the literary supplement of *Zhongguo shibao* (China times), June 8, 1985. This translation is from Liu Shaoming and Ma Hanmao, eds., *Shijie zhongwen xiaoshuo xuan* (The commonwealth of Chinese fiction) (Taibei: Shibao wenhua chuban gongsi, 1987), 2:525–31.

of warm wind stroking the tender grass, the wind carrying his cry: "A beautiful, alive woman." Just as if in the whole world, there was no one except the two of them. But him, he had another woman.

Xiaoni moved blindly with the crowd, completely forgetting the visit to her sick friend. Before she crossed the road, she looked at the red traffic light and abruptly awoke to the fact that the Hongyu that she knew was only a superficial version. She knew that he was a famous reporter who covered the political page, she knew that his various incomes added up to a monthly salary of HK $8,000, she knew his ideas on the parliamentary government system, she knew who his mother played mahjong with yesterday. But as for his inner self, she knew almost nothing. The two of them had been together for three months, but he had never brought up his past love life. It wasn't possible that a twenty-nine-year-old man had not had any girlfriends! But because he didn't bring it up, she willingly decided that he had not had any, decided that he was the same as she was, and this was the first time he had thrown himself into something. She was truly blind. Maybe in these three months he had had another all along as his daytime girlfriend, and she had been his nighttime woman. She had been cruelly deceived!

Xiaoni arrived at the pier in a daze and gazed at Hong Kong Island opposite, the island they had known and loved together. In the muggy May heat, gray clouds clustered oppressively, the island strangled in thick gray fog; for three months, she had been in a fog, thinking she was enjoying the softness and light of love. But the fog of Hong Kong Island was not white, it was gray tinged with black. It was true, only this moment had she awakened and realized that he had not been so good to her after all, in fact, he actually had been cruel. Like last month on her twenty-fourth birthday, when they had made a date to go see the foreign movie *Passage to India*, and then go to a Japanese restaurant; but he called and said "I'm busy so I can't come," making her wait until two in the morning until he returned. No fresh flowers, no birthday present, no apologies; not even an explanation as to where he had been. But she still had not been angry at him because she was used to accommodating herself to him. Why had she conceded so much? When she thought of it now, it was because he was a different person in bed, absorbed and considerate, making her believe he deeply loved her. She forgave everything else. Women were really useless, so easily offering up their hearts and bodies.

The yellow sand stirred up on the streets of Macao softly covered Xiaoni's body, and she was as if sealed in dust. This was good, she needed this separation to remove far away the shadow of those two who had walked out of the pornographic movie. Right up to dusk, she traversed the streets and alleys, and just when her legs ached so she could no longer walk, she saw a small hotel—Round Moon Inn—and went inside. This hotel had seen quite a few years, and the outer walls were made of small green bricks.

As soon as she entered her room, she collapsed on the bed. The air conditioner had just been turned on in the room, and it was still dry and hot; she felt her entire body was wet and sticky, as if even her mind was covered with sweat and dust. She got up and walked vacuously into the bathroom, turning on the cold shower and rinsing herself from head to foot. Only then did she really come to, look about, and immediately discover that she was standing clothed in a bathtub, with her pale green dress, bra, and underpants all soaking wet. Fortunately, this was an old-style hotel, so a nylon line to hang clothes was hanging in the shower. She took off all her clothes, squeezed them out, and hung them on the line.

She looked at her naked self in the bathroom mirror, the body every inch of which he had loved. Pint sized, she was only four feet eleven inches. He had once laughingly said that whenever he was at the window display of an arts and crafts store and saw the ancient beauties carved out of ivory, the kind reclining naked about as big as your palm, he would think of her. Now, under a fluorescent light, her skin gave off a greenish white, her face was haggard as if recovering from severe illness, and her eyes were like two black stones baked in the sun until they turned gray. She no longer wanted to face her shape, so she returned to the bed and clutched the pillow closely, mumbling, calling wildly in her heart, "It is time to part! He doesn't love me, he doesn't really love me, he should have told me long ago there was another. Those who love each other at least should let the other know where they stand, but he didn't even do this, he just doesn't love me, I have to leave him. . . ."

Suddenly someone knocked on the door. She grasped the pillow tightly, ignoring it. But the person knocking had great patience and kept on continuously, lightly rapping. She had no choice but to get up, wrap the white bed sheet around her naked body, and open the door a crack:

Outside the door was a very young girl, tall and thin. When she saw Xiaoni's unhappy expression, she stuttered fearfully, "There's a man to see you."

Xiaoni looked out the door but did not see anyone. The tall, thin girl pushed the door and came in, saying, "He said he would wait for you outside."

The girl entered the room and pointed to the window. Only then did Xiaoni see that there was a round window on the wall. The girl walked to the window, stretched out her hand, opened the window, and pointed outside. She was a whole head taller than Xiaoni. The window was very high, and Xiaoni could not see outside, so the girl helpfully pushed the small endtable over for Xiaoni to stand on. Xiaoni thought to herself, who could it be? Could it be Hongyu? She stepped on the endtable.

Outside the window was a road bordering the sea. The embankment looked like a long, curving, cream-colored snake. A man was sitting on the bank, his face toward the ocean and his back to her, and it really was Hongyu! Xiaoni almost yelled out "Hongyu!" but she covered her mouth, thinking to herself, didn't I just decide I was going to leave him? Then I shouldn't pay any attention to him. She stared at his strong back and was moved: he really did love her after all. Who knows how many hotels he had to go to until he found her. Maybe she was just imagining things, and he had not come out of the theater with that woman. Maybe they were just friends. She saw him holding his head in his hands as though he was miserable, and she could not stand the pain, she had to call out to him. But another idea flashed into her head: if she called him, wasn't she giving in again? It was clear that he already had found the hotel, so why didn't he come up and step inside, and knock on her door? Did he have to make her come outside to meet him? He still wanted her to accommodate him? She should be a little stronger and tougher. She bit her lip and did not call out his name.

He took his hands from his head and put them down, then turned his head to the side, but he was still unwilling to look at the hotel. In the western skies the bright red of the sunset reflected off the side of his face. She saw him take something out of his pocket; he took out a chain with a heart-shaped aquamarine hanging from it. It reflected the setting sun, shining and sparkling. This was a token of their love that she had given him! That was the second time she had given herself to him. He had not been like the men in the novels she read, after it was over turning over and falling into a deep sleep. After it was over, he took the pale blue, heart-shaped stone he had been playing with on her neck and wedged it between her two breasts, saying: "Between two peaks, like a lake in the mountains—very pretty!"

"My mother gave it to me, I have worn it for ten years! It has become part of my heart."

"Then give this part of your heart to me!"

So she gave the blue heart to him. He tied it to his belt and carried it around like a piece of jade, but that was only in the first month.

When she saw Hongyu clutching the blue heart tightly in his hand, Xiaoni's heart nearly jumped out of her breast. She was about to stick her head out the window and call his name loudly. But this time she also controlled herself, because she remembered she had only a bedsheet wrapped around her naked shoulders and body, and there were two other men talking on the bank. If she were to call out, they would surely look at her. Basically, Xiaoni was a conservative girl. She gazed at Hongyu's profile and felt a stab of pain. She urged herself strongly, "Be a little tougher! This time you really cannot give in!"

She jumped off the endtable and staggered over to the bed, burying her head in the pillow. She cried loudly, she finally let the tears come out! She had decided not to give in to him this time, but in her heart she already knew that Hongyu, with his personality, would not come in to see her, and the two of them would be separated to the far ends of the heavens by just a short distance. Be strong, this was the end, the end! She cried her heart out, crying on and on in a daze.

She did not know how long she had cried, but half in a haze and half awake, she was starting to feel tired from crying. She still was thinking about him— maybe he had already gone! Xiaoni turned around and looked at the window, and was immediately stupefied. There wasn't any round window on that wall, just a wall curtain! She jumped off the bed naked and ran over to the window, opened the curtain, and looked outside. When she looked out she saw that there was a street, with stores across the way that were still open, their lights on in the dim of the night. The road was not next to the sea at all, and there was no embankment.

Xiaoni was in shock. Had Hongyu come or not? Had she erred in viewing that street scene, or had she been dreaming? She walked back, but her foot kicked the endtable, and Xiaoni was amazed again. If it was a dream, how did the endtable get under the window? Then it was real, Hongyu had come! Suddenly her heart trembled. She lifted her head and saw, directly across from the bed, a rope hanging down from the beam with the lower part tied into a circle.

Xiaoni backed up two steps. This had to be a noose! Who wanted to commit suicide? Could it be that in a daze she had made plans to kill herself? But she was sure she had not done this! Could it be that that tall, thin girl wanted to kill herself? She remembered that her sharp, whittled face showed a streak of sadness. She had to find her and clear this up! Xiaoni dashed to the door and had her hand on the handle before she remembered that she didn't have a stitch on. She quickly returned to the bathroom and saw her clothes scattered on the ground. The nylon clothesline was gone. She realized that the nylon clothesline was the same rope hanging from the beam. She hurriedly picked up the wet clothes on the floor and put them on.

She walked rapidly up to the counter. Two women were sitting behind it: one a middle-aged woman, and the other a girl of fifteen or sixteen. But she didn't see that tall, thin girl. Xiaoni asked, "Last night did you send someone to my room?"

The middle-aged woman said, "Miss, you must be mistaken, you didn't even check in until after six this evening."

Xiaoni changed her question, "Did someone just come to my room?"

The two women looked at each other for a moment, then shook their heads uncomprehendingly at Xiaoni.

"I mean that tall, thin girl who came."

Surprise flashed across the women's faces, and the middle-aged woman quickly said, "Who did you say you saw?"

"That girl with the peaked face, where is she?"

The middle-aged woman immediately stood up and said, "Please wait a moment, I will go find the manager to exchange rooms for you."

Xiaoni watched the receding image of the middle-aged woman with great perplexity and then asked the girl suspiciously : "What's going on?"

The girl said in a low voice: "Last month that girl hanged herself in your room, and others have seen her too. . . ."

Xiaoni stood in shock, mouth open and tongue tied, for a long time. With great difficulty, an idea finally came to her: "When he grasped my blue heart, if I had stretched my hand out the window and called to him, what would have happened?"

My Son, Hansheng

Xiao Sa

Translated by Eve Markowitz

WHEN Hansheng moved away from home in his third year of college, he didn't need to give many reasons because his father supported any independent action and I too was not a conservative mother. I have always made every effort to keep up with the times, hoping I would still be a resourceful woman, emotionally and mentally alert, not just to prevent a generation gap between me and my children, but also since my husband, one year older than I, had always been an energetic, handsome man. At forty-six, I couldn't let myself become a tottering old lady. And so, people who knew Hansheng couldn't believe that I was his mother. Although this was good enough praise as the years went by, I realized that the mother-son relationship between Hansheng and me was becoming more and more distant and indifferent.

A mother could spend three days and nights explaining how adorable and amusing her son was as a baby and still not say enough. This was certainly the case when I talked about Hansheng—how fair he was as a baby, how plump and well-behaved, and when he smiled, his eyes were always large and round instead of closing into slits. At the time, both our salaries were low, all we could rent was a small attic room above another family. We managed all right in the wintertime, but in summer it was so hot it was unbearable. Heat rash covered the child's body with red spots; he looked like a mutant hedgehog. I didn't put any pants on him, just let him crawl all over the place. In the evenings, Yude would translate articles for a publishing house to earn a little extra money, and Hansheng would crawl over near his feet and hug his calf, kissing and biting it. Yude loved him dearly and would scoop him up with one hand, kissing and biting him back. I said that father and son were cannibals, as Yude would always say that chubby children aroused people's desire to eat them up.

Children were like this—until he became a teenager, with pimples growing on

The original appeared in the literary section of the *Lianhebao* (United daily news), June 27–29, 1978. The translation was first published in *The Chinese PEN* (Autumn 1980) and is reprinted by permission.

the tip of his oily nose, his chin covered with acne, and dark hairs sprouting out around his lips. His gaze was no longer frank and trustful but had changed to a kind of suspicious glare. While he had not yet done anything really bad as a junior high school student, Hansheng had begun to argue with me and to oppose his father. For example, we wanted him to continue his violin lessons, but he had a hundred different reasons for refusing to do so. Taking him to visit relatives was more difficult than climbing up to heaven. It seemed that walking along the street with his parents and his only sister was a source of great shame for him.

"Leave him alone! Children his age are all touchy," his father said.

Regarding the children's education, both Yude and I felt that they should study hard and pass the entrance exams into good schools. We didn't necessarily want them to become scholars, but at least to have the basic learning with which to develop their individual talents. We knew that the growing up process of each child could bring his parents some worries, but we never guessed that Hansheng would cause such serious problems.

Hansheng was still considered to be diligent when he was in junior high school. He did well in every subject and passed easily into the high school of his first choice. By then, Yude had already been promoted to editor-in-chief of the newspaper. We had our own home, and gradually our life seemed to acquire some style. I quit the library job I'd had for over ten years and concentrated on starting my own business—not just busily trying to keep the family going. Some friends and I established a publication for teenagers, directing it toward people between the ages of ten and fifteen. I believed I understood the subject and was interested enough in it. Besides editing, I started a column in which I chatted with the children, explaining and commenting on problems concerning them. Yude supported me all along; he felt that action to be part of a serious attitude toward life. This isn't to say he was a strict, stereotyped man. Not at all! He is an interesting man with many dreams. Is Hansheng like his father? I have always hoped that he would be.

When Hansheng got to high school, competition was so fierce that he could not rank among the top three students again. While he could not be blamed for that, his grades fell sharply when he was in his second year. Only when he couldn't pass English, mathematics, physics, and chemistry, flunking every one of them, did we realize this wasn't such a simple situation. I learned to do what many mothers do and searched his bedroom behind his back. Hansheng didn't keep a diary, but I did find a pretty wooden cookie box filled with letters and photographs. Hansheng hadn't told us about his penpals. The letters had all been mailed to a post office box. His penpals were from all over Taiwan, and there were even some from Hong Kong and the United States. Leafing through photographs of seventeen- or eighteen-year-old girls with hair all about the same length, the one that caught my attention was a frizzy-haired, attractively dressed, smiling black girl with white teeth.

I never took Hansheng to account for this because in the drawer under his bed

I also discovered more than ten sets of new and old locks and keys. Ranging from a high-quality, Spanish-style spring lock to an ordinary combination lock, there were all sorts and varieties. It made me remember the time Hansheng had brought a classmate home to play. When I'd returned from my office, I happened to see the two of them sneakily bending over, pressed against my bedroom door, pushing a copper wire into the keyhole, trying very carefully to remove something. I coughed once and scared them both. Afterward, Hansheng told me his classmate had bragged he could open any lock. He was only letting him try. Naturally, I believed him for I had never locked my bedroom door; the child couldn't have had any other reason to close it intentionally and then open it again.

But what did Hansheng want with all those locks and keys?

"Just playing!" he said.

I had once read a novel about a seventeen- or eighteen-year-old high school kid who wasn't interested in anything. All he liked to do was pick locks. His one ambition in life was to be able to crack any lock. Could it be that Hansheng too was a little unbalanced?

"*Ai-ya!* Don't make a big deal over nothing!" He frowned, and said impatiently, "Half the kids in my class know how to pick locks. Anyway, it's only a collection."

"A collection? Isn't stamp collecting fun? Why do you want to play thieves' games?"

"Ma! You make it sound horrible. It's also a kind of mind training."

To my surprise, his father approved of this explanation.

Aside from mind training, they also gained an opportunity to test their nerve. In the middle of the school term, I received a phone call from Yude at the office. He said that Hansheng was at the police station and asked if I would go there with him to guarantee his release. They were a gang of six, all with the same crewcuts, yellow khaki school uniforms, and unfathomable bitter expressions on their faces.

"You all come from good homes. Why would you want to steal books from a bookstore? For fun? Lock each of you up without food for three days. Then you'll see if it's fun."

A fat policeman pointed to the boy who had come to our home trying to unlock the door, saying, "He's got the most talent. The others are still learning. He's the one! He'd picked up a stack of more than ten books and was ready to take off."

Back at the house, I hadn't had time to begin my lecture when Hansheng took advantage of the opportunity to lash out: "Oh! That damned Ah-cai! If he weren't so greedy, we wouldn't have been caught! We had already gone to four shops. This was the last hit."

"You . . . how can you steal people's books?" Exhausted, I dropped onto the sofa, thinking my son was a thief and I was an editor of a magazine for young people, acknowledged to be an expert on teenage problems! Wasn't this incredibly ironic?

"*Ai-ya!* Who stole books? We just made a bet to see if anyone had the nerve to take them!"

I always believed in strictness when teaching children. When Hansheng was small, he once picked up a pencil and brought it home with him. I made him take it back to school and give it to the teacher. When he was in the fourth grade, a friend from next door came and told me Pan Hansheng had taken a pen from a student in his class. That night I bound his hands and feet firmly and used a feather duster to hit him more than ten times on his buttocks. The next day his father bought him a new pen. But now? Facing a son taller than ourselves, Yude and I both felt rather embarrassed.

I predicted long before that when the boy arrived at this point, another incident would soon follow in its wake. It happened in early summer, near the end of the school year. The security chief of the school Hansheng was attending telephoned our house. I answered. He wanted me to come to the school immediately.

"Hansheng—what's happened to him?" My first response was to fear for the child's safety.

"Pan Hansheng is fine, his classmate has a problem." The voice at the other end of the telephone had a nasal twang with a slight touch of humor.

I rushed to the school. At the end of a long hallway in the red brick building there was a large, dark office room where several elderly men were absentmindedly marking notebooks with red pens. It seemed the only sound in the office was the whirring of an electric fan on the ceiling. Listening to it, I began to perspire even more.

"Whom are you looking for?"

The unexpected sound from behind my back gave me a scare. I figured the man wearing an olive-green military uniform and three plum blossoms on each of his broad shoulders must be the security chief.

"I am Pan Hansheng's mother."

Following him into his office next door, I immediately saw Hansheng standing with his hands behind him, his back to the door, looking out of the window. I didn't call him. I only felt a rush of weakness and hurried to sit down on the sofa in a corner.

"Mrs. Pan! Don't get so nervous. Try to relax." The security chief smiled amiably as he slowly and steadily stretched his left arm toward me with an object held in his hand.

"Do you recognize this?"

It was a one-inch-wide hunting knife. The blade was sheathed in a ragged black leather case. The handle, ivory-colored, was crudely carved with designs that had been worn out with time and dirt into a brownish color. It looked familiar, but only after looking at it for a long time did I remember: There was a knife like this in our study, in Yude's large drawer. It was a keepsake from his youthful days.

"It looks like my husband's . . . my husband's keepsake. But I can't say for certain."

As if to say it didn't matter, he smiled and moved the knife a little closer to me.

"Pan Hansheng also says it's his father's."

"He . . ."

The security chief nodded his head solemnly.

"His classmate, Lin Zhengyi, was stabbed in the arm. Up to now, neither of the two will say why. The injured one has already been sent to the hospital. It's not serious, but Pan Hansheng will get at least two demerits for this."

The security chief allowed Hansheng to go home with me. We sat beside each other in the car, mother and son, but neither spoke a word. Looking at the angular lines of the face that he kept turned away, his eyes angry as ice, a sudden coldness filled my heart. I could not understand. What could have made my child so furious, so spiteful, so mean. . . .

"Why? Can you tell me why?" I asked him, gazing at him earnestly. I felt like patting him gently on the shoulder, coaxingly, to get him to tell the truth. But I waited for a long time. In his room, filled with piles of records, reference books, and other things, it seemed like the entire world was quietly standing still. I only wanted to hear his reason for trying to kill.

"There's no reason!" Under the circumstances, totally unwilling, he answered stiffly, "Don't take it so seriously."

So seriously? I called Yude and said I wanted him to come home right away.

"I'm in a meeting!"

"Your son is a cold-blooded murderer and you're staying in a meeting?"

Yude really let go this time. For an hour he lectured his silent son on everyday morals and how people should behave in the world. I followed him in and talked heartrendingly for two hours. We finally found out that it had happened just because of a single cigarette. The boy called Big Head wouldn't lend him one, then cracked a joke (Hansheng refused to say what the joke was), whereupon Hansheng angrily pulled the knife out and stabbed him in the arm.

Yude and I looked at one another, as if we both felt the reason for what had happened had been oversimplified.

After I left Hansheng's room, Yude stayed behind to talk to his son. I sat in the living room, straining my ears to hear, but all I could catch was Yude's voice. About half an hour later, Yude pushed the door open and came out, his face actually filled with excitement as he told me:

"Seventeen-, eighteen-year-old boys are all like this. Everybody goes through it. Don't be too sensitive."

"Me, sensitive? He wounded someone!"

"They're friends to the end! When Big Head saw that his arm was bleeding, he took off his khaki shirt, wrapped it himself, and got ready to go home. The

security chief found out only when the other students started yelling about it.''
Yude put his pipe in his mouth and played with the hunting knife in his hand. In
an almost approving tone of voice he said, "He had it sharpened. After all these
years, I'd forgotten it. It was given to me by an uncle of mine, a very interesting
man. He was always helping the underdog. He almost got himself killed for
sticking his nose in other people's business.''

"If you're afraid he'll get himself killed, give him a gun next time.''

I, of course, was referring to Hansheng.

Hansheng's punishment was to continue his studies at school but under special surveillance. To reduce his emotional pressure and to give him a change of
environment, we waded through all the red tape involved in transferring him to
another school. The new one was a private high school in the suburbs, on a
mountainside by a river, very quiet. The students lived and studied there. They
were permitted to go home on Sundays only.

Suddenly there was one person less in our home, and none of us could get
used to it. Hanlin had not been especially close with her brother, but she also
said, "I really miss Elder Brother!''

Hanlin was always a well-behaved, intelligent child. A good student at
school, a good daughter at home, and among relatives and friends she was
considered a sweet little princess. Every movement, every expression was perfectly charming. Even her pampered nature reflected a certain innocence. It
seemed she didn't have the trace of a flaw.

But with a child like this, can one really be sure that there is nothing to worry about?

"Yude! Hanlin is spoiled enough. It might be better if you didn't pamper her
so. Even if she is fortunate and will never have to go through the hardships we
had before, disasters may happen, people may change, and in trying to adjust, a
girl like her will be the first to be weeded out.''

"Oh! Hanlin isn't very tough, but what do you have in mind? Send her to a
deserted island for survival training?''

At a time when Hanlin couldn't have been doing better at school, a registered
letter came from the school Hansheng had recently transferred to. It said
Hansheng had been expelled for publishing and distributing pamphlets slander-
ing the faculty.

"You wanted to start a newspaper? Your father's been a newspaperman for
years. If you wanted to begin a newspaper you could have discussed it with him first!''

"I don't want to start a newspaper!'' The veins on Hansheng's temples were
pulsating, purplish-blue cords of anger. Choosing his words slowly he said, "I
did it for the sake of justice. I said what the others didn't dare to say. Hou
Zhengqun isn't fit to be our teacher. He's neither knowledgeable nor moral. As
the head of extracurricular activities, he steals funds from the school newspaper.
He's that kind of man! Dirty dog!''

"What does it have to do with you? You tend to your studies! What does it
have to do with you?''

"Why doesn't it have to do with me? I want to run the school paper. How can it not concern me?"

It seemed that any second his tightly clenched fist would explode like a firecracker. He was like an enraged young tiger. But could he possibly understand how I felt as a mother? Long ago I had stopped focusing my anger on any one of his criminal acts. I was truly worried about his future. Long ago he had transgressed what was normal. Could this kind of a child ever become a successful man? I was totally depressed, thinking of my two so very different children. It was perhaps the greatest defeat in our lives.

From then on, Hansheng stayed home for a period to study; he wanted to take the entrance exams for entering college without a high school diploma. Yude and I seldom bothered him, so naturally there was little opportunity for us to have any communication. In July they announced the results. Hansheng had managed to squeeze in at the end of the list of acceptances into the sociology department of a university. Even in our disappointment, Yude and I tried hard to think of the bright side. Since the main issue was already settled, we could feel slightly comforted that, for better or worse, Hansheng was now an adult and would be going to college. We hoped he wouldn't make any more mistakes.

At college, Hansheng was in fact very hard working. He began to enjoy reading, and he became most interested in the humanities. By asking around, we learned that he had a girlfriend surnamed Huang in the same class. Several times we wanted him to invite her over to the house for dinner, but Hansheng always refused, his expression vague and distant. Was it shyness? Or unwillingness to have his father and mother meddle in his affairs? Yude and I were both open-minded on this point and decided not to interfere. Anyway, the fact that he had a girlfriend was an expression of stability on his part.

Two years later, when Hanlin passed the entrance exams into the foreign languages department, which was her first choice, Yude suggested that the family celebrate. Hanlin wanted to go up to the Grand Hotel for a steak dinner. Although it was common to spend one thousand or eight hundred NT dollars to go out and have a good time with the family, it was still rather extravagant to go to the Grand Hotel for steak. When Yude was promoted to president, we had only invited relatives and friends for a family party at the Heavenly Kitchen restaurant. But this time was different, it was for our daughter! And, without any qualms, Yude promised. It was rare that Hansheng was also home. My daughter and I hurriedly dressed, and the four of us happily drove up to Yuan Shan in our car.

At that time, the Grand Hotel had not yet been remodeled into a skyscraper. The hand-carved and red-painted Qilin,* Golden Dragon, and Jade Phoenix buildings were still nestled against the mountainside, elegant in the palace style of ancient China. The Golden Dragon was actually three halls. In the exact

---

*An animal from ancient Chinese fables, supposedly with supernatural powers; often used as a symbol of power.

center of the entry hall was a five-clawed golden dragon coiled up in a tranquil fountain. From ceiling to floor, it was elaborately and magnificently decorated. When people, all dressed up, walked in, they would naturally hold their heads high, straighten their backs, and walk in a slow, dignified manner so as not to destroy the general atmosphere of elegance.

The Western restaurant was very different, simple and clean with white table-cloths, high-backed teak chairs, and tables set with bright, shiny silverware. We chose a table by the window. You could see the flickering lights below the mountain and even the iridescent reflections in the waters of the Tamsui River.

"Ma! The view from here is wonderful! We must come and stay here some night."

"Nonsense! Nobody stays in a hotel for no reason." Then I remembered to ask Yude, "On Sunday the Han family is celebrating their son's marriage on the second floor of the Sichuan Yangzhou restaurant. And I have a farewell dinner that night for Mr. Wu of our office. Will you have time to come?"

"Sunday? Impossible! There is also a wedding at the newspaper and I'm presiding. I think Hansheng and Hanlin can go. How about it?"

"Fine!"

Hanlin reluctantly promised to go, but Hansheng didn't say anything. He just kept staring at a distinguished-looking young couple sitting at a distance from us.

"What are you looking at?" I asked him.

"Nothing! Look at those two, so young and already looking so snobbish."

Yude ordered aperitifs, four orders of T-bone steak, oxtail soup for the children, salad, and clear oyster soup for us two.

I have never had a great appetite for Western food. Fried or roasted steak dishes have always seemed especially flavorless to me. But the quiet atmosphere in Western restaurants always gives one a peaceful, romantic feeling. No wonder some people say that eating Western food is eating atmosphere. Naturally, the one member of our family who was best adjusted to this kind of environment was Hanlin. She elegantly chose a small roll from the bread basket and daintily nodded her head to let the waiter dish vegetables onto her copper plate. Each move was according to the rules of etiquette. Hansheng was very different. He was frowning the whole time, and he didn't eat much. I thought to myself, maybe it would have been better if we had invited his girlfriend to come with us.

After dinner, Hanlin reached out from the back seat of the car and wrapped her arms around her father's neck, kissing him over and over again. I guessed she was up to something again, and sure enough she said pleadingly in a winning voice, "Dad! Let's go dancing, all right?"

"Let your father drive! That's dangerous!" I pulled her two arms away from around Yude's neck.

"All right? Ma!" Now she was pleading her cause with me.

"Why don't you ask your brother!"

Actually, this was my way of saying yes. We might as well take advantage of our good spirits for the whole family to have some fun together.

Nobody expected Hansheng to burst out with, ''I'm not going!''

''Come on! Elder Brother, say yes!''

''I won't go! There is nothing under the sun more boring than dancing. Couldn't we find something significant to do with our time?''

''Humph! Hansheng is a wet blanket! He hates everything!''

''So I do!'' Since Hansheng had just had a little wine, his face reddened as he became animated. It seemed that blood would spurt from his face. ''You don't seem to realize! We just had a meal that would keep a normal family going for a month.''

How could I not realize? But by the time I wanted to argue this point it was too late to speak up. No one said anything more, our faces set and distant. My stomach felt queasy, the steak we had just eaten turned sour and curdled in my throat. I rolled down the window and looked out onto the streets at the bright neon lights flashing unearthly colors over the faces of the pedestrians.

Our car turned smoothly onto Nanjing East Road and we drove straight home.

That night Yude and I were not in the mood to chat. When I woke up the next day and saw the bright sunshine I thought of all the many things I still had to do and had no desire to inflate the boy's unintentional words into material for an argument.

On Sunday, Hansheng refused to attend the Han family's wedding reception. A week later, he accompanied a school club on a social service trip to the east. The third day after he returned, we had yet another confrontation. At the dinner table I'd mentioned that the couple's aunt had recently taken an eleven- or twelve-year-old girl from the country into her home to do some simple house-work. I had heard that she paid the girl's family NT $50,000.

''Isn't that selling people?'' Hansheng frowned, his face filled with an expression of disgust.

''Nonsense! When she's about sixteen years old they will send her back home. They're giving her room and board, teaching her manners, and showing her how to work. What's wrong with that? Now that she has arrived, she doesn't even want to go back!''

''Ma! Why don't you take a girl in to help Hong-Sao! Another person around the house would make things livelier!'' Hanlin said.

''Nonsense, we couldn't do a thing like that.''

I had never been interested in having a girl like that, but seeing Yude so solemnly serious about it, I couldn't help but put in a word for the couple's aunt.

''Isn't taking a child into a house like ours better than letting her good-for-nothing father sell her into the streets? I really believe . . .''

''Ma! Don't you think that's immoral?''

Never had I thought that I might be an immoral person. And to think that the idea came from my son.

''Then you think her father's forcing her to become a prostitute is moral?'' It was the first time I fought back, talking to my own son as if I were facing an opponent.

"We can build a better social system to stamp that sort of thing out. If we work hard we can rectify the situation. Then we won't passively sell people into child labor rather than have them become prostitutes." He was all solemn dignity. "Our society closes its eyes to this phenomenon. Every person selfishly looks to himself, never giving a thought to others, never sympathizing with his fellow countrymen whose lifestyle is poorer than his own. Frankly, I hate your way of life. If one day you realize that there are others who eat salted vegetables and fat meat at every meal, you might understand what I mean. . . ."

Hansheng's talk suddenly made me feel that I was but a self-indulgent, wasteful, shallow-minded parasite of society, and his father was a selfish degenerate "'bourgeois" who only knew how to throw a thousand dollars away on a steak dinner and had never given a thought to our social problems.

That degenerate, mean father finally opened his mouth:

"Hansheng! Your mother and I feel that lately you seem to be totally dissatisfied with our family. I can't say that you are wrong. You're still young. You still have much to go through. But go slowly. Don't get impatient. You can go and do anything you want to do except always attacking others, especially your own family."

Yude and I didn't feel like sleeping that night. Sitting on the second floor balcony gazing at the distant moon, I could not prevent myself from complaining. How could he say we did not understand life's difficulties? Soon after Hansheng was born, Yude was sent to the south for half a year. In order to afford powdered milk for the baby, we ate pickled cabbage, dried shredded fish, steamed bread, and congee almost every meal. When I was pregnant with Hanlin, Yude was in the United States again for training. Pregnant women are always hungry, but since I couldn't afford to buy anything special, I would spend one NT dollar on peanuts and share it with Hansheng. Hansheng and Hanlin grew up in that small wooden upstairs room, an area of only 200 square feet on Jiuquan Street. The child doesn't remember where we slept and ate. But we do. . . .

"What good does it do to say these things?"

"What Hansheng says is unfair! . . ."

"Leave him alone! He's a big boy. Everyone has his own way of thinking, and we can't say he's wrong."

After summer vacation, not long after school started, Hansheng moved out, saying that being closer to school was more convenient for going to the library. We gave him a set allowance and he also did tutoring on the side, so he was able to get along. Because we saw each other less, the relationship between Hansheng and his family naturally became more distant and polite. Yude and I seldom heard his complaints and criticisms any more. Every Saturday night we would get together for family dinners. The next day, early in the morning, Hansheng would leave. Although we seemingly never interfered in his activities, as parents we couldn't help being concerned about him. Through the introduction of friends, we got to know Mr. Li, the dean of students at Hansheng's school, who told us that our son was a sincere, compassionate, enthusiastic young man. He was very involved in school activities, particularly those dealing with social services, so he was actually applying what he had learned!

When Hansheng graduated, the whole family went to congratulate him. He received quite a few large and small awards and prizes; we were very proud. Hansheng also took us to see the room he rented. This was the first time we were granted permission to enter his universe. The room was long and narrow. There was a metal bunk bed. As we walked in the door, we saw a large poster of Albert Schweitzer pasted onto the wall, assorted books, notebooks, and clothes. His roommate, surnamed Chen, a tall skinny fellow with bright eyes, was there too. He looked intelligent but seemed somewhat unreliable. However, I don't usually judge people completely by their looks, so I didn't feel there was anything amiss.

During dinner at home that evening, Yude asked Hansheng about his plans after graduation. We already knew he didn't want to leave the country for advanced studies. Hansheng shook his unruly head of long hair and said that he would decide once he completed his military service. He wanted to find work himself. He was implying that he didn't want his father to arrange anything for him.

The lot that Hansheng drew obliged him to do only two months of reserve service. Afterward he moved back to his little place. His roommate Chen did not have to do military training because he was rated a C in physical fitness, so he too continued to live in the room. Through the introduction of a professor, they both got work with a social education association earning monthly salaries of NT $4,000 each. We heard the work was light, just doing surveys and statistics, but it was because the work was too light that problems developed. Since Hansheng couldn't stand monotony, after two months he decided to quit and find another job. He wanted to develop and realize his grand ambition to work for the people and contribute to society.

Hansheng soon joined a service center for the wounded and disabled. There he specialized in helping some sadly handicapped people solve their psychological problems, train for employment, and locate jobs. It seemed Hansheng did his work enthusiastically and felt that this could be the kind of social work he would devote his life to. But it so happened that three months later he changed jobs once again. This time it was with a miners's welfare organization. He told me:

"It's not that I don't like helping the handicapped and disabled. I feel that if by talking to them I can help them discover a new understanding of life, it's very significant work. But I really couldn't stand some of my colleagues. All day long they would complain that the salary was too low and that there wasn't any future in the work. And they were so selfish. They gave the good opportunities to people they knew or liked, never giving a thought to those who really needed work. It was better just to leave than to get angry watching them."

"But they couldn't all be that way."

"A few like that was enough."

"But aren't you also complaining?" I asked.

Hansheng was quiet for a while, then declared: "What I'm complaining about is that over there I could only work for some of the people, for the minority. I think the work I have now is more suitable for me. I think I'll be able to improve the welfare of more people."

Not long after Hansheng had begun his new job, I learned that he had broken up with his long-time girlfriend. The reason was, Miss Huang could no longer uphold Hansheng's lofty ideals. Seeing her classmates either going abroad or getting married, she also needed to come to some sort of decision. But Hansheng kept changing jobs all the time, and it seemed that he was not getting anywhere. He had disappointed her.

Miss Huang angrily left for Japan, and Hansheng was naturally very depressed. When he came home he would be despondently quiet, never saying a word. None of us dared provoke him, hoping that his work would eventually soothe the pain. We didn't dream that soon after he would quit again. The reason, he said, was that he felt restrained by people at the top. He wasn't free to do his work the way he wanted to, so he found it uninteresting. Yude and I excused him since he was still feeling so emotionally depressed. We didn't say anything.

Hansheng remained unemployed for two months. Noting his air of defeat, Yude asked a friend to get him a good job in an advertising company, but when Hansheng heard about it he got mad, threw his bowl and chopsticks on the table, and ran from the house.

In Taibei, looking for work without connections is really not too difficult, but to find a suitable and interesting job is not so easy. Hansheng asked friends, wrote résumés, and responded to various advertisements. Finally he responded to a life insurance agency ad.

"Why don't you wait a little longer?" I tried my best to encourage him, saying, "Maybe you'll find work more suited to you."

"What's the use of waiting? Isn't it all the same?" he said exasperatedly.

Yude tried to discourage him from selling insurance. He said it was an unstable, underhanded business, that most insurance companies use people they get through ads to earn money for themselves. And yet he still took out an NT $200,000 accident policy. On top of that, after Hansheng was more himself, out running all over the place, realizing that selling insurance was not as easy as he had imagined, and accomplishing very little after a month, Yude secretly helped him out. Only then was he able to meet his one million NT sales quota. Seeing Hansheng looking so totally frustrated, I guessed that he wouldn't last long in the insurance business either.

It turned out that the company not only required a certain percentage of his sales, but also since he had already reached his maximum, they placed other salesmen under his supervision. This time he was to go out and exploit other people. Eventually Hansheng pounded the table, accused the insurance company of cheating, and walked out. But Yude had to continue paying insurance fees every month!

Later, Hansheng once again passed a test into an advertising agency as a market research analyst. The pay was decent and the work was simple. At first he was satisfied with the new environment and the new colleagues were interesting, but soon after, he again began to feel that the work was dry and meaningless. When he came home he would complain that the manager was unfair to his subordinates and flattering to his superiors. The section chief was sly, taking the credit for other people's work; every one of his colleagues were crooks and devils, eagerly in pursuit of money and fame, always ready to squeeze their way into any favorable position.

"That's the kind of ad agency it is! Dog-eat-dog. Disgusting!"

"Isn't it the same everywhere else?" I said.

"I don't believe that!"

A short time later, Hansheng quit again. In truth, I didn't worry about Hansheng's stubborn pride. It takes guts not to rely on other people, not ask for help. When Yude and I were young, we never relied on anyone but ourselves. Yude had come to Taiwan alone and worked his way through college, doing whatever job came along. My family hadn't been wealthy either. All I had for a dowry was a blanket and a pillow. As our new home, we rented a one-room wooden shack that stood in the backyard of someone else's house, and it was only after our landlord refused to fix our leaky roof that we finally moved out. Whom did we ever depend on? What really worried me was whether Hansheng actually had any plan in his mind. Did he know what kind of a person he wanted to be in the future? What type of work he wanted to do? Though Yude and I did not have any concrete plans at the beginning, we nevertheless had never been lazy, for we knew if we did not take things seriously, all our daydreams would inevitably turn to dust. I thought this was an important way of looking at things. I didn't know whether Hansheng could understand this, but it was too late for me to try and teach him now; this was a matter of the spirit, not something out of a teacher's manual.

"Ma! Hansheng and Dad say he's decided to drive a taxi. You'd better talk to him!"

Hanlin's voice was very nonchalant so that for a moment I didn't even realize what had happened.

"What does your father say?"

"Father says to let him do what he wants!"

Was this what Hansheng really wanted to do?

Hansheng, and also his roommate Chen, had been unable to find satisfying work so they had asked some friends and classmates to get together and form a mutual investment group of $3,000 NT per person per month. This lump sum would be deposited for a specified length of time, and each member of the group would take turns in drawing out the interest for his own use. At the end of the first period, Hansheng and Chen together drew out a total of over $60,000 NT. They bought a secondhand cab, spray-painted it, installed air conditioning, and the two of them started to work.

"Have you tested for your license?"

As I suppressed my surprise I asked a most meaningless question.

"Uh! An operator's license test is really difficult to pass. I tested three times!" Not in the least bit ashamed, he sat down facing me and crossed his legs. Now that his hair had been cut short, his youthful face seemed happy and lively. "I don't know how you and Dad feel about it. Perhaps you think it's losing face, but as far as I'm concerned, this is like starting a business. We have to earn money. Once we have money we can do what we really want to do."

"Can't you earn money doing other things?"

"How many other jobs can offer the same independence and need so little to start out with? Ma, isn't it good to earn one's own living?"

"Earning one's own living is fine." I tried hard to change my way of thinking. It wasn't shameful to have a son graduated from college driving a cab, but I did want to understand more fully: "Do you plan to drive a cab all your life?"

"Of course I don't want to drive a cab all my life. As soon as we have earned enough money, Ah-chen and I plan to open a good bookstore. You consider a bookstore a cultural enterprise, don't you?" The way he asked this was almost spiteful. "Once business picks up at the bookstore we can open some related outfit. Above the bookstore we could open an intimate coffee shop, a publishing house, or a magazine office where we could say what we wanted to say and give society the information it needs to know. . . ."

I couldn't deny that although his plan was not well enough thought out, it certainly was ambitious.

Hansheng came home to tell us about the first humorous thing that happened on the job. His first passenger had turned out to be someone from his class, so naturally he gave him a free ride.

Hansheng and Ah-chen drove the car on day and night shifts. I heard that each one of them could make over $800 to $900 NT in one day, and when it rained or there was a festival they earned even more. Aside from keeping a small amount for pocket money, Hansheng gave all the rest of his daily income to Ah-chen, who was good at keeping accounts. Ah-chen was responsible for paying their monthly investment payment of over $1,000 NT, over $10,000 for gas, and also their biannual payments of various taxes. There wasn't much money left over, but it was all duly deposited. In two years, they wouldn't owe anything. They would also have some money in the bank and own their own car.

"Then we can rent the car to someone else to drive and collect a fixed monthly rental." Hansheng happily explained to me.

Behind his back, Hanlin would smile and say to me, "Isn't he exploiting people himself?"

No matter what, Yude and I were hoping that those two years would pass quickly so that we could see the beautiful vista described by Hansheng. But in reality, it was never to be that simple. Half a year later, Hansheng came home and said that he and Ah-chen had moved.

Moving wasn't such a big deal, but we found out that they had moved in with a pair of sisters who worked in a dance hall.

"What kind of business is this?" His father was furious. It was the first time I had seen him this angry. "We've gone along with everything he has wanted to do but we're not going to let him go down the drain. You! You go find out about this."

His face almost purple with anger, Yude sat depressed in the study all night, refusing to speak to anyone. Although he went to work as usual the next day, he didn't look at all well. And no wonder Yude was angry! It didn't matter that a child was bull-headed or even stupid and incompetent, still he was our child. But we could not allow him to cheapen himself.

That afternoon, I went straight from the publication office to a four-story apartment building with a rusty, broken-down metal front door. One of the doors hung limply on its hinges, the other one stood halfway closed. I climbed to the third floor. Facing twin apartments; the one that was marked No. 18 didn't have a doorbell. I pulled open the dark, dirty screen door and knocked crisply a few times before I heard movement inside. The door, secured with a chain lock, opened just a crack. I could not see clearly, I only knew it was a woman.

"What do you want?"

"May I ask if Pan Hansheng lives here?"

"He's not home!"

The woman tried to shut the door, but I resisted and pushed against it.

"I'm his mother."

There was no sound from within, the door closed, and the woman removed the chain to open the door again. She had on a light pink silk nightgown with a black satin slip inside. She had a very good figure, but as she had just woken up, her eyes and face were bloated. Looking at her bleached brown hair carelessly pushed behind her ears, I thought of a rotten, stale peach.

"You're really his mother? I couldn't see! You're still so young!"

"I'm not young anymore!"

I sat down with my back to the French windows on the sun deck. The living room was connected to the dining room. It seemed spacious enough, since there was little furniture, but it hadn't been cleaned for a long while. A layer of dust covered the floor, the table, and the chairs. Newspapers and magazines were strewn all over the place. Plums seeds, watermelon rinds, empty cans, and cola bottles had been left on the table. Near the ceiling, some cockroaches ran back and forth, preparing for an attack. It turned my stomach.

"Obasan doesn't come in until Saturday. We have the place cleaned twice a week. It's a mess."

She shrugged her shoulders, as if it weren't really any of her business. Then, unexpectedly, she went into the kitchen and brought out a large paper carton of milk with two glasses.

"How about a drink?"

"Don't stand on ceremony! May I ask your surname?"

"Just call me Annie!"

As she ripped open the carton, milk splashed onto her finger. Unselfconsciously, she put her finger into her mouth and sucked.

"Hansheng isn't home?" I asked again, in order to start a dialogue.

"This week Xiao Pan drives in the daytime and doesn't come home till night. Ah-chen drives at night. He's still asleep!"

"You work in a dance hall, Miss Annie?"

"That's right!"

Frankly, Annie's unselfconsciousness made me feel better. Conversation came easily.

"Miss Annie, I want you to know I haven't come here with bad intentions."

"Eh? I never thought you came with bad intentions. Ask anything you like. If I can answer, I will."

"I'd like to understand the true relationship between Hansheng and yourself."

"Xiao Pan and me? There's nothing between us at all!" She laughed uninhibitedly, so hard that she rocked backward and forward, and tears filled her eyes. She said, "But . . . but he and my younger sister Helen get along well. Helen is out."

I felt terrible. Annie picked up a Long Life cigarette from the table and lit it. She exhaled thick smoke and said, "But really, it won't last."

"Why?" I asked anxiously, as if I hoped it would.

"It's hard to explain. Anyway, it just won't. I know my sister well. She doesn't inspire lasting emotions in people. You don't have to worry!"

I smiled bitterly. I really didn't know what to say. Annie certainly was talkative. In detail, she explained how they had gotten to know each other. Helen had met Ah-chen by riding in his cab. She often called for his car after that. Then she got to know Hansheng, and they became more and more friendly. Since the house was empty, the girls invited them to move in. With men in the house at night they felt safer.

Before I left, Annie swore to me several times that Hansheng and Helen were bound to break up. She said I shouldn't worry about it. She also said she thought Hansheng and Ah-chen had financial troubles. She did not know the details, but she thought I should bring it up with Hansheng.

That night our friend Youning and his wife came to our home for dinner. Youning, Ruizhen, Yude, and I were friends from college. After graduation, when Yude entered the news business, Youning left the country to study for a degree. The next year Ruizhen followed him. Life was difficult in the small wooden house and our spirits were low. I would sigh and say, "It's probably finished between Youning, Ruizhen, and us. They will return as Ph.D.'s and professors, they won't be the same."

Who could have dreamed that now we would have a large, two-story house in which to entertain guests? It wasn't a luxurious villa on Yangmingshan, but still it was a comforting achievement.

Except for a few more wrinkles on her forehead and using a bit more makeup, Ruizhen had retained the refreshing, elegant look of her youth. Youning had put on weight, just like Yude. I teased them, saying that, to preserve their figures, they should continue to play singles tennis as they had years before. In school, they had been on the school tennis team.

After dinner Youning kept praising my cooking, saying the food I served could compare with anything served by many large restaurants he had visited since he came back. Yude said that once he retired we would go straight to New York to open a restaurant. Youning immediately said, "Oh, Yude! This isn't a joke! Many people who are involved with cultural work are now promoting Chinese culinary culture in New York!"

Ruizhen liked Hanlin very much. She said that their Zhenxing was growing up in America without many Chinese friends. She hoped that Hanlin would write to him and be his friend.

"Next time, you should all come back together. I heard that Zhenxing got his bachelor's degree at the age of nineteen and he now has two Ph.D. degrees! That's really good! Youning! We're old now, we should retire and give way to our children."

This was the first time I'd heard Yude admit the fact of growing old.

"Nonsense! We're still in our prime! No way!—No way!"

Youning hadn't really made a joke, but we all laughed heartily at what he said. In the midst of our laughter, we heard the doorbell. Ah-hong went to open the door. It was Hansheng, wearing a cheap sweatshirt, jeans, and sandals. His hair was long and messy, as if he hadn't had a haircut for a long time, and his cheeks were covered with stubble. It startled us to see him this way.

"Hansheng! Come over and meet Older Uncle and Auntie Qin."

It was Yude who first addressed him. It looked like he had already forgotten the day's incident, but I knew he hadn't.

"What, calling me Older Uncle? I remember I'm six months younger than you. Come!" Youning got up, stretched his hand out, and enthusiastically grabbed Hansheng's, saying, "Call me Younger Uncle. You've gotten sturdy! What are you doing these days?"

"Driving a cab!" Hansheng announced truculently, as if he were angry with someone.

Everyone continued to laugh and chatter, but I felt that the sound of the laughter was not as natural as before.

When Youning and his wife had gone, to prevent a confrontation between father and son, I went into Hansheng's room alone.

"If you want to find me, why couldn't you telephone me?"

Hansheng was lying on his spring bed with his arm covering his face. He looked exhausted.

"I wanted to see where you were living. I also wanted to see Helen, but she wasn't there."

"There's nothing between Helen and me."

"Hansheng!" I sat down on the edge of the bed. Gently, as if I were talking to a newborn baby, I said, "It's not that Ma wants to scold you, but why don't you pull yourself together? Build a real career, going on like this isn't the way!"

I waited a long time but still didn't get a response. I thought of saying something more, but I heard him choking with tears beneath that husky arm of his. I couldn't believe my ears. I was so upset I didn't know what to do. I decided to wait for his tears to subside, for him to get it out of his system. It was only when he was quiet again that I leaned closer to him, almost kissing his thick head of hair. I was afraid if I sounded the least bit harsh I would never receive an answer; I very carefully asked, "What's wrong? Please tell Ma!"

"It's nothing!" Suddenly he sat up, turning his face away as he rubbed his eyes, just as he had done as a child when he came home after having been in some trouble outside.

"Annie says you have been having some money problems."

"Annie talks too much!" Hansheng got out of bed, picked up a wad of kleenex, and blew his nose. "Who cares anyway? I'm sick of it!"

He hadn't cried about that, but it had to have something to do with it.

I tried very hard and eventually got it out of him.

"Don't know what Ah-chen has been up to. He said three of his friends took off with their interest money and the mutual investment group fell through. We, the initiators, must pay all the others who are involved. I asked him if we had enough savings to do so and he said that we really didn't have any, what with payments for gas, for upkeep, for . . . *Ai!* What a mess! All this has made me unable even to drive any more, and then people have come to pressure us for money. Ah-chen says we should sell the car to reimburse them. How . . . how can I begin to explain. . . ."

"Then sell the car!" I suggested gently.

"Even if we sold the car we wouldn't have enough! . . . The more I think of it, the more ridiculously useless I feel. I've wasted half a year of my life. If I had only realized this earlier, it would have been better to have stayed at the advertising agency earning $7,000 NT a month, no matter what! I could have gotten married. I've been a fool! Incompetent! An idiot!"

The next day, Hansheng got up early and left. We didn't know what he went to do. Yude and I talked it over and decided that if the money he received from selling the car wasn't enough, we would pay the rest for him. Then, by mortgaging our two-story home, we could open a bookstore for him on Zhongxiao East Road, with a family-style coffee shop on the second floor, just as he had wanted. The question was, would he want it? We had no way of knowing. And in our hearts, both Yude and I had the same contradictory feelings. We desperately hoped that he would want to work at building up his own business smoothly, but we were also afraid that he would agree with us! It would seem so unlike the sternly righteous Hansheng who had wanted to struggle, to be independent, to be a model for society.

Shangri-La

Wang Zhenhe

Translated by Michael S. Duke

AH-DUAN had so much on her mind, she didn't sleep well all night.

The morning sky had barely begun to lighten when she decided she might as well get up, start a fire in the wood stove, and prepare breakfast. She specially cooked a plate of fried rice with bitter-tea-oil for Xiao Quan. She had often heard people say, "A bowl of fried rice with bitter-tea-oil is the most nourishing thing to give a child who stays up all night studying," so she had asked Ah-li, the country woman who sold betel nuts by the roadside, to bring her a jar of it. Nowadays no one ever sold such old-fashioned items on the streets any more. Quite some time had passed and she hadn't heard a word from Ah-li. It seemed she had forgotten!

Day before yesterday, she had anxiously reminded Ah-li again: "Xiao Quan is going to take the high school entrance tests day after tomorrow! Why haven't you brought the bitter-tea-oil I asked you to buy for me? My Xiao Quan is studying day and night, and I'm really afraid his health will suffer!"

The following day Ah-li brought her a half-used jar of leftover bitter-tea-oil from her own home, asking her to make do with it anyway because, even in the countryside, it was now difficult to buy the genuine kind.

Taking the jar from her, Ah-duan had opened and smelled it, then immediately frowned. "It really smells bad! More like kerosene! How can Xiao Quan eat something that smells so terrible?"

"You don't have to put in too much of it, just two spoonfuls will be plenty; then beat in a couple of eggs and add some chopped scallions—it won't taste so terribly bad!"

She sautéed the rice according to Ah-li's recipe, tasted it, and felt that it wasn't that hard to swallow. She also fixed him a bowl of his regular favorite, Japanese *miso* soup.

The original appeared in the literary section of *Zhongguo shibao* (China times), August 8–10, 1979. The translation first appeared in *The Chinese PEN* (Spring 1983) and is reprinted by permission.

When she had finished packing Xiao Quan's lunch, she glanced out the window and saw that the sky was turning a light gray. She heard a rooster crowing somewhere far away. She glanced at the small porcelain clock on the table—it was nearly five-thirty!

Must go and wake Xiao Quan! Late last night, before he went to bed, he had asked her repeatedly to be certain to wake him up before five-thirty. He wanted to review today's examination subjects once more. *That child is just too conscientious about his studies; he shouldn't ruin his health that way*, she thought to herself as she walked into his room.

There was no window, and only a faint shaft of light seeping through a three-foot space between the plank wall and the ceiling illuminated the room. Day and night the room was always as dark as a small air-raid shelter.

Sitting on the edge of the bed, she turned on the light and saw Xiao Quan snuggled in his blanket, sleeping on his side, facing away from the wall. He was smiling slightly—no doubt dreaming that he had passed the high school entrance exams. Just as she was about to reach over to awaken him, her hand suddenly stopped, motionless in mid-air.

He's sleeping so soundly; why not let him sleep a little while longer?

Ever since the day she had decided to let him take the entrance exams, she had not seen him sleep a full eight hours. Every day, early in the morning, he would get up and start studying in the dark; most of the time he would still be buried in his books at eleven or twelve at night. He had been going on like that for two whole months already! Drawing back her hand, she sighed softly.

Poor boy! Let him sleep a little while longer!

Suddenly she noticed what looked like small beads of perspiration glistening faintly on her son's forehead. Reaching out to touch it, she realized that he was sweating, and his neck too was soaked with sweat. She hurriedly lifted the blanket, then found a small towel and gently wiped the sweat off of his forehead and from under his chin.

Turning slightly, Xiao Quan faced upward and stretched his legs out fully so that his body seemed very long, much longer than she expected. She looked him over carefully several times, her eyes brimming with surprised joy. *This child has really grown up! When his father died, he . . . he was not quite three years old! And now . . . he has graduated from elementary school and is going to take the high school entrance exams—it all seems like such a short time.* Gently, she reached out to wipe his face, filled with a deep tenderness.

Just then Xiao Quan's eyes fluttered open, peering at her, then suddenly, with eyes wide open, he let out a yell as though he had been bitten by a snake: "Ma, what time is it? What time is it?"

"It's still early! Sleep a little longer." She kept on wiping his cheeks. "You sleep a little longer and I'll come back and wake you up in a few minutes."

"I don't want to!" Xiao Quan rolled out of bed, slipped on a pair of wooden clogs, shot into the kitchen, grabbed the little porcelain clock from the table, and let out another loud yell.

"It's . . . it's almost six o'clock already! You didn't wake me up and you still want me to sleep some more! I told you last night to wake me up before five-thirty!" He was pouting, his lips puckered out so far that a bottle of Hualian's special Deer Brand soy sauce could be hung from them. "Ma, what's the matter with you? You didn't wake me and I still have to go over my Chinese language notes again!"

Ah-duan turned off the light, went back into the kitchen, and smiled as she pulled Xiao Quan around to face her: "It won't hurt anything if you sleep a little longer. If you don't get enough sleep, how can you have the energy to take the exams?"

She could see from Xiao Quan's expression that he was quite unwilling to accept her explanation, so she pinched him lightly on the cheek. "Go wash your face and brush your teeth! You've still got plenty of time to review your lessons. 'Haste makes waste,' remember; what's the hurry? Take it easy!"

"The teacher said I should start out by six-fifty because it takes over forty minutes to walk to the examination hall!"

"You'll definitely make it." The water on the stove was about to come to a boil when the charcoal fire began to die out, so she picked up a paper fan from the floor and quickly began to fan the embers until the fire flared up again. "You'll definitely get there on time. There's nothing to worry about."

Xiao Quan had hurriedly washed up and dressed and was already sitting at the table studying his notes. Having filled the kettle, she set out her son's breakfast, looking around to make sure there wasn't anything else to be cooked before she poured some water on the fire. The briskly burning fire immediately hissed as if in pain and, with a puff of thick white smoke, noiselessly died out.

At the same time, as if in similar pain, Xiao Quan suddenly let out a loud cry. "What's the matter?" she quickly put down the lunch box she was packing and looked at him.

"Ma, this rice . . . ," Xiao Quan pointed at the rice, his face contorted with surprise, "What kind of rice is this? It tastes terrible!"

"Oh," she said, thinking to herself, "so that's it." She walked over to sit down beside Xiao Quan, smilingly explained that it was fried with bitter-tea-oil, and although it didn't smell so good, it was very good for his health and he should just swallow it without worrying. Seeing that Xiao Quan still looked troubled and unwilling, she repeatedly urged him to eat it. Finally Xiao Quan could do nothing but push in another mouthful and, with a bitter grimace, swallow it without even chewing, after which he gulped down a spoonful of *miso* soup to wash away the kerosene taste from his throat and tongue. All the while he kept muttering, "It tastes terrible!"

"You've got to chew before you swallow! You don't want to choke!"

Xiao Quan didn't care to listen; he just kept right on swallowing large gulps of rice followed by spoonfuls of soup, interrupted only by an additional "It tastes terrible" until he had done his duty completely and eaten the whole plate of rice. Then he put his plate and chopsticks in the sink. As he turned around, he caught sight of his lunch box all wrapped up on the table and let out another shout. "Ma . . . ," he quickly picked it up, "is this full of that terrible rice too?"

She smiled, shook her head, and told him that bitter-tea-oil had to be eaten in the morning on an empty stomach to be of any use; if he wanted to eat some more, he'd have to wait until the next morning!

"It tastes terrible. I never want to eat it again!" His tone of voice was very resolute, just like a martyr refusing to surrender.

She couldn't help laughing when she saw him pouting again so that a soy sauce bottle could be hung from his lips. Just as she was trying to figure out what she could say to break down his firm resolution and persuade him to eat it just once more the next morning, she heard him utter another loud exclamation.

"What's the matter now?"

Pointing at the small porcelain clock, he exclaimed, "Look! It's already six-thirty! Ma, did you eat yet?" Seeing her shake her head, he began to stamp his feet. "Ma, hurry up and eat! We have to leave by at least six-fifty or else we'll be late. Ma, you hurry up and eat and I'll go pack my school bag; we'll take off at six-fifty."

"I . . ." Before she could finish speaking, Xiao Quan had already run into the bedroom, picked up his school bag, and come back to stand in front of her. She went on eating her rice gruel as she watched him open his school bag and dump the contents out on the table. After that he took out a slip of paper from his shirt pocket on which were neatly written all of the things he would need to take with him that day. Then, as he read out each item on the list, he placed them into his bag one by one. She listened to him reading with great interest:

"One, examination entrance permit; two, *Guide to High School Promotion*; three, Chinese language notes; four, history notes; five, science notes; six, pencil box; seven, inkstand, ink, writing brush . . ."

He hadn't forgotten a thing. He had even written "lunch box" and "clear water to mix ink with" on his list! The things he had to take that day were nearly all stuffed into his bag and he was just about to close it when Ah-duan suddenly pushed the little porcelain clock in front of him.

"Take this too!" Seeing the puzzled expression on her son's face, she pushed her breakfast things to one side, pulled his bag over, and carefully placed the clock inside.

"You said your teacher said it would be best to take an adult's wristwatch into the examination hall so you would be able to control the time during the exams and not become too anxious. Nobody in our family wears a watch, but fortunately this clock is not too big; it's just right for you to take into the examination room."

"I don't need it! Without a watch I can still take the tests!"

"Well, take it anyway! With a clock you won't be worrying." She buttoned the school bag and gently pushed it over to her son. "Ma is really hoping that you can make good marks on the exams."

"All right!" Xiao Quan stood up and hoisted his bag onto his shoulders. "Ma, hurry up and eat! Otherwise we're going to be too late."

Oh Lord! The problem that had kept her awake all night had finally come up.

"Xiao Quan, Ma . . . ," Xiao Quan's eyes grew big with apprehension as he stared at her, and she suddenly felt as if something were stuck in her throat; no matter how she tried, she couldn't speak. She struggled a while but could only continue to gaze at Xiao Quan, her mouth open yet wordless.

"Oh, yes!" Xiao Quan said as if he had suddenly remembered something very important, and then went on to ask her, "Ma, where's your lunch box? Didn't you fix up something for yourself to eat too?"

" . . . "

"Didn't you?"

" . . . "

"Didn't you?"

She had to say it. "No, I didn't!"

"You didn't?" His voice was filled with surprise.

"Xiao Quan, Ma . . . ," She had to tell him; she just had to tell him. She felt terribly pained, and her eyes began to redden. "Ma cannot go with you!"

"Why? Why not?" Xiao Quan's face fell with disappointment. "Last night you said you would; you promised you would go with me to the examination site today! What happened? How come you say you can't go now?"

" . . . "

Seeing that she just stood there with her mouth open without speaking, he immediately went on, "How come you can't go now?" She felt as if an iron claw was tearing at her heart, tearing with such force that the pain nearly made her weep.

She really had promised him the night before that she would go with him to the examinations.

Yesterday afternoon the teacher had taken Xiao Quan and his classmates to the examination site to look around and familiarize themselves with the surroundings, and it was five or six o'clock before he came home. As soon as he came in, Xiao Quan exuberantly told her how the high school had such a big auditorium, such a big playground, and there was even a swimming pool and a gymnasium, and . . . , he continued thus with joyful animation just as though he had already passed the exams and was about to start studying there. Finally he related that his sixth-grade class had been assigned to examination section number five inside the big auditorium.

Even as they sat down to dinner, Xiao Quan's report was still not finished!

"Many of my classmates' parents are going to go with them to the examination site! Zheng Zhiwei said his mother and father were too busy in the morning, so they told his older brother to go with him; but in the afternoon they will go to see him. Zhao Zhengxiong's father has gone to Taidong, but he is going to hurry back tonight so that he can take him to the exams on his bicycle first thing tomorrow morning. . . ." He reeled off the names of many fellow classmates whose parents were all going to the exams with them; the more he talked, the more excited he became, as if he were relating some earth-shaking news. "They're so lucky! They all have somebody to go with them! Oh, they're so lucky!"

"Ma will go with you too!"

"Really?" He was so elated he threw down his chopsticks and clapped his hands. "Really, Ma, you really will?"

"Ma is not really very happy about you having to walk such a long way all by yourself!"

"Then tomorrow you'll have to close down the shop?"

"That seems like the only way."

She picked a piece of meat out of the salted cabbage soup and put it into Xiao Quan's bowl. "But tonight I'll have to finish up all the clothes that people have ordered. When we leave tomorrow morning, I'll have to leave them at Ah-li's place so that my customers can pick them up."

After she had put Xiao Quan to bed, she busied herself straightening up the shop and preparing to close up for the night. Just then her younger brother—her only relative in Hualian—came riding up hurriedly on his bicycle. Before he'd even gotten off his bike, he shouted out that the railroad office was working overtime and there was no way he could have come over earlier to see Xiao Quan. Knowing that Xiao Quan had already gone to bed, he didn't come into the house but just stood there at the door asking her very solicitously what time Xiao Quan was going to begin the exams tomorrow morning, how many subjects were to be covered, and whether he was was fully prepared in all of them. He even told her not to pressure Xiao Quan too much as it was bad to make a child feel too nervous. . . . Finally he said that early the next morning he had to test a train; otherwise he could take Xiao Quan on his bicycle to the high school at Meilun for the exams.

Her brother left right after he helped her close up the shop. She then opened the door just a little to let in some cool air. The wooden house that she lived in had a sheet metal roof; even after nightfall the heat radiated from the four walls like an oven. Even though the electric fan that her brother had built out of scrap materials continued blowing away at her feet, her perspiration just kept on dripping like rain as she sewed, working away under the yellow lamplight. By the time she had finished the lot, locked the door, and got into bed, it was already nearly two o'clock in the morning. It was not until then that the heat of the previous day began to subside a little.

Just as she was about to turn off the light and lie down, she noticed that Xiao Quan, who was sleeping on one side of the little room, didn't have anything over him. Fearful that he might catch cold, she quickly pulled up the blanket that he had kicked off and laid a corner of it over his stomach. Then she reached out one finger and, as if she were caressing her most prized treasure, lightly traced a line from his forehead down past the soft, petal-like lips all the way to his chin. *Child, you must know, all Ma's hopes are with you.* Her finger moved gently upward again, from his rounded chin past his soft lips, his slightly quivering nostrils, and back to his forehead. *If you can only pass the entrance exams, Ma will work like a horse to let you continue to go to school.* She bent over and kissed him ever so gently on the forehead, then she turned off the light and tried to sleep.

Only then did she finally begin to feel that her back and her legs were really hurting badly. Except for just before New Year's, she rarely pushed herself to work day and night like this! She urged herself to hurry up and go to sleep so that she could get up a little earlier in the morning, but she could not stop herself from wondering how Xiao Quan was going to do on the next day's exams. *Will he be able to pass or not? What should I take tomorrow?* Just as she was thinking that in this terribly hot weather she had better take some Eight Trigrams Pills or some Tiger Balm, she suddenly gasped out an "*Ai ya!*" the way Xiao Quan always did when he was puzzled by something; then she said to herself over and over again, *I can't do it! I can't do it! I can't do it!*

If she let all the neighborhood women know that she was actually going to close up shop in order to accompany her son to the examinations, who knows how they would ridicule her behind her back?

Knowing that she was a widow, the neighborhood women had very little to do with her; it was as though they felt that she wasn't fit to be living with everyone else on that bustling market street. Some of the local wives even regarded her as a star of ill omen and avoided her whenever they saw her for fear that she would infect them with some sort of terrible misfortune.

She also kept very carefully to herself. Unless she had some truly compelling need, she very rarely went over to her neighbors. Even so, no matter how hard she tried, she was constantly being harassed by a great deal of sarcastic gossip.

Last year, at New Year's, she had used some leftover cloth to make a new suit of clothes for Xiao Quan. He had been out of the house for less than half a day when Ah-li came over to tell her angrily about Mrs. Ji from the medicine shop across the street. "The way she can't stand to see anyone else wearing nice clothes or eating well, she must have been weaned on piss instead of milk! What business is it of hers if Xiao Quan wears new clothes? Just listen to the way she curses people—saying that Ah-duan has too many hairs on her ass, plain as anyone can see, and so she shows her ass off like it was her face! Just listen, is that any way for a person to talk?" Time after time, she kept repeating, "Is that any way for a person to talk?" And the more she said it, the angrier she became. "The nerve of her saying such evil things in the first month of the new year! I told her she'd surely come to a bad end. She has a little money and she starts bragging away like the God of Wealth himself, and ever so highfalutin and smug! She doesn't stop to think, if the Japanese hadn't been defeated and left that shop behind, her old man would still be their flunky. Huh! What is there to be so proud about having found a little money on the road? Huh!''

The next day she told Xiao Quan to change into his school uniform; but as she was putting those new clothes away in the closet, she could not help weeping bitterly with secret pain.

Then again, not too many days ago at lunchtime, Xiao Quan had felt too hot inside the house, so he took his rice bowl out and sat in the doorway to eat. Just then Mrs. Li, who runs a bookshop next door, walked by; and when she saw that Xiao Quan had a big piece of pork spareribs in his bowl, she laughed derisively:

"So . . . today you're eating spareribs! And sitting in the doorway to show off!'' Mrs. Li was so fat you could not even see her neck, and her laughter always rose straight up from her stomach to her mouth with a great roar. "Ha! Why don't you go sit out in the middle of the street so that everyone can see you eating such a delicious piece of spareribs! How about it, Xiao Quan, why don't you?''

From that time on, no matter what, she would never again allow Xiao Quan to eat in the doorway.

Such troubling things happened almost all the time. She lived in almost constant fear, as if walking on thin ice, ever watchful lest she do something that they might belittle her for.

If she allowed those cruelly watchful neighborhood women to find out that she was actually abandoning her work tomorrow in order to accompany her son to the examinations, they would certainly seize upon it as an opportunity to ridicule her further.

But she really did not feel good about Xiao Quan walking the forty or more minutes to Meilun all by himself to take the exams. What if something unforeseen were to happen? Then . . . she resolved again to go with him, but she was still afraid of her neighbors' gossip. Thus she kept on worrying and debating back and forth in her mind, tossing and turning all night long without even once falling asleep.

Finally, however, she did make up her mind—she would not go with Xiao Quan.

"Ma, why can't you go now? Why can't you go? Why . . . ?'' Xiao Quan kept on asking repeatedly.

She lowered her head, hesitating a moment before she slowly raised it again, her eyes looking off into the distance, not daring to look at Xiao Quan.

"Ma didn't get all of the clothes finished last night. I've got to hurry and work on them this morning. I promised those people they could pick them up this afternoon.''

"Last night you said for certain you would go!''

"Ma thought the clothes could be finished last night and didn't know it wasn't possible." Seeing the extremely disappointed look on Xiao Quan's face, her heart was pierced with pain. "Ma really can't go with you. Ma really . . ." Her voice choked up and she could not go on.

Seeing that she was about to burst into tears, Xiao Quan quickly moved forward, wanting to comfort her but really not knowing what to say. He just stood there looking at her anxiously, his hands fidgeting nonstop with his school bag. His face was filled with an indescribable look of confusion and distress.

She sighed and pulled him into her arms. "You must understand, Ma can't go with you because there's no choice. If there was, Ma would do whatever was promised. You understand? Ma can't go because Ma has no choice. You understand?"

He quickly nodded his head that he understood.

"It's almost time; hurry up and go now! You don't want to be late!" She pointed to the school bag on his back, "You've got everything, right? Have you got your examination permit?"

Xiao Quan nodded his head several times again.

"You won't lose your way now, will you?"

"Don't worry, Ma! The teacher just took us there yesterday!"

After she had given him a round of last-minute advice—"Be sure and do your best! Read all the exam questions carefully before you answer! Whatever you do, don't get too nervous. . . ."—Xiao Quan turned and walked toward the door, calling over his shoulder, "OK, I'm going!"

With the door closed, the shop seemed rather dark. All around were piles of grass mats, straw hats, brooms . . . clusters of black shadows. Xiao Quan deftly threaded his way through those familiar shadows to the front door. He pulled aside the door latch, and as he opened one side of the door a ray of light burst in. Outside, it was already quite sunny. Just as he was about to go out the door, his mother called to him from behind. Halting abruptly, he turned to see his mother already standing before him in the full light of day.

"You forgot to take your drinking water!" She stepped closer to help him shoulder his small canteen.

Before he'd finished calling out, "Ma, I'm going!" Xiao Quan had already bolted out the door. There were already quite a few people and vehicles on the street. Several clerks in the bookstore next door were busy sweeping up and getting ready for business. Her shop faced west and the morning sun had not reached it as yet, but on the other side of the street the sun was shining everywhere in one great patch of brightness. *With the sun so strong, Xiao Quan should have worn a straw hat.* Just as this thought came into her head, she also remembered that she should have admonished him to be very careful when he had to use the brush pen for calligraphy in answering the Chinese language questions, not to tip over the inkwell and mess up the exam paper. She was about to hurry out and call to Xiao Quan to tell him all of these things, when out of the corner of her eye she caught sight of Mrs. Ji, the owner of the pharmacy across the street, walking over with one hand on her head to block the sun and carrying some large lotus roots in her other hand, exclaiming loudly, "This heat is really enough to kill a person!"

Mrs. Ji stopped on the sidewalk in front of the bookstore and gave the lotus roots to one of the clerks who was sweeping there.

"Here's something fresh for your boss's wife; they picked them from the pond just yesterday and sent me a whole basketful!" Her voice was very high-pitched as if she were singing Peking opera. "You mean your boss's wife isn't even up yet? She certainly has a good life!" She brushed the dust off of her hands, placed them on her hips, and peered around with her binocular-like eyes, perking up her ears like a cat listening intently for any sound.

If she let this woman whose mouth had two tongues hear her admonishing Xiao Quan, who knows what sort of gossip she would make up? Who knows what she would say to ridicule her? . . . *Ai!* All she could do was to stop in her tracks and go back inside!

When she stuck her head out again to look, Xiao Quan had already reached the big banyan tree at the end of the road, and she saw him turn the corner onto Zhongzheng Road. Then she could no longer see him with his school bag and canteen on his back.

Mrs. Ji was once again crossing the street with her hand shading her forehead, all the while shouting out, "This heat is really enough to kill a person! . . . enough to kill a person!"

The clerks at the bookstore next door were busily opening up shop, and the noise they made resounded like a thunder clap.

She also opened her door without the slightest sound and swept up the sidewalk in front of her shop, again without the slightest hint of a sound.

As she was sweeping the sidewalk, a student who looked like he was going to take the entrance exams brushed by her. The child's mother was going with him. And the child also had a newly plaited straw hat on his head.

"Mrs. Zhang!" Mrs. Ji shouted from across the narrow street with her hand still over her forehead as if it actually grew there, "Where in the world are you taking your boy in this awful heat?"

When she heard her shout, the boy's mother turned her head to look, and, seeing that it was Mrs. Ji, she slowed down and pointed to her son walking beside her, "Taking him to the high school entrance exams. Today is the first day."

"You're truly fortunate to have a boy taking the high school exams!"

"Not really. . . ."

"You're not taking the bus?"

"Too many people. We couldn't squeeze on. It's really faster to walk over!"

After waving good-bye to Mrs. Ji, the mother and the boy wearing the straw hat quickened their pace, hurrying to the corner where they turned and were lost to sight. Ah-duan remembered the expression of extreme disappointment on Xiao Quan's face and could not help feeling very sad.

He's still only a child and rarely ever goes out by himself; I should have gone with him! I should have gone with him!

As if she had overheard what she was thinking, Mrs. Ji then stared straight over at her: "Ah-duan, isn't your Xiao Quan taking the exams today too?"

"He's already gone!" Lowering her head, she kept her voice very low and didn't dare speak up for fear that people would say she was making a noisy show of the fact that her son was taking the exams.

"You mean you're not going with him?" Mrs. Ji looked ever so concerned, and she raised her voice high enough to drown out the noise of the car horns. "This'll never do! Xiao Quan is going off to pass the examinations in first place, become a first rank official, and you, the mother of a *zhuangyuan** and a future lady and mother of a top-ranking official, you don't even go with him. . . . How can this be?"

Just as she was about to force herself to answer by saying, "Mrs. Ji, you really know how to joke," three cars drove up along the street and stopped, waiting to proceed, effectively cutting her and Mrs. Ji off with a wall of steel and noise. She quickly made use of this opportunity to pick up her dustpan and broom and hurry back into the shop without paying any further attention to Mrs. Ji.

She was extremely resentful of Mrs. Ji's derision. Even as she gathered up the straw hats, grass mats, straw rain capes, rolls and rolls of yellow toilet paper, and brooms made of plaited reeds that were piled up in the shop and moved them all out to the front for display, she was still feeling angry.

Then she thought of how she didn't have a man beside her and how badly off she was financially, so how could *she* argue with anybody about anything? She figured the best she could do was to keep quiet and swallow her anger.

She picked up the feather duster and busily dusted the wooden clogs; then she hurried on to sweep the floor inside the shop until everything was clean and neat. After that she took advantage of not yet having any customers to wash and hang out yesterday's dirty clothes. She then asked Ah-li to watch the shop for her while she hurried over to the market to buy a few vegetables and some things to put in Xiao Quan's lunch box the next day. She actually kept herself so busy that the sweat was pouring down her face, trying her best not to think again of Mrs. Ji's recent insults.

It was after eleven o'clock before she finally finished running around. By the time she sat down at her sewing machine and prepared to do some alterations on the clothes she was making, she had nearly given up caring about Mrs. Ji; but she could certainly not stop worrying about Xiao Quan.

I wonder how he's doing in the exams? I wonder how he's . . .

When her husband died, Xiao Quan was not quite three years old. At that time

---

*The scholar who made the highest marks in the civil examinations during A.D. 606–1905 was given the title of *zhuangyuan*.

the American planes came every day to bomb and strafe, so she had taken him to the countryside to live with her family away from danger. Her own family was too poor to support her, and she and Xiao Quan had to rely completely on her doing some sewing for people in order to barely eke out a living. After Restoration, a close friend of her husband took over a number of shops that had belonged to the Japanese and gave her the smallest one on Zhongshan Road to make her living by sewing and selling general everyday goods. Although their life was still quite difficult, at least the two of them, mother and son, had a way to get by.

At the time they first moved here, Xiao Quan had not even begun to go to school. When Xiao Quan asked her whether she would let him go on to take the high school entrance exams and continue studying after elementary school graduation, she was startled to realize how quickly time had passed. Time had truly flown by, and now Xiao Quan had actually graduated and was taking the high school entrance examinations!

"The teacher told us to come home and ask our parents," Xiao Quan had said as he handed her a questionnaire asking her to fill in whether she wanted her child to "prepare for high school" or "apply for employment." "If we're going to go on in school, the teacher will help us review our academic subjects; if we're going to go to work, the teacher will teach us the abacus and accounting."

"What do *you* want to do now?"

"I . . . ," Xiao Quan lowered his head as though he found it hard to say what he wanted to.

"Let Ma hear what you think."

"I . . . ," As he raised his head, Xiao Quan's cheeks reddened as though he were very embarrassed. "I want very much to go on to high school. But I . . ." Swallowing hard, he lowered his head again, "I know—I heard my classmates talking—it costs a lot of money. Zhuang Xinyi, Wang Fuxiong, Lin Haisheng . . . their families don't have any money, so they're not preparing to go on to high school. We don't have much money either, so I think it would be best if I go to work first and help Ma make some money. Once we have some money, then I can still go on to high school just the same!"

He raised his head, glanced at his mother, and then, as if to give her some time to think, looked out the door right into the sunlight streaming in from the west. It was about the end of April or the beginning of May then, the one time of the year when the weather in Hualian was most pleasant and comfortable; even the setting sun was an especially beautiful deep orange hue, and it lit up Xiao Quan's clear, pure face as if it were plated with gold—suddenly the Golden Child from the temple was there before her eyes!

Putting down her sewing, Ah-duan put her arms around the Golden Child standing before her and hugged him close. "My good and understanding child!" She caressed his ever so short hair. "You know the only desire Ma has in this life is that you have a good future and that people will not look down on you.

Since you want so much to go on studying, then Ma will let you study. If you can pass the high school exams, Ma will find a way for you to go on studying, no matter how hard I have to work.''

"But Ma . . .''

She stopped his mouth with her hand. "Don't say any more, I've already figured it all out. There are only two of us, mother and son, and we don't have any big expenses; if we save a little on everyday things, it should not be too hard to send you to high school." She handed the school questionnaire back to him. "Here, you just fill in 'prepare for high school' for me and that's it.'' She patted him gently on the shoulder. "Did you hear me?''

Xiao Quan nodded his head, too happy to speak.

The news certainly went around fast. In only a couple of days everyone on the entire street knew that the widow woman Ah-duan was actually going to let her son go on to high school. Once again, all sorts of vicious things were being said all around her, especially by those neighborhood women whose children had taken the high school exams without any success. Their jealousy grew into a sort of righteous indignation.

"Going to high school is not the same as going to elementary school—it takes a lot of money! And besides, nowadays if you only go to junior high school and don't continue on to senior high school and college, it's of no use anyway. For a widow like Ah-duan to think of sending her son to college, that's really too much!''

"If I were her, I'd be a little more reasonable and send the boy off to learn a craft; after only three years, he'd be a journeyman and able to make some money for her. Who's she trying to fool? Sending her son off to high school without counting the costs! With only that small shop of hers and that little bit of sewing work, and she thinks she can produce a golden *zhuangyuan*? She's dreaming!''

"Doesn't even have the ass to shit, why try!''

The neighborhood women did their best to make sure that she heard all of the terrible things they had to say, and this caused her to waver badly in her resolution to allow Xiao Quan to go on studying. Thinking about it over and over, she still could not decide what was really the best course. *The boy is only going to take the entrance exams and there's already so much gossip; if Xiao Quan actually passes the exams and I really let him go on to high school, who knows what vicious and insulting things the neighbor women will think of to say?*

"I really don't know what's the right thing to do. What's the right thing to do?'' She told her younger brother all about her terrible dilemma in hopes that he would help her to decide. After he heard her story, he angrily stamped his feet.

"Sis, how can you come down to their level?'' He raised his voice as high as he could so that he could be heard a long way off. "Who made it a rule that poor people's children can't go on to high school? Even the government is trying very hard to help poor people's children go on to a higher education. Who the hell are they to try to prevent people's children from going on in school and trying to get ahead? Truly, they're no better than dogs and pigs!''

Listening to him yelling like that, she became so nervous that she jumped up and frantically waved her hands to get him to stop. He must stop talking that way!

"You may be afraid of them, Sis, but I'm not afraid. . . ." He had originally intended to go on with something like, "Whoever picks on my sister is going to have to deal with me," or some such warning; but when he saw that his sister's eyes were reddening and she was about to burst into tears, he had to swallow back his words.

"Sis, you're always so weak, just letting people run all over you; just letting . . ." He sighed, then stopped talking.

After she sat down with a tired and despondent look on her face, he finally urged her not to come down to the neighbor women's level—if Xiao Quan were to pass the high school exams, then of course she'd have to let him go on to school. It was a matter of importance for the boy's entire life, he said, and she should not ruin his future just because of a little malicious gossip. Furthermore, he said, if there was any problem about money, he would certainly do all he could to support her; he would do everything he could.

In the end she accepted her brother's advice and fully resolved to permit Xiao Quan to continue on in school if only he had the ability to pass those examinations.

Was Xiao Quan destined for such good fortune? Did he really have the ability to pass the exams? She didn't know; she kept on thinking of this all morning and didn't have any mind for working. Customers came in to buy things, and she couldn't keep her mind on what she was doing with them. Once she even gave a customer too much change! As she was trying to cut out a dress pattern, she kept worrying about Xiao Quan going out on such a hot day without wearing a hat. *What if he was unable to stand the heat, like what happened on a school outing last year when he got dizzy and fainted? These past few months he's never had enough sleep at night, his health has surely been weakened. He definitely won't be able to stand the heat; definitely.* Then she thought of a number of things to comfort herself, like *I fed him fried rice with bitter-tea-oil for breakfast this morning; surely nothing will happen . . . nothing will happen.* Then she began to think of other problems: *What if he should lose his way? What if he didn't arrive on time? Could he understand the examination questions?* There was simply no way that she could stop worrying about Xiao Quan, and she could not concentrate on her work either. She had been cutting on one piece of material for a long time and still had not cut out a proper pattern; she had very nearly cut the wrong way and ruined her customer's material!

By noon the sun began to heat up. She really didn't feel like starting a fire and cooking lunch just for herself alone, so she went over to the noodle shop at the end of the block and bought a couple of steamed rolls. As she was eating the rolls, she wondered to herself whether the lunch she had packed for Xiao Quan was enough for him to eat. Then she thought that she ought to cook something nourishing like pork liver for Xiao Quan to take with him the next day.

In the afternoon her thoughts were all the more concentrated on Xiao Quan, and there was no way she could stop thinking and wondering: *How is Xiao Quan doing on the exams? Can he answer all of the questions or not? Did he have enough to eat for lunch? When he did his calligraphy for the Chinese language questions, would he knock over the inkstand and ruin the exam paper? Would Xiao Quan faint from the heat? Would he lose his way? Was he late this morning? Was he . . . ? Did he . . . ? Could he have . . . ? Mightn't he . . . ? Didn't he . . . ? What if he . . . ?*

The more things she thought of, the more agitated she became; she wished she could hurry over to the examination site and see for herself that very minute.

I should have gone with him—such a long way; such heat—I really should have gone along with him. I . . . Ai!

She raised her head and looked outside. The sunlight was already streaming into the shop! *It must be about four o'clock already!* Ah-li had long since moved her stand and all of her wares over under the big banyan tree to escape the heat. When a customer came to pick up her clothes, she had also asked her the time and she told her it was ten minutes past three. That was nearly an hour ago. She could not be mistaken. *It must be nearly four o'clock by now, Xiao Quan should be home by this time. The afternoon exams last until three, and with an hour to walk home, he should be home by now.*

She looked out the doorway several times but didn't see any sign of Xiao Quan. Then she ran down to the corner and looked down the road several times, but she still did not see him. After watching her dashing up and down the street and asking what time it was every minute, Ah-li laughed as she asked her, "Who are you waiting for? And in such a state too! Are you waiting for Xiao Quan?"

Seeing a big crowd of neighborhood people all sitting there under the banyan tree, she didn't answer Ah-li; just smiled as she went by.

She stood there about ten yards from where all those people were leisurely sitting under the banyan tree; stood there with the hot sun bearing down on her head and face, looking down the road . . . searching everywhere down the road with her eyes. Aha! Suddenly her eyes brightened. Just at the intersection of Zhongzheng Road and Mingli Road, about five hundred yards away, right there in front of the Hualian General Hospital, she saw him—she saw the image of a child, a child that looked very much like Xiao Quan, a child that looked exactly like Xiao Quan. She blinked her eyes and looked again, carefully. Heavens! Wasn't that Xiao Quan? Walking slowly along with a school bag on his shoulder, and with every step he took the canteen hanging at his side swayed back and forth. Wasn't that Xiao Quan?

Her nose tickled, as if she were just about to burst out crying. She hurried forward a few yards, then stood by the side of the street and tried to control her rising emotions as she carefully watched Xiao Quan walking along step by step.

Oh! Xiao Quan saw her! Xiao Quan waved to her with a big smile and began to walk faster! She could almost hear the water swishing around in his canteen as he came toward her.

Xiao Quan was almost close to her, almost—then there he was! She reached out and pulled him close. There were so many things she wanted to say and to ask that for a moment she didn't even know where to begin! Just at that moment the sound of loud singing blared out from behind them. She looked back and saw a pedicab advertising a movie pulling out slowly from the alleyway. The cab was plastered on all sides with brightly colored posters, and as it peddled slowly in the direction of Hualian General Hospital, a loudspeaker blared out a song:

> Oh! This beautiful Shangri-La,
> This lovable Shangri-La . . .

In a short time the music faded away and the pedicab stopped. She saw the man in the cab pick up a microphone and begin to blare out his propaganda:

"Good news! Good news everybody! Starting tomorrow the China Theater proudly presents the newest and finest nationally produced musical extrava-ganza—*The Oriole's Flight*. *The Oriole's Flight* is the biggest, brightest show yet, with the most dazzling array of singing and dancing. *The Oriole's Flight* brings together the beautiful Ouyang Feiying, the handsome and heroic Yan Shu and Chen Tianguo, and the old-time favorite superstar Wang Yuanlong in an unforgettable group performance. . . ."

When she went into the house, the blaring sound of "Good news! . . . *Oriole's Flight* . . . !" was still buzzing in her ears. Then, after another moment, she heard the singing start up again; seemingly like that same song of a moment ago, "Shangri-La . . . Shangri-La . . ." something or other; then the sound finally began to fade off into the distance.

Only then did she finally recall all of the things she wanted to ask Xiao Quan. She held his hands and anxiously asked him a spate of questions: How did he do in the exams? Did he have enough water to drink? Was he allowed to take the little porcelain clock into the exam room? Did he feel dizzy walking all the way under such a hot sun? Did he read any questions incorrectly? Did he tip over the inkstand? Did he . . . , did he . . . , did he . . . , did he . . . ? All of the questions that had piled up in her mind came tumbling out all at once. Finally she asked him why was he so late getting home. Didn't the exams let out at three o'clock? How come it was nearly five o'clock before he finally got home?

"I was reviewing tomorrow's examination subjects with my classmates."

"Oh, so that's what you were doing." Seeing that Xiao Quan's forehead was covered with beads of sweat, she hurriedly took a handkerchief out of her pocket and wiped it off for him. "Ma thought something happened and was so worried!"

Turning on the electric fan and letting it blow on Xiao Quan, she asked him if he were thirsty; would he like to go down to the corner shop and have some iced herbal gelatin?

Xiao Quan shook his head.

A customer came into the store. She told Xiao Quan to sit over closer to the fan and then went to take care of the customer. The customer bought a bamboo broom, a package of toilet paper, and some women's shampoo. After seeing the customer off, she went straight into the bedroom, carefully locked up the money she'd just received in the clothes locker, then sent Xiao Quan in to take a bath and busily began to cook dinner.

At about seven o'clock, she put the food on the table, turned on the light, and sat down with Xiao Quan to eat dinner, at the same time keeping an eye on the store. Xiao Quan's appetite was very good. He ate two bowls of rice and asked her to dish up half a bowl more; he also ate up the fish she had fried especially for him, without leaving a scrap.

"You're eating just like a cat, not even leaving the fish bones behind!" She laughed out loud. "I'll fry another fish for you tomorrow."

"Ma . . . I . . . ," suddenly his lips pouted again, so far out you could hang a bottle of Deer Brand soy sauce on them. "I don't want to eat any more of that fried rice with bitter-tea-oil tomorrow morning! That stuff smells awful!"

Watching the way he spoke with such obvious indignation, she couldn't help laughing out loud again. She pointed at his forehead and said, "Look at you . . . !" Then she grew serious and asked him a string of questions about the next day's examination subjects: Had he prepared them all? Did he feel confident? Was he sure he could pass the exams?

"Ma, do you know . . . ," Xiao Quan put down his chopsticks and his face grew very grave, as if he wanted to announce something of great importance, "Do you know who are the candidates for president of the United States? We know one is called Eisenhower, but no one knows who the other one is. Ma, do you know?"

"Ma never reads the papers and is only a woman; how could I know a thing like that?"

"We just don't know who the other candidate is!"

"You're not going to be tested on that; why do you want to know?"

"It's going to be on tomorrow's exam!"

She stared at him in consternation: "They're going to test you on that tomorrow?!"

Xiao Quan's eyes opened wide as he nodded his head, then he explained to her that tomorrow afternoon's oral exam would be mainly concerned with current events. She quickly asked him what were "current events." Xiao Quan answered that he was not all that clear about it either; all he knew was the teacher had told them that in the oral exam they would have to answer questions like, "Who is the premier? Who is the speaker of the House? Who is the provincial governor? Who is the chief commander of the army? Who is our ambassador to the United States?" and all sorts of similar questions.

"My classmates and I all know that Chen Cheng is the premier, Wang

Chonghui is the head of the judiciary, Jia Jingde is the head of the Examination Ministry, Rankin is the U.S. ambassador to China . . . , MacArthur is the supreme allied commander in Korea, and Eisenhower is a candidate for president of the United States, but none of us knows the name of the other candidate!'' He looked very worried, and drops of sweat came out on his lips.

"Why didn't you ask the teacher? Such an important question, why didn't you go ask the teacher?" She was worried too, and she raised her voice. "Didn't the teacher go in today too? Why didn't you ask the teacher?"

"We didn't get together to review until the afternoon. This afternoon the teacher was busy and didn't come in." Xiao Quan knitted his brows. "The teacher said he cannot come tomorrow either. Tomorrow he has to go to Taibei."

"Then what can you do?" Her voice was trembling and sounded as if she were talking on an extremely cold day. "What are you going to do then? What if they really ask you that question tomorrow and you can't answer it; isn't that going to influence your score?"

Suddenly realizing that he might fail the exams because he could not answer this question, cold fear creeped up her spine just as though a snake was crawling up her back. *What was to be done? Who should she ask? Who would be a good person to ask?*

In her anxious confusion, she finally thought of someone. Without further reflection, she sat her bowl and chopsticks down on the table with a thump and stood up.

"You finish eating; I'm going next door to ask Mr. Zhang. They take a newspaper, and he's also a citizen's representative; he'll know for sure."

Before Xiao Quan even had a chance to answer her, she had already run quickly outside. The sky was completely dark, and she could feel the slightest touch of light breeze against her face; it was after all a little less stifling than during the daytime. The lights of all of the shops across the street were lit up as bright as day. There was a large cloth banner hung across the door of the pharmacy, and she could see very clearly written on it in large gold characters: "Master He Ji's Pain Killer."

She turned to the right and walked four or five paces in the direction of the bookstore when she suddenly saw Mrs. Ji, Auntie Jin, Mrs. Han who sold cooking oil, and the Mrs. Zhang from the bookstore who was so fat you couldn't make out her neck. They were all sitting there by the doorway near the roadway to keep cool and had their heads together chattering away with great animation. She stopped abruptly. Mrs. Ji was going on about something, ceaselessly gesturing up and down with her thick round arms. Ah-duan heard something like, "lotus roots . . . very fresh . . . ," but could not understand the rest of what she vaguely heard. She just saw Mrs. Ji's heavy round arms waving up and down without stopping, as if she were beating up somebody in a great rage!

She wanted to turn back and not go on to ask her question, but then she thought again: *Xiao Quan might very possibly fail to pass the entrance examina-*

tions because he could not answer who were the candidates for president of the United States! That child loves to study so much; if his hopes come to nothing just because he cannot answer this one question, he will feel so hurt! So terribly hurt! I'd better just screw up my courage and go on over and ask my question. But just at that instant, she began to be apprehensive. *Mr. Zhang was such an important personage, would he be like his wife, like Mrs. Ji, Auntie Jin, and Mrs. Han . . . ; would he look down on a widow woman like me?* She immediately tried to encourage herself: *He wouldn't be that way! Men are always more reasonable, and besides, he's a citizen's representative.*

Pulling out a handkerchief, she wiped her face, drying the perspiration on her cheeks, and, straightening her skirt, she finally continued on toward the bookstore with her head bowed. From her home to the bookstore was only a distance of about ten yards, but she felt as if it were ten miles, as if she would never make it.

She finally reached the right side of the door to the bookstore, still some distance from where Mrs. Zhang and the rest of them were sitting. She stood there in the doorway timidly peering into the bookstore.

The lights were shining brightly inside the store. There were no customers, and the clerks were scattered about the store, standing or sitting, chattering idly. She craned her neck again to peer into the store, but she still did not see Mr. Zhang. She hurriedly asked a nearby clerk. The clerk said that Representative Zhang was just then having dinner; if she had something to see him about, she should come back a little while later!

Just as she was about to turn around and leave, she caught sight of Representative Zhang coming out from behind the curtain in the back of the store. Probably due to her overexcitement, she could not stop herself from blurting out loudly, "Mr. Zhang! Mr. Zhang!"

Suddenly everything was deathly still. She couldn't hear the sound of the clerks talking. She could no longer hear the voices of Mrs. Zhang, Mrs. Ji, and Auntie Jin chattering away. All she could hear was the hurried beating of her own heart.

During the stillness, broken only by the sound of her own heart beating excitedly, Mr. Zhang walked forward, picking his teeth, and in a surprised tone of voice asked what he could do for her.

"Mr. Zhang, excuse me for troubling you, but . . . ," she was terribly worried and afraid lest she say something wrong, as if she were addressing the emperor himself, "I'd like to ask you; I'd like to please ask you who are the two candidates in this year's American presidential elections? Could you please write down the list of names for me?"

Mr. Zhang's eyes opened wide, and he stared at her as if he had not understood what she said. "Wha-a-t? What did you say?"

"I wonder, Mr. Zhang, do you know who the candidates are in the American presidential elections?" All of the clerks, Mr. Zhang, and Mrs. Ji all crowded in around her. Her heart was beating so fast now that she felt it would come right up and choke her, and she didn't really know how she managed to ask her question the second time.

Mr. Zhang suddenly burst out laughing as if he had just heard something excruciatingly funny; he laughed so broadly that his mouth gaped open wide enough to toss a soft ball in between the rows of yellow teeth.

Mr. Zhang's great burst of laughter made her extremely ill at ease; she stood there nervously wringing her hands, and the sweat began to trickle down her forehead from out of her hair. She kept asking herself insistently, *What did I say wrong? What did I say wrong?*

After he had laughed for some time, Mr. Zhang finally removed the toothpick from his mouth, tossed it on the floor, and said, "Why on earth do you ask that? What do you want to know that for?"

All of the clerks and Mrs. Zhang crowded in closer, staring at her and waiting for her response.

"I . . ."

Without even waiting for her to finish, Mr. Zhang smiled broadly as he pointed at her and said, "Can it be that you too want to go and run for the American presidency? Are you going to go and run?" Her face was crimson from the neck up. "Ah-duan, I tell you if you run for president, as citizen's representative I'll definitely cast my ballot for you! I'll definitely vote for you! Why, even Ah-xi and all of them . . ." he pointed to neckless Mrs. Zhang standing there at his side, "would also cast their ballots in your favor! Truly, I'm not fooling, if you . . ."

Holding her hands tightly over her mouth in order not to cry out loud, she turned around suddenly and ran back home as fast as she could; she could still hear Representative Zhang saying to the others around him, "I was only having a little fun with her . . . only making a little joke. . . ."

Running all the way into the back room, she threw herself desperately on the bed and began to sob quietly there in the dark. She sobbed with all the force of her injured dignity. Representative Zhang's "little joke" had hurt her bitterly.

Seeing her run into the back room with a troubled expression on her face, Xiao Quan quickly put down his rice bowl and hurried inside. Hearing her sobbing heartbrokenly in the dark, he was so frightened that he didn't know what to do. After some time he finally walked slowly up to her and gently touched her shoulder.

"Ma, don't cry! Don't cry!"

Gradually she calmed down and stopped sobbing. Turning on the light and blinking her tear-swollen eyes, she reached up to clasp the small hand that was resting on her shoulder and squeezed it tightly in hers.

"Ma can take anything, can endure anything, just as . . . just as long as you make something of yourself, just as long as you make something of yourself for Ma in the future!"

Xiao Quan nodded his head.

After that she told Xiao Quan to finish eating, then take his books into the front to review his lessons while he watched the store. Xiao Quan very quickly nodded his head again. He had turned around and was just about to go into the front room when her eyes suddenly lighted up and she called out to him, "Where does your teacher live, do you know?"

Xiao Quan looked at her with a puzzled expression, "I know. I went there once. It's over at the foot of Huagang Mountain."

"You think you could find it at night too?"

"I could find it!"

"Well then, let's go there together!" She smoothed back the hair that had fallen over her eyes and wiped the sweat from her neck. "Let's go to your teacher's house and ask him. If they really should ask that question on tomorrow's exam and you didn't know the answer, wouldn't it influence your final score?"

After hurriedly bathing, she picked out a clean new dress to wear. Looking in the mirror, she saw that her eyes were no longer as red as they were a few minutes ago. Then she ran over to Ah-li's to tell her that she and Xiao Quan were going out for a while and to ask her to please watch the store while they were gone. Ah-li gladly agreed.

The most direct way to go from her house to Huagang Mountain was to go left past the bookstore and then go left again down Zhonghua Road, but she and Xiao Quan turned right along Zhongzheng Road and went in the direction of Mingli Road so as not to pass in front of Representative Zhang's store. Just as they went out the door, she caught sight of neckless Mrs. Zhang, Auntie Jin, Mrs. Han, and Mrs. Ji once again sitting there huddled together in their original place merrily gossiping away. Mrs. Ji was going on again about God knows what in that shrill voice of hers while all the time flailing her thick round arms up and down without stopping. Representative Zhang was standing there beside her with a rapt expression on his face listening intently to whatever she was saying.

She held Xiao Quan's hand as they walked up to Mingli Road. On both sides of the road were planted huge eucalyptus trees. As they walked along under the trees she could feel a light breeze blowing, and with it there came floating the sweet smell of eucalyptus leaves. She felt fresh and relaxed all over, and the painful sadness of a moment ago seemed to be completely banished from her heart. Just as they were nearly in front of the General Hospital, someone seemed to be calling them from behind.

Looking back over her shoulder, she saw her younger brother hurrying after them on his bicycle. He said he had been working overtime and had only just gotten free to come and see them. Ah-li had told him she was walking in this direction. He got off of his bike, grabbed Xiao Quan, and began to ask him about the exams: How did he do? Did he make any mistakes? What were the next day's subjects? As soon as he heard that she was taking Xiao Quan to his teacher's house to ask him some questions, he told Xiao Quan to climb on his bike and he would ride him there. After telling them, "Go quickly and hurry back," she turned around and headed home. After walking a little way, she suddenly thought that on such a hot night she ought to buy a pound of herbs and some ice and make some sweet iced herbal gelatin for her brother and Xiao Quan to cool off with when they got home. She then made a turn and started off in the direction of the night market. Before she had gone very far, she came upon that pedicab advertising *The Oriole's Flight* coming down the street directly toward her. The lights were on all around the pedicab and lit up the posters, as bright as snow. The pedicab driver was stripped to the waist and peddling along with great difficulty while the hawker was sitting in the cab smoking a cigarette and looking like he had already yelled himself hoarse and didn't want to say another word. He just kept playing over and over again that same song, and Ah-duan listened as she walked along:

> Oh! This beautiful Shangri-La,
> This lovable Shangri-La,
> I'm so in love with it,
> I'm so in love with it . . .

Number Nine Winch Handle Alley

Chen Jiangong

Translated by Michael Day

"GAN-QING!" This was yet another Beijing colloquialism. When saying "gan," you should drag out the sound, put a real effort into it. The "qing" should have a soft pronunciation, a gentle but quick release, just enough for its sense to be grasped. Whenever anyone says anything of some importance, you should be quick to tack a "gan-qing" onto its tail. This is the same as saying "That's right" or "That goes without saying," and one could even go so far as to suggest that it means "Every word of what you say is true."

Actually, the phrase is often heard in Beijing. It can be heard uttered up and down the avenues, streets, and alleys of the city, and it may not seem to be worth all this attention on my part. But at Number Nine Winch Handle Alley there is something unusual about the way the phrase is used. There is an old widow by the name of Feng who lives there. She's like other old ladies in that after someone has made some comment worthy of note she likes to jump in with a "gan-qing," meaning "You certainly don't want to forget that." Widow Feng's "gan-qing" is certainly not easy to come by. If you don't have enough of what it takes or are not able to make her envy or respect you, you'll not hear a sound pass her lips.

Take her son, Da-shan, for example. A man of near forty, he was recently elected manager of the neighborhood factory. After a few months he had turned it around from being a money-loser into being a profit-winner. When one talks about being good with the brain, the tongue, or the hands, where can Da-shan be said to come up short? At the factory, those bewhiskered and wrinkled old men and women are always hovering about their manager, and whenever anything of any import is spoken, is there ever a shortage of mouths to chime in with a "gan-qing"? At home, however, does he suffer less scolding? "Your ass is out of the house all day long. You only come back to eat and sleep. Do you think this is some kind of hotel? Turning on the lights, burning up the oil, you're only an

---

The original appeared in *Beijing wenxue* (Beijing literature), no. 10 (1981).

insignificant manager of a busted-up old factory. This is the good life? What the hell's so good about it? . . . What? You're a Communist Party member? What Communist Party? It's more like a labor party! Take a look at the neighbors—the Lius: two of every three days he goes off with his cart to haul bricks. Now that's communist! You belong to a Communist Party? It's rather a labor party! All day long working and slaving away, using up all your strength and energy. If that isn't a labor party, what is it? . . .''

Of course, when Widow Feng curses her son it consists of three parts abuse and seven parts praise. After all, the scolding is for the whole neighborhood to hear. And one can't blame her. Do you think being widowed at thirty or so and raising a boy and a girl on her own was easy? Yet, just listen to the tone of her voice—does it sound like she's holding anything back? Is he or is he not her only son?

Let me tell you that when anyone has Widow Feng's ''gan-qing'' added to their conversation it is a near certain indicator of that person's status in the courtyard. How would it be possible to talk about Number Nine Winch Handle Alley without first telling you all this?

To my knowledge, there are two Winch Handle alleys in Beijing. One is in the western part of the city, and the other is in the southern part. The one that I'm talking about here is in the south. The alley is not long, and, like the winch handle of an old-fashioned well, there's a little bend in the middle. When the gateway numbered ''9'' is reached, you have also reached the turn in the alley. The entrance-way to Number Nine is nothing to marvel at, there aren't even any mounting stones such as were used by horse and carriage riders in the old days, much less stone lions out front. The residence itself? This is no less than the pride and joy of a traditional Chinese family—a true quadrangle and its court-yard. Have you seen a traditional Chinese quadrangle before? According to the results of research by one scholar of architecture, the Temple of Heaven is patterned after the universe; Sydney Opera House is patterned after the sea; the pyramids of Egypt are somehow based on the moon; and the Sears Tower in Chicago is something like a mountain. But what about a Chinese quadrangle? It is said that the layout of the quadrangle is based on the patrilineal order of the traditional Chinese household, which is meant to ''lead along one's sons and womenfolk.'' This explanation seems to have a very human flavor to it, does it not? Doesn't this just make us common folk of the quadrangles pause and feel good about our dwellings? However, don't you think that ''leading along one's sons and womenfolk'' is not as appropriate as saying ''hugging one's sons and clutching one's womenfolk''? If you don't think so, take a look for yourself. The quadrangle still exists today, but where has the courtyard gone? Which courtyard isn't crammed full of lean-tos and wooden sheds? If a small courtyard stuffed solid with several families isn't ''hugging one's sons and clutching one's women-folk,'' then what is? . . . But, of course, there is no alternative to this situation. The ever-increasing number of us sons and daughters of the dragon has made "leading along one's sons and womenfolk" quite impossible. Is there any alternative to intensive "hugging" and "clutching"?

Number Nine's courtyard holds five families, exactly in the pattern of "hugging and clutching. . . ." Widow Feng, of whom we were just speaking, and her son and daughter live in the west-side house.

Someone asks: Does the courtyard of Number Nine really hold a personage whom Widow Feng can truly admire, from the bottom of her heart, and who is worthy of having the widow's "gan-qing" tailing his or her words? It does, my friend! Not only Widow Feng, but who in the whole courtyard, save Teacher Zhang who lives in the "knife-back house" that leans onto the south-side house, and Widow Feng's son, Da-shan, doesn't feel honor in the awful presence of Han Delai in the south-side house? Thanks to Han Delai, the residents of Number Nine's courtyard stick out their chests before the rest of Winch Handle Alley. He has given them good reason to feel proud. Whenever a resident of the courtyard gets into an argument with other residents of the alley, he or she only has to say: "Old Han says that this is so!" and that person will be sure to return home victorious.

Han Delai is now retired. A few years ago he had been the boiler-keeper at a paper factory. Is a man's life a paradise or a disaster? Who dares say? During the spring famine of 1943, Han Delai was wandering about the roads and villages of his place of birth to the west of Beijing with a dog club in his hands. Those days, when the land was barren for a thousand miles and even the bark was stripped off the trees for food, where could one turn? Where could one go? The land was infested with wild dogs satiated with the flesh of humankind, and they would just as soon eat a man as look at one. When a man's eyes got that glazed look in them that indicated he was about to drop, the dogs would come trotting up behind with their tails wagging expectantly.

Han Delai didn't even have the strength to raise the club to frighten off the dogs! Just when Han's eyes were starting to glaze over and he was about to drop to the road as dog food, he ran into Li Sanshu, a man from his own village. Li gave him a sweet potato and also a means of survival—he taught Han how to sing a few popular songs and how to perform drum tales,* and then he took Han along with him out into the world beyond the village. If one went to those remote and wretched places where the famine had not yet struck, one could get a bite to eat for a song. On the strength of his acquired skills, Han was able to wander the land and survive. A folk proverb says that if you don't die during times of calamity, you will survive in times of personal good fortune. And there is so much truth to it!

In 1969, boiler-keeper Han Delai unexpectedly was transferred to the Workers' Mao Zedong Thought Propaganda Team. Not long after, to everyone's surprise, he became some kind of "representative." It is said that he entered

---

*A form of storytelling sung to the accompaniment of a small drum.

Zhongnanhai,* went to banquets, and even spent a night there. Make no mistake about it, his full name was printed in the paper for all to see.

Is that hard to believe? All the residents of Number Nine, no, everyone in Winch Handle Alley immediately began to look at Han Delai in a new light. That time when he returned from shaking hands with Chairman Mao, he couldn't even bring himself to wash his hand for a day and a night. He waited until he was within the confines of the courtyard and then let loose with "I shook hands with Chairman Mao!" Young and old, men and women alike, from inside the courtyard and up and down the alley rushed up to get a hold of his hand. Who doesn't want a chance to get close to a legend, an immortal?

Widow Feng rushed out of her west-side house, grabbed Han Delai's hand, and started squeezing it with all her might. It was at this moment, in contravention of her own rule, that she first started to go on about the hardships and glories of her long chastity: "Life . . . is it easy? Nowadays, women of my age can be seen prancing up and down the streets making fools of themselves in the arms of their old men. Is there anyone else around like me, keeping watch over an old devil's bones my whole life? I haven't even batted an eyelash at any old fool! Do you think it's been easy?"

The people in the courtyard knew nothing about state banquets and Zhongnanhai. Widow Feng argued with the young people in the courtyard, claiming with dead certainty that even the latrine cleaners at Zhongnanhai were high-ranking cadres. As far as state banquets were concerned, you could most certainly eat as much pork braised in brown sauce as you wanted. To settle the matter she went especially to old Han to get a verdict. The result itself is of little importance as, in any case, he had firsthand knowledge of the subject. It was plain to see that he was no ordinary fellow, certainly not one of the common herd.

From that day on, Han Delai had only to come out with his mug of tea and sit himself down at his front door and Widow Feng would come bustling over, carrying whatever she was busy at with her, to listen to him hold forth. And, of course, at all the appropriate moments, one could be sure of hearing Widow Feng's "gan-qing."

"I tell you, if we workers hadn't gone into the universities to get things under control, it would have been a real disaster." Old Han was once more starting in on "the occupation." "It was all those capitalists' and landlords' kids who didn't stick to their studies and who set up those Petöfi clubs!† At first we thought they were just clubs and at most all they do is have a bit of fun and play some card games. No way! They were rotten to the core! Highly educated people spending all their time reading books about immorality! There was one book

---

*The official residence of the leadership of the Communist Party of China, near Tiananmen Square.

†Sandor Petöfi, Hungarian poet (1823–49), wrote many intense nationalistic poems and love lyrics.

called *Thunderstorm* that was about a stormy day and a house full of loose and immoral people! Even the eldest son was involved with his younger sister.* What do you call that! I gave those kids a real dressing-down: immorality is running rampant here! Aren't you convinced yet? What do you think?! If we workers hadn't taken things in hand, wouldn't they have gone from bad to worse?''

"Gan-qing!" Widow Feng's shriveled lips twitched in contempt, just as if her loathing of those people was every bit as strong as Old Han's.

"Bloody Hell, you know what? Even the Soviet revisionists and American imperialists have got Red Guards now!" Han Delai had turned to international matters. "Hey! The Cultural Revolution was a pretty smart move. Just you wait, before long Khrushchev (he only knows Khrushchev's name), Nixon—they'll all be up on the stage with placards around their necks, and that'll be the end of them!''

Of course, there was a time when Widow Feng was rendered speechless and had no desire to chime in with a "gan-qing." That happened only once, when Han Delai had returned from another banquet. On that occasion he probably had had a little too much to drink. He entered the courtyard and, without going into his house, called to his wife to bring out his tea. Then he sat down in the courtyard and began to cut loose.

"Uncle, which leading cadres did you see this time? Anything new?" said Widow Feng as she crossed the courtyard clutching a wok.

"Is there any need to ask?" Han Delai looked askance at her and shook his head in a self-satisfied way. "Me? I saw our Second-in-Command Lin's . . . woman."

"Really! You didn't shake her hand and talk to her, did you?"

"Need you ask?"

"What did she look like? I'm sure you took a good look at her!"

"She wore a military uniform, naturally." Han Delai sipped at his tea and puckered his lips as if he were savoring a mouthful of wine. He darted a glance at Widow Feng and, in a low voice, said, "And later, can you guess what she did? Heh, she took off the uniform and put on a little white gown. The bitch! Her tits were sticking out for all to see. Heh, heh . . .''

What was said later was even less dignified. In order not to make everyone quite ill, no more will be recounted here. In the meantime, Widow Feng had not been following her custom and interjecting her "gan-qings." She screwed up her lips, her eyelids drooped, fluttered once or twice, and then she quietly turned around and returned to her house. Just before she reached the door she thought of something and turned about. She went to the clothes-drying pole and took a bra and panties down, rolled them up into a ball and took them into the house with her.

---

*This is a famous spoken drama by Cao Yu and was regarded as a classic criticism of the "old society" until the Cultural Revolution.

Despite Han Delai's alcohol-induced indiscretion, which caused Widow Feng to lose her appetite for his conversation that one time, she still didn't eliminate his "gan-qing" privileges. Rather, not long after this, she acted as if she had forgotten the matter. After Lin Biao bit the dust, Han Delai said, "I saw early on that that crowd was bad news. That man was a dangerous character! That woman . . . was a fox fairy!* How could they have come to any good?" As for Widow Feng, what did she say? —"Gan-qing!" She even screwed up her lips as if she, like Old Han, had been wise to it all along.

And this was the way it went: Old Han having his say with Widow Feng's accompaniment every evening over a cup of tea or after dinner in the tiny open space that was the courtyard. This aimless gossip practically became their—no— the whole courtyard's constitutional "fourth meal." It goes without saying that Widow Feng needed only to ring up one "gan-qing" and she would immediately feel good all over. What about the others, you ask? Other people were not up to the mark, of course. Naturally, she always came out. The Manchurian banner-man living in the northern house—Old Lady He and her husband—could they dare stay away? The old man had worked with the Japanese puppet regime in Manchuria during World War II. When the houses were being searched, all their riches and finery were hauled out and displayed. In this way, the Hes were reduced to the lowest rung on the courtyard's social ladder. Every few days the two of them still had to go to the boss of the "revolutionary courtyard," Han Delai, report their recent political thought, and receive a lecture. Could they dare miss out on such an opportunity to receive an education? Take a look for yourself! When were fat old lady He and her old skin-and-bones husband not sitting out there listening quietly? Of course they lacked the courage and qualifications of Widow Feng that allowed her to interject her "gan-qings." They could only continuously nod their heads and make approving noises: "Certainly. How true. . . ." Even when Old Han was swearing and cursing to beat the band, they had to sit by and listen.

Wang Shuangqing and his wife lived in the south-side house. They were both workers with primary school education, forty-three or forty-four years old, with a young one and an aged one to care for—the aged one was a bedridden, paralyzed grandfather, and the young one a school-aged daughter. The Wangs both had mute temperaments, looked rather sickly, and were very, very timid. Of course they were sure to come out and attend court. It didn't matter what was said, just being close to someone like Old Han would be enlightening: it was an important matter. In those unpredictable times, one would at least be able to catch wind of things early on and somehow feel more assured about it all. A person would be able to avoid a lot of trouble. For example, during the October Grave-Sweeping Festival, when there was that trouble in Tiananmen Square, hadn't Old Han

---

*In traditional Chinese fiction, a fairy who could change from a fox to a beautiful woman to betwitch and lead men astray.

given advance warning? "I'm telling you, shut the courtyard gate! Don't go out with no good reason. They'll be more than likely setting up machine guns in Tiananmen! You'll be looking for trouble if you poke your head out there!" And wasn't it the truth? Wasn't the third eldest Song family son who lived at the top of the alley taken off to jail? Without Old Han, was the peace and serenity of Number Nine possible? . . . The Wang Shuangqings only had to get a glimpse of Old Han coming out to roost and they would rush over, making sure not to miss a word he said.

In the whole courtyard, only Zhang Chunyuan was not respectful to Old Han. Zhang Chunyuan was over thirty. His parents had lost their lives during the chaos of the late 1960s. When he came back from his stint in the countryside, he went to work as a high school teacher. Now, with his family living outside Beijing, he lived next to Wang Shuangqing in an addition on the south side, in a "knife-back house."

Every time Old Han sat down to shoot the breeze, Zhang would stand off to one side with his arms folded. Sometimes, from the movements at the corners of his mouth, his nose, and his eyes, it seemed that he was sneering. Wasn't he making a deliberate attempt to dampen the spirits of the others? What made Old Han lose face the most was that time when everyone was reclining in the shade. He looked at those around him and sighed, "The party has wonderful policies." No fault can be found in this. But what was the cause of Old Han's sigh? "Hell!" he said. "Even a creature like Wu Faxian has been released. Who says the party isn't magnanimous enough, or wise? Because of this matter I wasn't able to get to sleep at all last night! . . ."

Han Delai's meaning was clear. Widow Feng contributed her "gan-qing," the Wang Shuangqings let out approving gasps, and even the Hes were moved to chime in with an excited chorus of "How true, how true. . . ." No one expected then that a killjoy would come out to pour cold water on their parade. Zhang Chunyuan was standing off to one side with his arms akimbo again, saying, "Master Han, where did you hear this? How is it that I haven't heard?" Han Delai said: "So you don't know? There are a lot of things you don't know." Zhang replied: "Well, you must have some proof!" Han Delai flared up: "Proof? The fellow has even received foreign visitors, what more proof could one want! Go look at the paper! It's in the house!" The paper was brought out and everyone was unable to repress their laughter: it was a few years old—a 1969 newspaper!

Of course, Zhang Chunyuan was not able to shake everybody's worship of Han Delai just because of that one incident. Rather, Han Delai came to hate him. It didn't matter when, Han Delai had only to see Zhang standing by with his arms folded to start talking about the occupation of the campuses and the "stinking old ninth category"* in the vilest and most abusive way possible. If this

---

*Class enemies; intellectuals.

wasn't an attack on Zhang Chunyuan, what was it? After two or three doses of this, either because he was afraid of being abused or because he didn't have the time to listen to Old Han talk anyway, Zhang didn't come over any more.

"Abusive? I can see that you don't have the guts to call a spade a spade!" Han Delai felt even better about himself. Often when he was pouring forth strange and unheard-of things, he would suddenly lean forward and say softly (it almost seemed that he deliberately lowered his voice), "Hell!" Then he would sip at his tea and continue on with his animated and fulsome accounts. At other times he would sound off warnings about changes in the political environment, at which times he would always put on a displeased look and, turning toward the Hes, say, "I'm telling you, another revolution is on its way." Then he would elucidate, going on and on about the Cultural Revolution or some coming campaign, being as graphic as possible till the Hes were shivering with fright like birds that had just escaped the hunter's arrow. In a sea of respecting yet fearful glances, accompanied by "gan-qings," Han Delai would swell up with pride and self-worth till it seemed he would burst! All around him were the eyes of the cowed and dumbfounded. His words brought Old Lady He and Wang Shuangqing to him to make anxious reports on their political thought and to make nervous inquiries about the latest developments. This one leaves trembling in fear, and that one goes as if having been administered a sedative. Han felt pleased with himself, and there seemed to be no end to his happiness. This was what was meant when they said, "The working class is master in its own house!" Whenever he was free, he would go out to sit by his front door, and if two or three people didn't come over to listen to him discourse, he would feel offended. If a day went by when he didn't give the inhabitants of the courtyard a lecture, his throat would get itchy!

Not long ago, he gave his neighbors some much-needed reassurance. One of the residents of the courtyard heard that the nation's economy was "in the red." Of course, no one knew what "in the red" meant, but it sounded none too healthy. There was a vague sense that it had something to do with rising prices, and people started to get panicky. Han Delai saw the old ladies whispering together in a corner and grew angry. "Hummph! Look at all this lack of patience! In the red, in the white, what are you frightened about? I'm telling you our government has everything under control—otherwise why would they always be saying that the situation is excellent? Do you think they're just saying it? Let's just talk about water for a minute. Even China's water is worth money! Haven't you heard that over in Shandong, the water of Mount Lao is worth tons of money! Fill a bottle up with water and send it overseas to the 'big noses' and fork over the money please! Hell, water—will we ever run out of it? This alone should be more than enough. No? A leader said that in the future we have to be careful about our bottles and not break them. These days we've got lots of water, it's the bottles that are causing the problems. When we have more bottles, we'll be swimming in oceans of cash!

Only four modernizations? . . . We can do eight. . . .'' These words put Widow Feng into a fit of ecstasy, and the ''gan-qings'' flowed like water, too. In fact, everyone's spirits were raised; it seemed that they were all feeling much more secure. After he finished speaking, Han Delai let his eyelids droop and sipped his tea in an ocean of smiles and laughter. On the surface he looked calm enough, but inside he was bursting with his own self-importance and contentment.

Ah, but there are always two ways of looking at things. A real man doesn't talk about his past exploits, as those are all water under the bridge and past history. This great talk about the water of China being worth buckets of cash was Han Delai's most memorable heroic feat. Because, after that, although people didn't stop gathering about him to listen to his words of wisdom, Han became gradually aware that fewer and fewer people were coming, and those who listened to him were not as enthusiastic as before. There was not so much excitement outside his doorstep anymore. It was like the old proverb about ''eating a faithful dog, or packing away the trusty bow,'' . . . a very sad situation.

For example, look at the He household. They were recompensed with cash for all the valuables that were taken away during the ''destroy the four olds'' campaign.* Today they buy a clothes washer, tomorrow a television set, and they ostentatiously bring them into the courtyard. What do they think they're doing? Han Delai got upset watching this: ''Showing off, provoking people!'' he would say.

The event that rubbed Han Delai the wrong way the most was when Old Lady He shrilly announced to the whole courtyard that the sesame-flavored bean curd that she had not eaten for ten years, since the days of the Red Guards, was now available. You should know that bannermen and their old wives pay most particular attention to face. Any time there is something new or different to eat they become more willing to invite their neighbors to join in. It's a friendly act, but also common courtesy. With regard to the sesame-flavored bean curd, it is particularly understandable. Old Lady He, like so many other bannerman wives, really relished this food. To make proper fried sesame-flavored bean curd you must be sure to use ''sheep's-tail'' oil, real green soy beans, and dried hot red peppers that have been cut in half and fried to a crisp. When you taste the dish, it has a sesame flavor, but it's also sour and hot. Actually, this bean curd is no big deal. In the old days it was your standard ''poor man's feast.'' Who would have thought that the revolution would also revolutionize sesame-flavored bean curd out of existence for ten years and longer? The luxury of the bean curd was due to one of the relatives of Old Lady He's husband, who had heard the old lady going on about her bean curd and, after running all over the city searching for some, had finally obtained a small pot of bean curd, which he then presented to his mother-in-law. When, to her utter astonishment, the sheep's-tail oil, green soy

---

*A Cultural Revolution campaign to stamp out old ideas, old culture, old customs, and old habits.

beans, and dry peppers were all gathered together too, was it any surprise to see Old Lady He so jubilant? She burst out to Widow Feng, who was standing in the courtyard: "Da-shan's mother, I was thinking that I would never get another bite of sesame-flavored bean curd before I lay down in my coffin. Who would have thought that we would see it again! Now that we have sesame-flavored bean curd, do you need to worry about whether you will ever be able to drink the fermented soy-juice that you like so much again? It looks like there's hope that we might once more see real Heavenly Spring brand pickled vegetables and Bargain Lane pickled duck." This trumpeting was really nothing, but the neighbors were shaken by this unexpected news and were invited to partake as well. Especially excited were those old Beijing residents, even people from outside the courtyard, who were in their seventies and eighties. Third Aunt and Second Grandma were all cackling away nonstop. Troops of bound feet hobbled in. "Come on!" "Slowly, be careful of the hollow by the door there!" "All right, you've come. No matter how much you eat, your sharing in our food will be great flattery to us." So everyone fell to the sesame-flavored bean curd with chopsticks or spoons, commenting on and admiring Old Lady He's new acquisitions. None of this escaped Han Delai's notice. This grand event certainly did not take a back seat to Old Han's return from the state banquet.

Actually, what was wrong with all this? The Hes had benefited from the implementation of state policy. Their courage was restored, they had some money, and now they could do what all Beijing natives like to do: in the summer eat roast mutton; in winter eat boiled mutton; on the second day of the lunar New Year eat moon cakes; on the twenty-third day of the twelfth lunar month eat candied-melon. . . . No matter what, you'll never go hungry. Why couldn't Old Lady He eat some good food, too, and enjoy her old age?

Han Delai watched all the people coming and going from the Hes' house on the north side of the courtyard, choking back his resentment, until he saw Old Lady He's son, Er-zhou. Then he got really mad. Even Er-zhou had become a big shot in Winch Handle Alley recently. He'd bought a Suzuki 80 motorcycle, and it had brought out everyone in the courtyard when he rolled it in. On another day he pulled a different trick. Who knows where, but he bought a pair of pants that looked like they were made out of denim but weren't. They even had a foreign name, something like "Levis 501 Double X Jeans." He put them in water and while they were still dripping wet put them on, saying that they would shrink and in that way fit better to his body. . . . After saying that, he got up on the motorcycle, fired the engine, and blew out of the courtyard singing an advertising jingle: "Seiko, Seiko, high-performance watches . . . ," leaving the surrounding children with stars in their eyes.

Han Delai almost burst out: "Hummph! Still have to fix your political wagon. I'll take care of you sooner or later!"

Han Delai's anger had no effect; his tricks didn't attract any people at all now. Even the old ladies and men from neighboring courtyards didn't pay any attention to him—they would run over to Old Lady He's as soon as they stepped into the courtyard. They talked about some "old well-known store having re-opened," saying they should take a look at that "talking box that can record your own voice," and so on. As far as the young people were concerned, they gathered around Er-zhou and sang, "Seiko, Seiko, high-performance watches . . ." This spread to Widow Feng's house, where Han Delai heard factory manager Da-shan talking about "product information feedback." And even outside Number Nine's courtyard at the "youth-awaiting-work-assignment" kiosk, they were mulling over "lower profit margins bringing in more customers," and going to some make-up class to take a chance on a university entrance exam. . . . It goes without saying that all people have mental powers that are comparatively supe-rior or inferior: Han Delai's line was no longer effective, it was ignored. He himself understood the situation, but what could he do? Old Lady He's following was strong, but who could Old Han still frighten or awe? He wasn't a "representative" anymore—he was retired and living at home, and he couldn't find out what was going on politically. Shaking out the old stories and names had lost its efficacy through constant usage, and the Cultural Revolution looked to be gone for good. If any semblance of it did turn up, would there be anything novel about it? In those days they were having campaigns left, right, and center: they would scoop up a dozen or so people at a go, the handcuffs glittering, and whisk them away in a flash. In those days, the telling of such an event would turn everyone's face white, but today, what can one talk about? . . . Ai, even the courtyard's most hopeless household, the Wang Shuangqings, caught everybody off guard when they exploded their bombshell. It kept the whole alley buzzing for quite some time. But Old Han? No one asked him the time of day; he was old news and out of it.

Someone asks, what wicked thing did the Wang Shuangqings do that kicked up such a fuss? It was nothing wicked, rather, it was something rich. Not long before, Wang Shuangqing's old father died from some sickness. The burial put them so much into debt that they dragged out some old pottery that had been tossed in a corner and took it off to sell. They thought that now that the "four olds" campaign was long past and the pottery was lying about the house, it would sooner or later be broken, so they might as well go to see if any money could be made out of the stuff. They took the pottery to an antique shop, and what a surprise they had when the proprietor was stunned by their piece and even asked if they had any more at home. Wang Shuangqing thought for a while: "Yes, there's one more." The proprietor asked, "Why don't you bring them both in?" Wang Shuangqing hemmed and hawed for a bit. He was embarrassed to say. Can you guess why? The pot was at home being used as a urinal. He raced home and cleaned it out. What was it? A palace knickknack: an article of tribute to the emperor that had been especially made at Jingdezhen during the Daoguang reign period (1821–51). It was recorded in the Qing Dynasty Records Department Register of Valuables for all to see, and it was priceless. . . . This time there was even more of a hullabaloo, and things were really jumping at the Wang Shuangqing's. All the old wives from up and down the alley came by to pay visits, and they felt no compunction about garrulously inquiring as to the actual price of the pottery. When they came out, they either rushed home and emptied out their old rice pots and flower vases, wrapped them up, and took them over to the Tianqiao district, or walked out cursing, "Damned spawn of rabbits,* they smashed my pair of transparent vases. If I still had them today, there'd be enough to feed me for three lifetimes."

People! If at first you were the center of attention all day every day and then all those people disappear, leaving you behind lonely with an empty pot and a cold hearth, how angry and depressed you would most certainly be. And so Han Delai was angry and depressed, left out in the cold with nothing to do. He would eat his supper, brew his tea, and go out to sit at his front door. Any time neighbors came by he would chew an idle bone or two with them, but he knew that if he tried to hold them longer, what he said would amount to no more than an odorless fart. Those people had no desire to listen to what he had to say; the present never matches up to the glories of the past. Even Widow Feng, today over at the Hes', tomorrow the Wangs', here a "gan-qing," there a murmur of approval, rarely gave Han Delai the benefit of her "gan-qing" now. After sitting with his spirits very low for a while, Han Delai suddenly began to tap out a beat and to sing the traditional opera ballad "Fourth Son Visits Mother":

> *Yang Tinghui*
> *sitting in the yamen*
> *thinking to himself and sighing.*

His head swayed, as if he were of the same mind as Yang Tinghui.

> *Thinking back*
> *back to that time*
> *so very, very heartrending.*
> *I'm just like*
> *a bird in a cage*
> *having wings but not flying . . .*

Just you listen. He definitely has used those clappers before, sung drum songs; he even has the enunciation and diction of a Beijing opera singer.

That same day, at dusk, Han Delai was again at his perch "sitting in the yamen / thinking to himself and sighing," when Zhang Chunyuan came walking by.

"Master Han, nothing to do, huh?"

---

*Refers to the Cultural Revolution Red Guards.

When Old Han saw Zhang Chunyuan, anger immediately welled up inside him. These days Zhang was acting like some kind of big shot, too. Inside and outside the courtyard, the parents of hopeful high school students were seeking him out. One could hear "Teacher Zhang" to your left, "Teacher Zhang" to your right, and they wore the depression in front of the "knife-back house's" door deeper and deeper. But this was nothing. What was even more annoying to Old Han was that every few days he saw Zhang receiving massive envelopes in the mail with the name of some editorial department or publishing house stamped on them in red ink. If one asked him what it was, he wouldn't answer or would at most mumble a few words, then turn away and stride off. Later, Old Han heard that the fellow could write novels. Would he never be satisfied? . . . When Old Han heard Zhang's words, he was certain that he was rubbing salt into his wounds. Old Han gave Zhang a sidelong glance and drawled out his answer: "Nothing to do," then added, "What? When I had things to do you didn't like it, now that I'm taking it easy it also bothers you?"

Zhang Chunyuan rolled his eyes and put his tongue into the side of his cheek. He couldn't help laughing, "Can I help but be happy if you have nothing to do? Still, you shouldn't hang around here feeling sorry for yourself. Why don't you brew black tea fungus or practice *qi-gong,**—do something to make your old age longer and healthier? Or else, you could do what Old Man He is doing and keep birds. . . ."

"Great," Han Delai interrupted Zhang huffily, "longer and healthier old age! From what I can see according to ancient tradition, if you don't die at sixty you sustain a living death!" He gave out another "hummph" and darted a look at the north-side house: "Follow his example? Keep birds? There's no possibility of that. I'm a worker! My hands full of bird-cages all day long, swinging them back and forth? Even in the days when Old Man He was struggled against and swept the streets, he didn't have to work so hard. Serving birds, feeding them thirty cents of seed each day—back then he wasn't even so filial to his own mother. . . ."

"Okay, okay! You don't have to take my advice. You can sit here. Sit, be depressed, and sing your old opera songs." Zhang Chunyuan was mad. "I saw you sitting here looking bored and came over to try and help you find some way to drive away your low spirits, but instead you get hostile with me and then put the spurs to someone else! You can sit here and do whatever you like, it's no skin off my nose, it doesn't bother me. By all means continue singing, go on singing about your bird in a cage."

Han Delai's eyes followed Zhang Chunyuan back to his house. He felt a bit strange. Oh, so you're concerning yourselves over me and my problems and making fun of me! What problems do I have? I don't have to worry about food or clothing. There's nothing for you lot to be happy about! He thought about it for a while, then he got up briskly, rushed into the house and yelled out to his

---

*An ancient Chinese health exercise.

wife and children, "I'm going to a movie!" Then he shuffled into his shoes and tottered out the courtyard entrance.

Actually, when Old Han said he was going out to see a movie, they were only words said in anger. It was getting dark; where could one go to see a film? Yet, as Han Delai came out of Winch Handle Alley and wandered up to Zhushikou Avenue, he couldn't help but notice the flashing neon lights of the Zhushikou Theater through the murky light of dusk. As he moved closer, he made out a long line of people in front of the ticket window. They were selling tickets for an American film, *Singing in the Rain*, to be shown on the morning of the next day. "Line up!" he had heard someone say. Han Delai entered the line like a man who would miss out on something if he didn't.

When it came to Han Delai's turn to buy tickets, he hesitated: how many tickets did he want? Because he had spent so much time in the line he wasn't satisfied with buying just one ticket. He pawed at his pocket—he had a dollar and twenty cents exactly. "I'll take four tickets!"

What do you think this means? Is it possible that all people who spend time in long lines are liable to do this sort of inexplicable thing? In fact, they probably don't need to buy so many—they are simply buying for the sake of buying, otherwise they feel they've been had. It was like this with Han Delai: the next day he came to see the movie alone; the children had to go to work and his wife, once she heard that it wasn't some traditional opera film, wouldn't come on her life. Now Old Han had four tickets in his pocket, an excess of three. He would have to return those three.

When he was still a couple hundred meters away from the theater, Old Han passed groups of two or three young people anxiously standing at the intersection clutching their small change and asking, "Comrade, any extra tickets?" "Master, spare me a ticket please!" Han Delai walked past them. Suddenly, a certain emotion rose in his breast. He knew that he had four tickets and they had nary a one. He felt it hard to part so lightly with the extra tickets in his pocket. Having those extra tickets concealed on his person and listening to those desirous pleadings was actually a form of enjoyment! He put on a stern expression and shook his head at several young men who offered their money to him: "Don't have any. None to spare." He straightened up, stuck out his chest as far as he could and continued to reply off-handedly to their inquiries. Among them was a youth wearing sunglasses and sideburns, just like the He family's Er-zhou, who thought he might try his luck on Old Han. Old Han ignored him completely, thinking to himself, "If I sell them to anyone, it certainly won't be to you!"

Finally he reached the movie theater entrance, went up to the top of the two flights of stairs, and watched the great lines of people stretching off to the east and west, all waiting to return tickets. There was an even greater number of people searching for tickets. He pulled out a cigarette, smoked, narrowed his eyes, and watched those young fellows surrounding the people wanting to return tickets, pushing, shoving, pursuing people into alleys. He felt happy. He put his hand into his pocket and gave the tickets a twist. Secretively, he slid a ticket into the palm of his hand and walked over to a pitiful young girl clutching thirty cents who was watching the others fighting over the tickets. Without a word he passed her the ticket.

"Oh!—Thank you! Thank you so much!" The girl was so overjoyed by her unexpected prize that she jumped up and down.

Han Delai waved his hand nonchalantly.

"Comrade, any more? Sell another ticket!" "Master, spare me a ticket! ..." Woosh! Sharp-eyed, many people stumbled over one another as they rushed forward and surrounded Old Han, their hands clutching their money and shoving it out toward him. Calling out "Comrade," "Master," "Uncle," they pressed in about him.

"What are you doing, what are you doing!" Old Han had put on his stern look again. He parted the crowd and pushed his way out, brushing aside handful after handful of money. "I don't have any more to sell, just that one! I just have my own ticket left, no others!"

Some people walked off disappointedly, others continued pleading for his favor. Old Han shook his head and smiled contentedly.

Thus, one by one, he returned the tickets. Each time he had returned a ticket and was confronted by a clamoring crowd of people, he would put on a serious face and say, "No more, no more." He was experiencing an indescribable kind of happiness. He felt as if he were floating on a cloud.

By the time he had sold the third ticket, the people searching for tickets were of the unanimous opinion that he still had lots of tickets on his person. They followed him from the movie theater to the alley entrance, and from there into the public toilets, pulling at his arms, clutching at his clothing. Some told him how rare an opportunity it was for them to watch a film. There were all types of people—it was mind-boggling. Han Delai was already happy beyond his wildest dreams, and in the end, he sacrificed the ticket he had been keeping for himself. Even though he had no more tickets left, he enjoyed the thrill of being surrounded by a clamoring throng for quite a while longer.

There is no way for me to convey what kind of happiness Old Han was experiencing at that moment. Those old feelings of ease, of satisfaction, of self-worth were all there again. Was it something like eating ice cream or a fudgecicle during the dog days of summer, you ask? That kind of comparison is just a bit too far off the mark. Possibly only once in Han Delai's life, when he gave that talk at Number Nine Winch Handle Lane that had left the Hes with fear in their eyes and had brought him the pleasure of Widow Feng's "gan-qing," only then had he enjoyed this same sense of ease and comfort. Of course, he himself could not make such a comparison or connection. He only felt that with so many people crowded around him, chasing him, playing up to him, and worshiping him, his bones had turned to jelly and his days would be full of contentment and happiness once more. There would be no need ever again to sit alone in the courtyard, drink tea, and sing to himself.

Thereupon—and I'm not trying to show up the faults of an old man—Old Han developed a nasty habit. He would sit, depressed and bored, in the courtyard for two or three days, and then he would totter out onto the street, out past the Zhushikou Theater. If he saw a line there, he couldn't resist rushing over, buying tickets, and later selling tickets and getting his fill of those feelings of happiness and contentment. Sometimes he would keep a ticket and go in himself to see a film. Holding a ticket and walking through a crowd of envious eyes into the theater was also a delight for Old Han. If he was in a good mood, he wouldn't keep even one ticket but would use them all to help others. Afterward, when he had struggled free of the crowd and was on his way home, some foolish youths even went to the extent of pursuing him into Winch Handle Alley, right up to the entrance of Number Nine. Could the people living in the little courtyard make head or tail out of what Old Han was up to? He had nothing to do, so he would go out for a walk, then when he came back and closed the door to the street, he appeared rejuvenated, reinvigorated, as if he were coming back slightly drunk from another state banquet.

To put it crudely—Old Han looked like he had taken heroin and was without a care in the world! Once he was back in the courtyard, though everyone was courteous and thoughtful, greeting him politely and paying their respects and so on, were they like the people that gathered about him pleading for tickets at the Zhushikou Theater? Did they address him as they would when begging their grandfather for a favor, or when talking to their mothers or children? In the past, the courtyard had been that way, but now no one concerned themselves about anyone else. Who feared any other person now? One day when Han Delai was returning from the theater he bumped into Old Man He at the mouth of the alley, two bird cages, one in each hand, and each covered with a blue cage-cover, who was just on his way to the Temple of Heaven. Han Delai went forward to meet him. Having just come from the theater, Old Han's vitality had probably not yet dissipated, and he thought out beforehand the words he would use to annoy Old He. . . . "Old He, you seem really at ease these days. Socialism even lets you keep birds. It certainly can't compare to the old days in Manchukuo, huh?" Who would have thought of it? He hadn't yet thought out how to lead into them when he almost ran head on into Old He! When Han Delai saw Old He before him, he said, "Hey, Old He, taking the birds out? What type of birds have you got?" As he said this he reached out to lift a bird-cage cover. This was how he would lead into it! "Don't touch," came the response. He hadn't thought that Old He would use his bony old hand to stop him. "If you want to see, wait till I get back. You can come by the house to see them. In this place, forget it. The birds will try to imitate the traffic noises. . . ." As he said that, he bowed slightly and then walked off, the bird cages swaying as he went.

Han Delai was fuming, choked with rage. Not only didn't he get an opportunity to say what he wanted to say to Old He, but even that sense of youthful vitality and vigor was gone. Who does he think he is? he thought. He used to come to me every day, morning, noon, and night, to confess his sins. I had him so that he would run into his house and hide under his blankets when he wanted just to fart! But today he's getting arrogant too? . . . From Old Man He he went on to think about the rest of the people living in the little courtyard, and this again called forth those melancholy thoughts of fading glory and the passing of spring. It was still early, why should he go back? Why upset oneself watching them? He made a turn and entered a small street bar.

Old Han had yet another bad habit: when he had nothing to do he would slip into this small, dark den and order twenty cents worth of roasted broad beans, two ounces of strong liquor, and drink. Actually, a lot of bottles of alcohol that his son and daughter had given him as gifts were hidden away under the bed at home. In the beginning, his son used to buy him some cheap but strong sorghum-based spirits. He would pick it up and fling it out into the courtyard. "Are you trying to palm this garbage off on me—me who has even drunk Mao Tai?" From that time on it was usually higher-quality liquor that was put under the bed. Do you think he should go home where the drink is good, the food is tasty, where it's peaceful and quiet—a much nicer atmosphere? There's no possibility of that. Once Old Han is back in the courtyard and sees those familiar faces, he feels like he's being suffocated. Should he go back there to drink? Let them see him and think again that he's feeling depressed or lonely and taking to drink? Wouldn't that make them just so happy that even their sweat pores would start to grin? Old Han wasn't willing to do it; he would rather eat broad beans and drink "old white heat."

You probably haven't seen the kind of little bars that are common to Beijing: they have only two or three round tables and ten stools or so. Besides alcohol, there are also candies, cigarettes, tea, and so on. Some are husband-and-wife operations, others are run by a few old retirees. At the entrance there are always a few carts and three-wheeled delivery bicycles with empty wrappings and coils of rope hung on their handle bars. One look is enough to tell you that these are the haunts of the ordinary working people of this city—the heavy-load movers, roofers, drivers, hawkers, and the like. As soon as a glass of liquor has gone down the gullet, they look for someone to talk to. First one talks about the flavor of the alcohol, and then talk turns to all kinds of news and gossip, local or national. By the second glass one has usually got oneself a friend to unburden oneself with. A makes some comment and B says, "Gan-qing." B makes a remark and A says, "Gan-qing!" Slowly it gets so that A, B, C, and D's foreheads are all starting to shine from so much talking, and they begin to feel very good about themselves. Naturally, Han Delai also shared in these pleasures, and can you blame him for lingering there? Besides, if he didn't come by here so often, how would he have heard the news that they were going to start publicly criticizing people again! It was really so. An old man who had been drinking with him told him so; the newspaper was still in his hand at the time. He only knew that the objects of criticism were those "story writers," but who they were, he couldn't remember, and what the criticism was for, he didn't ask either. But he made a particular point of getting a look at that paper and, using his finger as a guide, carefully noted the date: year, month, day, he read each number painstakingly. There was no mistake this time—it was a recent edition. It was too good to be true—some more excitement was on the way! He hurriedly picked up his glass from the table and in two or three gulps finished off the alcohol, got up, and left.

Probably he drank those two mouthfuls of alcohol too quickly, because as he hustled down the alley it felt like there was a layer of cotton laid out on the road and that the soles of his feet didn't seem to touch solid ground. At first, he only looked forward to being the first to announce the news to the whole courtyard. Hummph! If it frightened them to death, it would serve them right! Later, he thought of Zhang Chunyuan. Hadn't he heard somewhere that Zhang was writing novels? Weren't all sizes of letters being delivered to his house? And hadn't he been acting so aloof and uppity lately that he didn't even respond to questions directed to him? This time you've had it, Zhang. Go ahead, be aloof, because more than likely you'll catch it! . . . A little later, the accumulated grievances of the past few years, like an opened Pandora's box, began to toss about in Old Han's mind. Hummph, he should have fixed this guy's wagon long ago! Didn't I say that sooner or later it would happen? Is Old Zhang only a "writer of novels"? It is just like in those movies in which men and women embrace and kiss. How disgusting! It's not only the movies, though. The peasants aren't staying down on the farms working the fields any more—they come into the city, sell their vegetables and other things, make furniture, and each household has its own fields. Aren't they going too far? I've heard that down in Shanghai people are wearing just about anything! Grown women wearing their skirts so short that you can see their panties! It's unspeakable! Further down, in Canton, they can watch what they like! If they want Hong Kong television, for instance, they just turn a knob and there it is. . . . That's okay, don't worry, this time the party'll clean up the whole lot of them! . . . Old Han began to think of the Hes again. Was the work he did for the Japanese Manchukuo puppets forgotten and past history? It was no problem, was it? All day he shows off, strutting about with his tail up in the air. Even his son is a good-for-nothing. He got his hands on some Western and Japanese things and is now leading all the children in the alley into evil ways! Who knows when another Cultural Revolution will come along and take care of the lot of them. As for Widow Feng, she's just an old brown-noser; she'll come to no good end. How about Wang Shuangqing? He's not really a bad sort. I heard he gave those treasures to the state and was given a bit of a reward for it, not too much, though. But he still needs a bit of education. As for those parents who bring their girls over to Zhang Chunyuan's and only care about getting their kids into college, at best they have muddled thinking only. . . .

The moment Old Han arrived back in the courtyard, Widow Feng came out of Old Lady He's house. She saw Han Delai, said hello, and went to the water tap to wash vegetables. Han Delai walked to the door of his house, pulled out a stool, sat down, and began singing a happy little ditty from an opera.

"Shuda's father, why are you so happy today?"

"With some excitement to watch, why not be happy?"

"Excitement?" Widow Feng gave him a sidelong glance, "What excitement?"

Han Delai puckered up his lips, and a matchstick that he was using to pick his teeth with wobbled back and forth under his nose.

Finally, he spat out the matchstick and said, "Haven't you heard, they're organizing criticism again! Can't help but be some excitement!"

"Criticism? Criticize who?" Widow Feng bustled over to Han Delai.

"A novel writer's being criticized. It was in the paper. No doubt about it!"

"Really? You're talking about Zhang Chunyuan, aren't you? Isn't he always in there writing?"

"Zhang Chunyuan?" Han Delai put on a stern countenance and a serious, dignified look came into his eyes: "Whether he's in trouble or not, we have to get a look at what he's been writing. Hummph! With the way he's been acting lately, could he be up to any good?"

While they were talking, Old Lady He got wind of what they were saying and came over. When Han Delai raised his voice and said, "Do you think it's only a problem with novel writers? I know the things that the Gang of Four did were a load of shit, that goes without saying, but some of the things that people are doing today won't lead them to a good end either! Will the Communist Party let them continue to run riot like this? Capitalism, bourgeois attitudes, getting back at people to avenge past wrongs, blindly worshiping things foreign—don't worry, we'll clean up the lot!" These days, although Han Delai was almost a forgotten man, when it came to matters like this he still had some influence left.

As soon as Widow Feng heard that something was up, she quickly put on a smile and said, "Gan-qing!" If she hadn't said it, that would have been the end of the matter, but when she said "Gan-qing!" it only served to stoke Han Delai's fire further. Huh! he said to himself. You're quick to jump the fence! Just now you were over there licking her ass, and now, in a shake, you're back here with me. It's not so easy, let me tell you!

"Gan-qing?" Han Delai retorted, and laughed icily. "During these two years lots of things have sprung up that need to be taken care of. For instance, your Da-shan in the factory is in a precarious position. They're holding elections for factory manager, for the director's position. Is the Communist Party still in power or not? Will they allow this sort of troublemaking? What happened to the enterprise responsibility system? It's more like they've been given a license to rake in the dough! If something goes wrong, that'll be in the fire too!"

This time Widow Feng couldn't bring herself to manage a smile or a "gan-qing."

After he had said his bit, Han Delai cold-shouldered the two old ladies, put on an air of disdain, and, not wanting to waste another word on them, turned about and went into his house.

After being left on Han Delai's doorstep, Old Lady He and Widow Feng felt quite put out. Neither of them doubted what he had told them. Listening to the way he said it and seeing the way he acted, something was definitely happening. From the sound of it, Zhang Chunyuan was sure to be criticized. In truth, Old Lady He and Widow Feng couldn't care less about Zhang's ruin. At first they even felt a perverse joy at the thought of his demise—the jealousies and hatreds of a communal courtyard are many. Just think, Zhang Chunyuan is all day hard at work with the lights on, and whenever he writes he stays up half the night. This really gets Widow Feng's goat! As for the rest of the people in the court-yard, don't they all hit the sack when it gets dark? But Zhang's special, acting as if electricity were free. Originally the whole courtyard was on one installed electricity meter, but the Hes put in their own meter, and the Hans and Wangs followed suit. All who were left on the other meter were the Fengs and Zhang. Widow Feng made the calculations that by sharing with Zhang she was footing a large portion of his bill. Didn't that upset her even more? Someone suggested that Widow Feng have her own meter installed and thereby solve the problem. Logically this should be the solution, but Widow Feng is hoping that Zhang will install one first. If he installs one, she won't have to, thus saving herself more than twenty dollars! But this other business will fix him. It doesn't matter if Zhang Chunyuan installs a meter or not, because once he's criticized he won't be writing anything any more. He'll be in bed early, asleep, with the lights off!

Old Lady He had an even bigger bone to pick with Zhang Chunyuan. Zhang was always preoccupied and never found time during his comings and goings even to say hello. Finely mannered Old Lady He had him pegged as someone who was too haughty to show respect to his elders or be concerned for the young. This was a secondary grudge, however; the door of the ''knife-back house'' that Zhang lived in was directly opposite Old Lady He's north-side house door, and it was this that bothered Old Lady He the most. Who lives in ''knife-back houses'' these days? It leans up against a wall with a slanting roof like an extended eave, and there isn't even a ridge pole. Don't all knowledgeable people in Beijing know that this is an inauspicious house? Before Zhang Chun-yuan, a teacher by the name of Li used to live in that house. At that time Old Lady He argued with Li, ''Remodel the house as fast as you can, it's unlucky.'' Teacher Li didn't listen, and what was the result? He was struggled to death during the Cultural Revolution. If you're not afraid of the inauspiciousness of your house, that's fine, but your ''knife-back house'' is opposite someone else's door! That's great! Sure, the Red Guards searched through your house, but didn't they come and search over here too? . . .

So the house to the south became a sore point with Old Lady He. With Teacher Li's death, Zhang Chunyuan moved in, and the old lady went over to exhort him as well. Who would have thought that he, like Teacher Li, didn't believe her? Recently, of course, things have been quite rosy for Old Lady He; there was only that "knife-back house" that gave her such lingering misgivings. "Here we go again, just look, didn't I tell you, aren't you in trouble now, Zhang Chunyuan? And it's all the fault of that 'knife-back house!' It's too late to run now! It serves you right! Why didn't you listen to the words of your elder? Didn't you walk into it with your eyes wide open?"

Actually, these were only fleeting vengeful thoughts that Old Lady He and Widow Feng entertained. Such thoughts didn't make them feel good at all; gradually they even began to feel a bit uneasy, especially Old Lady He. After all, that "knife-back house" was still there opposite hers. Now that Zhang Chun-yuan was in trouble, could she be sure that things wouldn't turn out the same as before? Would disaster not descend on the north-side house as well? And from the look of Han Delai and the none-too-friendly tone of his voice and comments, Old Lady He was even more scared. Capitalism? Settling old scores? Who does he mean? Is he talking about my family? Worshipping things foreign? He must mean Er-zhou, no doubt about it. When she thought of these things she hated Zhang Chunyuan even more for bringing disaster down on the heads of his neighbors. You can see other people passing their days prosperously, but you can't leave them in peace!

Widow Feng had long ago returned listlessly to her house, and not a sound was heard out of her for the rest of that afternoon. She waited until her son came home and then confronted him with a bout of cursing and yelling: "What have you come back for? Why don't you go back to straighten things out! Having raised you to this age, can't I pass a few worry-free days? Making you waistcoats in the summer and padded jackets in the winter, and what for? For what, I ask you? Just so at the age of forty you can bring trouble to the door and give me sleepless nights?"

Her son was stunned: "What do you mean?"

"What do I mean? You aren't satisfied with being a good worker, no, you go out and want to be a manager! Elections, elections, this time you've done it, it's about to get rough again. . . ."

Her son laughed, "It won't happen. The leaders have said they aren't going to carry out a political campaign."

How could Widow Feng believe that? And so she carried on with her scold-ing. It happened that at this time Da-shan was worried about some other matter concerning the factory, and as he listened to the old woman go on and on about nothing he grew angry: "Stop talking nonsense! If it comes to a campaign, you won't be able to escape it either! Going on all day long about the 'Communist Party' and the 'Labor Party'; you think the neighbors can't hear you? I've done some silly things, but you haven't?"

This was very effective; Widow Feng didn't say another word. After a while she rose to clean up the dinner dishes, thinking to herself, "If it's true, won't it be just like in the days of the 'Gang of Four'? Up at five, late to bed, those who work hard are out of luck, and the shirkers and the tricky ones do just fine for themselves? . . . Even I, an old widow in my seventies, will have to speak cautiously, or, if things get bad, I'll be branded a counterrevolutionary, won't I . . . ?"As she continued to think in this vein, she became somewhat indignant about the things Han Delai had said. Suddenly she began to feel some compassion for Zhang Chunyuan. She even momentarily forgot about their problems over the electricity bill.

How, you say, can we fittingly describe Old Lady He and Widow Feng? Can we say that Widow Feng is selfish? Having brought up a son and daughter on her own for so many years, and even now she's not really so well off, is she wrong to get so upset about an electricity bill? Can we say that Old Lady He is too superstitious? Who arranged it that by chance the two men who lived in the "knife-back house," Teacher Li and Zhang Chunyuan, should both meet with misfortune? Who arranged it so that Old Lady He would be roped in with them? Can she be blamed for being frightened? . . . But the two old ladies are still good people at heart because, although in the beginning they were none too happy about Zhang Chunyuan's predicament, they quickly realized that real trouble was on its way. If a Cultural Revolution–style campaign was really in the works for all of Number Nine, no, the whole of Winch Handle Alley, and the whole city, the whole country, those hellish days would be back once more. If that happened, no one would have a good time of it, no one would be able to escape, including oneself and one's family—everybody would be in deep water. That night as they lay in their beds, as they thought of ways and means to control the calamity that was about to fall upon their families, they even went to the extent of trying to think of ways out for Zhang Chunyuan, though, in the end, they had to admit that if something truly was in the wind, Zhang and they themselves would have absolutely no place to turn. True enough, but because of this idea, these two old ladies helped to bring about a tragicomic farce.

On the morning of the second day, when everyone in the courtyard had gone off to work and Old Han had also gone out—probably back to the little street bar to pick up on some more gossip—only the two old ladies remained in the courtyard. A little past ten, a stranger aged about forty came into the courtyard. He said he was looking for Zhang Chunyuan, and upon enquiry it was learned that he was from the editorial department of some magazine. How wonderful! The two old ladies had been looking for a person to say good things about Zhang Chunyuan to, and out came the tea and cigarettes. The visitor saw that Zhang Chunyuan was not in, but he was not able to resist the boundless generosity of the two elderly women, so he sat down in the courtyard on a small stool and began chatting with them.

Who would have thought that the visitor's questions made the two old ladies feel very uneasy. He asked about Zhang Chunyuan's accommodations, his family, his age, and even about his political background. That's it, there was no escaping it—Zhang Chunyuan was in serious trouble! The two elderly ladies answered his questions listlessly, all the while stealthily passing meaningful looks to each other. Finally, Widow Feng couldn't hold back anymore and said, "This Zhang Chunyuan, you couldn't find a nicer person on this whole earth if you went out looking for one. But of those in the writing profession, who can avoid slip-ups every now and then? If your newspaper is going to criticize him, could you do it without using his name? Leave him out of it. . . ."

Old Lady He quickly followed her with, "His wife and child live out of town, far away. If they see him being criticized in the papers, won't they think it's another case like *The Three Family Village*?* Isn't it sure to frighten them to death?"

"What? He's been criticized? Where?" The visitor grew anxious after listening to the old ladies talk.

"In the paper. It said a story he wrote had some problems. How's it possible that you don't know?"

"What was the name of the story? Which newspaper?"

"Ai-ya, you're asking us! Old Han who lives in the east-side house told us. And make no mistake about it, he said he read it himself."

"Oh?"

"What, you didn't know about this? Then . . . why're you looking for him?"

"Me? Oh, nothing, nothing at all. . . ."

He didn't say anything more. Widow Feng and Old Lady He sat on either side of him and continued to say nice things about Zhang Chunyuan as if the visitor had some control over his fate. But the visitor didn't seem to listen, and not much later he rose and bade them farewell. They told him that Zhang Chunyuan would be back soon and he should wait, but he wouldn't; they asked him to leave a message, but he wouldn't do that either. This perplexed the two old ladies even more—what had this person come for anyway?

Zhang Chunyuan came back at noon. The two old ladies were hidden away in the Hes' house where they had been whispering quietly for quite some time; they didn't dare tell Zhang about the visitor. It was not until nighttime, after the lights had been turned on and they could see Zhang through a window at his desk writing, that they could stand it no longer. Both of them slipped across the courtyard and into the "knife-back house."

The unexpected visit of these two old ladies seemed very strange to Zhang Chunyuan. They sat in front of the desk and exhorted him together, "Teacher Zhang, is it worth the trouble? Every day you're hard at it till late at night, and this is what you get as a reward. Haven't you taken the hint yet—no, still in here writing away!" And again, "Even if you yourself are willing to go on regardless, you have to think about your wife and child too. You are the only one left of your family, and you still don't live a quiet life?" . . . This confused Zhang

---

*A group of writers criticized during the early 1960s.

Chunyuan even more. When he finally figured out what the old ladies were talking about, he couldn't help laughing out loud.

It was actually quite a heartbreaking matter, and the two old ladies were completely mistaken about it. Yes, Zhang Chunyuan was writing novels, but he had spent seven or eight years at it and not one had succeeded, not one had been published. How could he be criticized for anything? Those envelopes that had so angered Old Han and seemed so mysterious to the old ladies were all manuscripts returned from various editorial departments.

After the ladies told him of the visitor who had come earlier in the day, Zhang Chunyuan stopped laughing. His face paled and he anxiously inquired, "Really? Did he say anything? Which magazine's editorial department? What was the person's name?"

Of course the old ladies didn't know the answers to any of these questions; they could only repeat for him what the visitor had asked and what they themselves had said. As he listened to them, Zhang Chunyuan felt he was going to cry: "My dear ladies, I really want to thank you. It was really nice of you both to try and help me, but, instead, you have destroyed the one big opportunity I have been looking forward to all these years!"

"Really?" The two old ladies were stunned.

Zhang Chunyuan said, "You don't know. Every time my manuscripts were returned, they didn't even write me a letter. This time I hit the jackpot—they came to visit, and they probably wanted to publish my writing. When you two ladies told him that I had been criticized, you more than likely frightened him away."

Upon hearing this, Old Lady He and Widow Feng were dumbfounded.

It isn't necessary to relate what happened later, because you will be able to guess most of it. The false alarm that Old Han raised in the courtyard of Number Nine Winch Handle Alley passed away. Still later, it seems that even after there really was criticism of a writer in the papers, name and all, it didn't amount to much. The writer kept on writing, and his works kept on being published. As far as Han Delai's "clean-up" that was "sooner or later" going to happen was concerned, nothing seemed to occur at all. The taut bow-string in everyone's heart gradually loosened even more: Old Lady He is still as ostentatious as ever; she still holds frequent get-togethers with her old cronies, today sending her son to Qianmen District to buy "Wang Zhihe's" fermented french-fried bean curd, tomorrow sending her daughter off to Bamian Cao to buy "Puwu Fang's" dumplings. But she still broods about Zhang Chunyuan's "knife-back house," saying, "It's unlucky, can there be any doubt about it? Writing for seven or eight years and not a word printed. He had just that one chance, and we even tried to give him some well-intentioned help, but what was the result? Disaster! If it isn't the fault of that 'knife-back house,' then what is it?! It also caused my second son to get a bad score on his college entrance examination!"

How about Widow Feng? She's still the same as before: this day over at the

Hes', that day visiting the Wangs, saying her "gan-qings"; she doesn't even try to avoid going into her "Communist Party," "Labor Party" dialogues. At the same time, she's still angry at Zhang Chunyuan for staying up late and burning the midnight oil. Every two or three days she presses him to buy his own electricity meter. As far as the Wang Shuangqings are concerned, when they heard that something was up, they were quite pleased with themselves for having given the palace treasure up to the state. They immediately stopped their daughter from going over to be coached by Zhang Chunyuan, but after four days they sent her back to him. Their daughter's original name had been Wang Wenge,* and this had been a good thing during the Cultural Revolution. Their daughter was born just at the time when factional fighting was taking place. As they didn't have to go to work, both husband and wife stayed at home for seven or eight years. They didn't have to spend money on a nanny or on daycare, and they themselves raised their child on the salary that the state continued to pay them. Now, to fall in step with these good times, they have changed the child's name to "Cultural Pavilion."† They hope she will be able to get into a key middle school and then on to university and a good "iron rice bowl" job.‡

You are sure to think that Han Delai is the most crestfallen person in the courtyard, but you would be wrong to think so. Han Delai is still saying the same things: "Hummph! They'll take care of the lot of them sooner or later." And he wasn't without something to crow about either. Didn't He Er-zhou have to push his Suzuki 80 over to the Ganshi Qiao free market for motorcycles and sell it? Isn't it true that Er-zhou no longer dares to go prancing about in those Levi jeans? Hummph! If one didn't put the fear of god into people once in a while, what might happen? If Er-zhou had the money, he'd buy another vehicle to cruise about in! He'd probably walk about the streets with his bare ass hanging out! Of course, Han Delai didn't know that Er-zhou sold his motorcycle because the authorities were cracking down on them and gas was hard to steal. Recently he'd heard that they wanted people to pay road upkeep fees and insurance. Who could afford to pay ten dollars or more a month just to keep a bike on the road? He decided to get rid of the motorcycle quickly, to sell it while there were still buyers. How about the jeans? Because he often wore them while they were still wet, they had shrunk so that all the curves of his lower body bulged out. Unfortunately, a bad case of "nettle rash," or so it seemed, popped out all over. He had no choice but to put them away. He decided to cure the skin disease first and then think about wearing them again later.

The thing that finally caused Old Han to lose heart happened a couple of weeks later. Again, as before, he got bored sitting around in the courtyard and went out for a walk. As he walked past the Zhushikou Theater he saw that they

---

*Abbreviated Chinese form of "Cultural Revolution."
†Also "Wenge" but a different *ge*.
‡A job with a state-run enterprise.

were selling tickets for a film called *It's Really Maddening*. From the sound of the name it seemed interesting. The movie poster said it was a "comedy," so, as always, he bought four tickets. If no one at home wanted to come, would there be any possible problem selling them?! More than likely people would fall over each other to get at his tickets! Who could have known that the next day, just prior to the film's showing, as he went to stand near the theater entrance, there were no crowds of people waiting for returned tickets! He immediately understood that he had been fooled! The waste of money was not so great a problem, but begging people to buy his tickets injured his pride and he felt resentful. Yes, *It's Really Maddening*. What was most maddening, though, was that behind him some riffraff were also selling tickets. What were they yelling? . . . *Casandra Bridge*,* very erotic! Who will buy? . . ." And there really were people buying tickets from them. Han Delai went over to look and was infuriated. Right, they were ticket scalping, and at one dollar a ticket! He grabbed a young man by the arm and accosted him: "What are you doing! Huh? What? Scalping, profiteering, come on, we're going to the police station!" The young man pulled his arm loose and shouted: "Brother, don't be in such a hurry. Oh, so I've taken away your business have I? Don't give me that line! You sell yours, I'll sell mine. Whoever can sell tickets should stay, whoever can't, should blow. Who do you think you are, threatening people with your damn police station?" Han Delai became even angrier. So the punk thought he was also scalping tickets. "Don't you dare mistake me for one of your kind! I have extra tickets and I sell them at the original prices." "Old man, don't pretend to be some saint with me. Do you think I haven't seen you? You come here every two or three days! Do you always come to sell extra tickets? And at their original prices? You're just looking to make trouble. Don't give me that line! Police station? Okay, if you want to go, we can go together. Do you think you'll be able to get off scot-free?" On and on they disputed. Pushing and shoving near the theater entrance, the two of them drew a large crowd. A policeman came over and led both of them away.

Do you think that Han Delai was able to explain himself once he was in the police station?

"You also go there often to sell tickets?"

"Yes."

"What do you sell them for?"

"The original prices."

"What's the idea of always buying tickets and then reselling them like that?"

". . ."

There was no way to explain it!

The police weren't able to settle the case, so in the end, they sent a young policeman to Number Nine's courtyard to find out more about Han Delai.

---

*A Polish film about World War II.

Who would be so wicked as to say bad things about Old Han? Everyone unanimously agreed that the old man had been depressed and bored and had nothing to do and, as a result, had gone in search of some diversion. Er-zhou was even more gracious: he changed his past tune and equated Old Han's actions with "studying Lei Feng's example, and doing good things for others."* The young policeman brought Han Delai back, and before he left he said, "Bored or not, don't go back there and do that sort of thing again. If you want to watch a movie, buy yourself a ticket and then go in and watch it. Don't go looking for trouble. You say you're too old to do such a thing, and we believe you, but if you get kicked or hit by those hoodlums, won't you be in danger of losing what's left of this life?"

Even without the policeman's warning, this one last place where Old Han could find pleasure had been lost to him. These past two days he has gone back to his old routine. He doesn't leave the courtyard. He brews his tea, sits despondently at his doorstep, strikes up a rhythm and starts to sing:

> *Yang Tinghui*
> *sitting in the yamen*
> *thinking to himself and sighing.*
> *Thinking back*
> *back to that time*
> *so very, very heartrending.*
> *I'm just like*
> *a bird in a cage*
> *having wings but not flying.*

You only have to hear him sing it once and you'll certainly admire his voice. He sings so well; his diction and enunciation are just perfect.

---

*Lei Feng was an ordinary soldier who was made into a model of proletarian virtue for propaganda purposes and is still held up by the authorities as a paragon of self-sacrifice. The reference to him here is ironic in the extreme.

Race Day

Bai Luo

Translated by Richard King

ON THE SCREEN, a dozen thoroughbreds lined up in their starting stalls. During the parade before the race, the blue of the ocean and the complementing green of the turf had delighted Zhang Fanzhou, but that delight was wiped out now by the tension that gripped him as he waited for horse number seven to break from the stalls.

From the instant the stalls opened, he had eyes only for number seven. Over a straight kilometer, the key to the race is the sprint finish over the last few dozen meters. His heart throbbed convulsively to the beat of the pounding hooves, an insistent rhythm that stopped abruptly as number seven sped past the finish post in first place.

He heaved a sigh of satisfaction and turned the television off. The rest of the card was of no interest to him. Two thousand Hong Kong dollars, half of his savings, had been riding on number seven.

Playing the ponies was something he had learned to do in a month or so, an indication of how well he had adapted to the local ways in the half year or more since he had fled the village school in Guangdong Province to a shack on the island of Hong Kong. But his past wagers had never been more than a hundred. This time it had felt like do or die.

His wife Mo Jinlan had gone out, taking three-year-old Xiaohao with her. She had told him she was going to Guntong to see her cousin and make arrangements to rent an apartment. Tomorrow afternoon, his parents would cross the bridge at Luowu, coming from China to share their life in the "paradise" of Hong Kong. "Paradise" for him was a cramped space between wooden slats, which he had taken for a thousand Hong Kong dollars shortly after he arrived. It was hard enough for the three of them to turn around in the few square feet they had, how

---

The original was taken from *Selections from Hong Kong Literature, Series II* (Hong Kong City Government, 1981). It has also been reprinted in Liu Shaoming and Ma Hanmao, eds., *Shijie zhongwen xiaoshuo xuan* (The commonwealth of Chinese fiction) (Taibei: Shibao wenhua chuban gongsi, 1987), 2:532–41.

could they fit another two people? Jinlan was probably right—they'd have to find some way to let the old folks live in comfort for the first while at least, then think again in a few months. That way they wouldn't be too let down when they arrived.

But what about the rent? He had his own way of looking at it. Jinlan was always nagging him, complaining that his mind had been "struggled" out of him by the village schoolchildren. The only thing those little hooligans wanted to learn was how to beat people with billy clubs and ransack homes. When they came to his house, there wasn't much for them. But they still called him an overseas Chinese bastard, and when they discovered copies of the cadre newspaper *Reference News* which he had stashed away under his bed, they accused him of "stealing state secrets" and gave him a vicious beating. Thus the farce was played out. Had they really beaten the sense out of him? His mind couldn't be completely useless—if it was, his boss at the restaurant would have been worried that he'd be forgetful, and would never have hired him to make deliveries.

Jinlan also nagged him about playing the ponies. But he'd only done it three times. Once the guys at the restaurant had clubbed together for a quartet. In order to get in with them, he'd pitched in fourteen dollars. They hadn't won, but he'd benefited from their loss. By putting in the fourteen bucks, he'd become one of the boys—now they called him "Ah-cheung" instead of "Mainland Cheung." As a graduate in mathematics, he knew how to calculate whether something was worthwhile.

Another time was on his birthday. In a burst of inspiration he had tried his luck with a daily double using the numbers for the month and the date, and this time he won. He didn't make that much on it, since both horses were heavily favored, but he was in bliss for days—Zhang Fanzhou's luck wasn't so terrible after all! The only thing that was terrible was that when he told his wife about his triumph, she'd chewed him out for being "without ambition" and "never getting ahead."

The third occasion was after Jinlan had been rushed to hospital with appendicitis. It had cost them a thousand dollars, which was more than they could really afford. He had hoped that the ponies would take pity on him and let him win back the money he had spent on doctor's bills, but this time his hopes were dashed and he lost a hundred dollars. It was just as well he no longer dared to tell Jinlan, or she might have got mad enough to take a turn for the worse, and then what would he have done? That was the most miserable day since he had come to Hong Kong!

But today was his happiest day. Five hundred dollars to win on a hundred dollar stake, and five hundred to show, multiplied ten times! He did some sums in the column of the newspaper and worked out that he would be picking up seven thousand dollars in winnings from the betting shop. Shaking with elation, he looked at his wife's picture on the wall. He wanted to shout: "Jinlan, I was only worth two grand yesterday and now I have eight!'' But in the end he said nothing. He was afraid that Jinlan would still insist there was something wrong with his head, and even more afraid that she would fly off the handle again because he had been playing the ponies, and making such huge wagers!

He remembered that time when he had come back to the restaurant from making deliveries to find he was over twenty dollars short. After he got off work, he'd told Jinlan about it and she'd scowled and told him off: ''They really did beat the sense out of you! Just a three-figure number, a schoolchild could handle it. You've got a math degree and you still screw up!'' He didn't want to give up on this one and kept racking his brains in an attempt to remember which house it was that had underpaid him. The only explanation he could come up with was that somehow he had lost it himself.

Forget those minor irritations. Today he was a different man. He walked with easy strides, whistling a little tune. Then it occurred to him that it had been years since he had whistled; hurriedly he pulled his lips in and returned to his usual expression.

After picking up his winnings at the betting shop, he folded the thousand-dollar bills up small and slipped them into a hidden pocket in his pants behind his belt. Then he went down a side street, found his boss at the restaurant, and asked for three days off. Originally he'd planned to take only one day off to meet his parents, and to let Jinlan worry about everything else. She was at home with Xiaohao anyway and was quite prepared to look after his parents. Today, with money in his pocket, he felt different. Now he thought it would be fun to show them around Hong Kong and Kowloon.

After he'd had some dinner, Jinlan and Xiaohao came home. He asked Xiaohao if he'd eaten, and the child nodded. Jinlan just frowned when he asked her about renting a place.

''Nothing suitable?''

''Rents are too high.''

''Don't fret, it's bound to cost a few bucks more to live in a high-rise.''

''You can say don't fret, did you get rich all of a sudden?''

He said nothing, but whipped his hand away from the secret pocket. He'd been afraid she would ask him where he was going to get all that money from.

He said nothing, and Jinlan spat out her resentment: ''Just one small apartment is twelve hundred a month, and that's all you earn! Maybe the landlord will tell us we can't cook, and then we can feed the old folks on air!''

''So what do you think we should do? They'll be coming tomorrow, we've got to have somewhere for them to move into, and you keep saying that this place is . . .'' What had seemed like a heavy weight in his secret pocket was starting to feel lighter. Twelve hundred! His eight thousand wasn't even seven twelve hundreds, how many twelve hundreds was he going to need. . . ?

He watched as his wife unlocked her camphorwood chest and took out an ornate box that she kept wrapped in a silk handkerchief. Xiaohao was playing on the bed with his building blocks, but when he saw the pretty box he crawled from the foot of the bed to the head, reached up, and begged for it. Jinlan glowered at him, and the boy was well enough trained to know he should pull his hand away and go back to his blocks.

When the box was opened, a pair of glittering gold earrings came into his view, engraved with the inscriptions ''heart's desire'' and ''good fortune''; these were followed by a gold chain with a locket in the shape of the peach of longevity. He remembered when he and Jinlan had met her father at the Overseas Chinese Hotel in Canton, after he had come all the way from Penang to see them. The wizened old man had opened the little box and said, ''Lan, the fates were against your mother; she couldn't live to see you married. I'm not much better, either—I have nothing to offer you as a wedding gift but these few pieces of jewelry. With them I wish that you will have your heart's desires and good fortune and always be happy together.'' Poor old man! When they got to Hong Kong, they discovered he'd died the month before. He hadn't told them how sick he was, since he was afraid it might prevent them from getting their visas to leave China and take care of him. . . .

He stole a glance at his wife. Tears had sprung to her eyes, touched off by the gifts and the memory of the giver. He was about to talk about it when Jinlan wiped her eyes and said, ''There's more than three ounces of gold in these, you'll get at least ten thousand for them. That'll pay the rent for the old folks for a year or so, and we can work out what to do after that.''

He choked with emotion: ''How . . . how can we? That's all we have to remember . . . we shouldn't . . .''

She cut him off: ''We've your parents to think of, they'll be here right away. We only got their telegram a couple of days ago, and we don't have any time to raise the money any other way. If we don't rent a place now, there may not be anyplace later on. There's no time to hunt around. We've paid a month in advance, and bought a bed and a quilt. You can sell the jewelry first thing in the morning, then pick them up at the station and pay the landlord for another two months to secure the lease. That way they can rest easy for the evening.''

Xiaohao was bored with his building blocks. Realizing he was being ignored, he let out a yell, knocked down the beautiful house he had been building, and howled for his mother to pick him up. Jinlan hugged the child to her breast, patting him gently on the bottom to get him to sleep. The child was exhausted after being out all day.

He replaced the lid on the box and wrapped it in its silk handkerchief. Maybe the sense had been struggled out of him, but he still understood her. Jinlan was a good wife, kind and upright; to be honest, she was more concerned for his parents than he was himself. Sure she complained, but who wouldn't when the rents were so high! But here she was, ready to sacrifice those pieces of jewelry that she had risked smuggling through customs in order to keep them and the memories they held. This wasn't just any jewelry!

He patted his secret pocket again but didn't dare come clean about it. She was bound to refuse to spend money that he had come by in this way, and they wouldn't be able to celebrate the fact that his good luck meant they could get out of selling her jewelry. He was starting to resent his wife's inflexibility, but he also had to admit that her judgment was seldom wrong.

His wife and son were already in their world of dreams, but he couldn't get to sleep himself. Fortunately, this week there was Saturday and Sunday racing, so tomorrow would be a race day too. Back and forth in his brain flashed the images of galloping thoroughbreds and golden rings and lockets.

Bright and early the next morning, Jinlan wrapped her treasures in their silk handkerchief and gave them to him. She instructed him to go to Guntong, sell the jewelry and bring the money home, then set out to meet his parents' train at Honghan. She figured that the train wouldn't get in till three, so they could be there in good time.

He draped his jacket over his shoulders and slipped the transistor radio from the dresser into one of the pockets. Then, after sliding his feet into plastic thongs and running his hand through his tangled hair, he trudged wearily out of the house. For all his exhaustion, he was acutely aware of two things. One was the jewelry in the silk handkerchief, which he clasped tightly to his chest. The other was the wad of banknotes, which he patted constantly to make sure it was still there.

When he got to the bustling Guntong market, he went to a restaurant for breakfast. By his watch it was only just after nine, and he knew that most of the stores would not be open yet, so he ordered another coffee and opened the paper to pass the time.

He flipped to the racing page and was instantly mesmerized. Once again, galloping horses and glistening jewelry flashed before his eyes. Now was the time to marshal his mathematical talents to assist him in his deliberations. He had more than ten thousand dollars worth of jewelry and just over eight thousand in cash. There was no way he could make a switch without Jinlan getting suspicious. He just had to get the money, right now! He wasn't going to put up with his wife sneering at his mental powers. What he needed most of all was a sum of money to get him out of his present bind. A grand sum, that would be best, enough not only to save the jewelry that had been left to them as mementos, but also for a spacious apartment for his parents, for Jinlan and Xiaohao, enough to rid them of all their anxieties. He was as exhilarated as if he were himself astride some wild steed in full gallop. He jerked himself to his feet and strode out of the restaurant.

The atmosphere of the betting shop exactly suited his mood. The booths for filling out betting slips were crowded with people, packed so tight you couldn't even get water in between them. Latecomers, convinced that the ponies would treat them well this time, hunted out a place to squat or stand, then spread out their newspapers and betting slips and decided on a plan for the campaign ahead.

Those with well-thought-out strategies had already joined the ranks heading into battle. When their turn came at the window, they fired off salvos of money, confident that the receipt from the cash register would soon be transformed into the spoils of war.

He squeezed in among them, oblivious of time, like a warrior locked in mortal combat, summoning up his last ounce of courage to defeat the God of Death, and await an anthem of victory. On such a day, a stake of a thousand to win was but an outmoded dagger. Only a bet of a thousand to win plus another thousand to show in each of the first four races would qualify as the heavy artillery of modern warfare. His firearm was primed, now he must set forth with guns blazing, to return only when the enemy's general was killed and their standard seized.

For all his modest appearance, there was something so manifestly heroic in his posture that it caused a stir in the line. Those close enough to witness it looked as if they would burst out cheering. His mind was set on the first four races of the day: if he could only win a succession of victories in these skirmishes, he would go home loaded down with booty—twenty thousand, thirty thousand, maybe even more! Intoxicated with the thought, he lurched forward, hardly aware of the direction he was headed in.

On he tramped, on and on, and when finally he looked up, an opulent aura of pearly light shone from the window, spraying his face with myriad jets and splashing him into wakefulness. From his torrid fantasy he returned to cold reality: his wife had instructed him to go to the goldsmiths and sell her jewelry. She had told him to be back by lunchtime and go with her to meet his parents. How was he going to manage it—racing didn't start today till one! How could he have failed to realize there would be a problem with the timing! He scratched at his head and cried out in anguish: It's true! With all their struggling, they've made me crazy!

If he were just to step right into the goldsmith's, the transaction could be completed in a couple of minutes, and he'd be able to get home in time with the money in his pocket. But how could he part with the "heart's desire" and "good fortune" rings and the longevity pendant, and never see them again? It had pained Jinlan so much to part with them, could he leave her with only an empty case? He couldn't sell them! He couldn't!

Suddenly decisive, he strode into a restaurant across the street and dialed a number. He spoke into the receiver without a pause: "Something just came up, it's urgent. I can't come home right now. You and Xiaohao go ahead to the station, and I'll meet you there." He slammed the phone down before his wife had a chance to answer.

Never before had making a phone call taken so much out of him. Bone-weary, he slumped down on a stool. Maybe because there was racing today, it was quiet for a Sunday, so quiet he could hear his own heart pounding. He needed the peace for a while to sort out the chaos in his mind.

The waiter brought him a glass of water. Idly he glanced at his watch. It was almost one, so he might as well have something to eat. Which reminded him he should turn on his transistor. He fished it out of his pocket and held it to his ear. The familiar voices of the commentators were chattering away, giving their listeners the returns on the various stakes and introducing the horses. The voices were like an entrancing melody to him, instantly capturing his full attention.

The waiter brought a bowl of borsch and croutons. Mechanically he stirred it around with his spoon. The sense of hearing had taken command of his body, reducing the sense of taste to a vassal status.

The main course was spaghetti; this too he just pushed around on his plate. His pushing and stirring came to an abrupt halt; his fork stopped in mid-air, the noodles it had carried flopped to the table. The campaign had begun in defeat. He had lost the first race.

The tangle of spaghetti on his plate was knotted like his stomach. But to his ears came the sound of the beacon fires being relit; the prospect of the renewal of hostilities rekindled the hope in his heart. The waiter, who was bringing the dessert, was unperturbed. Such shows of temperament were commonplace on race days.

Dessert was a dish of pineapples in syrup, but he didn't even glance at it. He leaned back, eyes closed, waiting for them to come under the starter's orders. At the words ''They're off'' his body hunched forward involuntarily. His spoon lifted the morsels of pineapple into his mouth to the rhythm of the commentary, now slow, now fast, now slow again, then clattered from his hand to the table in final despair.

Half the empire was lost, but his valor was still as great as that of Xiang Yu, the hegemon of Chu. For all his conviction, he couldn't help feeling just a little panicky. He found himself starting to plead for mercy. He was going to call to the waiter to bring something to drink when he discovered a cup of black coffee had materialized on the table beside him to revive his sense of taste. He only realized as he lifted it to his lips that it was bitter; he had forgotten to add sugar.

The bitterness had at least aroused his taste buds, breaking the absolute supremacy of the sense of hearing. Gradually he regained his other senses; the return of sentiment triggered in his brain the image of Jinlan. Through a haze he saw his parents standing at his wife's side, the four members of his family peering anxiously into the crowd, desperately looking for him.

He hung his head and prayed to High Heaven to protect him, to change his luck, to see defeat turn to victory in the next race before it was too late. He let his mind go blank for a moment, waiting for the moment when his luck would change. The atmosphere was stifling, like a lead weight on his heart. But he survived his suffocation, and the time came! Within a minute, the beautiful bubble was burst again.

Hysterically he poured the whole cup of bitter coffee down his throat, lurched to the till to pay his check and blundered out of the restaurant. He stumbled toward the goldsmith's store across the street and pulled out of his breast the little package that Jinlan had given him. He unpinned the package, set the handkerchief aside, and with a trembling left hand took hold of the golden jewelry, which sparkled all the more in the sunlight. He closed his eyes. Then, just as he was about to step into the goldsmith's, a piercing sound erupted from the transistor radio in his jacket pocket: And now for the next race! The next race!

Eyes agog, he recoiled and whipped the stub of his betting slip out of his jacket pocket. In a final burst of lucidity he said to himself: They still haven't run the fourth! I still have the fourth! His strange behavior aroused the suspicion of the man in the goldsmith's store and attracted curious glances from inquisitive bystanders. But he just stood there staring at the jewelry in his left hand and the betting stub in his right, as if he was trying to judge their weight, unconscious of the world around him.

The sight of a policeman's billy club jolted him from his daze like an electric shock. Everything in his hands fell to the ground.

"What's your game?" demanded the policeman. "Got your I.D.?"

His eyes clouded over, he was dumb. The policeman lost patience: "Put your hands up, I'm going to search you!"

"Clubs . . . still the fourth race . . . my . . . mind . . . ," he moaned, before he too fell to the ground.

The policeman pulled out his I.D. and notebook. Then he gathered up the betting stub and the items of jewelry one by one, went into the goldsmith's and made a call. One of the shop-clerks said a word to him. He walked back out of the store and picked up the silk handkerchief that lay nearby. The white silk was muddied by feet that had stepped on it.

A siren sounded. The ambulance had arrived.

Wrong Number

Liu Yichang

Translated by Michael S. Duke

CHEN Xi was lying in bed staring at the ceiling when the telephone rang. It was Wu Lichang. She invited him to go to the five-thirty movie at the Leimoutoi Theater. His spirits were instantly buoyed up and he shaved, combed his hair, and changed clothes with alacrity. As he was changing clothes, he softly whistled the currently popular tune "A Courageous Chinese." Examining himself in the mirror after dressing, he decided that he really must buy himself a famous brand shirt. He loved Lichang and Lichang loved him. As soon as he could find a job, they could go to the Marriage Bureau and register. He had just returned from America, and, although he had his degree, he still had to rely on luck to find a job. If his luck was good he would find a job very quickly, but if his luck was bad he might have to wait for some time. He had already sent out seven or eight letters in answer to job advertisements; some replies should be coming in this week. It was on this account that he had been staying at home for the past few days waiting for phone calls from those companies and not going out unless absolutely necessary. But since Lichang had called to invite him out to a movie, he definitely had to go. It was already four-fifty; he had to step on it to get to Leimoutoi on time. If he was late, Lichang would be angry. And so he went forth with long strides, opened the front door, pulled back the steel grating, stepped outside, turned around, closed the front door, locked the steel grating, got into the elevator, went downstairs, left the building, and strode off in the direction of the bus stop with a feeling of breezy relaxation. Just as he reached the bus stop, a bus came speeding along, swerved out of control, careened up onto the bus stop, ran into Chen Xi, an old woman, and a little girl, and crushed them into bloody pulp.

Chen Xi was lying in bed staring at the ceiling when the telephone rang. It was Wu Lichang. She invited him to go to the five-thirty movie at the Leimoutoi

---

Written in 1983. This translation is from Liu Shaoming and Ma Hanmao, eds., *Shijie zhongwen xiaoshuo xuan* (The commonwealth of Chinese fiction) (Taibei: Shibao wenhua chuban gongsi, 1987), 2:473–75.

Theater. His spirits were instantly buoyed up and he shaved, combed his hair, and changed clothes with alacrity. As he was changing clothes, he softly whistled the currently popular tune "A Courageous Chinese." Examining himself in the mirror after dressing, he decided that he really must buy himself a famous brand shirt. He loved Lichang and Lichang loved him. As soon as he could find a job, they could go to the Marriage Bureau and register. He had just returned from America, and, although he had his degree, he still had to rely on luck to find a job. If his luck was good he would find a job very quickly, but if his luck was bad he might have to wait for some time. He had already sent out seven or eight letters in answer to job advertisements; some replies should be coming in this week. It was on this account that he had been staying at home for the past few days waiting for phone calls from those companies and not going out unless absolutely necessary. But since Lichang had called to invite him out to a movie, he definitely had to go. It was already four-fifty; he had to step on it to get to Leimoutoi on time. If he was late, Lichang would be angry. And so he went over with long strides, opened the front door, and . . .

The telephone rang again.

Thinking it was one of those companies calling, he turned around quickly and ran over to answer it.

"Hello!"

A woman's voice came through the receiver:

"Is Uncle there?"

"Who?"

"Uncle."

"There's no uncle here."

"Is Auntie there, then?"

"What number are you calling . . . ?"

"Three nine five seven . . ."

"You trying to call Kowloon?"

"Right."

"You got the wrong number! This is Hong Kong."

Indignantly slamming down the receiver, he went out with long strides, pulled open the steel grating, stepped outside, turned around, closed the front door, locked the steel grating, got into the elevator, went downstairs, left the building, and strode off in the direction of the bus stop with a feeling of breezy relaxation. When he was about fifty yards from the bus stop, he saw a bus come speeding along, swerve wildly out of control, careen up onto the bus stop, run into an old woman and a little girl, and crush them into bloody pulp.*

---

*Author's note: This story was written on April 22, 1983; that day the papers reported a fatal bus accident in Taikoshing.

Night Revels

Hai Xin

Translated by Gu Yaxing

WHEN the last bit of the deep orange sun, its glistening crest, was swallowed by the sea, the valley world turned a primordial gray. At this time the evening breeze carried some strange noises over—the sound of pop music, Guangdong opera played by *suona* horn, *sheng* pipe, and *xiao* flute mixed with gongs and drums, and the wild beating of tins and bamboos.

What was the matter?

The family had been settled in at the top of this twenty-two-story apartment house located on the east slope of the valley only about ten days. Before moving in, this family of five—Mr. Ye, a bank manager, Mrs. Ye, principal of a kindergarten, white-haired Old Granny Ye, eldest daughter Xian-xian and second son Chang-chang, and their thirty-some-year-old maid Ah Qing Sao—had lived in a noisy roadside building in Bei Jiao, paying more than HK $1,000 for rooms of no more than 500 square feet.

Mr. Ye got a raise in salary recently. The chairman of the board appreciated his services on behalf of the bank over the past ten years or more so much as to choose to install him at the top of this east-slope luxury apartment house recently built by the bank and to rent it to him at a rather low rent. Old Granny Ye, however, learned from some female neighbors in the Bei Jiao apartment house that both the east and west slopes of the valley were gravesites. Disposed to worming their way into every crevice, the real estate agents had finally cast their greedy eyes upon it. Thus the graves were removed and the ghosts driven out. That was followed by large-scale construction, several apartment houses being erected. The Ye family was in fact the first family settling in at the top of the first house. Lighting the first lamp, they led the way in.

The original appeared in Hong Kong's *Wenhuibao*, May 18, 1980, and was reprinted in *Tai-gang wenxue xuankan* (Taiwan and Hong Kong literature) (Fujian), no. 2 (November 1984). This translation is from that text as reprinted in Liu Shaoming and Ma Hanmao, eds., *Shijie zhongwen xiaoshuo xuan* (The commonwealth of Chinese fiction) (Taibei: Shibao wenhua chuban gongsi, 1987), 2:476–83.

It was out of her unwillingness to contend with the ghosts for living space in this manner that Old Granny hesitated to move in. Yet, in spite of her feelings and her sympathy for the evicted phantoms, Mr. and Mrs. Ye insisted on accepting the bounty bestowed by the bank. Therefore, they moved in at last and settled down at the top of the apartment house which was situated at the foot of a hill, beside the sea.

Since she had to obey her son in her old age, Old Granny had no way out but to follow them, though she kept complaining all the way. The only remedy she could think of after settling in was to burn incense, candles, and funerary money earnestly and sincerely every day, and beg the homeless ghosts for forgiveness. She promised that in July she would make some special effort to help release them from purgatory.

The balcony at the top of the apartment house faced those west-slope graves yet to be removed. Standing erect on the slope was a three-story, fort-like villa built distinctively in the British style. In front of the villa lay an open lawn. A swimming pool was on its far side. Being deserted, the villa fortress had grown derelict with an air of sad desolation. It was now gloomily awaiting the day when it would be demolished and replaced by high-rises of some twenty-odd stories.

What Old Granny dreaded most was walking out onto the balcony, raising her eyes, and seeing the remnant of the graveyard and the run-down villa-fort on the west slope across the valley. Whenever she stood on the balcony, she reminded herself that they were really living next door to ghosts and breathing a most gruesome and ghastly air

That day was on a weekend. In the evening Mr. and Mrs. Ye were to take part in a banquet celebrating the birthday of the chairman of the board. A little after six, they went downstairs and drove downtown.

At home were Old Granny, Xian-xian, Chang-chang, and the maid Ah Qing Sao. It was so quiet in the house that the singing of the insects and the croaking of the frogs on the slope could be heard.

From the west slope the sound of pop music, *suona*, gongs and drums, and the wild beating of tins and bamboos mixed with the joyous shrieks of men and women . . . became clearer and louder as the sky grew darker.

The first person who was drawn onto the balcony was Old Granny. She strained her eyes, gazing at the fort-like villa across the valley. The lawn was scattered with lanterns of various colors as well as fluorescent lamps. Bonfires could be seen everywhere. Around the empty swimming pool were lines of candles placed in good order, their tiny flames flickering. In the pool some figures were moving to and fro, and some more bonfires were lit. . . .

At the sight of this, Old Granny turned pale. Involuntarily putting her palms together, she muttered, "Lord Buddha preserve us!" But right after this she exclaimed, "Ghostly revels! The he-ghosts and she-ghosts like to have their parties on the weekend too. How ridiculous!"

The granddaughter and grandson were drawn outside by her remarks. They walked onto the balcony, lifted their heads and looked over at the west slope. A moment later Chang-chang hurried to his father's bedroom to fetch his binoculars. With them in his hands Chang-chang looked up and down the villa and the lawn.

"Superstitious! That's a bunch of trendy boys and girls. They're just having a classy open-air party!" said he.

Impatiently, Xian-xian snatched the binoculars from her brother. Gazing through them, she said, "Yah! What a classy party! They're all decent men and women. Oh, there's a band too! Look, some people are dancing, some are barbecuing, some are laughing merrily on the veranda. They're having an evening party in the garden!"

Ah Qing Sao, who had retired to her room, had certainly caught the nonsense of the old woman and later the description by Chang-chang and Xian-xian of what they saw through the binoculars. She went over to the window, raised her head, and looked at the villa-fort and the lawn on the west slope. Her face broadened into a complacent smile.

She thought—how could it be a ghost party? a classy get-together? or a rich folks' soirée?

She remembered that after 3 P.M. that day, while grocery shopping in West End market, she saw some long-haired and dirty-faced beggars who were in those soiled uniforms usually worn by members in the undertaker's band. They were buying out Chen Niu-ji, a frozen meat man—drumsticks, chicken wings, pork steaks, beef, and sausages.

"Niu-ji, you gonna sell your frozen meat to us beggars at a discount, eh?" said one beggar, whose face was so filthy that one could hardly tell his eyes from his eyebrows.

A big, tall guy, Niu-ji said, "Twenty percent off."

"Niu-ji, wanna drink beer with us this evenin'?" said a short beggar with a long beard. "What are you up to—usually you guys never spend a single penny on food!" said Niu-ji.

"Us West End beggars are gonna have a garden party!" said a tall beggar, whose long hair was done up in a bun, making him look like a Daoist hermit.

"Beggar's garden party!" Disbelieving, Niu-ji opened his eyes wide.

"Don't you fine people like some variety in your food and drink and party much of your time away? We beggars just wanna get together!" The beggar with the long beard jumped up and down.

"Where will you have this party?" asked Niu-ji.

"In the villa-fort on the west side of Jin Hu Shan valley!"

"Aha, Goddam smart, that villa is a real nice place," said Niu-ji, holding up his thumb in approval.

"Besides, we're gonna invite all the down-and-outs who run the streets to have a good time with us this evening."

"This really is interesting news!" Niu-ji reached out his hand and put it on the arm of the beggar with the bun.

"We old women *soldiers* were sent to fruit stores for damaged fruit. When the storekeepers learned about the beggars' evening party they let us have their seconds of apples, pears, and bananas for nix!"

"Ah Shui has managed to borrow some tapes and a tape recorder. We're gonna have a great time this evenin'!"

"All us fellows think we're gonna have a hell of a party celebrating the beggars' birthday!'

Old Granny pulled the binoculars from Xian-xian's hands, pressed them hard on her eyes, and stared at the old villa-fort on the west slope with great concentration.

"What is it, Grandma?" Chang-chang asked.

After a prolonged stare, Old Granny yelled, "Ghosts, ghosts, I've found a bunch of male and female ghosts in weird get-ups. Look, there's a she-ghost in flaring crimson dress with a red turban on her head. . . . There's another she-ghost who's in purple from top to toe and her face is greeny blue. . . . Oh, how awful, there are a couple of he-ghosts whose hair's so long it's touching the ground, one of them is wearing a floppy theatrical costume and the cap of a Daoist priest. Another's in a long gown and a mandarin jacket. A third one looks like a clown in a circus troupe. Some men are dressed like women, some women made up like men. . . . Good God! They're demons and monsters! Why did we move right here to live in the middle of this hell? May Buddha preserve us! May Buddha preserve us!"

Chang-chang grabbed the binoculars from his grandmother and put them to his eyes. After he gazed for a while he laughed heartily, "Grandma is so superstitious! How could this be a ghost party? All of them are cool youngsters. They're having a masquerade. They're wearing fancy dresses on purpose. Oh, they're wearing masks too!"

Xian-xian took the binoculars from her younger brother. She couldn't help laughing, "Grandma, do you really believe that so many demons and monsters from the graveyard are having their fun there? What a scream! Actually they're men and women from good families. It's an outdoor garden party that they're having!"

Standing by the window in the servant's room, Ah Qing Sao raised her eyes and scrutinized the villa-fort on the west slope as well as its surrounding lawn. Overhearing the conversation of Old Granny and her granddaughter and son, she smirked sarcastically.

Naturally, she could recall what she had come across in the evening: on her way from the market, where she bought some vegetables, to Zhang Ji Store for butter and canned goods, she passed Heng Jia Street and saw two women taking a bath by a roadside fire hydrant. People often saw them walk up and down the streets, carrying gaudy umbrellas opened above their heads and jabbering incessantly. But now, under the babbling water from the hydrant, with all their ragged clothes off, they were rubbing themselves down with soap, both looking very happy.

On each side of the street was a big crowd of men and children; of course there were women too. They watched these crazy nude bathers with great interest, just like watching a porno film.

The two nude bathers jokingly voiced their protest in unison, "What's the attraction?" "You have never seen a woman clean her body before?"

The lanky woman who always loved to rouge her cheeks added arrogantly, "We're going to have a garden party this evening. We're all paying five dollars!"

The other woman, a dumpy, swarthy one, said, "A party with goodies galore for only five bucks. What a deal!"

They were apparently devoid of a sense of shame. None of those glaring eyes would deter them from cleaning their bodies in preparation for the garden party.

After the bath they put on their new clothes. Ah Qing Sao gasped, "Aren't these clothes stolen from the Puppet Troupe? . . . They're the prettiest stage costume worn by the leading lady in that old play. Who said you were crazy? My good ladies, you do have some taste in dress for your beggars' get-together!"

At that moment Old Granny raised the binoculars once more. She cried out as if she'd discovered something grotesque:

"That's it! Just last evening I saw a couple of families down the valley joining together to ask some Buddhist monks to chant scriptures to bring blessing and ward off misfortune. They burnt a paper mansion, two paper airplanes, and a whole lot of paper cars. . . . Look, the male and female ghosts have parked more than ten paper cars in the square under the old fort of a villa! The ghosts must have got all those cars and raced over to attend this night revel!"

Chang-chang seized the binoculars from his grandmother and looked through them for a long while before he said, "Grandma's really mixed-up! The cars parked in the square are all A-one racers. There are fancy new electric mopeds too. For you, everything has got to do with ghosts. Lame-brained!"

Having searched for a good while through the binoculars, Xian-xian commented, "They aren't ghost cars or racers. They're all specials from famous manufacturers: Rolls Royce, Mercedes-Benz, Volvo, Bluebird . . . all privately owned by celebrities!"

In the servant's room, Ah Qing Sao couldn't help tittering: she had been to the square beneath the villa-fort on the west slope. It was in fact a wrecker's yard for used-car parts. Her husband had the job of taking out seats there, covered with iron rust all day. A couple dozen cars of various makes ready for disassembling were parked there. She wondered how even the magnifying glasses or binoculars did not help these people of three generations to discern reality.

The binoculars had turned into a favorite toy for those three, who fought with one another to get hold of them. It was true that Chang-chang, being younger and quicker, had almost totally controlled the binoculars. Again and again he stared at the grand party on the lawn in front of the west-slope villa. So in the end the old grandmother had to call on her prestige as a senior. She ordered her grandson to surrender the binoculars to her and let her follow the ghost party closely.

Reluctantly, Chang-chang put the binoculars into her wrinkled old hands.

Once again, with the aid of the two cylindrical enlargers, the old lady succeeded in cutting down the distance and getting a good look at the west slope. She stared very hard and suddenly let out a loud cry. It seemed that something serious had happened.

"What's the matter, Grandma?"

"Bull-heads and horse-faces, yes I see a lot of bull-heads and horse-faces running up the slope and into the fort. They're pushing and hauling those monstrous demons down the meadow slope."

Xian-xian snapped up the binoculars from her grandmother, gazed for a little while, and shouted, "Robbery! Some thieves are looting the ladies and gents of their jewelry. The robbers have disguised themselves as police officers and stormed the fort!"

Chang-chang quickly caught the binoculars, put them to his eyes, and yelled loudly, "How can it be a robbery? It's obvious that a lot of policemen have dashed onto the slope and are taking in these smart kids who have been puffing marijuana and having a sex-party down the hill."

From the servant's room, A Qing Sao could see clearly without the binoculars: squads of policemen had surged onto the slope and were dragging the male and female beggars who were having their nighttime revel down the hill. She heaved a sigh: "You mean to say it's a crime for beggars to hold a soirée on a deserted lawn over a graveyard?"

Aunty Li's Pocket Watch

Liang Bingjun

Translated by Kirk Anderson

EVERYBODY in the office had gone home. I was the only one left, finishing up copying the accounts, when all of a sudden the telephone rang. I picked up the receiver.

"Hello."

"Get me Director Wang on the line." On the other end of the phone was a slightly deep voice with a commanding tone. I recognized who it was and almost immediately stammered back.

"Uh, is this Aunty Li? Director Wang's gone."

"What time did he leave?"

"At 5:00. Quitting time."

"You must be joking! It's not even 5:00!" She slammed down the phone fiercely, and suddenly all I could hear was the sound of the dial tone. My ear was hot, but I didn't know if it was because of the scolding I had just endured or what. I looked at my watch. I had five after five. I looked back and the clock on our wall also read five after five. Director Wang obviously left according to the time on the wall. This time he really had bad luck. I silently turned my watch back five minutes, then, thinking about it, set it just a little earlier. I'd have to check it against Aunty Li's time, then it would be right.

In our factory, only Aunty Li's time is accurate. Nobody knows how long she's been working here. Some say she's been here since it started; others say she's related to the boss. No matter what, from the time our company was just a little Chinese-style sewing shop, with just a few seamstresses, up to right now, having developed into a large-scale Western-style garment factory, Aunty Li has always been here. No one knows exactly what her position is, but if you considered our factory a big family, then she would be the strict and authoritative

---

The original appeared in *Sihai: Tai-gang-haiwai zhongguo wenxue* (Four seas: Hong Kong, Taiwan, and overseas Chinese literature), no. 3 (1986). This translation is from Liu Shaoming and Ma Hanmao, eds., *Shijie zhongwen xiashuo xuan* (The commonwealth of Chinese fiction) (Taibei: Shibao wenhua chuban gongsi, 1987), 2:542–52.

grandmother. She's always been here, issuing the rules, passing out rewards and punishments. If the seamstresses have a complaint, or if a staff member has an idea, for the most part they meet with her. We've heard a lot of stories passed on, of her promoting new people and extending benefits. But those are just stories. There are also those that hold her ability to determine right and wrong in the highest esteem, but that's just hearsay too. At least we're too young and didn't have the chance to witness the glory of her former days. By the time we started working here, her power was already supreme. We also never had the opportunity to see how it had been tested. She was already a symbol of legislation and enforcement. We're all quite afraid of her. If anything isn't to her liking, she immediately makes a phone call. We only have to hear that slightly deep voice with the commanding tone, and we know there's a problem.

Aunty Li's sense of time is as serious and principled as her sense of right and wrong. She has an old pocket watch that never leaves her person. People say it's one of the rare treasures that came to China during the Qing dynasty that her father passed on to her. The accuracy of that watch is well known. In any of the rooms of our factory, if any clock is slightly off, it always ends up being reset according to Aunty Li's pocket watch. Similarly, if there are any disputes between personnel, it's always Aunty Li's judgments that are the standard. Aunty Li and her pocket watch have really become a kind of law in our factory.

So, the next day as I was telling Director Wang about Aunty Li's call, he looked a little frightened. Although he was still talking tough—he said something about managing affairs according to the clock—he obviously had a guilty conscience. He had lost confidence in himself and the clocks in our office. It wasn't too long before he was called in to see Aunty Li. He was gone for about half an hour, and when he came back he didn't look very good. I didn't dare ask him how it went.

At quitting time Director Wang was afraid to leave right away. He pretended like it wasn't any big deal, shuffling papers around. I obviously couldn't expose him. He stayed past five after five (that was the time by the electric clock on the wall; my watch, which I changed yesterday according to Aunty Li's time, read just 5:00), he took a deep breath and wasted a few more minutes, then, seeing there was nothing out of the ordinary, left quickly.

When it was five after five according to my watch (the wall clock was now at ten after), I put my things in order and was just about to leave.

But the phone rang suddenly. It was Aunty Li; she was looking for Director Wang.

"He left at 5:00." I could only be honest.

She didn't say a word. I got nervous and asked, "Aunty Li . . . what time do you have?"

"Just 5:00!"

I promptly set my wristwatch back five minutes. You just can't trust these ordinary watches we have, I mean look, Director Wang's in trouble again.

The next day Director Wang was again called into Aunty Li's office; this time he was in there even longer. Old Feng and Old Zhu of our accounting department were talking. Today they weren't talking like they usually did about our company's lack of benefits, the problems of promotion, or the meagerness of incomes. They were discussing Director Wang's situation. They felt like I did about it. Although it seemed Director Wang was being treated a bit too harshly, he had mistakenly believed the inaccurate wall clock, so what could we say? We were just like the other office workers, simply rejoicing in the fact that it hadn't happened to us, and calculating how to consider our own best interests. Afterward we'd just pay careful attention to the time. We both respected and feared Aunty Li, and luckily we had her to look to as a model, especially as a way to check our clocks. We should obviously follow her example. As Old Zhu said, if we're gonna work, we have to follow someone else's rules. At this point Director Wang came back. He looked even worse than yesterday, so we all just shut up.

Director Wang was quiet all day; he looked as though he felt he had been wronged. I lowered my head and didn't look at him. Anyway, the work was already enough to keep me busy. In the afternoon, the manager of the maintenance department (some people said he was related to Aunty Li) came with a technician to our department. My eyes, hidden by my work, looked ahead and saw a black pair of socks. The technician had taken off his shoes to stand on my desk to adjust the wall clock. The manager dialed Aunty Li on the inside line, then looked at the clock on our wall. He said to the technician, "Slow it down by fifteen minutes and it'll be right."

I looked at my watch, and although I had adjusted it yesterday, it was wrong again now. I set my watch back another five minutes. I'd have to watch out for myself, be especially careful. I'd have to check it every day to make sure it didn't deviate from Aunty Li's standard time.

Then I heard the manager talking into the phone, saying, "The clock in the accounting department's fixed, now we're going to the factory."

After they left I saw Old Feng and Old Zhu lift their wrists to adjust their watches according to the time on the wall. Director Wang got up and hesitated at first, then he did it too. In the quiet office all you could hear was the clicking sound of the gears of the clock.

From that day on, time was the popular topic of conversation in our office. The next day Old Feng shared with us a bit of inside news. He said because the company was approaching the day of our annual pay increases, they were paying particularly strict attention to the conduct of the employees. And Old Zhu followed with another piece of news: because of the economic depression, the garment industry was in a slump. The company was going to lay some people off, so it was a very serious situation. I heard these two different pieces of information with both joy and dread. We were insignificant office workers and would naturally give priority to playing it safe. In days past, they piled the work up on me; I always had the most work in the accounting department. I was also the last person to leave the office. The present situation seemed very different. At five o'clock, nobody was thinking about leaving, they were all still sitting obstinately in their seats. Today was Wednesday, but Old Feng, who loved to bet on the evening races, was surprisingly in no hurry to leave. Instead he asked, "Do you think we should call and ask what time Aunty Li has?"

"Yes!" Old Zhu dialed the phone unbelievably quickly. I heard him say, "Is this Aunty Li? This is Zhu Jiming in the Accounting Department. Can I ask what time you have right now?"

Then he said completely submissively, "It's 4:55? Thanks, thank you."

He didn't seem surprised in the least. He immediately took off his shoes, climbed up on my desk, and set the clock back five minutes.

All I could do was set my watch back five minutes. *Ai*, wrong again. It's lucky Old Zhu called to ask. These days you just can't trust your watch.

At this point Director Wang lifted his arm, then put it back down. I didn't know why he was hesitating. Then he suddenly said, one word at a time: "Couldn't—it—be—that—Aunty—Li's—pocket—watch—is—wrong?"

I stared at him stunned. I hadn't anticipated that he'd say such a thing. And both Old Zhu and Old Feng, not knowing what to do, lowered their heads as if they hadn't heard anything. But no one heard it better. To come out with this kind of statement was not something to be taken lightly. And moreover, on what grounds could he doubt Aunty Li? She always maintained morality and discipline; she was both honest and strict. She was a model reproduction of the traditional Chinese mind. And her pocket watch was famous for its accuracy.

After Director Wang said this sentence he let his head droop down. He didn't look like he felt any better. It was probably because he'd been scolded that he was in a bad mood and had come out with this indignant statement.

The next day Director Wang didn't say a thing all day. The atmosphere in the whole office was a little bit stiff. I really didn't like it; in the past we had all been talkative and jovial. Director Wang would sometimes joke around, saying our factory was a harmonious combination of Chinese and Western elements, but we didn't have any of the benefits—only the disadvantages of both. For example, there aren't any measures taken for Western-style bonuses or material benefits, but there is the Western work system. There isn't any of the Chinese-style affectionate camaraderie, but there are redundant employees as a result of Chinese-style personal "connections." Afterward we could criticize the meagerness of the salaries, the gloominess of the future, and all that. But despite the fact that he'd said it, wasn't everybody still acting in the same old way? If you put it that way, though, everyone still seemed happy. And I know: Director Wang has always been inclined to respect Aunty Li. He'll occasionally pour out his grievances but he'll also say: it's lucky there are still people like Aunty Li who hold firm to impartiality. But now Director Wang was just silent, he hadn't said a thing. Maybe he just couldn't help but change his way of thinking.

I really couldn't bear the silence. The days seemed terribly long; it wasn't easy making it to the end of the day. Everyone tidied up their things, and I heaved a sigh. Director Wang looked at his watch, then looked at the clock on the wall. 5:01. He hesitated. He waited a bit, then finally cleaned up his things and left.

I just couldn't get the drawer of my old desk to close. I tried hard to shove it in, then swore at it, and grumbled that it hadn't been thrown out earlier. Just as I was straining, struggling with my desk, the telephone rang.

Old Feng answered it. I just heard him say, "He left."

I knew it right away: this time Director Wang was really in a mess.

I heard Old Feng ask what time it was, then he climbed up on my desk again and set the clock back five minutes. So now the accurate time was 4:58, instead of 5:03.

So it really wasn't quitting time yet. I abandoned my struggle with my desk, sat down, and continued transcribing.

Right after work I got a ride to the theater. I had a date with my girlfriend to see the five-thirty movie. When I got there I didn't expect to see her turning around to leave. I chased her. She ignored me completely, then finally gave me a good cursing. I didn't know what it was all about. She said I was half an hour late. I checked the time on my watch, which was set according to the clock at the office which was set according to Aunty Li's pocket watch. It was 5:30. But her watch and the clock in the hall at the theater both said 6:00. According to the man at the door of the theater, the movie had already been playing for thirty minutes. I never thought that I'd end up a victim of this clock question.

But compared to Director Wang's disaster, my problem was really nothing.

The next morning when Director Wang came in he was immediately called into the office. After hardly any time he came back out, indignantly packed up his things, and left. People said he had been fired. No one dared ask him anything. Someone said he suspected that comment about Aunty Li's pocket watch was one of the reasons for his punishment. But it probably wasn't true, because when somebody got fired, no one was really very clear about it. As Director Wang was packing up his things, tearing up pieces of scrap paper, the calm expression on his face couldn't hide his rage. In the whole office, the silence was broken only by the mechanical whistling sound of tearing paper. Finally he left without uttering a word.

After he left, I had a feeling that something wasn't quite right, but I didn't know what it was. After a while I heard the sounds of talking and laughing behind me. I couldn't hear clearly, but it seemed to be Old Feng jokingly calling Old Zhu "Director," as if, since Director Wang was gone, his position was there for Old Zhu to fill.

But after a few days Old Zhu was disappointed. Aunty Li brought someone named Li onto the scene and introduced him to us. During the introduction, in passing, Aunty Li made a stern comment about justice. She mentioned the importance of submitting to discipline and respecting one's seniors. She especially stressed the traditional Chinese virtue of punctuality as something we mustn't neglect. I thought what Aunty Li had to say was very significant. In an industrial organization, discipline is very important. Director Wang's situation was extremely unlucky, but since things ended up the way they did, no matter who comes on the scene, we insignificant office workers will just have to keep on doing our work. As for Old Zhu, I don't know if it was because he coveted the potential connections of the position or what, but afterward he told us that the new director Li was really Aunty Li's cousin. But we didn't know whether to believe him or not.

The days passed as they had before, the only difference was that each day before quitting time Director Li would call to check Aunty Li's time. Each day we would discover that our watches were five minutes fast, and we'd promptly correct them according to her time. Each day when work was over we'd call Aunty Li, adjust our watches, then we'd correct the clock on the wall. It had become part of our daily routine, just like those letters full of official jargon were part of each day's work, it was an indispensable verse of our closing song. And now each day, climbing up on the desk to slow the clock by five minutes according to Aunty Li's accurate time had become my responsibility. And of course I followed the director's orders, without the slightest doubt. I was just doing the work that was assigned to me. We can really do things without thinking.

At the beginning there was no problem. The days passed one at a time. Our factory gradually seemed to become a world apart from the outside. In each department our colleagues began to miss the bus and train. Missing the beginnings of movies and arriving late to parties gave rise to husbands' suspicions and wives' complaints for everyone. Nothing could be done about meeting the kids after school or missing night school. As for me, my girlfriend went from being mad at me to asking me rather humorously if I was working according to daylight savings time. But finally she couldn't take it anymore and we broke up. But how could I say anything about it? I could only talk about Aunty Li's celebrated pocket watch, and about her strictness and her impeccable sense of time. I brought up several historical examples. From the time of the resistance during the Hong Kong occupation through a decade or more of prosperous economic development, Aunty Li's pocket watch played an important role in our organization. But my girlfriend—she just curled her lip and said we were completely crazy, and that we had fallen behind the real time and didn't even know it. Several of our colleagues were worried in the same way. There was no way they could persuade outsiders to believe Aunty Li's time was really accurate and that the outside world was a quickly passing mirage. People on the outside weren't in our organization, so there was no way to make them feel the soundness of Aunty

Li's authority. Half the time we were in the office, and the other half the time we were in the outside world; it started feeling like two different time zones. It was really a big hassle.

The days passed like this one at a time. Each day we'd leave work according to Aunty Li's time, but each day the color of the sky seemed darker. When other people went to work we were still at home sleeping; and when we got off work the streets were already peacefully without human shadows. I was really jealous of the outside world's night life, but all I could do was resent the fact that the external world's sense of time wasn't the same as Aunty Li's standard time. Everyone felt about the same way: some upheld Aunty Li's accuracy and spurned the reality of the outside world. Others started, as Director Wang had, to doubt Aunty Li. But these were both minorities; most people did things according to the rules, living one day at a time, where accidentally complaining was bad luck.

Each day when we got off work there were fewer and fewer people on the street. At first everyone thought we were the crowd coming out after the last movie, but a little while later people thought it was an illegal meeting and sent out the police to suppress our demonstration. In the early hours of the morning as we dispersed onto the completely empty streets, whether we were returning to the meanest alley or a new section of town, no one would believe that we were just coming home from work. The men were frequently searched by the police but even more frequently mugged in the stairwells; and a day didn't go by without a woman being attacked. But these sorts of things happened so often, and of course everyone was affected, so this also became a part of our daily routine.

Despite the fact that all the employees of the factory were coming and going according to Aunty Li's standard time, the rise and decline of the garment industry wasn't under the same control. Under the influence of the depression, the industry's tendency to grow was reduced; orders were down, and so was production. Within the factory, rumors were steadily increasing. Everyone was saying that America and Japan, and even a consortium of Eastern European countries, were going to buy into our company. The old look of our company was apparently going to change. I didn't know whether or not to believe this kind of gossip, until this one day when Aunty Li had me bring the account book to her office. As a result I saw an unfamiliar middle-aged man talking with her there. She passed the account book over to him. I stood to one side, bored, waiting, just like a page boy. He glanced at a few numbers, then said several things I didn't quite understand. I stood blankly behind him, leaning against the wall, practically falling asleep, when finally I saw him look at his wristwatch and say: "It's almost 5:00, we'll talk again another day."

When I heard this, I couldn't contain my fright. I thought this guy would get a scolding. Behind him, the clock on the wall (no doubt adjusted each day to

Aunty Li's pocket watch) now read 11:00 A.M. His watch, like most of the watches in the outside world, had clearly not been adjusted to Aunty Li's standard.

I waited for an angry rebuke. But nothing happened. I just saw Aunty Li amiably shake hands with this man, smiling as they parted. Not a comment was made about what he said. I thought maybe she didn't hear him, but ordinarily that wouldn't be the case. But then why? She opened the door to see the man off, then came back in and sat down without noticing me. I stood there behind her, trying my hardest to make a small sound to let her know I was there. But she didn't hear; she was concentrating on turning the pages of the account book on the desk. She had obviously forgotten I was standing there, watching her from behind. After a while she closed the account book, then fished her pocket watch out of her pocket. She opened it, looked at it, then put it on the table. She stared into the empty space in front of her. After a minute she held her forehead as if she had a headache, then put her head down on the desk. I really didn't know what to do. Should I just stay here behind her, or go for the door? Now it seemed like I was behind her looking for other people's secrets. But it wasn't intentional. I could swear it was absolutely unintentional. I just couldn't bear staring at Aunty Li's full head of white hair. A moment before she had the bearing of an ordinary sickly old woman, displaying the frailness of her wrinkles. This really didn't fit in with my resolute, serious image of her.

Thinking about what had just happened, a faint feeling of uneasiness came over me. I felt like a worm was nibbling at me. Why hadn't she reprimanded that middle-aged outsider like she did the people in our factory in order to keep a proper sense of time? I really didn't understand. It was this that drew out my suspicions. It forced me, who had always just followed orders, to start thinking about it. It was this that got my courage up quietly to take a step forward to look at that famous pocket watch.

It was the first time I had ever seen a pocket watch in my life. It was next to Aunty Li's prostrated head. Set off by a few fragile white hairs, it was very different than I had imagined. All I saw was an ordinary open pocket watch, very old looking with a few greasy stains. The shell and the hands of the watch were rusty, and the numbers were blurred beyond recognition. Frankly, I couldn't tell if the hands were still moving or not. I just watched, and from a crack in the shell of the watch suddenly emerged a little brown worm.

Mother Lode

Zheng Wanlong

Translated by Jeffrey C. Kinkley

THE LIFE had gone out of the fire. Its wet logs crackled and smoldered, while the ends that had felt the ax blade exuded a milky liquid and an acrid smell that made you itch. It was all Strapping Wang's fault, for not going out far enough to gather dry wood or strip some birchbark. Staring through the blue flames at the muscles rippling down Wang's back but not daring to open his mouth was Hipless Li, or "Li-about-to-Lose-His-Pants," who seemed too thin to hold his clothes up. He was afraid of Wang's eyes. They were like a wolf's.

That bastard was capable of anything. Old End-of-His-Rope, before he went off, had said right in front of everybody that he was giving his deerskin to Sun Hanba. Sun had slept in the wet and got ringworm all over—scratched himself so much at night that everybody went crazy itching. But here was that deerskin now, spread out under Strapping Wang's ass. He'd said his hemorrhoids had flared up again.

Hipless Li tightened his belt and then let it out again as he left the campfire to pluck some weeds. He twisted them together and spread them out on the rock where he laid his head. He hadn't gotten up and looked at the ravine now for three days running. When he walked he felt tight in his chest and had difficulty breathing. If it hadn't been for the special instructions Old End-of-His-Rope gave when he left, Strapping Wang would probably be driving him like a dog right now to go out to cut wood and build the fire. He'd never be able to figure out this big bear of a man. His face glowed like a young fellow's, but Old End-of-His-Rope himself had said he was over forty. Those wolf-like eyes had fixed on Li and refused to let him go from the first time they met. The fire in them could burn you to a crisp outright; they'd frightened him to the point he'd awakened crying several times in the night. But for the fact that the surrounding expanses were just as scary, and there was no place to go, he'd have packed up his bedroll and made off that first night. That was last year, when he was only

---

Translated from Zheng Wanlong, *Shengming de tuteng* (Life totems) (Beijing: Zhongguo wenlian, 1986), pp. 92–106.

319

fifteen. His father had died in the Pantou gold mine, and Old End-of-His-Rope had brought him here. "What a fuckin' sweety you are boy—I'd bet your ma was real easy to look at." The boy had just burrowed into his bedding when Strapping Wang grabbed him. His eyes burning blue-hot, Wang snorted a little laugh out his nostrils. Shoving him away, the boy drew up his trousers and said, "Leave my ma out of it." Then he'd grabbed Li again, clasping him tighter still, and stroking him all over with his other hand, chortling, "I've never touched myself a woman. I guess this must be what your ma feels like." Wang pulled him onto his breast and bit his shoulder. After that, every encounter with Wang seemed like a brush with the devil. Wang wouldn't let him be for a single day—he'd curse him, fondle him, kick him, pull his ears, slap him around. Only when he was mistreating the boy did a smile show itself on Wang's broad face. He was usually grim as a rock.

The pot hanging over the fire began to hiss and send out the sweet aroma of dog meat. It made Hipless Li's whole stomach ache. The men struggled to a sitting position and moved close to the fire, away from the wind. They didn't bother to breathe through their noses; they opened their mouths wide and swallowed again and again. You could hear them gulp. Hipless Li downed his saliva as it came; each mouthful burned his stomach like a fire. But Strapping Wang lay on his back, resting his head on his arms, facing up at the empty sky and gnashing his teeth.

There wasn't much salt left, just a pinch for the whole big pot. An extra pinch and the aroma would have been that much stronger and unbearable to all. They did have another pinch, in the oilskin packet inside the deerskin pouch—it would be rationed out over the next two days. If Old End-of-His-Rope wasn't back by morning three days hence, they'd have to make do with something else.

They'd already been without food for nine days. Two fellows must have eaten some kind of poisonous root or mushroom. Their ashy white faces swelled up as they died; they cried in anguish the whole night through, clawing through the stuffing in their jackets down to the flesh beneath. Now they lay buried under that lightning-struck oak tree. Even Strapping Wang hadn't the extra strength to dig pits for them. They'd just piled up rocks over the corpses. Hipless Li didn't dare close his eyes that night. He kept hearing the two men moan beneath the tree. He imagined he saw their hands, scratched all bloody, reaching out through the cracks in the rocks.

"Let me have a bit of the broth, huh? I beg you everybody, just a mouthful, all right?" Sun Hanba was the oldest of the seven survivors. He slowly rose with his pitted brass bowl, staring with fright at all those gaping eyes as he gradually advanced toward the hanging pot.

They all lifted themselves up on their arms as though singed by the fire and stared in terror at his bowl. Their faces were quivering like jelly.

The brass bowl clanked against the top of the pot. Before Sun Hanba could drink the soup he'd scooped up, Strapping Wang pounced on him from behind the campfire like a leopard. Wang knocked him over and choked him, using his two hands like pincers.

"Aargh—!" Sun Hanba rolled over on the ground, squealing like a pig.

"Let him go, it was just one gulp." The group struggled to their feet to restrain Strapping Wang.

Sun Hanba's eyes were practically squeezed out of their sockets, but as soon as Wang let him go, he flipped himself upright on his feet like a fish and went looking all over for his bowl. It was dry. He couldn't even see where the broth had splashed. Taking his bowl in both hands, he began to cry like a child—so loud that everyone bowed their heads, afraid to look at him. Only Strapping Wang was on his back again, resting on his arms and looking up at the sky.

They'd been stuck here for more than six months, and it was now seventy-two days since the store at the Pantou mine had stopped sending supplies. They hadn't mined a grain of gold since they'd got there. They'd gone a whole month for "naught" and spent three excavating "strata just above paydirt." They'd gone through one pickax handle after another and still no hint of "the yellow stuff" in their pans. The whole crew wore an angry look. Maybe there just wasn't any gold *in* this fuckin' place. An artilleryman from the Oroqen tribe had been through here and bagged himself three stags in one day—and a gold nugget that weighed seventy-five grams. Must be fate.

Hipless Li was so hungry he was resigned to whatever might come. How often he'd thought of slipping away at night when everyone was asleep, but he didn't know his way and had no horse. Those who fled earlier had died along the way. Old End-of-His-Rope had ridden off on their only horse, a gray-colored one. Right now the fate of them all was in his hands. But would he ever return? When they'd come to this new site and written out their I.O.U.'s at the store, Old End-of-His-Rope himself had had a head full of dreams. He'd said that if he could mine a thousand grains of gold, he'd roll up his bedding and head south of the Great Wall to his old home. He'd buy a few acres of land, build a three-room house, and get his brother a wife. He'd drunk two bottles of liquor that night and staggered over to Widow Wei's house. She was the comeliest woman in Pantou Gulch, and no one dared to compete with Old End-of-His-Rope, not even the manager of the store. The old man wasn't just good at using his money, he was greedy. People had followed him into Bear Gulch and settled there homestead by homestead, on the strength of his name and experience in these parts. There were more than three hundred souls there at the peak. Now only seven were left.

As the sun sank behind the tops of the trees, Hipless Li suddenly lost the smell of the dog meat. He blacked out.

They divvied up the dog meat before it was fully done.

Everybody feared they wouldn't live to see it get tender. They felt themselves becoming spider webs hanging from the trees. If something suddenly tore them apart, they'd be lost to oblivion.

When they scooped the dog meat out from the hanging pot, the broth was distributed first. With that soup, Hipless Li came back to his senses. Everybody grew steadier as they stared at Strapping Wang dividing the meat. He went into the woods and selected a smooth, glossy birch tree. After girdling the truck with slits up above and down below, a single stroke of the knife down the grain of the tree, not too deep and not too shallow, produced a neat birchbark cylinder the diameter of the trunk. He sewed up the two ends watertight, using the knife point and steel wire. Without so much as a glance at the several pairs of eyes gaping at him, he slowly walked back to the fire. He whittled two round wooden stoppers with lightning speed, then stuffed one of them into one end of his birchbark tube. It was getting dark as he cut the dog meat into pieces and stuffed them one by one into the tube, so he had Hipless Li light pine torches. Using a wooden stick, he pounded the dog meat into the birchbark tube until it was packed firm, stoppered up the other end, and marked off the tube into seven equal sections with a ruler. Rolling himself a cigarette and lighting up, he slowly lifted his eyelids and surveyed the wizened and bedraggled faces around him. "You all saw me do it. This is our food for the next three days. Each person pick out a section of the tube. When you've made your claims, I'll saw them apart. But don't wait till I've cut the fuckin' thing and then say somebody else's portion is better than yours."

You couldn't see the dog meat behind the birchbark, so picking out a section was leaving everything to luck. Yet they all took fully an hour to make their choice, staring at the tube until their eyes were tired. Strapping Wang put on a scowl again and, rubbing his saw blade against his pants, cut off the sections one by one. No one made a sound. Hipless Li felt as if his own body were being sawed on.

By the time the pine torches were burned out, the birchbark tube was all cut into pieces. Each person hid in the dark with his own segment; it was as if everybody had suddenly disappeared. They all went to sleep. In the empty expanses around them, not even a ghost could have heard the intense gnawing and munching.

The night went by with equal silence.

The next day before dawn, Hipless Li began to wail.

"Son of a bitch! Which of you pricks could have . . ." He gave a start as if bitten by a snake, jumping up in horror with the wreath of dried leaves on top his head, crying and cursing, "What son of a bitch pulled such a fucking trick? My meat's gone."

The night before, this young buck had laid on a pile of dry leaves and straw. After eating one third of his meat, he went off to sleep with his section of the birchbark tube enfolded in his arms. Actually his mind stayed awake the whole time. The place where he lay faced the stand of birches at the mouth of the gulch. Their leaves were yellow now. Above them was a flock of tiny migrating stars, invisible unless you sought them out. Flashing like fish darting in a stream, they tinkled clearly and melodiously. A long, fine silver mesh seemed to be descending from the sky to stroke his face—so soft, like falling into his bother's bosom. When he awoke from this warmth and brightness, he just couldn't find those tiny sojourning little stars again. The birchbark tube hidden in his breast had been ripped open and thrown on the ground.

Hipless Li's weeping startled everyone awake, but no one moved. They were all checking their own dog meat.

"Mother-fucker, that wolf carried away my dog meat too! I'll hump his grandmother." Sun Hanba threw his section of the birchbark tube into the fire, which was already down to ashes. Taking a twisty knife out of his bedroll, his eyes swept the scene like the twin barrels of a rifle. "Being as I'm his father,* I'm gonna have it out with him! To the death!"

Sun Hanba swung his knife with a whoosh, like the wind. Standing up amid the glint of steel, Strapping Wang sent out a cold stare with his eyes that was enough to make you shiver. "Me being *your* old man, I wanta know what you'd do if I did eat it? A mother-fucker like you doesn't deserve any dog meat."

Nobody quite saw just how Strapping Wang sent Sun Hanba's knife flying out of his hands. Sun took a blow to the jaw, too. Then he was hurled sideways, five or six feet, into the marsh grass. The mud splashed up high into the air when he landed.

Unlike the others, Hipless Li saw everything, but he felt his head shrink down into his neck, and his shivering beanpole legs go weak and numb.

"Baby Hipless, you little prick, the bastard got your meat, too. Why isn't your knife out by now?" Spitting out a mouthful of blood and mud, Sun Hanba struggled to his feet and came reeling out of the marsh, his eyes big as chicken eggs and howling like a wild animal. Lunging forward, he jumped on top of Strapping Wang.

He was thrown into the marsh again, with Strapping Wang in pursuit. Wang grabbed him by the throat like a chicken, then relentlessly pummeled his head, alternating fists. As Hipless Li watched, the knife in his hand clunked to the ground. So did his heart.

"Stop it, stop it," the spectators to the fight began to yell with fear in their voices, but no one came forward to restrain Strapping Wang. Instead they ripped open their own birchbark tubes and began wolfing down their meat, chewing noisily and swallowing it just as loud.

Suddenly hurt, Strapping Wang yelped. He stepped back, his hands covering his crotch. The sweat ran down his face in a stream. He threw himself down on the fire, drew himself in like a beetle, then rolled over and over.

"Did you get bit?" Strapping Wang was covered with ashes from head to foot; his head was buried in them. He wasn't moving. Hipless Li took out the packet of medicine Old End-of-His-Rope had left them. He want over to Wang

*His elder and thus his better.

and turned him over. "Swallow some, then rub a little of it on."

"Look . . . gimme a little water."

Hipless Li looked at the blood on Wang's trousers. It was oozing out from his crotch and between the cracks of his fingers.

"Go get it! Are you waiting for me to strangle you to death too?"

Taking another glance at Strapping Wang's bloody crotch, Hipless Li picked up his brass bowl and followed a crude trail they'd trampled out with their feet to a stream beside the hillside. A gentle breeze silently shook the willow saplings on the bank. Their leaves sifted a dazzling patch of golden light onto the water surface. Suddenly the stream grew dark as a school of "willow roots" swam by. But they fled without waiting for Hipless Li to come up. If they hadn't, you still couldn't eat them even if they leapt up into your bowl. It was a rule of the mountains—you didn't eat the flesh of anything that didn't grow hair. He blankly watched the quiet waters, wondering if they'd been fish anyway. Perhaps they were only the shadows of clouds.

When Li came back with the water, that son of a bitch Strapping Wang had stripped naked in front of everyone, putting medicine on that thing of his and wrapping it up with strips of cloth. "This is my own thing. I'll fiddle with it any damn way I please! By the looks of you, you bastards must be scared to death of it."

Hipless Li shifted his eyes to the raggedy bedroll under the tall, thin oak tree under which Strapping Wang slept. As if running from lightning, he let out a whoop and jumped toward it: "My dog meat, it's my dog meat!"

A powerful force had thrust him sprawling lengthwise before he ever made it to the tree.

Lying on the ground, he watched the stark naked man stuff the meat into his mouth one big chunk after another, without the slightest noise. It was as if he were filling up a mineshaft.

When Hipless Li pounced on that naked body a second time, Wang seized both of his arms with one hand, crunching them like dead branches. The remaining meat was in his other hand. Raising that arm, he suddenly threw the meat up into the oak tree.

Once caught up on the branches, it became a blackbird; however much Hipless Li shook the tree or threw stones to knock it down, the meat would not budge. Under the white sun he saw a faint glimmer of blue all over the blackbird's body. Its feathers made a tuneful sound as it flapped its wings and its two demonic eyes looked like the stars he'd seen in the night.

At the start of the fourth day they were still lying there as before. The mountains surrounding them on all four sides in the gorge seemed much taller, and the forests looked a lot thicker. Since the wind off the Amur River couldn't penetrate, the whole of Bear Gulch seemed to be rotting. Marsh grasses were faded and curled, the leaves were losing their color, and mosquitoes were dying in droves among the thick reeds, turning them black. Scum formed on the fen as yellow bubbles splashed and popped on the surface, emitting an unbearable stench.

Hipless Li shook the crown of weeds off his head. The first thing he saw when he opened his eyes was that blackbird up in the treetop. It was still flapping its wings, still faintly glowing, but it was just too far away, seemingly up in the sky. He looked at the men lying down around him in desolation. These men burned incense and prayed to the all-seeing Lord God of the Mountain when they first entered the gulch, and swore oaths to the heavens above, but nobody cared about anybody else now. The men's faces were stiff and withered, like oak leaves with mildew on them. They gave off a rank body odor. He could smell his own. It was a stench of rotting flesh. He was going to die here. He didn't know what death was like, but he felt that it must be something growing out of his own body, something that brought both itching and numbness like an insect bite, something that broke a hole in the skin and let the blood run out, let it flow till the body was drained. He wanted to smile—he ought to smile at that devilish blackbird before he closed his eyes. He exerted all his strength in order to grin. He didn't know whether or not the bird caught it, as his eyes slowly went shut. His last sight was of that bird, gradually growing smaller, making an eerie sound with its wings and flying up to the sky on a wind that beamed golden rays. Its beak was breathing out bubbles, like a fish. Clear, iridescent bubbles were all over it. Suddenly everything went white. He couldn't see anything at all now. He only felt that he was burning up.

As the fever quietly receded, Hipless Li dimly heard someone singing opera, accompanied by the low and melancholy plucking of a *liuqin* fiddle. Hoarse as a chain saw came the lyrics: "I remember how I guarded the Guzhou Ferry in a one-man stand, I the one-stand man: armor flashed, spears glinted, blood flowed; then came the sable skins, the medals, the victory toasts; never enfeoffed, I was ennobled, allowed my boasts; now graying at the temples, I know no worries. . . ."

He knew without looking that the singing was from the Shandong fellow named Guan (Reed). Two nights before he'd somehow fallen ill and moaned the whole night through. This old bachelor had thrown away all the money he'd ever earned on those women at the house of ill repute in Heihe. When he got to be fifty, he said every year after that would be a bonus. He wasn't afraid of death—only of not having his liquor. They'd run out of that even before they ran out of food. He was the first to lose his ability to stand, and from the day he did, he hadn't ever gotten up again.

The plucking suddenly stopped. Sun Hanba yelped as if he'd been bitten in the rear by a wolf: "He's dying! The Shandong Reed is dying."

He ranted on for some time, but no one budged. Maybe they couldn't. Hipless Li felt cold goosebumps welling up all over his body. His blood felt as if it were creeping up and down his skin like an insect.

"Strapping Wang, I beg you, get him some water." Sun Hanba's voice grated on your ears like he was crying—or like a whirr from the sky that crashed into the undergrowth, leaving nothing but torn leaves.

Hipless Li saw Strapping Wang rise beneath his oak tree and lean against it, half dead, without even a glance at Sun Hanba or the "Shandong Reed." He seemed to be talking to the wind, which had grown fearsome: "I can smell the fish in the river. There's going to be a change in the weather."

"Hey, Strapping Wang, the Shandong Reed is practically dead."

"What are you yelling about!" Strapping Wang's eyes, burning like charcoal, seared Sun Hanba. "What the hell do I care if he dies or not. If that son of a bitch Old End-of-His-Rope doesn't come back by tonight, I'll go to the abandoned pit all by myself and dig out the gold hiding there." Suddenly he gave a grim laugh. It filled the ravine like a great gust of wind, making Hipless Li feel his whole body draw inward, as if he were weightless. He dug his fingers into the earth, afraid that he might float away, like dry leaves.

"I'm not willing to die—I'm not going to rot here. There are people who will miss me, like the young widow in the Gao family over at Dalalatai."

"I have a wife and kids, too, back at home in Zaoqiang. And my father, who'll soon be eighty. When I came here, my baby boy couldn't say 'Papa' yet." Without waiting for Strapping Wang to finish, Sun Hanba began to wail, as if he were crying. Hipless Li's goosebumps came back. This time his skin wasn't just cold but itchy. Perhaps Sun Hanba really was crying tears, but Hipless Li couldn't imagine what he was feeling.

"You're just waiting for them to burn spirit money for your deceased soul!"

Strapping Wang lay down again. He always laid himself out flat in the same place, never moving an inch. The son of a bitch really knew how to save his energy. Hipless Li thought to himself that only Wang still had half a tube of dog meat. The prick was truly devious! But fate was fixed in heaven. There was no telling who really would go first.

Nobody spoke today. Everyone quietly awaited his death, hoping that the others would die first. They thought about whatever little merit they had accumulated in the past; perhaps these good deeds would serve them in good stead now. Hipless Li had nothing much to think about, and Strapping Wang didn't occupy his mind either. They both went to sleep, surrounded by the wind that was growing colder by the gust.

That night the weather did change. The wind brought with it a damp feeling of morning. Just as the treetops were suffused with white light, the rain came down, and shortly afterward came granular snow coarse as sand. When it hit your face it was like pinpricks, or being singed by the fire. Soon the wind ceased and the snow came down steadily. The ravine was covered in white.

As the snow buried him, Hipless Li began gradually to feel warm all over. He opened his eyes and looked at the campfire. It was in the same place where they had cooked the dog meat. Golden flames danced among the logs. Sometimes the tongues of fire would stretch out like arms and lightly stroke Li's face; sometimes like devils they would leave the fire and float straight up, suspended in midair. Everyone Hipless Li knew was among those flames: his father, his mother, and the sister he'd grown up with; Old End-of-His-Rope, too. If only the fire didn't go out, they'd never leave him.

"Shit, I see you still expect me to wait on you sons of bitches."

Hipless Li was awakened from his hallucinations of "warming himself by the campfire" by Strapping Wang's cursing. He was suddenly aware of being buried deep in the snow. The cold had gone straight into the marrow of his bones. After struggling for quite some time, he raised himself up through the snow and saw Strapping Wang. Wang had put up a frame for a shed from newly cut birch poles and was covering it with straw mats, saying "shit" every other word.

When it was covered, the light of day was peeping through. Strapping Wang picked up the men buried in the snow one by one and bore them on his back to the shed. He cursed them out as he carried them, including their ancestors three generations back, not forgetting Old End-of-His-Rope. Everyone knew that this storm would snow them in. Old End-of-His-Rope wouldn't be able to get in, and they wouldn't be able to get out.

As he carried these characters, stiff as corpses, into the shack, Strapping Wang gave off steam from both the top and the bottom of his head, like a bamboo bun-steamer. Gasping for breath and eyes glazed, he fell face down into the snow several times and had a hard time getting up.

"I'm only carrying you out of love for your mother," Strapping Wang said as he hurtled Hipless Li onto the straw in the shed with the strength of a bear. Wang stretched out and pinched Li's jaw in one hand. "Son of a bitch, do you take me to be your daddy?"

Hipless Li pushed his hand away and averted his face.

"Hah, you son of a bitch, still not willing for your ma to lie with me? Once I do, you'll have an easy life! Your daddy here has plenty of money!"

Laughing offensively, Strapping Wang kicked Hipless Li with all his might and wrenched his neck again. Tucking in his head, Wang exited the shed.

He packed snow all around the shed, tamping it down firmly, then gathered two big armfuls of straw and brought them in, kicking Sun Hanba: "Well men, take off your clothes, I've got work to do outside and I can't do it without clothes."

"We'll freeze to death." Sun Hanba groped for his knife underneath where he lay.

"Put that fucking knife away!" Strapping Wang put his foot down on the arm that held the knife. "Would I let you freeze to death, you sons of bitches that even a wolf wouldn't touch? I'll cover you with straw. When you wiggle into your little straw nest, you'll find it comfier than your mama's breast. You bastards'll die of happiness."

Strapping Wang donned all the gowns and pairs of pants one by one, each with their own peculiar body odor and fishy stench. Off he went, with a pickax and shovel on his shoulder.

He was on his way to the abandoned pit. It was in a little gully on the other side of the mountain ridge. No one had ever got any gold out of it, but just before Old End-of-His-Rope left, he'd sworn they'd strike it rich there. It was on that account that he'd gone back to the store to negotiate for more food and liquor.

The gully was far away from the shed and separated by a ridge and a dark birch forest, yet Hipless Li still could hear Strapping Wang's pickax. When the bugger worked he always went at it like a madman. Sparks would fly from the tip of his pickax and his beads of sweat would vaporize on the rocks.

In fact, everyone in the shack could hear Strapping Wang's pickax. The noise traveled through the ground. It thundered so loudly that no one could sleep. They cursed to themselves with envy: "Here it's cold enough to make you clench your teeth, and this son of a bitch gives up life itself to please his women!"

It was dark and Strapping Wang still wasn't back.

That night, the people in the shed were so cold they couldn't stand it. Sun Hanba took out his steel and flint, about to light the straw to keep them warm. They all pounced on him, starting a melee that continued close onto dawn. Thanks to the wrestling, they all worked up a good sweat. Without that, their very brains might have frozen into lumps of ice.

At the light of the next day, Strapping Wang returned.

His face and body were all covered with ice that had congealed from blood and water. In his arms he bore a rock the size of a dog's head. He staggered to the entrance of the shed and fell down. The rock rolled away some distance.

"Young widow, oh my young widow!" he yelled in a scratchy voice, crawling like a big bear with the rock buried in his breast again. He got slowly up, his glazed-over eyes fixed on the men in the shack. Grinning so that you could see his blood-stained teeth, he chortled: "I'm the one who dug it out! Look at it. Look at it you sons of bitches, a 'dog's head' of a nugget, my mother lode. It must weigh a hunnerd-fifty or two hunnerd grams at least." Hipless Li stared at it dumbly. It was obvious that it was nothing but a rock.

"Why the fuck aren't you smiling? You sons of bitches." Strapping Wang pulled down one of the birch support poles in the shed and went outside, using it as a cane. He was headed for the snowy path that led outside the gorge.

He'd gone a far distance when Hipless Li heard him laugh and curse again: "You sons of bitches!"

Hipless Li felt his heart torn to shreds and blown aflutter by the wind whistling through the shack. Like snowflakes it drifted, out into the gorge.

Scritch, scratch, went the steel upon the flint. Sun Hanba yelped like a devil, then cackled with laughter. He'd lit the straw. The flames soared, burning a hole in the top of the shelter. Hipless Li watched the golden flames in terror, flames that danced around like demons. The ashes from the straw flew up from the fire like a startled flock of inky birds. The birds carried with them something from his heart. He followed them, soaring into the heavy blackness that hung overhead like a curtain of iron.

Dazzling Poma

Zhang Chengzhi

Translated by Steven L. Riep

AS THE WIND blew through the tops of the pine trees, wave after wave of shrill, string-like sound floated over the forest. The firs and the pines swayed gently back and forth and rubbed against the foot of the Tian Shan mountain range. Before the foothills a plain of goose-green grasses, which reached as far as the eye could see, waved gently in the breeze. They stretched silently down to the Tekes River, which lay in the darkness of dusk.

Every evening at twilight as I followed the green, grassy slopes down toward the river, I felt filled with a strange and indescribable joy. The shrill wind blew in the tips of the blue pines. Lost in reverie, I almost forgot Adiya and Suiwazi. Sometimes, as my hand moved, it would brush the coarse hair on the head of the black dog that ran beside me, but I didn't know what I touched. The ear-piercing wind seemed like the sound of zither strings snapping one by one. My eyes filled with soft yellows and greens, and in this confusion of colors, I headed toward the Tekes Valley. We always walked this way. We came out of the valley formed by the jutting, icy peaks of the Tian Shan range and followed the soft grasslands as we headed home. As I noticed Adiya and Suiwazi walking along with their arms flailing away at their sides, I thought that I had always walked in this manner. The vista before me was immense: even if I looked around, I couldn't take in all of the blue-tipped pines, the green foothills and the turbid river. I didn't bother turning my head, but walked along as if dazed by the scene with my blurred eyes staring straight ahead of me. In my mind, however, I visualized the awesome mists of the Tekes and knew that ahead of me flowed the soft grasses that carpeted the riverbanks and behind me the cold peaks of Mount Heaven grew ever more distant.

As I came to my senses, I suddenly caught my breath.

I stopped walking and looked around for Adiya and Suiwazi. I couldn't help laughing as I saw them panting from their hard run. They had the same round,

---

The original appeared in *Minzu wenxue* (Nationalities literature), August 1986. The author dedicates this story "to my teacher, Mr. Weng Dujian."

drum-like little bellies and the same shiny, dark little fannies. I saw four dirty little feet stained green by the pasture grasses, and below their waists they were covered with mud. Adiya looked nervous, and Suiwazi had a solemn expression on his face. The two of them hurriedly pushed ahead like two plucked, white chickens strutting down a road. The black dog jumped in the air, and with each jump, his hairy black head reached almost as high as the children's heads. When the boys noticed I had stopped, they began to whisper to each other, but I couldn't understand what they were saying. Their hands shook impatiently by their sides as they suddenly ran ahead.

They were hurrying home, I thought, because the sun was about to set.

As the sunlight shone through Adiya's fine, brown hair, I could see his small head rocking quickly back and forth. Below the head was a dirty, black neck that connected to the funny little body that strutted around like a white chicken's. And what are you wearing slung over your shoulders? Is it a sedge raincoat or a grass shawl? Is it blue or is it red? Perhaps it really isn't clothing at all—it certainly isn't one of the Elute people's unhemmed robes. Adiya, those tattered old rags that you wear create a style all your own. As I looked over my shoulder at him, my heart swelled with joy. Adiya certainly didn't understand me. His two spindly, black legs cut through the thick grass with a swishing sound. The sky quickly grew dark, and Adiya seemed to grow nervous. I knew he was anxiously thinking of the bowl of dumplings cooked in milk that awaited him at home.

Suiwazi and Adiya stood about the same height. From Suiwazi's dirt-stained face shone a pair of sparkling eyes. He was stark naked, so you could see his washboard-like bones and his shiny black fanny. He wore a hat that, though once white, now had green stains from the grasses, yellow marks from the melted snow, and black spots from the mud of the plains. The hot sun baked Suiwazi's shoulders, but I knew he didn't feel the heat because the cool evening breezes of sunset blew over the foothills of Tian Shan just as the slanting sun filled the grasslands with its golden hue. Suiwazi didn't pay any attention to the weather, he just took off on his grass-stained legs and ran toward Poma. At noontime, when Suiwazi's family built their cooking fire, they said they were going to make *guokui*, the flat breads the Mongolian people like to eat. Suiwazi's mouth watered as he thought of eating the fragrant *guokui*.

I knew the snowy mountain peaks behind me grew more distant with each step I took. As I couldn't see the source of the shrill sound that continued to pass over the treetops, I wasn't sure if it came from the wind striking the trees or the trees plucking the wind. After I came out of the mountains, my field of vision suddenly expanded and the soft, green grasses of the riverbank flowed ahead of me. Bathed in golden light, the two banks grew wider as they stretched toward Poma, which you could just distinguish in the distance.

Is this the mortal world? I asked myself. Is this the twentieth century? When I return to the inner reaches of Tian Shan to visit Poma each summer, I can't help asking myself these strange questions. Tian Shan is too beautiful, I thought as I swallowed hard. And Poma (I tried to change my train of thought), that beautiful spot that lay in the midst of Tian Shan. Well, it's our secret. Since I started working as a hydrologist, I have come to Poma each summer and have taken this place as my own private paradise.

Adiya and Suiwazi suddenly started to fight. In the bright sun, their small, dark bodies rolled about in a ball in the thick carpet of grass. Each pummeled his opponent's back and shouted a string of epithets that I couldn't understand. I was startled! You've started fighting, you two rascals! I rushed through the grasses and fell down just as I was about to grab them. Adiya started at me with eyes as big as a calf's and let forth a series of piercing cries. Suiwazi, whose dirty white hat now sat tilted to one side, drummed on his little black face and let out a stream of strange sounds—he was not ready to give up the fight. I couldn't understand them, and I couldn't do anything with these "Kings of the Mountain" but take them by an ear, one boy in each hand, and drag them to their feet. I lifted up the strips of cloth that covered Adiya's hindquarters, and I grabbed Suiwazi around the waist and gave each boy a good swat on the fanny. The two boys, now angry, ran ahead of me in a pout.

Panting hard, I finally caught up to them. I saw that the sun, which had already dropped low in the sky, now cast its golden rays eastward. Bathed in the sunlight, the boys looked like a pair of bear cubs standing on their hind legs. They quickly and angrily ran through the thick pasture grass of the foothills. Ahead of me I could vaguely see the semicircular outline of Poma's wooden bridge.

The two boys suddenly broke into a run, and their bare feet made splashing sounds in the mud puddles that dotted the plains. As they ran across the bridge, which was made of rounds of wood, it swayed back and forth and gradually I could see its side. A mud hut and a yurt seemed to rise up suddenly before me as I walked along. Adiya fell with a splat into a pool of mud, and I saw Suiwazi pull him to his feet by grabbing his collar. The two boys shouted unceasingly, but I couldn't understand what they were saying. The hut and yurt continued to rise before me until I could see all of them. The bridge, still swinging, looked like the side view of the spring inside an automobile shock absorber. Suiwazi ran up on the hill and Adiya kicked loose some gravel. Suddenly they separated and each went toward his own home—one to the black yurt and one to the half-buried mud hut. The smoke from the cooking fires swept horizontally along the grass-lands and obscured the two boys in a cloud of soft, gauzy, gray fog.

Poma's sun was about to set.

The wooden bridge had not deteriorated since my last visit. I took a bundle of rough pine poles and went down to the riverbank to take some hydrographic measurements. I didn't really need to check the water level every day, and the depth scale I'd stuck in the water was really for appearances only. Besides, the rainy season hadn't started yet in Tian Shan. The rushing water seemed to form piles of vivid green jade. While it wasn't flooding, I thought, I'd better keep an eye on the river anyway.

I happened to notice Suiye taking a bath, so I wrote a few comments in my notebook and carefully stepped back across the stones as I prepared to leave the riverbank. In the moment I glimpsed Suiye, I suddenly thought that the notes I made really didn't mean anything because I didn't necessarily record the depth reading. I turned to Suiye and yelled, "Suiye, are you bathing?"

Suiye suddenly stood up—I saw that he seemed to lose his footing as one of his feet plunged into the icy cold water. "Don't be nervous, Suiye, keep calm," I called out quickly. I hated myself for upsetting Suiye. "I brought the children back," I said absentmindedly.

"That grandson of mine," Suiye sighed. I couldn't understand Suiye's Gansu dialect. I only knew that he was "bathing" in the icy, snow-fed river. He was just like that precious grandson of his. Suiwazi loved the wilderness of Tian Shan, and Suiye enjoyed taking a dip in the icy waters.

As Suiye stood hesitantly in the river, I knew that he was waiting for me to leave. One of his bony feet remained immersed in the frigid river, the emerald-green snow melt flowing around it as bits of snow covered his legs. Suiye had a simple and honest face, which now bore a trace of fear on it. I didn't want to bother him any further, so I quickly jumped back onto the bank. "Take it easy, Old Sui, I'm leaving now." I quickly said good-bye to him and left the riverbank.

The thick, white smoke form the cooking fires blew over the bank. This was Poma, which sat opposite the steep slopes of the Tian Shan range. They had built the pinewood bridge at the narrowest point of the steep banks, and a road led back from the bridge in the direction I had walked. Two families took care of the bridge: Suiye's family, who lived in the mud hut, and Basengaba's family, who lived in a triangular black yurt. This was Poma, a small settlement nestled in the heart of the Tian Shan Valley. Here you won't see a herd of cows or a flock of sheep, not to mention another human being. For thousands of miles in all directions, the broad plains stretched as far as the eye could see. There wasn't anything except the snow-covered mountains, the pine forest, the foothill grasslands, the icy river water, and the billowy white clouds. Oh, and there was me, but I only came in the summers to inspect the condition of the river and to check the bridge. When I came, I just stayed with the two families—it's a pity I can't understand a word they say.

I sat down in front of Basengaba's door by the hitching post, let out a sigh of relief, and threw my notebook on the grass. Basengaba took off his sleeves and tied them at his waist like a Tibetan does. Beads of sweat rolled down his arms, and the relaxed muscles twitched beneath his bare, brown skin like small fish swimming about.

"Amoer saihan bainu?" I used my broken Mongolian to greet him. Basengaba responded happily with a long stream of words. As I looked at him, I couldn't believe that anyone could have such scarred, wrinkled, dark skin. Under the setting sun, Basengaba worked enthusiastically with a file to smooth his hitching post, and a pungent aroma of pine hung in the air. As he filed and rubbed, perhaps he thought that his flying tool would carve some strange and wonderful designs into the post. Basengaba used his arm to smooth the coarse grooves. He bent his hand and elbow and panted hard, and near his elbow you could see a bone sticking up perilously close to the surface of the skin. He used his forearm to polish the wood. He puffed hard as he worked, and the hitching post started to shine with a deep luster.

It gradually cooled off in Poma.

The sun grew closer to the western horizon.

Suiwazi took a bite of fragrant and crispy *guokui* and chewed on it with a crunch. As he chewed, he walked toward the yurt with his belly stuck out, and he was covered with mud below the waist. Adiya came out of the yurt carrying a bowl made of yellow poplar wood. When blown by the wind his worn robe looked like a tattered cape. Although he carried his bowl in both hands, the milk trickled out in a steady stream. While he wiggled his small fanny as he walked forward, he made a bit of a slurping sound—whether licking the skin off the milk or salivating, I'm not sure.

As twilight fell, the boys stood on the grasslands eating and drinking and trying each others' food. I lay on the ground and watched them with fascination. Adiya broke off piece after piece of the *guokui* in Suiwazi's hand and put them in his mouth and chewed them up. Suiwazi extended his thin, black neck and took sip after sip from the bowl of milk tea Adiya held. At that moment, the smoke from the cooking fires blew away and you could hear the clinking and banging of pots, plates, and cups being moved about.

I raised my head and saw Suiye stumbling back from the river. He looked at me and smiled, and also smiled at Basengaba. Old Baseng had finished filing his hitching post and stood up with an air of satisfaction, his skin covered with perspiration.

It's time to eat, I thought.

Both of the families ate their meals on the grasslands in front of their homes. Suiwazi, Adiya, and I ate food from both families. Basengaba and Suiye each sat in their own doorways and quietly ate their milk noodles, or *baoersake*, and crispy *guokui*. I noticed that the two old men ate in a very similar manner. They chewed at the same tempo, their mouths opening and closing simultaneously. A billow of black clouds, no, they were strips of clouds, obscured the setting sun and darkened the mountains and grasslands around us. The area surrounding Poma grew quiet in the deepening blue of dusk and the faraway peaks of Tian Shan became a giant carving. In the distance, the Tekes Valley receded into darkness and the milky-white, rushing river disappeared. I no longer heard the shrill, ear-piercing sound of the wind that had blown above the treetops.

I knew the secret that Suiye carefully concealed. Last year, when I brought the letter that announced that his name had been cleared of all crimes, Suiye just shook his head as if nothing had happened. "It's my business. No. No." When he shook his head, his eyes seemed to sink deeper into the shadows of their sockets. The casual manner in which he took this news startled me. He rubbed his worn robe and slowly walked to the bridge. Loud, thundering sounds rose from the river where floes of shiny, green ice rushed along and broke into fine pieces on the rocks and the bridge pilings. He walked toward the bridge without any concern for the piece of paper, and I didn't know what to do with it.

Last summer when the flood waters came, they torrented down through Poma and struck the bridge, creating a billow of fog like the smoke from firecrackers under the bridge. Suiye was an *akhund*, or Moslem leader, and one day in 1958 as he was reading scriptures, he was tied up and taken to prison. Suiye told them he was from a Qinghai family and that he had never had the good fortune to visit a nice place like Gansu. He stayed in prison for three years, and one day while he was being transferred to a work reeducation camp, he escaped and fled to Xinjiang. Suiye said he was a gold miner who had come to pan for gold and had followed the Altun Shan mountain range into the northern reaches of the province. I took the piece of paper and stuck it inside his mud hut and forgot about it. Somehow Suiye found it and threw it in the river where it floated away.

As Suiye ate his *guokui* I could see that he had trouble chewing. When he ate, he put his hand under his mouth to catch the fallen crumbs and stuff them into his mouth. Then he would close his mouth and his eyes and his cheeks would move as he chewed slowly and the numerous wrinkles in his face would stretch and form a happy expression. The vista of Tian Shan surrounded Suiye and he seemed to blend into its expanse.

Suiye took a yellow *guokui*, waved it before my face, and then squatted down. The colors of dusk deepened, the sun remained submerged within the black strips of cloud. Suiye broke the bread into two pieces. He panted hard and the silvery white whiskers on his red face shook up and down. He broke the *guokui* into four pieces and said, "Nu, wuge, chisha." The warm, yeasty smell came into my nostrils as he offered me a piece. "Nu, chisha," he said, forcing me to eat more *guokui*. There was nothing I could do. I knew that even if my stomach was full to bursting, I had to break off another piece; a big, round, well-browned *guokui* had already been broken into pieces for me, and you can't keep *guokui* once it's been broken up.

Suiye simply refused to pay any heed to the matters discussed in the letter. I couldn't help sighing as I picked up a fragrant piece of bread. Suiye returned to his place, crossed his legs, and continued to eat. He put a thin, bony hand under his mouth to catch the crumbs and shove them back into his mouth. Afterward, I saw him close his eyes and a contented smile appeared on his face.

Basengaba leaned against his yurt with a bowl of brown milk tea at his feet. When he saw that I had glimpsed him, a smile broke out on his simple, honest face. When he smiled, his eyes narrowed into thin slits. Basengaba relaxed and opened his robe, exposing his chest and the brown belly below it, which was filled with milk tea. Darker now, a soft, shimmering light fell upon Basengaba's round belly, and I thought I saw a drum or gong, or perhaps the rusted old helmet of a knight.

Poma was Basengaba's native place, he was born and raised here. I hated myself for not being able to learn the Elute language, because Basengaba could speak Kazakh, Uighur, and Kirghiz, he just couldn't speak the pathetic Chinese language. He had hunted, tended flocks, cut wood, and fought in battles, but he'd never left Poma. I looked at Poma's bewitching sunset and I understood why. Once you'd found a place like this, who'd want to leave?

Basengaba refilled the bowl before me. The Elute who lived near Tian Shan, like the Kazakhs, used large bowls to drink their tea. It was salty and warm and expelled all weariness from my body. As I drank, perspiration covered my head and I saw that Basengaba's body was also covered with sweat. He looked at me and smiled contentedly, and his two eyes formed two thin slits in his dark, brown face. Though Basengaba had a cow and a black dog, he didn't have a horse—he only had a hitching post. He had a special affection for the post because whenever he walked past it, he would let out a long sigh and carefully rub it.

"Ao, ao, taaoya." Basengaba pointed at the large bowl in front of me. I knew that he was saying "Drink, drink, drink it up." I took the bowl in both hands and took a long, gulping drink and then took a bite of fragrant *guokui*. Hey, I thought, fat people and sumo wrestlers grew up like this. They sat between two old people who forced them to eat even after they were full. How could you avoid getting fat?

Basengaba stood up, swaying as though he was drunk, and then staggered over to me. I wanted to stand up and take the teapot he held in his hand; startled, he made a frantic gesture for me to sit. I crouched down and watched him refill my bowl again and decided that even if I burst, I was going to eat with them until they finished.

Basengaba put his arm around his shiny and smooth hitching post and rubbed it clumsily like a brown bear would cuddle its cubs. Yes, and no horse, I thought sympathetically. I tried to imagine a fine horse hitched to the post, but I couldn't see one—perhaps Aba could. At that moment a reddish light suddenly shined upon the post. Startled, I raised my head and saw—Poma's sunset.

Everything in the world was plated with a golden-red hue.

Poma's sun sank behind the brilliant, roseate clouds.

Suiwazi, who was amazed by the sunset, stopped playing. He took a step forward and a vivid pink light fell upon him. A rust-colored light gilded the grasslands on which the boy stood and suffused him in red so that his white hat looked like a burning flag.

Adiya let out a cry of joy and ran barefoot across the crimson grasses, his tattered rags trailing behind him as he joined his friend and stood in silence. The wind blew from the distant horizon where the sun set solemnly. The blazing red light shone on Adiya one moment, and it was dark the next.

In an instant Poma had become an unfamiliar place. The Poma that I knew, nestled in the heart of the Tian Shan range, wasn't like this. I was suddenly afraid. I looked anxiously around me and noticed that the steep, cold mountain peaks had become molten swords burning with fire, and the grasslands had been transformed into a billowing, red sea. I again felt elated and realized that I was witnessing something solemn and dazzling. I reverently sat down and embraced my knees tightly. My mind seemed to soar into the crimson clouds and my bosom burned fiercely. How can a day end like this? The grasses that were transformed into an enormous painting, Tian Shan's strangely transformed sun, and the flourishing world of the living, how could one day end like this?

In the midst of the red-washed valley, two families and one bridge were the only things in Poma when the sun set. The crooked mud hut looked like a red boulder and the pointed yurt became a blazing umbrella. The river's water had turned to a molten red and the pinewood bridge glowed like a shining steel ornament. The two three-year-olds stood in wonder and gleefully extended their spindly arms. They looked like two hot coals, like two small bear cubs that accidentally fell into a burning sea. Each of the two old men sat in silence and leaned against his own home. I guessed that they also must have felt a burning feeling as their chests were also plated with a vivid, brick-red color. Is this the moral world? I was moved to the point of unbearable pain. Is this the twentieth century? I thought that I simply must be crazy to stare at this scene as if I wanted to drink in this rare moment of beauty with my eyes. And it would soon be over, I thought sadly.

The drunken, red sun had already sunk completely below the horizon.

Basengaba suddenly burst into song, and his manner interested me. He sat cross-legged and rocked forward and backward violently. Sometimes he bowed his head, sometimes his chin pointed at the sky. Hoarse and distant came the long tune:

"Amuer . . . sa'na . . . haiyiyouheyi . . ." I didn't know how many times I had heard that song. I'd only heard it sung frequently at Poma. This old hymn, "Amuersa'na," was the Elute's song of praise for a hero and a well-known song of revolt. No one had ever dared to sing it in Ili, Wusu, or Wulumuji, but this was Poma. Basengaba didn't read newspapers, and he didn't understand the gossip that other people told him about this old song. And if he sang it in Poma, who was going to complain? Who cared? I'd heard this tune so many times that I understood several lines:

"Amuer . . . sa'na . . . haiyiyou . . ."
"Hero . . . fate will protect you . . . heyi."

Basengaba sang as if he was insane or drunk. The long notes he sustained seemed to bid farewell to the rosy glow that filled the sky. He sat up straight and the hands that he rested on his knees returned to their brown color. The song sounded piercing and coarse, yet it also sounded fine and rich, and as the red color faded into blue, the rising and falling of Basengaba's singing filled the air.

I saw his eyes watching the beauty of the setting sun, and I observed a trace of deep sorrow. The stunning red clouds were about to disappear, I thought, and they'd appeared for but a moment. Basengaba used this song of praise to bid farewell to the fiery sky. When he saw the color fading, he must have thought of the fate of Amuersa'na, and perhaps he thought of the twilight years of his own life. I suddenly grew excited as I realized that this trip had not been wasted, for I had seen something reach its conclusion at Poma.

A wave of unidentifiable music floated over me. It was slow, as if complaining, hoarse yet moving, sad and resentful. I listened carefully to it and hoped and prayed. The icy, swift-flowing mountain river suddenly grew quiet, and something strange appeared in the bright blue skies that came before the black of night. The grasses started to wave about and the thunder of the flowing waters returned. I almost started to cry.

Suiye started his evening prayers.

Suiye had long knelt in front of his yellow mud hut with his lips vibrating as he chanted scriptures. His thin, wrinkled face, his anxious and focused sincerity, his suffering, and his deep hope truly moved me. Suiye continued to chant softly, and the wind bore his words and transformed them into music as it carried his sustained tones to the heavens. Suiye, like Basengaba, also faced the twilight years of his life, but his heart was as full as the ocean, and he had those experiences that he kept hidden from others. Whether they concerned inciting rebellion, leaving his native place, or facing the torments of prison, Suiye didn't talk about them at all. Suiye bathed in the river and performed his rituals in the purity of Poma—he didn't need a piece of paper to prove himself—he had his own, unbreakable heart as justification.

This was the end of the day. Poma ended this day under the deep blue sky that was washed just moments before by the roseate clouds.

Hand in hand, Suiwazi and Adiya played in the dew-damp grasslands. Since we adults had nothing to do, we watched with interest the boys play. Adiya, who wore his tattered robe, took giant stride after giant stride like a rider about to mount his horse. Suiwazi, naked as before, stuck out his dark little fanny. His white hat shone proudly in the bright sunlight.

The two of them suddenly started to argue angrily in a flurry of Elute, Mongolian, and Gansu dialect that none of us could understand. Neither boy spoke his family's language properly, but neither Adiya or Suiwazi seemed to care. Basengaba shook his head and laughed, so did Suiye. They looked at each other and shook their heads again. I knew that the two families could not communicate with each other and relied on the two boys as their communication link.

The two boys suddenly became friends again and grabbed each other and, laughing madly, rolled around on the bright grasses. The air filled with their clear, bell-like cries of joy. Each of the old men, seated in front of his own home, was captivated by the scene.

Deeply moved, I lay quietly on the grass between the two dwellings. This was one sunset I had witnessed at Poma, and in my young eyes, the day had ended with a dazzle. I lay quietly and didn't want to leave the still-warm grasses. I wasn't going to daydream anymore, I was just going to let my body absorb the warmth and wait for the first rays of the morning sun to shine upon me.

About the Authors

BAI LUO (Bai Lecheng, 1946–) is a native of Guangdong Province who now lives in Hong Kong where he is an editor and a writer of novels, short stories, and essays.

CAN XUE (Deng Xiaohua, 1953–) is a native of Changsha in Hunan Province where she now lives with her husband and son. Her family suffered greatly from the Anti-Rightist Campaign to the end of the Cultural Revolution, and she and her husband were able to survive by teaching themselves how to make clothes and becoming *getihu* (independent entrepreneur) tailors. She has published two short-story collections, *Huangni jie* (Mud street), from which "The Hut on the Hill" was translated, and *Tiantang li de duihua* (Dialogues in paradise, available in English translation).

CHEN JIANGONG (1949–) moved with his parents from Guangxi Province to Beijing in the mid-1950s. During the Cultural Revolution, he worked for many years as a coal miner. He was among the first group of post-Mao university students, receiving his B.A. degree in Chinese literature from Peking University in 1982. His published works include the short-story collections *Miluan de xingkong* (Bewildering firmament) and *Duanfeng yan* (Phoenix eyes).

CHEN YINGZHEN (Chen Yongshan, 1936–) is one of the most prolific and controversial writers in Taiwan, a man who spent seven years in prison for his alleged "subversive activities." A native of Taibei County, Taiwan, and a graduate of Tamkang University's Foreign Literature Department, he has been a fellow at the University of Iowa's International Writing Program. His collected works number in the teens, including his early masterpiece *Jiangjun zu* (A race of generals) and an ongoing series of stories entitled *Huashengdun da lou* (Washington skyscrapers).

HAI XIN (his surname is Zheng, but another pen name is Fan Jian, 1931–) came to Hong Kong from the mainland in 1947. He has held a number of jobs, such as bartender, barber, and factory worker, while publishing more than twenty books, including short stories, novellas, and novels, most notably *Qigai gongzhu* (The beggar princess).

339

HAN SHAOGONG (1952–) is a native of Hunan Province. After spending several years during the Cultural Revolution on a rural commune, he later graduated from Hunan Normal University and worked as an editor before becoming a professional writer. He now lives on Hainan Island. His best known of several short-story collections is *Youhuo* (Lure, 1986). He has won literary prizes in both the People's Republic and Taiwan.

HONG FENG (1957–) is a native of Tongyu County, Jilin Province. He had been a worker and a teacher before becoming an editor for *Zuojia* (Writers) magazine in 1984. He has written many short stories and novels since he started writing in 1983. "Shengming zhi liu" (The stream of life) won the Jilin provincial literary prize for best short story.

HUANG FAN (Huang Xiaozhong, 1950–) is a native of Taibei. His stories have won numerous literary prizes from Taiwan's leading newspapers, the *China Times* and the *United Daily News*. His many works include *Lai Suo, Yun* (Clouds), and *Wo pipan* (J'accuse).

LI ANG (Shi Shuduan, 1952–) is a native of Lugang in Taiwan. After graduating from the Chinese Academy of Culture, she received a Master's degree in drama at Oregon State University before returning to teach at her alma mater. She has published numerous novels and short stories, the best known of which are perhaps *Shafu* (The butcher's wife, literally "husband killer," translated by Howard Goldblatt under the former title) and *An ye* (Dark Nights).

LIANG BINGJUN (another pen name is Le Si, 1948–) is a native of Guandong Province. With a doctorate in comparative literature from the University of California at San Diego, he now teaches at Hong Kong University. His many works include *Shanshui renwu* (People in the landscape) and *Lei sheng yu chan ming* (The sound of thunder and cicadas chirping).

LIU YICHANG (Liu Tongyi, 1918–) is a graduate of Saint John's University in Shanghai. In the early 1950s he worked as an editor and writer in Hong Kong, Singapore, and other places before settling down in Hong Kong in 1957. He has published several volumes of short stories and essays.

MO YAN (Guan Moye, 1956–) is a native of Shandong Province. During the Cultural Revolution he left school and returned home where he worked as a part-time laborer in a linseed oil factory. In 1976 he joined the People's Liberation Army, and in 1984 he was admitted to the Literature Department of the Armed Forces Cultural Academy. He began writing fiction in 1981. His publications include a collection of short stories, *Touming de hong luobo* (The crystal carrot) and two celebrated novels entitled *Hong gaoliang jiazu* (The red sorghum clan) and *Tiantang suantai zhi ge* (Paradise County garlic song). The film *Red Sorghum* was named best film at the 1988 Berlin Film Festival.

QIAO DIANYUN (1931–) is a native of Xishaan County in Henan Province. He joined the People's Liberation Army in 1949, retired in 1953 to a production brigade, and began writing in 1955. He has written over a hundred stories about Chinese rural life and has won literary prizes in both Beijing and Guangzhou.

SHI SHUQING (1945–) is a native of Taiwan. She has a B.A. degree in Western literature from the Tamkang Literary Academy and a Master's degree from the State University of New York. She taught at Zhengzhi and Tamkang universities in Taiwan before moving to Hong Kong. She has published many collections of short stories and essays, including most notably *Yiyeyou—Xianggang gushi* (One-night journeys—Hong Kong stories).

SHI TIESHENG (1951–) is a native of Beijing. During the Cultural Revolution he worked on a rural commune in Shaanxi Province where he contracted a rare illness that left him paralyzed from the waist down. Confined to a wheelchair, he worked in a factory in Beijing until he became a professional writer. His short-story and essay collection, *Wo de yaoyuan de Qingpingwan* (My far-away Qingpingwan), contains the best of his early works, but his writing continued to improve in the late 1980s with the publication of numerous short stories and novellas.

WANG ZHENHE (1940–90) was a native of Hualian in Taiwan. A graduate of National Taiwan University's Department of Western Literature and a fellow at the University of Iowa's International Writing Program, he was a pioneer in the use of Taiwanese language and diction in his tragicomical fiction about the bitter lives of the poor and misfits in a rapidly modernizing Taiwan society. He is best known for his early collections *Jiazhuang yi niuche* (An oxcart for dowry), *Jimo hong* (Lonely redness), and *San chun ji* (The story of three springs). His voice will be sorely missed.

XI XI (Zhang Yan, 1938–) is a native of Zhongshan in Guangdong Province. Educated at Normal University in Hong Kong, she has been a teacher as well as a writer for many years. She has published numerous collections of poetry, essays, and short stories, including *Xiang wo zheiyang de yige nüzi* (A woman like me), *Wo cheng* (My city), and *Shao lu* (Sentry deer).

XIAO SA (Xiao Qingyu, 1953–) is a native of Taibei, Taiwan. She began writing fiction at the age of sixteen, has written over a dozen novels and short-story collections including *Riguang yejing* (Night scenes in daylight) and *Wo er Hansheng* (My son, Hansheng), and won numerous literary awards.

YUAN QIONGQIONG (1950–) is of Sichuanese extraction. She graduated from a commercial middle school in Taibei and did not become a professional writer until the age of twenty-six. Since that time her fiction has won many prizes, and she has published a number of books including *Chunshui chuan* (Spring water boat) and *Ziji de tiankong* (A place of one's own).

ZHANG CHENGZHI (1948–), a native of Beijing, is an ethnic Moslem of China's Hui minority. He spent four years as a herdsman in Inner Mongolia before returning to Beijing where he took a B.A. degree in archaeology from Peking University and a Master's degree in history from the Chinese Academy of Social Sciences. He has published several short-story collections, including *Beifang de he* (The northern river) and *Huangni xiao wu* (Yellow mud hut), and a novel entitled *Jin muchang* (Golden farm).

ZHANG DACHUN (1957–) is a Shandongnese born and raised in Taiwan and a graduate of Furen University's Department of Chinese Literature in Taibei. He has worked as a literary editor for the *China Times*, and his short stories have won numerous awards from the *Times*, the *United Daily News*, and other publications. His best-known collection before *Jiangjun bei* (The general's monument) was *Jiling tu* (Birds of a feather).

ZHANG XIGUO (1944–) has a Ph.D. degree in electrical engineering from the University of California at Berkeley and has taught for many years at the Illinois Institute of Technology. He is a prolific writer whose works include *Qi wang* (The chess master, available in English translation), *Zuori zhi nu* (Yesterday's anger), and *Buxiuzhe* (The immortals).

ZHENG WANLONG (1944–) was born in Heilongjiang Province but grew up in Beijing after the death of his mother. He worked eight years in a pharmaceutical factory during the Cultural Revolution before working his way up in the Beijing publishing world during the late 1970s. He has been chief editor of the Beijing literary quarterly *Shiyue* (October). The finest of his many short-story collections is *Shengming de tuteng* (Life totems).

ZHONG LING, who has a Ph.D. degree in comparative literature from the University of Wisconsin (Madison), is a writer, critic, and professor of Chinese and comparative literature. She has lived and taught in the United States, Hong Kong, and Taiwan, and her many works include English translations of ancient and modern Chinese women poets in collaboration with Kenneth Rexroth, *Lun hui* (Reincarnations), *Meili de cuowu* (Beautiful mistakes), and *Wenxue pinglun ji* (Essays in literary criticism).

ZHONG XIAOYANG (1962–) was born in Guangdong Province, went to primary and secondary schools in Hong Kong, and graduated from the University of Michigan. Her essays, short stories, and new-style poetry have won many Hong Kong literary prizes. Her best-known works are *Liu nian* (The fleeting years) and *Ai qi* (Beloved wife).

About the Translators

KIRK ANDERSON is a graduate student in Chinese at Harvard University's Department of East Asian Languages and Civilizations.

JOHN J. S. BALCOM is a frequent contributor to *The Chinese PEN*.

ERIC B. COHEN is a graduate student in Chinese at Harvard University's Department of East Asian Languages and Civilizations.

MICHAEL DAY received his B.A. degree in Chinese from the University of British Columbia's Department of Asian Studies. He now lives in Xi'an, China, where he teaches English and American literature at the Xi'an Institute of Foreign Languages, translates Chinese literature, and writes his own poetry.

MICHAEL S. DUKE is professor of Chinese in the University of British Columbia's Department of Asian Studies. He is the author of *Blooming and Contending: Chinese Literature in the Post-Mao Era* (1985), *The Iron House: A Memoir of the Chinese Democracy Movement and the Tiananmen Massacre* (1990), and editor of *Contemporary Chinese Literature: An Anthology of Post-Mao Fiction and Poetry* (1985) and *Modern Chinese Women Writers: Critical Appraisals* (1989).

HOWARD GOLDBLATT is professor of Chinese in the Department of East Asian Languages and Literatures at the University of Colorado, Boulder. His recent translations include Li Ang's *The Butcher's Wife*, Pai Hsien-yung's *Crystal Boys*, Zhang Jie's *Heavy Wings*, and Ai Bei's *Red Ivy, Green Earth Mother*. He is also editor of *Worlds Apart: Recent Chinese Writing and Its Audiences* (1990), a series of essays discussing many of the writers featured in this anthology.

GU YAXING received his Master's degree in modern Chinese literature from the University of British Columbia's Department of Asian Studies.

ROSEMARY HADDON received her Master's degree in modern Chinese literature from the University of Victoria and is currently completing her doctoral dissertation, ''Nativist Literature (*xiangtu wenxue*) and Chinese Homeland (*guxiang*) Poetics,'' at the University of British Columbia's Department of Asian Studies.

YING-TSIH HWANG is a frequent contributor to *The Chinese PEN*.

RICHARD KING is assistant professor of Chinese at the Centre for Pacific and Oriental Studies of the University of Victoria in British Columbia.

JEFFREY C. KINKLEY is professor of Chinese at St. John's University in New York. He is the author of *The Odyssey of Shen Congwen* (1987) and editor of *After Mao: Chinese Literature and Society 1978–1981* (1985).

JEANNE LARSEN is associate professor of English and creative writing at Hollins College in Roanoke, Virginia. She is the translator of *Brocade River Poems: Selected Works of the Tang Dynasty Courtesan Xue Tao* (1987) and the author of *Silk Road: A Novel of Eighth-Century China* (1989).

WENDY LARSON is assistant professor of Chinese in the Department of East Asian Languages and Literatures of the University of Oregon.

ROSS LONERGAN received his Master's degree in modern Chinese literature from the University of British Columbia's Department of Asian Studies.

EVE MARKOWITZ studied English and comparative literature at Pennsylvania State University and abroad. She is a frequent contributor to *The Chinese PEN*.

STEVEN L. RIEP is a graduate student in Chinese in the University of California at Los Angeles's Department of Oriental Languages.

JANE PARISH YANG received a Master's degree in Asian studies from the University of Iowa and a Ph.D. degree in comparative literature from the University of Wisconsin (Madison). She has lived and worked in both Hong Kong and Taiwan and is a frequent contributor to *The Chinese PEN*.